The
F.D.R. Memoirs

Books by the author

WHEN F.D.R. DIED
THE NEW IMPROVED AMERICAN
THE F.D.R. MEMOIRS

The

F.D.R. Memoirs*

★As written
by BERNARD ASBELL

Introduction by Anna Roosevelt Halsted

Doubleday & Company, Inc., Garden City, New York, 1973

ISBN: 0-385-08414-5
Library of Congress Catalog Card Number 72–92189
Copyright © 1973 by Bernard Asbell
All Rights Reserved
Printed in the United States of America
First Edition

For my wife
Marjorie
whose labor and love
are here
from first page to last.

Introduction
By Anna Roosevelt Halsted

More than six years ago Bernard Asbell described for me the format he planned for this remarkable book. I wished him luck and told him that it sounded like a formidable task.

Inwardly I wondered if it were possible for someone who was in no way connected with F.D.R.—either with his public career or personal life—to write a credible historical memoir in the first person. Also, it appeared to me then that the background chapters would require an incredible amount of sensitivity, insight, and research immersion, literally the ability to write as one living within the skin of another human being—and a very complicated one at that.

I am no historian and never kept a diary, and since Father's death have often hoped that someone would be able to re-create in writing Franklin Delano Roosevelt as a human being, as well as a statesman and public figure. So it was with great curiosity, mixed with considerable trepidation, that I started reading the manuscript. I don't think I'm given to euphoria, but I do know that by the end of Part I of the "Memoirs," followed by the background to that chapter, I was avid to continue.

Twenty-seven and a half years after I last saw "that man," whom I was lucky enough to call "Father" and "Pa," he was very much alive for me once more—in a realistic sense, as a human being. A human being with sensitive feelings and strong convictions; with bubbling humor and gaiety; with a zest for a battle of wits, whether in behalf of his own ideas or those adopted by him; yet who seemed to prefer a "poker-game approach" to a direct and personalized confrontation; who took pride (and didn't hesitate to show it) in his diversity of knowledge: world geography, people everywhere, history, and Nature with her own interrelationships with humans; and whose charm of personality flourished on a diversified audience and companionship.

This book startles with its clarity in showing the similarity between some of his public problems and some of those we face today. And somehow it's good to be reminded of the inception of programs initiated for the benefit of all kinds of people, programs so bitterly fought then and which now are accepted as ordinary necessities of life: Social Security for one and, more broadly, the responsibility of the federal government to help regions, states, and local governments. Problems affecting too many people and involving expenditures too great for a local entity to handle alone presented two facets of difficulties. One, the necessity for federal help in time of emergency. Two, the broader difficulty of devising long-range programs for federal-government participation without building opportunities for federal domination or local oligarchies. The answers to the last were not solved in Father's administration, challenged him to the last, and have not yet been found.

Like all writers of history, Mr. Asbell has of course brought to bear his own judgments and constructions of some of the whys and wherefores of plans and actions taking place during the period covered by the narrative, as well as some of Father's personal reactions. But in so doing he has managed in all his chapters to make alive, vivid, and sometimes poignant the tales of those historic years as indeed they might have been told by the architect of the New Deal and subsequent wartime leader—had he lived on. It is exciting reading.

Finally, because of my personal ties and my own construction of memories, of special fascination to me are Mr. Asbell's "background" chapters following each "memoir" chapter. Here is insight that rings amazingly true to me. Here are vignettes of people and incidents tied into the life and times of this man, from babyhood to within a few years of his too early death—all of which ring true to me too—though, as Mr. Asbell and I have talked, we have agreed that with the death of every human being die certain personal factors about which those left behind can only conjecture.

So, to me, the formidable task I foresaw has become a rare human and historical document and a highly credible piece of live literature.

President Franklin D. Roosevelt
The White House
Washington, D.C.

Dear Mr. President:

First of all, the absence of a date on this letter is intended as an assurance to you that my work in drafting your memoirs will proceed absolutely off the record, without a recorded history of its own.

My understanding of your main wishes is as follows:

(1) The draft I prepare for your editing and approval is to be designed for publication twenty-five years after your death, when, it is to be assumed, virtually all the main actors of the current national drama will have departed. Thus the manuscript shall describe events, name names, and explain the purposes behind your actions as truth requires.

(2) The memoirs are to cover the period between your first inauguration as President and the nation's entry into the present war—the period known as the New Deal. As I understand your thought on this, you wish your personal record of the New Deal effort for domestic reform and recovery—the effort for which you sought the presidency—to stand separate from any account you may one day undertake of the present war and the international events that led to it.

In preparing this draft, I will consider that I am serving you best if the pages tell too much rather than too little. My aim shall be to give you editorial options of subtraction, not burdens of addition.

There is an incident I have learned from one of your associates that I will take as a guide. I refer to it not for its bizarre subject matter, but its spirit. During your first year in office, you will recall, Speaker Rainey came to see you about some letters just discovered indicating that Lincoln may have been of illegitimate conception. The Speaker is said to have asked you whether the Library of Congress should suppress or destroy these letters. Your immediate response, so I have been told, was that they should not be suppressed, that Lincoln's parents were married before his birth, and that in any case the supposed facts had nothing to do with judging Lincoln's presidency. The greater harm would be done in concealing truth.

In this spirit I will set about my task. At the earliest date I can manage, the draft will be yours and ready for you to make it truly your own.

Most respectfully,

Bernard Asbell

MEMORANDUM TO THE READER

The foregoing letter was never sent to the President. Many acts went un-
finished upon Franklin D. Roosevelt's unexpected death, on April 12,
1945, while the nation—the world—was yet at war.

I am satisfied if the reader agrees merely to *suppose* that such a letter
existed, that the conversation it confirms took place. The fact of the
matter is that the project—whether undertaken by me or by anyone—
could not proceed as described.

A few years ago three men gathered at the end of a working day at a
New York club, the Coffee House, for drinks and trade talk: Samuel S.
Vaughan, then an editor, now publisher, at Doubleday; Eric Larrabee,
former editor of *Harper's;* and myself. One thing we had in common,
besides our trade, was a fascination with Presidents. Vaughan had been
involved in the publication of the *Memoirs by Harry S. Truman* and
later worked as editor on Dwight D. Eisenhower's several volumes of memoirs and recollections. I had written a book narrating the unforgettable
events immediately following Roosevelt's death.

With a wistful air of opportunity lost, Vaughan remarked, "What a
shame Roosevelt didn't live to do his memoirs." Agreed. Then he
turned to me and asked, "Why don't you do them for him?" Astonishment. He continued: "If Roosevelt had lived, his memoirs would have
been drafted, up to a point, by a professional writer. Why don't you be his
ghost?"

I said I'd think about it, and, to my surprise during the next several
weeks, found myself thinking about it seriously, at times certain the idea
was mad, at other times that it was too engaging to put aside.

What could anyone gain by reading "Roosevelt's" memoirs—written by someone else, without the final, crucial approval of F.D.R. himself? At best it would be merely a speculation on history. To be true to the tradition of presidential memoirs it would have to come out one-sided and self-serving. Perhaps that alone might justify the project, since it is possible today, after a flood of memoirs and published diaries by his associates, to study the twelve years of Roosevelt's presidency from the viewpoint of almost every leading New Dealer's experience—except his own. Yet F.D.R.'s own account of his presidency, done now and in this way, seemed to require something else. Was there some way the work might reveal—in a single volume, for the first time—the inner life of this man who continues to be described as an "enigma"? How could such an undertaking cut through what Robert E. Sherwood called F.D.R.'s "heavily forested interior"? By hearing F.D.R. talk about himself, how might we possibly discover something about him that he would not— perhaps could not—say?

Eventually I brought back to Vaughan a design for discovering Franklin D. Roosevelt, by writing his memoirs—and something more. Thus began the six-year labor of this volume.

Just as I would have done had I carried out this task for F.D.R., I would use as my main sources, in addition to his private files in the Roosevelt Library at Hyde Park, the diaries and papers of his associates. I would quote Roosevelt directly when—and only when—these diaries and papers directly quoted him. But what these firsthand observers saw the President do and heard him say are not necessarily what the President saw and privately thought. The men who recorded his daily actions did so as political men. Thus they added to the compounded shortcomings of much written history. They observed him politically, not personally, as though one aspect could be seen clean from the other. Others around Roosevelt—a son, a secretary, a housemaid—set down sometimes revealing personal anecdotes, not attempting in an important way to tie the revelations to the politics of the man. While surely a man of parts, Roosevelt was not to be understood in parts. He had to be sought in the whole.

I resolved to try to understand his public behavior by matching it against his private experience, early as well as late. What personal knowledge, what biases, what concealed remembrances of frustration and delight, what of his most personal self did he bring to each of a staggering series of great public episodes? How could I be *his* explainer of his presidency—how could I *be* F.D.R.—without at least searching for the buried current of personal urges that animated him?

I decided to borrow a tool of the dramatist. It is a frequent practice of playwrights, before writing for their audiences, to write for themselves.

A dramatist may want to introduce a character for a short appearance, perhaps only a few spoken lines. But those lines must be real, true. Before bringing him on stage, the dramatist may privately outfit the character with a concise biography. Who was his mother? How did he fare in school? What kind of town was his world? From what personal experience is he to speak his lines? If this background biography provides the author with understanding, the character's words come out true.

I decided that I must form this kind of concealed, background acquaintance with Franklin D. Roosevelt. For each crisis that I (he) was to reconstruct on these pages, I had to choose, at least to my satisfaction, the private learnings that may have caused him to act as he did. For each section—or Part—of the memoirs, I wrote a background memorandum as preparation for myself.

In doing so I found that episodes in the background did illuminate his actions—and many previously unexplainable motivations behind those actions—that the memoir chapters were to describe. Conversely, many of the puzzling actions of his presidency forced a new interpretation of his earlier and more private life. After months, years, of meshing presidential foreground against private background, Franklin D. Roosevelt became, at least in my mind, a fathomable, sometimes even predictable man. No less complex, but no longer an enigma.

In the book, I present each background memorandum *following* the Part for which it was written as preparation. By thus reversing the order of their creation, it is hoped that these memoranda will intrude less upon the memoirs, remaining truly as background. The memoranda are printed in the type face you now read.

If in places my own memoranda take off in flights of speculation that would hardly seem appropriate to a work of standard biography, the reader is asked to remember the private purpose for which they were written.

Contents

PART I   PRESIDENT-ELECT

PART II   MY FRIENDS . . .

PART III   THE FIRST HUNDRED DAYS

PART VII   SAVING LIBERALISM AND LIBERTY:
THE BATTLES JOIN

Part I

President-Elect

Most men in public life overestimate the complexity of economics and underestimate the complexity of politics. My predecessor in the White House and his associates fell into that error—but so did most of *my* associates and some of my best political friends.[1]

Economists and their disciples love to explain all of human existence by spinning elaborate formulas and unraveling long lists of statistics. They so befuddle the minds of us ordinary mortals (and, I suspect, sometimes themselves) that it's hard to keep in mind what economics is all about. Economics is simply the very real business of how men extract materials from the earth, process these materials through machines, distribute goods and human services among their fellows, and attempt to balance and control these activities to man's general advantage.

Materials, machines, and men—these are tangible matters. When economists get too wound up in the intangible symbols of these very real things—chiefly money, as though it is living an economic life of its own—they begin to theorize themselves off the track. Man is a theorizing animal. That is one of our imperfections. A good theory should help explain the real world we live in; too many theories try to explain a perfect, orderly world that simply does not exist.

Materials and machines—we may even throw in money—are almost entirely manageable by men. I say *almost* entirely. As long as foods and fibers grow from the earth and there are machines to make them into goods, men need never go hungry or poorly clothed or badly sheltered—provided that men can agree on how to use them. But getting men to agree? That challenge, which has little to do with economics, is enormously difficult, enormously unpredictable, enormously complex. That is the subject of *politics,* which economists and most public men insufficiently understand.

During the campaign of 1932, our mighty nation was close to economic collapse. Yet the elements of abundance surrounded us. Natural abundance? The orchards and furrows were bountiful as always, livestock fat, cottonfields in white bloom, and coal mines open for digging. Machines? The world's most vast and balanced collection of factories stood unnaturally idle, but poised for production as soon as men could organize themselves to make the wheels turn again. Men? Everywhere were men, hungry but ready to work joining nature and technology to satisfy their need for food, for garments and shelter, and for the dignity of useful work.

What had put everything out of kilter was not a shortage of real resources but a dislocation of money. My predecessor—and opponent in the campaign of 1932—spoke of a crisis of confidence. In this he was quite correct. As he saw it, however, people were losing confidence in their money. Thus he made the common error of focusing on the symbol and overlooking the reality. He sought a cure by trying to manipulate money instead of the true elements of prosperity: materials, machines, and men. Especially men.

Our real danger was that men might lose confidence in themselves, in each other, and in their government. The result would be revolution, turmoil, and anarchy—all very real prospects in 1932. The people needed a President who would address himself to the behavior of men, not the behavior of money. They needed to believe in their government as an organizer of the power of people, not merely a manipulator of the market price of gold.

They needed to feel that government was a friend, which means that they needed to regard it, in a way, as a friendly *person.* This was not an unreasonable need. The people, after all, choose a leader, their President, who can—and should—personify the spirit of government. That leader can—and should—go to the people, listen patiently, and talk plainly about their problems, their ambitions, their readiness to work in support of their families. He can—and should —lead them toward the real, controllable requisite of prosperity: getting men into harness with their natural and man-made resources.

In so far as a leader can, in a nation of more than one hundred million, I tried to talk about real things and as one person to another in addressing—and listening to—the people of our troubled nation. I think they felt this; and that may have had more to do with the success of some of our efforts than the design of the programs themselves. It would be gratifying to me if history judges that some confidence was restored in government during my years in office as a result of people feeling the presidency had been personalized.

This person-to-person concern was the intended tone of government during my administration. I intend it to be the dominant tone of these memoirs. These pages will not tell all there is to tell. By being selective, however, my purpose will not be to conceal, but to prevent boring my reader to slumber. Much of what happens in government is immensely boring. This is because much of what happens has little truly to do with the lives of most people. I remember President Wilson saying to me once: "Ninety-nine out of one hundred matters which appear to you and me today as of vital Administration policy will be completely overlooked by history, and many other little things which you and I pay but scant heed to will begin to be talked about one hundred years from now."[2]

If anything distinguishes the New Deal from previous eras of government, it is that after 1933 our government more than ever before legislated directly for people: creating jobs, providing electricity and controlling floods, supporting prices for farmers and protecting prices for consumers, asserting and defending human rights for all our citizens. On these matters—the continuing struggle to bring government into the service of the people—I will concentrate my accounts in this volume. Others I will largely ignore. For example, one of the matters pending before me when I entered office was the London Economic Conference, having to do with international monetary matters. This conference, of course, turned out to be something of a failure. That is not why I will ignore it, however. My reason for leaving this to others to write about is that even if it had been a success, it would have done little to change the lot of the forgotten man. In contrast, however, I want to deal in considerable detail with the monetary crisis at home, the threatened collapse of our banks. Every American family that had managed to put away a few dollars for a rainy day was deeply affected by the health of the corner bank. This

kind of choice of subject material will be a general rule throughout
this volume. Readers interested in greater detail in less vital matters
will hardly be without sources for finding out all they want to know.[3]

Properly, this account of my years as President of the United States
might begin with a statement of the philosophy and aims with which
I entered office. I shall not begin that way, however, simply because
in our first hours—and for many days—after assuming office, my
associates and I were prevented by extraordinary circumstances from
giving practical thought to long-range plans or philosophies or theories. Plans indeed we had. But the moment called for urgent, im-
provised action.

Only one President before me, Abraham Lincoln, had entered
the White House while the very life of the nation stood in such peril
from internal threat as in 1933. No previous President, including
Lincoln, had assumed office while a crisis was at its razor edge.

For fifteen years—since World War I—a national disease had been
developing, imperceptible to many, until mounting neglect led to collapse in 1929. One could begin the tale almost anywhere among
those days and years. Let us choose as our point of entry a night two
weeks before my inauguration, which was to take place March 4,
1933. In the American experience of passing leadership from one
elected head of state to another, which had involved thirty men before
me, that night was unique.

A group of New York City political reporters, calling themselves
the Inner Circle, were giving an annual fun-making dinner, something like the better known Gridiron Club affair held every year in
Washington. Close to midnight—it was Saturday night, February
18—I departed with a group of coworkers from my town home in
East Sixty-fifth Street to join these newspaper friends at the Astor
Hotel. As we drove across Times Square, I could not help but feel
heartened by the capacity of people in the streets to find gaiety after
three years of acute unemployment, scarcity of spending money,
malaise of the national spirit. On this particular Saturday night it was
indeed surprising. Four days earlier, in the great center of automobile
manufacture, Michigan, Governor Comstock had stunned the nation
by closing all the banks in his state to forestall many of them from
collapsing. Fear had led to panic—people draining banks of their deposits—and now panic threatened disaster everywhere to banks, to

savers, wage earners, small businessmen. How much deeper into trouble would the panic be permitted to sweep us? This was the disquieting question we carried with us across Times Square and into the Astor Hotel.

The after-dinner show at the Inner Circle, written and acted by newsmen, was grand fun and the laughter was good for the spirit. Amidst the merriment, a man whom I did not know tapped me on the shoulder, displayed a badge from the United States Secret Service, apologizing that he was under orders to come to me personally, and handed me a brown envelope addressed in handscript.[4] I was not a little surprised at finding it contained a ten-page letter, written in his own hand, from President Herbert Hoover. Trying not to show concern that might alert those around me, I began to read:

THE WHITE HOUSE

WASHINGTON

Feb. 18, 1933

My dear Mr. President-Elect:

A most critical situation has arisen in the country of which I feel it is my duty to advise you confidentially. I am therefore taking this course of writing you myself and sending it to you through the Secret Service for your hand direct as obviously its misplacement would only feed the fire and increase the dangers.

The major difficulty is the state of public mind—for there is a steadily degenerating confidence in the future which has reached the height of general alarm. I am convinced that a very early statement by you upon two or three policies of your admistration [sic] would serve greatly to restore confidence and cause a resumption of the march of recovery.[5]

What the President wished to "advise" me of "confidentially," it turned out in page after astonishing page, was not new information but pure speech material from the election campaign in which he had been defeated three months earlier. (The entire text of Mr. Hoover's remarkable letter appears as Appendix I.) By clear implication, the "steadily degenerating confidence in the future" was a general horror at the thought of me in the White House. Equally clearly, "a resumption of the march of recovery" depended upon Mr. Hoover's informing me when to make statements and what they ought to say. One might then wonder why the people had elected me, in whom they so lacked confidence, and defeated Mr. Hoover.

Instead of discussing the real emergencies that engrossed the people's minds—their pockets bare, children hungry, factories shut down—the President invoked the language of abstract symbols that still seem to possess most of the men of his party: "proposals to abrogate constitutional responsibility," "re-expansion of credit," "balancing the budget" (while scrupulously avoiding to mention that not one of Mr. Hoover's four budgets had balanced).

After nine pages of ideology rejected by the people, Mr. Hoover generously told me what the statement he sought from me ought to say: ". . . it would steady the country greatly if there could be prompt assurance that there will be no tampering or inflation of the currency; that the budget will be unquestionably balanced even if further taxation is necessary; that the government credit will be maintained by refusal to exhaust it in issue of securities."

Of course I intended to say no such thing. First of all, he, not I, was the possessor of presidential authority. He would use it or not, as he pleased; but he would not succeed in drawing me in as a partner in past failures. My second reason was stated best by Mr. Hoover himself the very next day. In a letter to Senator David A. Reed marked "Confidential" (and soon made available to Mr. Hoover's biographers), the President wrote:

> I realize that if these declarations be made by the President-elect, he will have ratified the whole major program of the Republican Administration: that is, it means the abandonment of 90% of the so-called new deal.[6]

I doubt that ever in our history has an outgoing President been so insolent toward a newly elected successor. How was I to reply? I could think of no way that would say what I was truly thinking, yet not appear reciprocally disrespectful of the man who still occupied the exalted office.

I decided to take the risk of not replying at all, a risk that soon required me to cover my tracks.

The President failed to read my clear hint of silence. On February

28, only four days before I was to assume office, he wrote to me again, and again in his own hand. This time he not only told me what to say, but what to do in running the government. After years of inaction which had led to his defeat, he urged upon me the action of calling Congress into session! This I fully intended to do, but hardly at my predecessor's behest. Mr. Hoover's second, even more remarkable letter began:

It is my duty to inform you that the financial situation has become even more grave and the lack of confidence extended further than when I wrote to you on February 18th. I am confident that a declaration even now on the line I suggested at that time would contribute greatly to restore confidence and would save losses and hardships to millions of people.

My purpose however is to urge you—upon the basis of evident facts —that the gravity of the situation is such that it is desirable that the co-ordinate arm of the government should be in session quickly after · March 4th. There is much legislation urgently needed but will not be completed by the present session. The new Congress being in majority with the admistration [sic] is capable of expeditious action.[7]

I could hardly avoid replying to a second letter from the White House. But, again, I could hardly reply with my true mind. Therefore I decided to create a fib. I prepared a letter responding to his first one, dating it as though it had been written nine days previously:

49 East 65th Street
New York, N.Y.

February 20, 1933

Dear Mr. President:

I am equally concerned with you in regard to the gravity of the present bank situation, but my thought is that it is so very deep-seated that the fire is bound to spread in spite of anything that is done by mere statement. The real trouble is that on present values very few financial institutions anywhere in the country are actually able to pay off their deposits in full, and the knowledge of this fact is widely held. Bankers with the narrower viewpoint have urged me to make a general statement, but even they seriously doubt if it would have a definite effect. . . .

Having dictated that, I proceeded to dictate a new letter in response to his second one. It began:

Dear Mr. President:

I am dismayed to find that the enclosed letter, which I wrote in New York a week ago, did not go to you, through an assumption by my secretary that it was only a draft of a letter.

Now I have yours of yesterday and can only tell you that I appreciate your fine spirit of co-operation, and that I am in constant touch with the situation. . . . I am inclined to agree that a very early Special Session will be necessary—and by tonight or tomorrow I hope to settle on a definite time. I will let you know. . . .[8]

Perhaps I should not embarrass my predecessor by now revealing this fib of many years ago. But it would come out. Any future student of this episode may find among my papers the stenographic notes of my two letters. They happen to be unusual notes, not written in a stenographic notebook, but on two small sheets of linen paper, the kind used for personal correspondence. Since the notes in this condition would make it clear to anyone that the letters were dictated at the same time, perhaps the best thing to do would be to destroy them. But I shall not—I cannot—bring myself to destroy historical papers. So let the record stand. The source of the discourtesy was not of my making.

To get back to the main line of the story, I ought to fill in some details of the bank crisis that occupied the outgoing President, the incoming one, and the people of the country—and I ought to recall something of how it came about. In doing so, let me freely confess that I share with most Americans—including some of our finest businessmen—a distaste for the details of banking. I wrote about this to James M. Cox, who had been my party's candidate for President in 1920, when I had the honor of being his running mate. In my letter I asked Jim Cox to become chairman of the Federal Reserve Board. In turning me down, he wrote:

My dear Frank:

. . . During all of my mature years my predilections, every one, have run clearly away from banking. I never bought stock in a bank, nor would I serve on a board of directors. In our whole economic set-up, banking is the one thing which never inspired the least degree of interest or enthusiasm on my part. . . .

I replied:

Dear Jim:

I do understand—fully—especially because I am like you, for I have all my life, as lawyer and business man, run away from banking. It is the last field of human activity that appeals to me.

That, however, was one reason why I had so greatly hoped that you would head the Federal Reserve Board even temporarily. I do not want anyone in that job who has a passion for banking! And, alas, because I know that you have a superabundance of old-fashioned common sense, business acumen, and with it all ideals, I felt you were highly fitted to help us put the whole financial structure on its feet. . . .[9]

In that spirit of distaste for banking and respect for common sense, I present this account of the bank crisis of 1933.

The trouble may be traced back to 1900, when pressure by Populists persuaded Congress to reduce the required capitalization of national banks from fifty thousand dollars to twenty-five thousand dollars. Almost any farmer or groceryman could start a bank in a crossroads town that hardly supported a general store. Between 1900 and 1920, the number of banks increased by almost a thousand a year, from 10,382 to 30,139. This rate of growth was far greater than that of either the population or the economy. But agriculture, the backbone of the economy, was prosperous, so most of these infant banks flourished.

Then came World War I. To provide food and fiber for a war-stricken Europe, farmers greatly expanded their acreage. At war's end, farmers found themselves the victims of their own abundance. As plentiful crops outreached the people's readiness to buy, farm prices declined. Many farmers met their need for dollars by producing even more, further depressing prices. To make ends meet, they were compelled to borrow. Banks were caught in a squeeze. They were lending money to foundering farmers on whose land and equipment these banks also held mortgages. A farmer who failed, thus represented a double loss to a bank: an unpaid loan secured by a farm that had grown unprofitable.

It is not surprising, therefore, that bank failures after 1920 occurred primarily in the rural states of the Midwest, Northwest, and South. Both major parties share responsibility for these failures: the Republicans because of their traditional view that government should take a passive role in the market place; the Democrats because they were mainly an urban party, not sufficiently mindful of rural problems—a parochialism I have worked hard to correct.

The earlier proliferation of banks now turned into a proliferation of failures. Between 1921 and 1932, 10,484 banks with deposits of nearly five billion dollars closed their doors. Of these, 1,571 were national banks, with aggregate deposits of more than a billion dollars. (It is worth noting here that the average number of failures for a *single* year of this period was more than twice the *total* suspended in the dozen years that followed the banking reforms that my administration was soon to bring about.) Now the carelessness of the 1900 law became clear. Of all suspended banks, 65.7 per cent had capital of less than fifty thousand dollars.

Other great changes were taking place in American life that tightened the squeeze on rural banks. Slowly, almost imperceptibly, but inexorably, the nation was shifting from a predominantly farm economy to a gigantic industrial one. This had two main ramifications: The first was that many marginal farmers abandoned their land for the higher wages of factories, leaving many a farm to be operated by less efficient old people and casual farm hands. This was accompanied by a disappearance of smaller industries in small cities; they took flight to the labor markets of big cities or were bought up by bigger companies. The withdrawal of their deposits added to the troubles of small banks. The second ramification was that banks, attracted by the growth of manufacturing industries, began investing heavily in stocks that were rising spectacularly.[10]

It is hardly necessary to recount here the disastrous crash of the stock market in 1929, except to observe that the foresight of some bankers was hardly better than that of the legendary newsboys and elevator operators whose speculations helped drive up the market to insane levels. When the New York Stock Exchange headily opened on September 1, 1929, the aggregate value of all stocks was some $89 billion. By July 1, 1932, these values had collapsed to $15 billion.

Stockholders—including many banks—had lost $74 billion, a loss of 83 cents of every dollar invested. The total loss was roughly three times what America had spent in fighting World War I, or, put another way, almost three thousand dollars for every family in the nation.[11]

It is indeed lucky that the nation's banks did not collapse overnight. If depositors had become aware immediately of the trouble their banks were in—if they had all appeared soon after the crash to take their money out and transfer it to a good, safe mattress—all parties would be almost broke, depositors as well as banks. The nation's 18,569 banks had about $6 billion in cash to meet $41 billion in deposits, the rest represented by securities and mortgages that had flattened in value, some made utterly worthless. The secret of the dire sickness of banks was made even more treacherous by bank examiners, both state and federal, who sympathetically permitted bankers to count bondholdings, including much paper that was entirely uncollectible, at face value.

The secret, of course, could not be kept for long, despite the buoyant, misleading verbiage of President Hoover: "the inherently sound condition of the banks" (November 15, 1929), "the strong position of the banks" (December 3, 1929), "the soundness of the system" (October 2, 1930), and "the strength of our banking system" (October 6, 1931).[12]

In the three years following the crash, while the incumbent President was reciting those words, five thousand banks collapsed, 2,290 in the most terrible of those years, 1931. No matter how grandiose the trumpeting of economists and their President, the collapse was brought about by simple defensive acts of simple people. They began taking their dollars out of banks. One story came to me of a schoolteacher who asked a twelve-year-old boy why he was scratching himself. She discovered that the child had $1,100 taped to his chest. He explained that his parents were afraid of banks. People stashed money in old baking-powder cans, under floor boards, within walls. As depositors made withdrawals, nibbling away at the dwindling supply of bank cash, banks called upon other banks to repay loans, spreading the disease and the insolvency.

The rising money shortage finally forced President Hoover into a bold step, in January 1932. He proposed and Congress created the Reconstruction Finance Corporation. The RFC borrowed money from the Treasury and lent it to cash-starved banks, salvaging many from ruin. The correctness of this overdue regulatory step was confirmed by an almost immediate decline in the rate of bank failures. In October 1932, closings numbered only ninety-seven.

Hoarding of money, however, remained pronounced. In July 1932, hoarding had reached an estimated $1.5 billion. Now, here is something important to keep in mind: Withdrawals for hoarding are not at all like normal withdrawals. Normally, when people take money out of a bank, they spend it, stimulating business and employment. Hoarded money is neither spent by its owner nor lendable by the bank. Thus it is subtracted from the country's money supply. The effects of hoarding were intensified when foreign depositors began to withdraw their balances, causing a flow of gold out of the country. This threatening flow increased when many large American investors sold their securities for cash, exchanged their cash for gold bars, and shipped them abroad. Between February 1 and February 15, 1933—only a month before the presidency was to change hands—bank withdrawals of gold and currency increased alarmingly from five to fifteen million dollars a day.[13]

At this point, along came a remarkable invention that was to have a great deal to do with my first few days in office: Money was disappearing from accounts so fast, a responsible bank could hardly tell from hour to hour whether it was solvent. An important bank in New Orleans, on which the stability of a whole region depended, needed a breather to analyze its books. That's when the invention came in. Governor O. K. Allen of Louisiana proclaimed a *bank holiday* on February 4, 1933. Of course, the governor needed to keep things looking right. So he consulted his almanac and declared the holiday "in commemoration of the 16th anniversary of the severance of diplomatic relations between the United States and Germany."[14]

Ten days later, Governor Comstock of Michigan seized upon the same invention to save the banks of his state. Although it was St. Valentine's Day, he ignored the ruse, knowing he could play no games. He closed all of Michigan's banks, not for one day but eight. The nation was thunderstruck. In the rest of the country's banks, gold outflow soared to $37 million a day, currency $122 million.

In Detroit, municipal laborers, carrying uncashable pay checks in their pockets, fainted from hunger on the job. Milk companies delivered on credit until their supply of milk dried up, because farmers needed cash for feed. Boston stopped paying its police. Chicago hadn't paid its schoolteachers for months.

Banks were stormed by frightened depositors wanting their money. While bankers and the administration were bare of ideas for preventing public disaster, depositors often showed remarkable ingenuity in personal protection. At one Bronx, New York, bank, women rented a squalling baby from a young mother to use as influence in getting to the head of the teller's line. Their rental charge for the baby was twenty-five cents a trip. In some places, bank employees had to be deputized to keep order.

During the week of February 20, a single bank, the Baltimore Trust Company, paid out $13 million, nearly half of it on Friday. That night, Governor Albert C. Ritchie of Maryland closed his state's two hundred banks for three days. The national tremor intensified.[15]

Clearly, somebody had to do something. Governors, by closing their states' banks, were at least doing the only thing they could think of. What was the President doing? Mr. Hoover seemed to be preoccupied with looking for simple explanations. I have often been accused of oversimplifying economic matters that others insist are terribly complex. In this regard, I bow to the clear superiority of Mr. Hoover. On February 21, three days after his remarkable first letter to me, the President wrote a more frank one to his own Secretary of the Treasury, Ogden Mills, in which he settled the matter of crashing banks, as far as he was concerned:

> The causes of this sudden critical development are simple enough. The public is filled with fear and apprehension over the policies of the new Administration. People are acting now in individual self-protection, and unless it is checked, it jeopardizes every bank deposit, every savings, every insurance policy, and the very ability of the Federal Government to pay its way. The indices of fear are hoarding and flight of capital. The drain of gold is not yet alarming, yet its wide spread is symptomatic. . . .[16]

This analysis by my predecessor might well stand alongside an analysis once offered by *his* predecessor, President Calvin Coolidge: "When a great many people are unable to find work, unemployment results."[17]

By March 2, two days before my inauguration, the country was gripped with terror. Total or partial bank holidays were in effect in twenty-one states. Secretary of the Treasury Mills and Eugene Meyer, Chairman of the RFC, were urging President Hoover to declare a national banking holiday. He did not do so.[18]

On that day, my closest coworkers and I departed for Washington, setting up headquarters at the Mayflower Hotel. The time was filled with ironies. The incumbent President was calling for action from me while he, still holding constitutional powers to do all manner of things, refused to do anything. Meanwhile I, refusing to act before acquiring authority, was actually choosing among possible courses, almost all of which would strain the limits of presidential power and perhaps change the tone of government for years to come. Here were the courses of action pressed upon me from various influential sources:

1. I had before me an urgent letter from Thomas W. Lamont of J. P. Morgan and Company reading, "I do not wish to be an alarmist: in fact, I am perhaps usually inclined to be too much the other way. But when I came back this morning from the south, on a hurry call, I found the situation far more critical than I had dreamed. I believe in all seriousness that the emergency could not be greater. . . . And it is your say-so alone that will save the country from a disaster." And what "say-so" did Mr. Lamont propose? That the government, through the RFC, bail out crippled state and national banks by depositing unlimited quantities of government funds without security. I *loved* his reasoning: "As you pointed out to me, it may cost the government a lot of money to do this, but it would be *cheap at the price.* [Italics his.] A billion dollars spent now and provided by the Federal Reserve Banks against their ample gold reserves may save the country from total prostration, and far greater expense later on."[19] What compassion he showed for banks and gold reserves! When I was later to use this same reasoning for bailing out American families by creating jobs, feeding children, and reviving the whole economy by generating spending money—that a billion dollars spent now would be cheap at the price—I was to be denounced for fiscal irresponsibility. Since Lamont's was the most sonorous voice among bankers, I considered his proposal with the seriousness due it, but with scarcely any intention of following it.

2. More radical cures were proposed by other doctors. One of my own staff group, Rexford G. Tugwell, about to become Assistant Secretary of Agriculture, suggested that the government, through its

postal savings system, take over the deposit and checking transactions of banks. A Republican senator from New Mexico, Bronson Cutting, was far more radical than Rex, the radical-in-residence of my staff. Senator Cutting's advice is most eloquently described in a reminiscence he was soon to write: "I think back to the events of March 4, 1933, with a sick heart. For then . . . the nationalism of banks could have been accomplished without a word of protest. It was President Roosevelt's great mistake." If the institution of banking was to be conserved, some radical step was necessary. But Cutting's radicalism was as ill-advised as Hoover's do-nothing conservatism, which would conserve nothing.[20]

3. I had before me another urgent memorandum, from Senator Key Pittman, the silver-tongued spokesman of the Silver State of Nevada. He alone urged me *not* to call Congress into special session. First, he advised, I should "start preparation" of an elaborate, gorgeous new banking law and get it "approved by the leaders of every school of thought in the Senate and the House before it is introduced. To call Congress into session before legislation is ready . . . would precipitate the introduction of hundreds of bills . . . Excitable speeches would disturb the country without accomplishing results or even giving hopes of results." This, of course, was a variation on doing nothing—doing something that takes far too long. I was to take office on Saturday, March 4. By the following Monday, without resolute action, the nation's money system could be a hopeless shambles.[21]

4. For two months I had been considering use of an obscure presidential prerogative tucked into an emergency law passed during World War I and never repealed, called the Trading with the Enemy Act. I would use this law to close all the nation's banks, except for certain prescribed activities. This, in effect, would take Governor O. K. Allen's invention and fashion it into a *national bank holiday,* permitting them to reopen when inspection showed the banks were sound and depositors safe in relying upon them. Now, this step involved some reading between the lines of the law. The provision of the Trading with the Enemy Act that interested me said: "That the President may investigate, regulate, or prohibit, under such rules and regulations as he may prescribe, by means of licenses or other wise, any transactions in foreign exchange, and the export, hoarding, melting or earmarking of gold or silver coin or bullion or currency."[22] The

clause does not give the President any specific power to close banks. But it permits him to regulate, in any way he sees fit, currency hoarding and export, too much of which was already threatening the welfare of the nation. One doesn't have to be a Supreme Court Justice or even a Philadelphia lawyer to see that if, in the President's opinion, temporarily closing the banks is the way to regulate these harmful activities, the law permits him to do it. I solicited and received an opinion from my Attorney General-designate, Senator Thomas J. Walsh (who died hours before taking office) that this law permitted me to close the banks. This opinion was confirmed by Homer S. Cummings, whom I named in Senator Walsh's place.[23]

The thought of using this Act was not original with me. The incumbent Secretary of the Treasury had urged it upon President Hoover. Hoover had refused, later calling it "a weak reed for a nation to lean on in time of trouble." What was his notion of a stronger reed? During his last week in office he inquired of the Federal Reserve Board in writing—no doubt in longhand—what it thought of a federal guarantee of bank deposits. The Board lamely responded on March 2 that it had nothing to suggest. No wonder former Secretary of the Treasury William Gibbs McAdoo was moved to exclaim, "Our entire banking system does credit to a collection of imbeciles."[24]

I did not plan to rely on the Trading with the Enemy Act entirely. I would call Congress into session immediately and ask the prompt passage of a law permitting me to close the banks and specify the conditions under which they might be reopened. Thus the courts would not be called upon to decide whether my use of the old Act was legal or not. The new law would have the matter over and done with.

That is the course I decided to take. It was a proper—a required—presidential thing to do, attacking a national emergency with any and every tool available within reasonable limits of the law. When your house is on fire, you may run to your neighbor for fire-fighting tools. If he doesn't answer his doorbell and the door is open, do you stop to worry about etiquette? Of course not. You go in. You don't let your house burn down. Suppose you don't find a fire extinguisher or even a garden hose, but over there in the corner is a bucket. You don't stop to wonder if the bucket is meant for washing floors. If it holds water, you grab it and run.

It is not the job of presidential leadership to accept every law from

Congress at face value, precisely as it is written, and act according to its instructions as though following directions on a soup can. If that were so, we would call him our National Clerk instead of our Chief Executive. It is the job of a President to probe and test what a law will permit him to do in the interests of the people. For a President, laws should not be prison bars but crowbars—tools for applying leverage to the job at hand, especially in emergencies. If the President oversteps the scope of the law, the courts will soon remind him of its limits. If he oversteps the intent of the law, the Congress will surely fence him in with a new one. If he succeeds in his new interpretation, however, he has been truly creative in finding new ways to meet the needs of the people. That is what we should expect of a Chief Executive under our system of checks and balances. Congress writes laws by passing them. The courts write law by defining what is and what is not permissible under the Constitution and the laws of Congress. The President writes law by using old legal tools for new purposes—and testing whether he can get away with it.[25]

One of the things often written about me—by writers who don't know me very well, who, in turn, must be informed by politicians who don't know me very well—is that the way to get anything out of me is to get me off by myself. Without the support of my advisers and speech writers, so the legend goes, I melt down into some sort of schoolboy who would never look anybody in the eye and say, "No." It's perfectly true that I do try to be pleasant with my visitors. I do try to listen respectfully. My friends have told me that I do have a habit of nodding when someone talks, which some visitors misconstrue as winning my agreement on whatever they're talking about. Really, all the nod means is "I get your point." I am sorry if this has confused some people who know me less well than others.

I bring this up as the only way I can explain the behavior of Mr. Hoover on the last full day of his presidency. He must have swallowed that "schoolboy" theory hard. We were to have a traditional tea—his family and mine—at 4 P.M. on March 3. As I entered the White House with Mrs. Roosevelt, and my son Jimmy and his wife, Betsey Cushing Roosevelt, we were greeted by good old Ike Hoover, the chief usher who had been there since before the days of Theodore Roosevelt. Ike said to me, "It's good to have another Roosevelt in the White House." Then he whispered, as though passing on mere social information, that the President would meet us in the Green Room and that as soon as the amenities were done with, the President would bring in Treasury Secretary Mills and Eugene Meyer, a Governor of the Federal Reserve Board.

What he was up to was perfectly clear. A fine cup of tea, indeed! As I later remarked to Jimmy, this was one of the most insolent bits of presumption I had ever witnessed in all my political years.

I asked Ike to call the Mayflower Hotel immediately and summon Raymond Moley, my chief adviser. If the President was going to play tricks, that was his prerogative, but I was going to have my witness, too.

The minute Mills and Meyer appeared, I asked that Moley be shown in. Bless him, he was already in the lobby waiting. The President then told me that he had been advised to invoke the Trading with the Enemy Act but that his Attorney General was inclined to think the Act became invalid with the end of World War I. I told him that my advice was precisely the opposite. The President then asked me to assure him that if he invoked the Act, the new Congress would not disavow its use. I told him that if he decided to invoke the emergency powers, my administration would regard his action with the greatest sympathy. But the risk of Congressional disavowal would be no jot or tittle smaller whether he invoked the powers now or I did later.

I was ready to take on this risk myself. Clearly he was not. At this late hour, he was still determined to prepare me as the goat should his action fail. When the impasse was evident, I attempted to avoid further strain by mentioning the custom of an outgoing President returning the call of an incoming one. I said, "I realize, Mr. President, that you are extremely busy, so I will understand completely if you do not return the call." For the first time that day, he looked me squarely in the eye and said, "Mr. Roosevelt, when you are in Washington as long as I have been, you will learn that the President of the United States calls on nobody." I was sure Jimmy wanted to punch him in the eye.

A few days after my inauguration, I arranged to pay a call on Mr. Justice Oliver Wendell Holmes on his ninety-second birthday. Climbing the steep, narrow stairs of his I Street home, I don't mind saying, was rather difficult for me. But Mr. Justice Holmes was due the respect. And Mr. Hoover was due the rebuke.

Most of my adult life had been engaged in political conflict. Disagreements rarely affected my personal feelings about other men. I bore no ill feeling toward Mr. Hoover resulting from the election campaign. But his preinauguration behavior overstepped gentlemanly bounds. I never asked him to visit me at the White House, and, I might add, he never made a courtesy phone call to me on his visits to Washington. Later, during World War II, many people advised me to appoint Mr. Hoover to some major post for the sake of national unity. As the record will show, I appointed many leading Republicans. But Mr. Hoover no longer interested me.[26]

BACKGROUND MEMORANDUM TO PART I

First off, I must clear my mind of the popular, legendary, and entirely erroneous notion of Franklin Roosevelt as a man of the common people. Besides misleading the reader, it can only distort my perception of him.

From his toes to the tip of his tilted cigarette holder, he was a patrician born and raised, and an adored only child to boot. Respect came easily, because he expected it. Affection rained on him, because he seduced it with the siren skill learned by children overfed on affection—or starved for it. And, strangely, he came by it both ways. He was bathed in adoration by his mother—but not by playmate peers.

How can a man become a man of the people when he was not a child among children? Imagine (as a child of the city streets myself, I really can't)—imagine never playing ball in a shouting gang; never fleeing in terror after breaking a neighbor's window; never sneaking off for mischief with a pal when Mom thought you were cleaning the cellar; never tasting the sound of swear words learned from a school tough; never being bullied or trying out the sweet supremacy of bullying another. Imagine never going to school. Imagine being taken daily in a carriage to share a tutor with the equally caged children of a nearby estate, sometimes catching a glimpse along the way of school children of the townsfolk running free along the road, playing tag, laughing, whispering, telling secret things one to the other—but never to him. What games did they play? What secrets did they tell? What excitement had they that he could never know? Had Franklin been a child of less curiosity, it would hardly matter; but on some days this child of lively mind longed to know—and knew he could never know. Surely what curiosity he brought to these glimpses also was nurtured by them.

There has seldom lived a grown man with a more hungry curiosity. Whether for the romance of history or geographical trivia; whether for gossip of royalty or details of a party given by one of the office girls—he'd question closely, with great appetite, about who was there, what was served, what were the best jokes and the best pranks.

What is curiosity—inordinate curiosity—but systematized hunger for experience, observed or imagined, but early denied? Oh, to know what those common children played at—without having to become one of them.

Uncommon strength is nurtured by feared weakness. Uncommon curiosity is nurtured by imagined inexperience. And suspected uncommonness—felt by an affection-hungry man—can deepen his hunger, nurture his learning of a common touch. He is perhaps most likely to have "ne'er lost the common touch" who ne'er legitimately gained it.

The truth is that this man of whom—*for* whom—I write, far from being a common man, is something of a priss, a compleat seducer, fearful of being caught a snob, a lover of being loved, and with a shade of manner that John Gunther, with delightful precision, called "feminoid."

But a softy? Certainly not.

Spoiled brats—and this is a classic description of one, although I really don't think that's what young Franklin turned out to be—are not softies. They are hard, with unreasonable expectations, unreasonable demands. But early vanity may mature into useful pride. It is a man of deep, strong, long-hardened pride who, while maintaining the good manners his mother taught him, seethed with umbrage at the behavior of Herbert Hoover. (For goodness' sake, let's finally give the man release. Let Roosevelt for once in public—a quarter century after he's gone—unload his real feelings about Hoover. It'll do his soul good.)

So much for this background to background—let's get to the point. Here's this man about to do the utterly implausible. In this chapter I must set the stage for the reader. We all *know* it happened, yet it defies reason. Pronouncing a ghostwritten homily about nothing to fear but fear, and radiating the seductive smile that elected him, Roosevelt closed down the crippled banks. Reopening them in less than a week, he got on the radio and asked the frightened people to bring their precious dollars back. And they did! By the hundreds of millions of dollars, they carried their life savings to the riskiest of "safekeeping." Implausible? Inconceivable! Preposterous! But they did. He said everything was going to be all right, and that made everything all right.

The man who spoke of "nameless, unreasoning" fear had been elected by nameless, unreasoning confidence. The people could not reasonably have been swayed by his stated "program"; it was too unformed and ambiguous. The people were swept by a desire to turn out Hoover and an even greater desire to find someone new in whom to believe. F.D.R. was exquisite for the role. While Hoover kept talking of confidence, F.D.R. hardly mentioned the word. He was the look, the sound, the very presence of confidence. He exuded it. The people, needing to believe, found a man who invited belief.

The source of the people's peculiar confidence in F.D.R. was F.D.R.'s consummate confidence in himself, and the only explainable source for *that* is in the cradle. It's not too much to say that if Roosevelt's mysterious aura of confidence saved the banks—and capitalism itself—a small medal ought to be struck for Ma-*ma*. That poor old lady has taken a public thrashing, eluding credit not only for what F.D.R. owes her but for what we *all* owe her. Dominant a force as Sara Delano Roosevelt may have been in the life of Franklin both as boy and man, it's entirely simplistic and wrong to regard her only as a repressive influence. She was the single most enriching fact of his life.

Another person who thinks the popular conception of Sara is all wrong is F.D.R.'s daughter, Anna, the oldest of his children, who grew closer to him than any member of his family. In my hours of conversation with her, I just needed to touch the "Granny" button to get an outpouring about the *security* she provided Franklin that never for a moment, so far as anyone could ever see, failed him:

"Oh she was a martinet . . . but I've always felt that he did have *always* this assurance. At the time things were going all to pot, from '28 on, let's say, to March '33, and this man suddenly came in"—Anna often falls into the detachment of saying "this man" when talking about Father in historical terms—"he stood for the self-assurance of a past. He had a way of speaking to people who had just been knocked out of their homes. But he was not about to be knocked over the way they'd been knocked over. He spoke from security."

"So, in a way," I suggested, "his mother's love served the whole country."

"Oh, helped *save* it. This is where I don't think anyone's given credit to Granny. The credit that she really is due."[1]

Sara Roosevelt kept Franklin fearless of fear by the direct means of shielding him from unpleasant experiences that inform fear: unattended pain, punishment for failure, undue scolding for bad behavior. Seldom has a young child been more constantly attended and incessantly approved by his mother.

Sara needed the companionship, the affection, the delight—the possession—of her baby almost as much as the baby needed hers. Her life had been more orderly and pleasant than fulfilled. As a young woman under the benign vigilance of a rich, proud father, she had turned suitors away, apparently to her father's satisfaction. Then, not altogether to his pleasure, at the age of twenty-six she gave her hand to her father's business associate and contemporary, very nearly the father's personality twin. James Roosevelt, a widower, became Sara's husband at fifty-two. When, a year later, in her bedroom at the Roosevelt ancestral home at Hyde Park, New York, she became a mother for the first and only time, she was about as distant in years from her husband as from her baby. The restraint and dignity required in acting the young wife to an aging aristocrat this energetic woman counterbalanced by active and emotional involvement with her infant possession.

For two months her child remained unnamed, his mother content to call him "Baby." When the parents finally brought themselves to name him Franklin, after her father's brother, for many more months Sara continued to speak and write of him as Baby.[2] Although she could afford a nurse and indeed employed one, she believed "that every mother ought to learn to care for her own baby, whether she can afford to delegate the task to someone else or not." For almost a year she breast-fed him. Other elemental attentions continued far longer. At age eight and a half, while visiting relatives, Franklin wrote his father with manly pride, "Mama left this morning and I am going to take my bath alone."[3]

Father, fifty-three years the child's senior, is often portrayed as more of a grandfather, a distant presence. After all, he had a son by his first marriage as old as Franklin's mother. This portrayal is not correct. Father James entered easily into Franklin's world, taking his little son for a gentle ride through the snow on a horse-drawn sleigh, a row down the Hudson River, a bird shoot. Before Franklin was two years old, they often rode together in a single saddle. Touring the estate, the child would observe his father as an active "man in charge," directing the labor of helpers. But there were times when James withdrew behind his muttonchop whiskers to the recuperative silences where grandfathers often go. Despite the active engagement of James in his son's life, there was little doubt as to whose claim on Baby was superior. Often Sara said, "Franklin is a *Delano,* not a Roosevelt at all." In his devotion to wife and child, Father James formalized this claim by an unusual provision of his last will and testament: "I do hereby appoint my wife sole guardian of my son Franklin Delano Roosevelt, and wish him to be under the influence of his mother." A wish could hardly have been observed more faithfully.[4]

Franklin spent most of his time in the company of adults. Acquiring, as any child would, the manners of those in his environment, no wonder the small boy impressed people around him as precocious and serious. At age

five he accompanied his parents to Washington for a social round of visits
with John Hay, William C. Whitney, and President Grover Cleveland.
Sara wrote, "Everyone is charming to us. Even Franklin knows everybody."
But behind the learned openness and good manners with elders, there also
grew an acute shyness. Mother wrote, "No one knew better than I what a
time Franklin had in hiding the self-consciousness he felt when he spoke to
anyone other than the members of the immediate family." Even servants
in the kitchen offering a cookie, she observed, could not lure him from behind Mother's skirts.

A cultivated use of words became a main vehicle for the mutual adoration of mother and son. She spent hours reading to him, at home, on their
sailboat the *Half Moon,* from *Little Men* and *Robinson Crusoe,* and twice
she read him *Swiss Family Robinson.* With everlasting patience, she
amused him with games. Sara has recalled a rare reprimand. Its tone is revealing of the absence in his early life of ill-tempered conflict, the constant
maternal awareness of shaping a young personality, by withdrawing and
restoring approval, toward a desired end. Playing a game of steeplechase,
the child sulked when he didn't win. Coolly, Mother picked up the toys
and informed the child she would play with him no more until he learned
to lose like a gentleman. With some apparent guilt at what was for her
extreme behavior, she later wrote, "I dare say I was thought a rather hard
disciplinarian at the time." What inevitably resulted in Franklin was a
desire to please and an acute skill—which his mother mistook for an in-
born intuition—at finding the means for attaining that end.[5]

If words were the main vehicle for transmitting Mother's adoration, the
child learned to respond in kind. At age five, when Mother was ill, he wrote
her his first letter. Addressing its envelope "Mrs. James Roosevelt/Hyde
Park/N Y," he enclosed a page of ink drawings of sailboats and carried
the communication to her bedroom upstairs. The letter said:

1887

Dear Sallie
    I am very sorry you have a cold and you are in bed   I played with
Mary [Newbold, a neighbor's daughter] today for a little while   I hope
by tomorrow you will be able to be up   I am glad to say that my cold is
better   your loving

Franklin D. Roosevelt

The harmoniousness of such an existence, if it does not dull one entirely,
is bound to release ebullience and joy—and a hunger for adventure, which
many years later was to manifest itself in an appetite for crisis as the nectar

of life. His second letter, written January 1, 1888, still before Franklin was six years old, was an explosion of fearlessness and zest:

> my dear mama
>   we coasted! yesterday   nothing dangerous yet, look out for tomorrow!! your boy.
>
>   F

To whom else but Mother was there to write, his early days so bare of other children? At large family gatherings he saw cousins from across the Hudson at Newburgh (Mother's side) or from Oyster Bay, Long Island (Father's). At one such party he played a horse, and a distant cousin, Eleanor Roosevelt, rode on his back. Except at these affairs, his playmates were almost exclusively the Rogers and Newbold children of Hyde Park, social peers whose homes were separated from his by the expanse of huge estates along the river.[6]

On October 22, 1888, when he was nearing seven, having already mastered his letters, spurred by mother's adoration, his formal education began. For two hours a day—still leaving most of his mother's day warmed by his presence—he went up the road to share with the Rogers children the instruction of their governess, Fräulein Reinhardt. Before long, he improved his loving letters to Mother not only in English, but sent one in German script: "I will show you, that I can already write in German. But I shall always try to improve it, so that you will be really pleased."

Three years later, when Fräulein Reinhardt departed for a "sanitarium" (a euphemism of the day for a mental hospital), he acquired a tutoring nurse of his own, Mlle. Sandoz from Switzerland, who added French to his repertoire. Also, the first signs of social consciousness. One day he wrote in a composition on Egypt, "The working people had nothing. . . . The kings made them work so hard and gave them so little that by wingo! they nearly starved and by jinks! they had hardly any clothes so they died in quadrillions." After two years, Mlle. Sandoz left to be married. In adulthood, Roosevelt enjoyed commenting that he had driven one governess to insanity and one to matrimony.

When he was nine and accompanying his parents on a summer visit to the German resort of Bad Nauheim, he had his only experience in an elementary school. He was enrolled in a small *Volksschule* for six weeks with the aim of improving his German. He wrote to a young cousin, "I go to the public school with a lot of little mickies and we have German reading, German dictation, the history of Siegfried, and arithmetic in which I am [up] to '14×71,' on paper, and I like it very much." Sara was less taken by the experiment in classlessness, writing that it was "very amusing, but I doubt if he learns much."

At eleven years of age, Franklin's home instruction was transferred from a nurse to a male tutor. Mother knew she could not keep him forever cloistered. When the gangling boy turned a pubescent fourteen, alas, she sent him away to Groton School. "It is hard to leave our darling boy," she wrote. "James and I both feel this parting very much."[7]

The departure from home was more difficult for Franklin than for most of his classmates, almost all of whom also had led early lives of protectiveness and exclusion. Normally, a boy entered Groton at the age of twelve. Franklin's peers had had two long years of sharing experiences, forming alliances, constructing a miniature society, before Sara brought herself to let him go. Much of *his* four years at Groton, although he never indicated it in his letters to Ma-*ma,* were lived under the stress of feeling, at least partially, an outsider. Franklin's wife-to-be, in her latter-day profuse autobiographical writings, lays upon this early stress much of Roosevelt's later need for seeking, and skill at winning, affection—not only from working associates but from the millions in crowds through the wave of a hand, the glow of a smile.

At Groton the budding man in Franklin sometimes showed signs of flowering, but the mother's son in him did not get much chance to wilt. Upon the outbreak of the Spanish-American War and publicized exploits of Cousin Theodore, Franklin and his roommate, Lathrop Brown, conspired to run away to do battle against the Spaniards. They were about to execute their manly little plan when their bodies broke out with telltale marks. The boys landed not in Cuba but in the infirmary with scarlet fever. Mother rushed to Groton. Forbidden by doctors to visit his quarantined room, she daily climbed a stepladder and sat outside his infirmary window reading to him.[8]

When not ill, Franklin wrote home at least twice a week in the most endearing of prose. While addressing letters "My dear Mama and Papa," he almost always referred to Papa in the third person, making clear whom he was really addressing. He acknowledged her equally frequent mail not by referring to "your letter," but always "your dear letter," as though that were all one one word. Mother saved his letters, every one, but not before dressing them up with omitted words she was sure he intended. In one, thanking her for sending the *Audubon Journals,* he wrote, "I shall spend every spare on it until it is finished." She inserted the word "moment." In another: "Your visit seems like a delightful now." With certainty of his intentions, she inserted "dream." In still another, writing that he was "dieing to see their new horses," Mother corrected his spelling before filing the letter for posterity (which apparently she never doubted would be interested in seeking it out).

Surely for Sara a high point of their correspondence, often cluttered with her admonitions of self-care and his requests for toothbrushes, dental floss, and sweaters, was reached when Franklin wrote: "When you send the other things please could you send the little picture of yourself [as a girl] in the little silver heart-shaped frame on my bureau, as I want it to put on my desk here."[9]

Now, really! Would a boy so snugly loving, loved, and secure, so nurtured by the warm reality of bosom, bath, and book, grow up expected to fear impending disaster from so remote and abstract a source as a banking system? What an ideal upbringing for a man who would one day say —just when people needed someone to say it: Bring your money back. "All we have to fear is fear itself."

The self-confidence that people perceived distantly in F.D.R., Roosevelt's associates saw close at hand. An observation by Raymond Moley is the most acute, describing not one incident, but two; contrasting, but reinforcing. The first of these occurrences came on February 15, four nights before the Inner Circle dinner. Roosevelt interrupted a Caribbean fishing trip to make an appearance in Miami, at Bay Front Park. After completing a short, informal speech, he sat atop the back seat of an open car leading a procession, waving to the crowd. In the second car, Moley and Vincent Astor, F.D.R.'s fishing host, exchanged odd speculations. Astor, new to the world of a presidential presence, remarked how easy it would be for an assassin to do his work and, under darkening skies, be swallowed up in the huge crowd. Moley replied that he had passed through such throngs in twilight so many times in the preceding campaign months that he had ceased thinking about the danger.

At that moment, five shots cracked through the crowd.

The point of describing the ensuing minutes is not in the event itself, but in Roosevelt's personal involvement and feelings. Therefore, it's his own recollection that is most revealing. Characteristically, Roosevelt's account, dictated the next day, makes no direct mention that the crazed gunman, a thirty-two-year-old Italian bricklayer, Giuseppe Zangara, while shooting five people including Mayor Anton Cermak of Chicago, missed his target, F.D.R., only by inches. The President-elect was saved only by the quick action of a woman in the crowd, who jostled Zangara's arm and deflected his aim.

"I have tried ever since last night not to confuse what I saw with all that was told me," Roosevelt dictated. "After I had finished speaking, somebody from the talking picture people climbed on the back of the car and said I simply had to turn around and repeat to them what I said.

"I said I would not do it. He said: 'We have come a thousand miles for this.' I said: 'I am very sorry but I can't do it.'

"Having said that, I slid off the back of the car into my seat. Just then Mayor Cermak came forward. I shook hands and talked with him for nearly a minute. Then he moved off around the back of the car.

"Bob Clark [a Secret Service man] was standing right beside him to the right. As he moved off, a man came forward with a telegram. . . . Just then I heard what I thought was a firecracker; then several more. The man talking with me was pulled back and the chauffeur started the car.

"I found that a bullet, probably the one that hit Cermak, grazed the top of Clark's hand. His hand was all bloody and scratched. . . .

"I looked around and saw Mayor Cermak doubled up and Mrs. Gill [Mrs. Joseph Gill, wife of a Florida utility magnate] collapsing. Mrs. Gill was at the foot of the bandstand steps. She was shot in the stomach. As soon as she was hit she must have got up and started down the steps. She was slumped over at the bottom.

"I called to the chauffeur to stop. He did, about fifteen feet from where we started. The Secret Service man shouted to him to get out of the crowd and he started the car forward again. . . .

"I saw Mayor Cermak being carried. I motioned to have him put in the back of the car, which would be first out. He was alive, but I didn't think he was going to last. I put my left arm around him and my hand on his pulse, but I couldn't find any pulse. He slumped forward. . . . For three blocks I believed his heart had stopped. I held him all the way to the hospital and his pulse constantly improved.

"That trip to the hospital seemed thirty miles long. I talked to Mayor Cermak nearly all the way. I remember I said: 'Tony, keep quiet—don't move. It won't hurt you if you keep quiet.'

"They rushed him to the operating room for examination. I remained in the hospital and later talked to Cermak for four or five minutes. I also saw the others except Mrs. Gill who was being operated on. They failed to extract the bullet. I remained at the hospital until about a quarter after eleven and then returned to the Nourmahal [Astor's yacht]. I went to bed about two o'clock." (The shooting had been at 9:35 P.M.)

The main point, at least for me, is found in Moley's subsequent recollection:

"Roosevelt's nerve had held absolutely throughout the evening. But the real test in such cases comes afterward, when the crowds, to whom nothing but courage can be shown, are gone. The time for the letdown among his intimates was at hand. All of us were prepared, sympathetically, understandingly, for any reaction that might come from Roosevelt now that the tension was over and he was alone with us. For anything, that is, except what happened.

"There was nothing—not so much as the twitching of a muscle, the mopping of a brow, or even the hint of a false gaiety—to indicate that it wasn't any other evening in any other place. Roosevelt was simply him-self—easy, confident, poised, to all appearances unmoved.

"F.D.R. had talked to me once or twice during the campaign about the possibility that someone would try to assassinate him. To that extent, I knew, he was prepared for Zangara's attempt. But it is one thing to talk philosophically about assassination, and another to face it. And I confess that I have never in my life seen anything more magnificent than Roose-velt's calm that night on the Nourmahal.

"The companion picture came four days later in the early-morning hours of Sunday, February 19th. . . . The Inner Circle was giving its annual jamboree. . . . The letter from Hoover announcing that the breaking point [of the bank crisis] had come somehow made the awful picture take on life for the first time. . . . I looked up at Roosevelt, expecting, cer-tainly, to see some shadow of the grim news in his face or manner. And there was nothing—nothing but laughter and applause for the play actors, pleasant bantering with those who sat at table with him, and the gay, un-hurried autographing of programs for half a hundred fellow guests at the dinner's end.

"I thought then, 'Well, this can't go on. The kickback's got to come when he leaves this crowd. This is just for show. We'll see what happens when he's alone with us.'

"But when we got back to the 65th Street house—Roosevelt and three or four of us—there was still no sign. The letter from Hoover was passed around and then discussed. Capital was fleeing the country. Hoarding was reaching unbearably high levels. The dollar was wobbling on the foreign exchanges as gold poured out. The bony hand of death was stretched out over the banks and insurance companies.

"And Roosevelt was, to all appearances, unmoved.

"It was not until I left the Roosevelt house at two o'clock that Sunday morning that the curious parallel occurred to me. Here were two sequences of stimulus and reaction—Roosevelt alone with his friends after the at-tempt on his life, and Roosevelt alone with his friends after hearing the news that the banking system was mortally stricken. And the responses had been alike!"[10]

Almost everyone close to Roosevelt—his wife, his children, his cabinet officers, his speech writers, his friends—if they have written about Roose-velt at all, have noted his peculiar lack of fear. It is as though he had lived

by the aphorism long before Louis Howe filched it for him from a depart-
ment-store ad: "The only thing we have to fear is fear itself."[11] One
friend, Morris Ernst, a lawyer, made the common observation in a somewhat overdramatized way. Yet in doing so, Ernst may have hit a psychological bull's-eye he did not intend. Ernst once wrote of F.D.R., "He had
humor and gaiety arising out of a deviation from the ordinary pattern of
man, which is fear of death."

In the years since Ernst made his strange comment, years that saw the
full bloom of the age of Freud, a school of psychological researchers has
interested itself in the wide variations of intensity with which different individuals fear death. Some of these researchers have perceived that adults
who inordinately fear death had more often than not, as small children,
suffered stress and anguish in early psychological separation from their
mothers. Conversely, those who with relative comfort can contemplate—
or at least accept—the idea of death usually had been children whose
separation from mother was known to proceed with a secure, gradual ease.
(While Roosevelt held death among those unpleasant subjects he didn't
like to talk about—he loathed attending funerals and avoided discussing
sickness—he clearly accepted it as a simple fact. One of the remarkable
documents of his life is a long memorandum he wrote by hand in 1937
specifying instructions for his funeral and burial, down to the number of
minutes for the service, the departure time for the train bearing his coffin,
the precise length, width, and height of his grave monument, and the exact
direction in which it should lie, even going so far as to limit attendance by
congressmen and the press to two senators, two representatives, three
cameramen, and three reporters.)[12]

Whether these psychological researches in the long run will hold water
or not, and whether or not they illuminate something of Roosevelt's
psychic make-up, one thing is certain. His separation from his mother was
gradual and secure in the extreme. There is reason to believe that the degree of maternal separation that many healthy boys experience by the time
of adolescence did not run its course, in the case of Roosevelt, until he was
almost forty years old. But more of that later.

Part II

My Friends . . .

If the nation's money system had collapsed out of fear, it would be restored out of faith. As head of the national family, my inclination was to do what I would have done in a comparable crisis at home: call a family conference. A national family conference was now possible. Over the past six years, radio stations around the country had connected themselves into national hookups. Inevitably, this would become a great instrument of education and leadership. Before the week was over I would bring about such a family meeting, via radio, called a fireside chat.

But first I had other words to deliver in a more formal setting. At noon on Saturday, March 4, 1933, a chilly, windy day, I took my oath at the Capitol. In the inaugural address, I tried to set a tone of faith that we would all need in the hours and days ahead:

"This great Nation will endure as it has endured, will revive and prosper. So, first of all, let me assert my firm belief that the only thing we have to fear is fear itself—nameless, unreasoning, unjustified terror which paralyzes needed efforts to convert retreat into advance. . . .

"Plenty is at our doorstep, but a generous use of it languishes in the very sight of the supply. Primarily this is because rulers of the exchange of mankind's goods have failed through their own stubbornness and their own incompetence, have admitted their failure, and have abdicated. . . .

"The money-changers have fled from their high seats in the temple of our civilization. We may now restore that temple to ancient truths. The measure of the restoration lies in the extent to which we apply social values more noble than mere monetary profit. . . .

"The people of the United States have not failed. In their need they have registered a mandate that they want direct, vigorous action. They have asked for discipline and direction under leadership. They have made me the present instrument of their wishes. In the spirit of the gift I take it."

The very people standing before me at the Capitol were caught in the financial emergency. Although few among them were poor, their pockets were empty, except for blank checks that were useless for exchange into cash. Shortly before dawn, Governors Herbert H. Lehman of New York and Henry Horner of Illinois had shut down the banks of their states, the main valves of the financial system. The nation had overnight turned moneyless. On the morning of the inauguration, a newspaper reported:

CAPITOL CROWD IN WILD
RUSH TO FIND CASH

Hotels Won't Pay Out Money

Telegraph Heavily Taxed

Appeals for Aid Are Sent
To Friends and Families
In Home States

WASHINGTON—The thousands of men and women visitors who left their hotels and rooming houses today to attend the inaugural ceremony went to Capitol Hill with worried faces. . . . Women in brilliant evening frocks and men in evening clothes scurried from bank to bank and from hotel to hotel, seeking any amount of cash to carry them on. They were too late. . . .

Shortly after 2 a.m., a wave of anxiety [had] swept from hotel to hotel as the words of the impending events were whispered and telephoned and shouted.[1]

I was struck by one reporter's impression of the day's mood: "I do not know how it may have been in other places, but in Chicago, as we saw it, the city seemed to have died. There was something awful—abnormal—in the very stillness of those streets. I recall being startled by the clatter of a horse's hooves on the pavement as a mounted policeman rode past."

I have already described how frantic citizens had been scrambling to get their cash out of banks. Now, on the very day of the transfer of national power, the richest nation on earth was in chaos because their cash was locked inside the banks. From across the country, a new wave of vivid vignettes flowed to our attention. It is important to recount a few of them here so that readers of future generations appreciate the unique—to many, the terrifying, to others, the humorous—mood of that Inauguration Day.

My new Secretary of State, Cordell Hull, had to mollify enraged diplomats who argued that their money was entitled to diplomatic immunity from "confiscation" by closed banks. Throughout the country, doctors, unable to buy gasoline for lack of cash, had to cancel visits to the sick. In New York, a traveling salesman sold his shoe samples in a hotel lobby for cash to get home. From Reno, Nevada, came word that fewer than half a dozen divorce cases were filed each day during my first week in office. Women who could well afford court costs and fees lacked cash for train tickets. We heard of a night-club entertainer who, in a rage, murdered his partner for accepting a pay check instead of cash.

One does not realize the dependence of national commerce upon small change until suddenly the banks—which control the flow of coins—are shut down. People with bills in their pockets—but no change—could not use a pay telephone, ride a streetcar, or buy cigarettes. We heard of one traveler who tried to buy shaving supplies, tendering a fifty-dollar bill. The store clerk, unwilling to part with his change, took back the supplies and advised the man to grow a beard. People would do anything for change. Word got around New York City on Inauguration Day that ticket clerks at Pennsylvania Station had a supply of coins. A crowd showed up offering hundred-, five-hundred-, and even thousand-dollar bills, trying to buy unneeded tickets to Newark just to get change. Next morning, Sunday, hotel managers in a fervor of evangelism ordered bellhops to church with the pious instruction to drop bills in the collection plate—and remove change. One Methodist minister solicited an offering of IOUs. These tales seem amusing now; they were not then. Storekeepers in Elgin, Illinois, upon hearing that a sixteen-year-old neighbor boy had saved 11,357 pennies toward his college education, were in no amused mood when they surrounded his home begging for the precious coppers. I confess that I was amused at the rumor that John D. Rockefeller had run out of dimes and had to give his caddy a whole dollar bill.

In history, of course, commerce preceded money, and now people found themselves regressing to old ways. Having lost their medium of exchange, some went back to mere exchanging. The story came down from Wisconsin of a wrestler who signed a contract to receive a can of tomatoes and a peck of potatoes for practicing his art. An Ashtabula, Ohio, newspaper announced that it would accept produce as payment for advertising. The most good-natured offer of barter, I thought, was made by the New York *Daily News,* which was sponsoring the Golden Gloves boxing tournament at Madison Square Garden. The *News* announced that any article worth a fifty-cent ticket would do at the gate. One lady was cheerfully admitted upon presenting a pair of silken step-ins, clearly worth the price.

One other item is worth mentioning. At the White House, late Saturday night after the inauguration, Mrs. Roosevelt came to me looking quite distressed. Our boys had to return to school and she had very little cash for their pockets. I assured her that somehow we'd manage. Mrs. Roosevelt often retold this story, always adding, "I began to realize then that there were certain things that one need not worry about in the White House."[2]

Before getting on to the important place of Fireside Chats in my years at the White House—the main story I want to convey in this chapter—I must sketch out the events that resolved the bank crisis, at least temporarily, during my first week in office.

On Saturday evening I received an assurance from Will Woodin, my Secretary of the Treasury, that, come what may, he would have an emergency bank bill ready by the following Thursday morning. On that assurance I called a special session of Congress starting that Thursday, March 9. I also drew up a proclamation to declare a national banking holiday from Monday through Thursday. The purposes of this holiday were to (1) prevent continued runs on banks, (2) permit the reopening of sound banks in an orderly manner, (3) keep closed the many banks that were insolvent and permit their orderly liquidation, and (4) enable the people to have confidence in the banking system when its normal operations resumed.

All day Sunday, federal reserve bank officials objected and bickered over this move, offering no alternative of their own. They harped on the "dubiousness" of the President's authority to close reserve banks along with others. When the proclamation was issued at one o'clock Monday morning, they were still bickering. Finally, at 2 A.M., Ray Moley, losing patience, demanded that if a President, two Secretaries of the Treasury (Ogden Mills of the previous administration was working right along with us), and the head of the Federal Reserve System couldn't order the closing of the reserve banks, who, in God's name, could? At that, they gave in.

Meanwhile, starting at ten o'clock Sunday morning and for four interminable days and nights, another group of bankers haggled over ways and means to reopen banks, especially how to get money back into circulation after so much gold had been withdrawn which normally was the security behind dollar bills. Woodin reported to me that they were at sea; all these vaunted experts, confronted by the unusual, could come up with no answers. They reminded me of a day in 1914 when I was Assistant Secretary of the Navy: I was traveling from Maine to Washington, riding the so-called Bankers' Special, listening to such gentlemen, the experts, discuss the outbreak of war. I asked their opinion of how long it would last. They all agreed, "Not more than three months. There isn't enough money in the world for a war to be able to last longer."

In the face of such wisdom, no wonder the tempers of reasonable men were now being strained. Old Senator Carter Glass of Virginia, a fiscal conservative if there ever was one, lost his temper before the week was out, stating (the underlying racial sentiment was his, not mine): "One banker in my state attempted to marry a white woman and they lynched him." And Senator Burton K. Wheeler of Montana added his contribution: "The best way to restore confidence in the banks would be to take these crooked bank presidents out and treat them the same as we treated Al Capone when he failed to pay his income tax."

Rather than stand with these exaggerations—which were indicative of a growing mood—I was more inclined to go along with Gerald Johnson, the historian, who had said a few weeks earlier, "It will be many a long day before Americans of the middle class will listen with anything approaching the reverence they felt in 1928 whenever a magnate of business speaks. We now know they are not magicians.

When it comes to a real crisis they are as helpless as the rest of us, and as bewildered."[3]

We simple politicians decided to find our own solutions. One of the ideas that had run through these fruitless discussions was issuance of *scrip,* a kind of temporary currency later redeemable for real money. While the bankers were theorizing on the pros and cons of scrip, in some places groups were already issuing it privately— and making it work. At Princeton University the student newspaper printed 25-cent scrip notes for students, issuing them on credit, and merchants accepted them. Mormons in Salt Lake City did the same.

Consideration of national scrip abruptly ended on Tuesday morning, when Secretary Woodin rushed into my office with an idea that saved the day. Old Will, an elf of a man, had been a manufacturer of railway equipment, never a banker; he wore a gray toupee, invented unforgivable puns, and composed songs on the guitar. One of his tunes had been the opening number of the Inaugural Concert played by the National Symphony Orchestra. He was better known as composer of *Raggedy Ann's Sunny Songs* for children, one of which went:

> Let us be like bluebirds,
> Happy all day long,
> Forgetting all our troubles
> In a sunny song.

Lying awake most of the night, Will's artistic mind had cut through the cloud of confusion raised by bankers who could not see the difference between gold and real wealth. He said, "I played my guitar a little while and then read a little while and then slept a little while and then awakened and then thought about the scrip thing and then played some more and read some more and slept some more and thought some more. And, by gum, if I didn't hit on the answer that way! Why didn't I see it before? We don't have to issue scrip." His fist crashed down on the table. "These bankers have hypnotized themselves and us. *We can issue currency against the sound assets of banks.* The Reserve Act lets us print all we'll need. And it won't frighten people. It won't look like stage money. It'll be money that looks like money."

That became the basis of the Emergency Banking Act—and the beginning of the end of gold as security for dollar bills.*

Still, however, gold *was* the accepted symbol of wealth. We decided to fight the slyness of gold hoarding with slyness of another kind. The Federal Reserve Board announced that, while banks were closed, it would advertise lists of hoarders who failed to redeposit their withdrawn gold by the following Monday, March 13. Bank doors would open to admit persons for that purpose. The plan worked beautifully. By the thousands, anonymous phone callers asked banks what would happen to people whose names were advertised. Bank employees were coached in answering vaguely but ominously. In pockets, in tin cans, in suitcases, gold certificates flowed back to the banks. People lined up in queues as they had in the preceding weeks' panic of withdrawals, mostly in New York, where $30 million was taken in in one day. One man brought in seven hundred thousand dollars, and one company, unidentified, delivered $6 million. So great was the return of gold that we had to issue far fewer of the newly authorized federal reserve notes—"Woodin money"—than we had originally anticipated.

At noon Thursday Congress convened. Writing of the emergency

---

* For those interested in the more technical provisions of the Emergency Banking Act, I quote from my summary of it in Volume II of my *Public Papers and Addresses:*

"This Emergency Banking Act confirmed all of the emergency measures which had been taken by the President and the Secretary of the Treasury since March 4, 1933; and also gave the President further emergency powers to control foreign exchange transactions, gold and currency movements, and banking transactions in general. It gave the Comptroller of the Currency power to appoint a conservator, when necessary, to conserve the assets of closed national banks without liquidation. It also authorized national banks to issue and sell their preferred stock to the Reconstruction Finance Corporation, a provision which permitted them to obtain funds without creating claims superior to the claims of their depositors, as was the case whenever they borrowed money from the Reconstruction Finance Corporation or elsewhere.

"The Act also made it possible for any member bank to meet all demands for currency so long as it had sound assets, regardless of the technical eligibility of these assets under the former permanent law, by borrowing against these assets from the Federal Reserve banks.

"On the previous Sunday, March 5th, when the Proclamation closing the banks was determined upon, it was obvious that we should strive to allow the banks to open just as soon as we could obtain reliable assurance of the solvency of each bank. To obtain this information throughout the United States would require at least a week. However, we thought it best to limit the first Proclamation to four days.

"It was necessary, as we had expected, to issue a second proclamation at the expiration date of the first proclamation (March 9, 1933), extending the bank holiday indefinitely until further Proclamation."

banking bill was not completed until one o'clock. Chairman Henry
B. Steagall of the House Banking and Currency Committee, as I
heard it, ran down the aisle of the House chamber, waving over his
head one of only two existing copies (the other was at the Government
Printing Office) and shouting, "Here's the bill. Let's pass it." Which
the House with record speed did. The same copy was then dispatched
to the Senate, which passed the bill with seventy-three yeas and seven
nays and promptly adjourned at 7:52 P.M. At 8:36, in the White
House Library, surrounded by unpacked books and pictures, I signed
my first bill into law—less than eight hours after it was written.

It is worth noting here that the seven senators who voted against
this emergency bill, while mostly Republicans, were classed among
the "progressive" wing of their party, or who officially wore the designation of the Progressive Party (Borah, Carey, Costigan, Dale, La
Follette, Nye, Shipstead).[4] That was my first—but not my last—
experience in learning that my "progressive" allies sometimes became
so engaged in theorizing about a Utopian world that they blinded
themselves to present realities. These "progressives" had a penchant
for confusing their *dream* of the possible with the *art* of the possible.
With full knowledge of the small minority they composed—and the
small minority they represented—they pressed for the impossible,
risking the national disaster of disunity when only unity could save us.

What they wanted—or some of them did—was for me to take advantage of the emergency by the radical act of nationalizing the
banks. Permanently. The American people were not asking to have
this done. But these senators wanted it, and were so convinced of
their wisdom that they would impose it upon the average citizen,
who was, after all, on his back helpless to object. "There will never be
a better time," Costigan and La Follette pleaded with me the night
before the bill's passage, never arguing that this is what the people
want. Well, there is never a better time to tell another fellow what's
good for him than when he is on his back. But once on his feet again,
that fellow will do some deciding of his own. And you'd better
watch out.

What we did in our Emergency Banking Act was not radical, but
bold. Banking depends upon make-believe, upon confidence. Instead
of undermining confidence, we sought to inspire it. We took unorthodox steps to support orthodox instruments: private banks and
sound dollar bills. The time called for new ways, but not for new

institutions. I go along entirely with Ray Moley's estimate written six years later: "If ever there was a moment when things hung in the balance, it was on March 5, 1933—when unorthodoxy would have drained the last remaining strength of the capitalistic system. Capitalism was saved in eight days."

There was a small but growing band of angry citizens, impelled by the hardships of the depression, who wanted to see the destruction of the capitalistic system. There were others, who were incapable of imagining the slightest change in their old, untroubled ways. Once their system was saved, they wanted no further tampering with it, no permanent reforms that would protect our capitalistic system—I almost said *theirs,* but I mean *ours*—against a recurrence of crisis. Because I later proposed such protective reforms, some of these comfortable ladies and gentlemen whispered that I was a "traitor to my class." Let them say it if they wish. And I say this: I certainly had not become President to be the servant of *any* class. If I helped save the system that happens to benefit those ladies and gentlemen more than anyone else, I helped save it because I believe it promises to benefit more people in more ways than any other system known. But it is a system, not a religion or a deity. It is a tool, invented by man to serve man. When it wears down and serves badly, men must sharpen it, renew it, perhaps even reshape it. The only alternative was one I was far from ready to accept—taking the troublesome old tool and throwing it away.[5]

We might have taken other ways—and others did. On the same day, March 6, 1933, that we closed the banks to conserve our system, another people on their backs, the frightened citizens of Germany, elected a majority to the Reichstag in support of Adolf Hitler. History was soon—and at unimagined human cost—to test whether our course of moderation or theirs of desperation was more in the service of humankind.

And so we come to our second weekend in office and the announcement, made on Saturday, that on Sunday at 10 P.M. I would talk on the radio to bring the people into our plans.

The idea had been growing in my mind all week. I had thought back to the time about three years earlier when, as governor of New York, I had been pressing for consideration of new controls over power companies. The legislature was recalcitrant. Well, I was confident where an informed public would stand, so I said to my staff, "I'll take the issue to the people." We arranged a state-wide hookup of radio stations. I explained in straightforward, conversational terms why I felt my position was in the interests of the people. Let the editorialists and power-company publicists proceed to say anything they please. I had stated my case in full, in my own words, independent of their interpretation. Let the public now express its will. They certainly did. Mail came flooding in to the legislators at Albany. That convinced me that the new power of radio, properly used, was an instrument of democracy. One may say that for the first time in centuries a public leader could again establish the intimacy with citizens once known in the small city-states of ancient Greece.

Of course, Presidents had spoken on the radio before. President Woodrow Wilson was first to do so. Warren G. Harding was first to cast his voice beyond a single city, over a hookup connecting Washington, New York, and St. Louis. Four years before my election, Herbert Hoover and Alfred E. Smith made the first campaign speeches over extended networks.

These early presidential appearances on radio were regarded as technical wonders, but were, in the main, political flops. Always, an appearance was "An Address." Never just a simple talk. The speaker would orate aloofly to a throng, never sit down for a friendly talk with a man and his wife. You always had the feeling the orator didn't have you in mind at all, but was talking over your head to people a hundred yards behind you.

In fact, Presidents considered it their duty to remain aloof, not only from the average citizen but even from leading men of affairs. When Woodrow Wilson finally consented to permit the installation of a presidential telephone, he had it placed outside his private office. My immediate superior in his administration, Secretary of the Navy Josephus Daniels, wouldn't dream, except in the most extraordinary emergency, of conveying a message to the President by telephone. Nor would the President deign to call him. Hoover was first to permit a telephone in his private office, but he used it only rarely.

I thought all this aloofness was silly play acting as well as highly inefficient. We immediately installed a switchboard in the White House, with private lines to many offices. About a hundred government officials were able to get through to me at will, without the formality of going through my appointments secretary. I spent about one quarter of my time on the telephone, which vastly enhanced the cause of prompt decision making.[6]

To help end this feeling of an unbridgeable moat between the people and their President, we hit upon the happy thought of calling my bank message a "fireside chat." The term caught hold so well, it was soon formalized by the press with capital letters, Fireside Chat. Actually, the talk was delivered in front of—well, not too far away from—a real fireplace, even though no one thought of starting a fire. The room was so cluttered with wires and switching contraptions, I am sure the engineers would not have allowed it. As it was, we had to remove James Monroe's gold dinner service and a barrelful of other museum pieces to make room for all the radio equipment in the oval-shaped room in the White House basement, which became our broadcasting studio.

About thirty officials, friends, and family members sat before me, enduring uncomfortable folding chairs. On the desk from which I spoke were a battery of microphones, a decanter of water, and a watch that showed seconds as well as minutes. In the margin of my reading copy, I had marked where I should be at precise points in my radio time. With a quick glance at the watch between occasional paragraphs, I could tell whether to slightly slow or speed up my reading, which they told me was normally about a hundred words per minute.

As it turned out, this careful preparation did me no good for the first "chat." Minutes before I was to begin, I asked for my reading copy, a special one, in pica type, triple-spaced. Everyone looked at everyone else. Nobody had it. There was no time to start ransacking the White House. The faces of my staff froze in terror. After allowing them a few moments to fear everything including fear itself, I motioned to a newspaper reporter to lend me his mimeographed, single-spaced text. It was not at all difficult to follow.

This was not to be the last Case of the Missing Speech. On the day almost nine years later, December 8, 1941, when I went to the Congress personally to ask for a Declaration of War, we returned to the White House, and my secretary, Grace Tully, asked me, "Where is the speech, Mr. President?" It was, of course, a document of great historical importance. I replied, "I guess Jimmy [my son] or Charley Fredericks [a Secret Service agent] picked it up." No one knew anything about it. Mike Reilly, the head of the Secret Service detail, undertook a big investigation. He traced it from the Capitol via Jimmy to the White House foyer, where it had last been seen on a shelf atop the coat rack to the right of the front door. It was never found. Somebody had purloined a most extraordinary souvenir that he will never be able to display on his mantel or safely show his grandchildren—or even donate to the National Archives without great embarrassment.

On the matter of furnishings and trappings for the Fireside Chats, one more deserves mention: my pivot tooth. It happens that I have a chip in one of my lower front teeth, resulting from a boyhood accident. While I doubt having lost many votes from thus offending the human eye, the imperfection does peculiar things to the ear. Sometimes the middles of my words come out a bird whistle, especially on the radio. So I've been fixed up with an extra, portable "pivot tooth," which, when my best behavior is called for, must be screwed into place. Well, frankly, I loathe the silly thing. I faithfully keep it in a heart-shaped silver case, but am less faithful in carrying it around. Just before broadcast time, someone would always say in a voice of sudden alarm, "The tooth!" And I would start digging around in my pockets. It was seldom there. That would set in motion what Mike Reilly calls the "pivot-tooth detail"—one of his boys walking with great dignity out of the oval room, then, once out of sight of the presidential guests, running like blazes up to my bedroom for the precious tooth. More than once when the network announcers, Carlton Smith, John Daly, and Bob Trout, were austerely pronouncing, "Ladies and gentlemen, the President of the United States," I was seen hastily screwing in that tooth. For that matter, careful students of history who take the trouble to listen to recordings of my Fireside Chats will detect occasions when the pivot-tooth detail didn't quite make it.[7]

The Fireside Chat on banking began with the salutation I used in every speech I recall making since the days, more than twenty years earlier, when I successfully campaigned for the New York State Senate among my farm neighbors in Dutchess, Putnam, and Columbia counties:

"My friends:

"I want to talk for a few minutes with the people of the United States about banking—with the comparatively few who understand the mechanics of banking, but more particularly with the overwhelming majority who use banks for the making of deposits and the drawing of checks. . . . I know that when you understand what we in Washington have been about, I shall continue to have your co-operation as fully as I have had your sympathy and help during the past week.

"First of all, let me state the simple fact that when you deposit money in a bank, the bank does not put the money into a safe-deposit vault. It invests your money in many different forms. . . ." And so on, in a summary of how banks work, how loss of confidence in them had made currency disappear, and the three steps promptly taken by our government: (1) proclamation of the nation-wide bank holiday, (2) passage of the Emergency Banking Act enabling me to extend the holiday if necessary and reopen banks gradually, and (3) regulations permitting banks to release payrolls and permit some withdrawals for family emergencies.

I went on to assure people that when banks reopened, the sound thing to do was not to make further withdrawals, but to make deposits: "It needs no prophet to tell you that when the people find that they can get their money—that they can get it when they want it for all legitimate purposes—the phantom of fear will soon be laid. . . . I can assure you that it is safer to keep your money in a reopened bank than under a mattress."

A message of this kind to the people must steer a careful course between the Scylla of unnecessary technical detail and the Charybdis of buoyant twaddle. The average man may not be qualified to walk into a bank and start running it. But talk to him about his own bank account and he may surprise you with his alertness and intelligence. When I dictate a speech, I try to wipe from my mind any awareness of bankers or government officials or university-trained experts. I try to talk directly to someone like Old Moses Smith, a farmer I have known all my life at my home town of Hyde Park. Moses is not a man of formal education, but he knows what's good for him. When I drive through the countryside of Hyde Park, I often drive past Old Moses' place, especially when I'm troubled by a new government crisis. I stop the car, call to him, and all I have to say is, "Moses, how are things going?"

He has never failed to help me out. He tilts back his hat, unloads some tobacco juice, leans on my car, and says, "Well, boy, I'll tell you. . . ." That's the only way he ever addressed me as a boy or as President. It kept us on good terms. After a half hour or so, I'd drive away refreshed, with a worthwhile new look at things.

After one of my early Fireside Chats, I was very pleased to hear from my old friend Felix Frankfurter, then a law professor at Harvard. In his estimable opinion, at least, my chats were beginning to fulfill what I think is a most important function of the presidency. He wrote: "Sunday night you again took the nation to school—as I hope you will, from time to time, take it to school. With . . . simplicity and lucidity you are making known to the nation what you are doing. But you are also making the people feel—and nothing is more important for a democracy—that in a true sense of the word it is *their* government, and that *their* interests and *their* feelings are actively engaged."[8]

For most talks, of course, I did not do all the preliminary work unaided. Certainly I was not about to emulate my predecessor, who once complained that he had to spend two or three weeks on a personal, longhand drafting of each talk. Such use of a President's time is hardly in the best interests of the people he serves. My inaugural address, for example, was drafted by Raymond Moley, with whom I had held the closest discussions about it during all the months since the election. He knew my thinking, and his preliminary draft expressed it. Still, his thoughts were not precisely mine. On the night of February 27, starting from the basis of his draft, I sat down at my Hyde Park home and, in my own hand, composed the address in my own language. A few days later, my assistant over many years, Louis Howe, who also knew my thinking as few others did, made a valuable suggestion or two that enriched the final draft.

Some people are cynical about such assistance, disparaging it with the term "ghost-writing." I think they are foolish. A presidential speech, while delivered with the personal touch of his own voice, is not—should not be—a subjective, highly personalized literary work. It is an expression not of a President's private soul, but his public policy. He speaks for his entire government and, one hopes, for all the people he leads. Why should not the best minds of his government and among his people help him? The important thing is that the message grow from the President's thoughts, mature with his own contributions of language, and, most important of all, that the President take total responsibility for the final text.

In brief, this is how these views on speech writing were applied to the first Fireside Chat: The task of writing a first draft was given to Charles Michelson, for several years a publicist for the Democratic National Committee. Michelson later confessed, "Technically, these matters of deep finance were, of course, clear over my head." Shielding the useless draft from my eyes, Moley stepped in and reassigned the task to Arthur A. Ballantine, Under Secretary of the Treasury, who, I might add for the edification of any who considered my tendencies too radical, was a holdover from the Hoover subcabinet. Ballantine, a classmate of mine at Harvard, did a fine job of building a sound, correct structure for the message. But, of course, it was on the dry side. I took his draft and dictated a new one— aimed directly at Old Moses.

During the next two years Moley was in charge of advance preparation of speech drafts. He had occasional assistance from Howe, Frankfurter, Donald R. Richberg, William C. Bullitt, General Hugh S. Johnson, and Rex Tugwell. In 1934 two protégés of Professor Frankfurter, Thomas G. Corcoran and Benjamin V. Cohen, worked on speeches with Moley and directly with me, among their other important government duties. Beginning in 1936, Judge Samuel I. Rosenman of the New York State Supreme Court, who had been my counsel as governor, took over speech preparation. This loyal and sensitive man was unique in his ability to present me with a draft, after I had discussed my thoughts with him, that expressed almost exactly what I would write myself. About the time World War II loomed over us, the playwright Robert E. Sherwood brought his remarkable artistry and intelligence into team with Rosenman's. Many a time I discussed a speech with them late at night, then went to bed, while that resourceful pair stayed up all night in the Cabinet Room—Sam fueled by sandwiches and cokes, Bob by whiskey and soda—revising draft upon draft and having a speech ready for me to work on in the morning.[9]

Soon after the Fireside Chat on the banks, which was broadcast over a transcontinental network of more than 150 stations, radio experts estimated for us that twenty million homes had tuned in, with an audience of sixty million Americans. That was grand, but what effect would it have on the fate of banks? The answer was not long in coming. Next day, Steve Early, my press secretary, handed me a

telegram he had received from Roy Roberts, a Kansas City newspaperman:

> YOU MAY BE INTERESTED IN KNOWING BANKS REOPENED HERE IN
> AMAZINGLY QUIET FASHION PUBLIC HYSTERIA SEEMS OVER MORE DE-
> POSITORS THAN WITHDRAWALS BUSINESS AND CROWDS SMALLER THAN
> USUAL FOR A MONDAY ASIDE FROM THAT NOTHING OUT OF WAY ROOSE-
> VELT SPEECH MADE A PROFOUND IMPRESSION LIVESTOCK AND GRAIN
> MARKET FUNCTIONING WITHOUT HITCH

And this wire from A. P. Giannini of San Francisco, chairman
of the Bank of America, the nation's largest bank:

> THE OPENING OF BANKS IN SAN FRANCISCO WAS VERY GRATIFYING
> NORMAL BANKING CONDITIONS PREVAIL EVERYWHERE STOP ON MY VISITS
> TO OUR BRANCHES I FOUND DEPOSITORS CHEERFUL AND MOST WILLING
> TO COOPERATE IN THE PRESIDENTS POLICIES I FOUND EVERYWHERE
> HIGH COMMENDATION OF THE PRESIDENTS SUNDAY SPEECH AND OF THE
> CONSTRUCTIVE ACTIONS TAKEN BY HIM I FEEL THE PRESIDENTS PRO-
> GRAM SUCCEEDING BEYOND EXPECTATIONS . . .

Next day Giannini wired again:

> . . . PRESIDENTS TALK LAST SUNDAY NIGHT DID THE TRICK AS FAR AS
> CALIFORNIA IS CONCERNED FINE REPORTS CONTINUE TO COME IN FROM
> ALL OVER THE STATE . . . YOU WILL ESPECIALLY BE INTERESTED IN
> KNOWING THAT THE AMOUNT OF ACTUAL CASH TAKEN IN THROUGHOUT
> THE BRANCHES OUR SYSTEM WHICH WERE OPENED MONDAY AND TUES-
> DAY EXCEEDED THE CASH WITHDRAWN BY ONE MILLION TWO HUNDRED
> TWENTY FIVE THOUSAND DOLLARS THIS CERTAINLY SHOWS THAT MONEY
> IS COMING IN OUT OF HOARDING KINDEST REGARDS

The New York Federal Reserve Bank alone soon reported an excess return of $10 million. By the end of March, more than $1.2
billion flowed back to banks in currency, half of which was in gold
coin, bullion, or certificates. By the end of the year, of the 17,796
banks operating before the panic had reached its crest under the
previous administration, 14,440 banks were in operation, with $33
billion in deposits. Of the remainder, some had been forced to fail,

but many reorganized by merging with others. The banking system had been saved.

Amidst all the heartening news that poured into the White House in the hours and days after my first Fireside Chat, only one message left me deeply puzzled. I still don't know whether to tell of it with pride or penance. My old friend John Lawrence, a New England merchant and banker—and an unflagging Republican—wired that in the banking crisis I had acted with the character of Lincoln and the timing of Coolidge!!!![10]

BACKGROUND MEMORANDUM TO PART II

What in the world was the secret source of his unparalleled ability—through *talk*—to court trust and love of millions whom he never saw and who never saw him in the flesh? It was an act of seduction unmatched in our political history. No need here to dredge up the illustrative anecdotes, the endless testimonials of the meek and the mighty, illiterates and learned, who tuned the radio to Roosevelt's voice and "had the feeling that the President was talking just to *me*." The task here is not to make it credible but to account for it. Something must power the development of so extraordinary a talent. Some urgent inner craving—perhaps some deep feeling of lacking something?—must lie behind the cultivation of a power to reach out and touch, personally, intimately.

On this elusive matter of his closeness to people, I have searched and pored over every printed and handwritten word I could find, diaries and letters, of family members and working associates, those who were closest to him. They lead to a single, inescapable conclusion. He was a singularly private, *un*intimate man. There is no hint of Roosevelt's opening himself to the risks of intimacy with any individual, whether friend or family. And there is reason to believe that—at least when he was younger—a yearning and craving to overcome this inability was a driving force in his life.

Look at what they say. Those who allude to his "closeness" to individuals really describe something distant:

Frances Perkins, his "Madame Secretary" of Labor: "He had that imponderable human quality which made people feel they were close to him. The rank-and-file politicians, the heads of little county and local committees, pulled up a seat and whispered their deepest hopes to him."

Raymond Moley: "His attitude was never either snobbish or patronizing.

. . . It probably sprang from a sense of unfamiliarity, a faint envy of experiences and interests he hadn't shared. I imagine that this is what prevented him from enjoying a genuine camaraderie with Al Smith, Robert Wagner, Jimmy Walker, and others with a Tammany background. Somehow, in the depths of consciousness, there fluttered a hint of the alien—not in them, but in him. In his dealings with [labor leaders John L.] Lewis, [William] Green and horny-handed Congressional brethren the same uneasiness is apparent. He calls them 'John' and 'Bill'; but there is always the suggestion of some inner watchfulness, some subtle incompleteness that makes intimacy impossible."

For a man of F.D.R.'s origins, "some inner watchfulness" is perhaps allowable in the presence of Al Smiths and John L. Lewises. But what happens when he lets his hair down among his closest working partners?

Sam Rosenman, whose sentences as ghost writer Roosevelt could hardly tell from his own: "This man was different—different in bearing, in speech, in personality. . . . He was friendly, but there was about his bearing an unspoken dignity which held off any undue familiarity."

The almost identical observation from Felix Frankfurter, as close an intellectual partner as F.D.R. ever had: "Our friend had, no doubt, the common touch. But he had also another quality—that mystical touch of grace, a charismatic quality that stirs comfortable awe, that keeps a distance between men and a leader. . . ."

And Harold L. Ickes, his troublesome but trusted Secretary of the Interior, describing a late-night drinking and singing party of F.D.R.'s inner circle: "It is delightful to see how the President can enter in at a party. He had as good a time as anyone there, laughing and talking and joking. Anyone not knowing him would not for a moment have thought that he was President of the United States. Yet, in spite of all his fun-making, no one ever presumes to treat him with familiarity. . . ."

Many men, of course, learn to keep a careful distance from coworkers, especially men in high office. They husband their intimacy—the spending and earning of trust—for those bound by flesh and blood. Was that the way of F.D.R.?

James Roosevelt recalls his childhood: "Father . . . was a busy, ambitious, and, I suspect, somewhat self-centered man. When he was around, which wasn't nearly often enough for us, he inundated us with fun and activity—and with love, too—but in his special way, which was both detached and overpowering. Sometimes we felt we didn't have him at all. . . ." And of later on: "Father had very few 'soul searching' conversations with any of us—Mother included—on matters other than public issues. . . . His great lack in life . . . was that, while he had lots of persons to whom he could talk, he had no real confidants. It was part of his rigid

Hyde Park upbringing that private, personal matters were a man's own business, not something to be discussed with a second party. Even his minister, the Reverend Frank R. Wilson, to whom Father was close, told me that their conversations never probed into Father's personal sorrows or disappointments or hurts. . . . Nowhere in the world really was there anyone for him with whom he could unlock his mind and his thoughts. Politics, domestic economy, war strategy, postwar planning he could talk over with dozens of persons. Of what was inside him, of what really drove him, Father talked with no one."

Mrs. Roosevelt: "I don't think I was his confidante either. He never would discuss an intimate family problem unless it was something that had reached the stage at which it just had to be discussed. Then we would talk it over, he would tell me what he wanted done, and I would do it. . . . He lived his own life exactly as he wanted it. . . . His was an innate kind of reticence that may have been developed by the fact that he had an older father and a very strong-willed mother, who constantly tried to exercise control over him in the early years. Consequently, he may have fallen into the habit of keeping his own counsel, and it became part of his nature not to talk to anyone of intimate matters."

Joseph P. Lash, a close friend of Mrs. Roosevelt for twenty-five years and her biographer, tells of a conversation with the President's wife: "She had to have contact with people she loved, Mrs. R. once said. . . . The President seemed to have no such bonds to people. Not even his children. He was completely occupied by politics and his public duties. What were his motivations in politics? I once asked. Some of her children thought it was his place in history, but she did not think that was quite fair or right. She thought he had a great sense of obligation to move the world forward, that progress was part of the historic process as well as a kind of moral imperative. But she could never get accustomed to his real lack of attachment to people. Except for Louis Howe, she could never conceive of the President doing a reckless thing for a friend because of personal attachment. . . . Each imagines he is indispensable to the President, Mrs. R. went on quietly. All would be surprised at their dispensability. The President uses those who suit his purposes. He makes up his own mind and discards people when they no longer fulfill a purpose of his."

The family member with whom F.D.R. seemed to have the warmest tie was his daughter, Anna, eldest of his children. While perhaps no more soul-baring with her than with the others, Roosevelt enjoyed having her around tending to him. Unlike James, who describes Father through the experience of his own childhood, Anna speaks of Father's childhood, beginning to touch at the roots we seek: "Remember, this was a boy whose nearest friend lived about a mile and a half away. That was Edmund Rogers, who just happened to be there, the only one, I think. When Father went to Groton at fourteen he no more knew how to get along with boys his own age than the man in the moon."

Anna's observation helps explain another, made by Mike Reilly the Secret Service man, which, simple as it is, engages the attention. Reilly never knew Roosevelt as a child but hardly let his eyes off him as President: "He went to Groton and Harvard, he was raised alone and he had just about everything he wanted throughout his youth, so it would be just a little too much to expect him to be 'one of the boys.' He never was 'one of the boys,' although he frequently made a good try. It was such a good try that it never quite came off."[1]

What boy does not yearn to be "one of the boys"? It is a natural yearning for easy intimacy and is indeed a relationship that feeds the learning of intimacy.

Intimacy is a learned thing. It must be learned early or the opposite may be learned—the skill of keeping a distance. Intimacy is learned when two children offer and elicit trust and have happy results in doing so. Such good experience is most likely to happen when a child has a range of children with whom to have good experiences and bad, of trust and occasional betrayal, and from whom to choose one for a special kind of mutual intimacy. From among many, a child chooses and says, "This one is my friend"—at least for now.

Franklin did not have this range of opportunities. No brothers and sisters with whom to play and fight, conspire with, tell secrets to, look up to or down upon. Only Edmund Rogers, "who just happened to be there."

Well, Edmund wasn't the only one "who just happened to be there." He had a slightly older brother, Archibald. When Franklin was seven, he visited New York City and wrote his first letter to a friend. A great deal of scholarly inspection has been made of Franklin's personal letters, but it appears to have gone unnoticed that his first non-family letter—his first to "one of the boys"—was not to the one later assumed to be his chosen friend, Edmund, but to Archibald:

"We are going to see Barnoms Circus and it is going to march through the streets and we are going to see it. . . . Send love to Edmund."

Before a year was out, Archie, the chosen friend, was dead of diphtheria.[2]

How is one to speculate on what the death of his closest playmate meant to lonely, eight-year-old Franklin; what it may have meant to his *trust?* Was Archie's death a betrayal? Was he not to count on the lasting fidelity of friends? Was death the teacher of Franklin's first lesson in the necessity of holding himself in reserve from others? Or from examining too closely his own feelings? An imponderable to a child's mind that is best not thought about? Who can know? But a casual event it certainly was not.

And so Edmund—not the one to whom Franklin wrote of the circus—was the only childhood friend left to him. What did this friendship teach him of intimacy—or the absence of it—between the ages of seven and fourteen? In all this time this much-traveled (Europe, New York, Campobello Island), prolific young letter writer wrote to Edmund only once. At the age of nine, he was sailing to Europe aboard the *Teutonic*. Lacking the verve of his many letters to Mama, the letter was distant, proper, taut: "The waves are quite high. When one is sitting down, one has to take care one does not slip off." (If anything is noteworthy about this communication to his remaining playmate, it is that he added a P.S. and signed it "F.D.R." —the first time those now towering initials are known to appear in his hand.)[3]

How close could he have felt to Edmund—what could they have taught each other of intimacy—considering that in four years at Groton, which they entered together in 1896, Franklin's hundreds of letters home mentioned Edmund only five times? Distant, dutiful mentions: "Edmund is doing quite well, I think, in everything except Latin." "Edmund has been in the infirmary nearly a week but is much better now."[4]

If a childhood shared with Edmund, "who just happened to be there," describes anything about Franklin, it reveals a childhood not of learned intimacy but of learned loneliness. Can it be that this is why he designed an adult life constantly surrounded—in fact, *cluttered*—by people, people, people, yet none of them, either coworkers, children, or wife, ever felt that he opened himself to them? Can it be that this loneliness, a never fulfilled yearning to be "one of the boys," underlies his getting on the radio to say, as no political leader has ever so effectively said: Let me be one of you. I will speak to you intimately, not as an orator but a friend. I will declare to you my most intimate trust if you will repay it with yours?

At Groton his quest for acceptance as "one of the boys" goes on. At first he made the error of seeking what he always could count on at home—the approval of adults. He wrote to Mama, "I am getting on very well so far. . . . I have not had any black-marks or latenesses yet," and won the punctuality prize. His sensitive radar for detecting affection soon taught him, however, that what appeals to adults is no help in the roughhouse peerage of a boys' school. Finding a soundly political middle ground, he wrote home triumphantly, "I have served off my first black-mark today, and I am very glad I got it, as I was thought to have no school-spirit before. Old Nutter Barbarossa gave it to me for talking in the schoolroom."

The thing that mattered—really mattered—at Groton was athletics. However his childhood had accustomed him to being the central jewel of attention, at Groton such status could be won only by excellence in football, baseball, and crew. In these he couldn't excel. He was only five feet three inches and bony when he arrived at Groton and remained thin while growing to his full height of six feet one before graduating. But he found an athletic competition he could win. It was the "high kick," involving such pain that only desperation would bring a boy through. A pan is suspended from the ceiling and a contestant kicks up at it as it is progressively raised. Franklin's winning kick was seven feet, three and a half inches—two feet higher than his head. Lord, how he must have wanted to win. With Spartan joy he wrote home: "At every kick I landed on my *neck* on the left side so the result is that the whole left side of my body is sore and my left arm is a little swollen!"[5]

So we have here two rivers of this man's personality that find their confluence in the extraordinary triumph of his Fireside Chats: First is the yearning of this lonely boy to feel not alone, not different from children playing along the road at Hyde Park as Franklin rode by in his carriage, not apart from those others at Groton who had arrived two years younger, and who seemed always more knowledgeable about being a boy. Second, as described in my earlier notes, is the serenity and confidence of a boy whose cultivation of words had become prominent in the earliest exchanges of affection with Mama, and with other adults, early and late— aunts and uncles, cousins and neighbors—who adored him for his felicity with words. His pride, his self-confidence, his knowledge of himself were all entwined with skilled use of words. He could rely on himself— totally—as long as he could rely on words. Lonely he may have been, but Franklin Delano Roosevelt he was, too—a Delano and a Roosevelt both.

Suddenly I remember some movie film I saw at Warm Springs that anyone can see who visits the house in which F.D.R. died. It was taken during the 1920s, soon after he began going to Warm Springs in search of a cure for his paralysis. There's something odd about movies taken before the days of talkies. In those days one did not associate sound with films. So, as in posing for snapshots, one may be visually self-conscious, but only visually. Roosevelt is sitting there with friends, self-consciously amused by the camera. He turns to a friend, smiles to the camera, then to another friend, then the camera again. But the striking thing is that while the friends smile and squirm shyly, Roosevelt never stops talking. His uneasiness makes his jaws go, go, go. Incessantly. Friends nod, laugh, fidget, while Roosevelt—and only Roosevelt—talks, talks, talks.

John Gunther, the author, makes an almost identical observation after meeting Roosevelt in his presidential office: "His face, the best-known face in the world except possibly Hitler's, was hard to study, too mobile, never at rest, almost hyperthyroid, quivering with animation. . . . In the midst of this crushing day, the President then proceeded to talk for forty-six minutes without a break. I managed to get a few words in, but not many. Yet the only excuse for my being there at all in circumstances of such pressure was that I might have something useful to say. . . . Like all really good talkers, the President was a good listener, too. . . . But exactly how and when he listened has always been a mystery. . . . People who saw him often came to adopt special techniques to deal with this phenomenon. 'My own method,' a well-known judge has reported, 'was to let him run for exactly five minutes, and then to cut in ruthlessly.' [Congressman] Vito Marcantonio once startled him by interrupting him in midstream, 'Sorry, Mr. President, but you're filibustering on *my* time!' . . . The simplest way to get at the President was to be invited to lunch. Then you could talk while he ate. . . . Leon Henderson . . . would pay no attention to his own food, watch carefully for the precise moment when FDR's mouth was full, and then let fire. Mr. Roosevelt, who never missed anything, was fully aware of this; he would try to outwit the doughty Henderson and throw his timing off. Or he would murmur slyly, 'Leon, what's the matter with you, you're not eating!' "

Gunther again, this time describing a press conference at the President's desk, a thick crowd of reporters pressing all around: "In twenty minutes Mr. Roosevelt's features had expressed amazement, curiosity, mock alarm, genuine interest, worry, rhetorical playing for suspense, sympathy, decision, playfulness, dignity, and surpassing charm. Yet he *said* almost nothing. Questions were deflected, diverted, diluted. Answers —when they did come—were concise and clear. But I never met anyone who showed greater capacity for avoiding a direct answer while giving the questioner a feeling he *had* been answered."

Raymond Moley in a letter to his sister: "He just enjoys the pleasant and engaging role, as a charming woman does. . . . He is wholly conscious of his ability to send callers away happy and glowing and in agreement with him and his ideas. And he particularly enjoys sending people away who have completely forgotten (under his spell) the thing they came to say or ask. . . . The man's energy and vitality are astonishing."

If talk was an act of love—or of seeking love—it was not to be squandered on the unlovable. Sam Rosenman: "Roosevelt hated to talk about government affairs with people who had offended him deeply or whom he disliked. He would at times carry this feeling to extremes—for example, refusing to see a committee of the Congress that had requested an appointment, because of his deep dislike of one member of the committee."

To talk incessantly as a means of incessantly charming, incessantly seducing attention and love, is not done without strain. He once remarked to a maiden cousin, Margaret Suckley, a quietly amusing, comfortable woman whom he liked to take on his semi-annual trips to Warm Springs: "You know why I like to have you around? Because I don't have to keep you *entertained* all the time."[6]

His reliance on talk—gay or serious, compassionate or objective, always openhearted as long as it never grew truly intimate—was at the deepest roots of his reliance upon himself. In talk he could call upon the security in which he was nurtured. Is it any wonder that as he took office in a country on the verge of falling apart, his first instinct was to sit down with all the people of America—bankers and depositors and Old Moses Smith—and start making everything all right by having a good heart-to-heart talk?

A final little item, poeticizing the paradox of the schoolboy so lonely and the serene national leader so confident in his power of talk. Which of these was he more? Or was he truly always both? Which was being described—the serene leader or the schoolboy—by the New York *Times* reporter who witnessed the first Fireside Chat and wrote: "When the broadcast was over Mr. Roosevelt waited in silence until the signal was given by the engineer that the White House microphone was off the air. Then he turned and asked, 'Was I all right?' "[7]

Part III

The First Hundred Days

I would like to feel—in fact, I am confident—that by the time these pages are made public it will be hard for any young American to imagine a time when millions walked the streets of our great cities hungry, frightened, not knowing how they would stay alive the next day. By then it will be hard to imagine a time when our federal government, amidst economic and social collapse, had no machinery for saving good American families from starvation; hard to imagine that some of our most "responsible" men—many in government— kept insisting that all that was none of the government's business.[1]

Before the New Deal was many years old, our opponents learned to chant a wearisome litany that in rescuing millions from dying— literally dying—the federal government had formed a dangerous habit of doing too much. Let it be remembered that those who voiced that chant were content in the time of our agony to do nothing.

When I took office the federal government was so aloof from the welfare of individual Americans that we had no definite method for learning something as basic as how many were out of work. Even that was not considered the business of government. So we could only make informed guesses. In the fall of 1932, *Fortune,* a conservative business magazine, put forward an estimate that 34 million men, women, and children—one out of every four Americans—were members of families that had no regular, full-time breadwinner. (The estimate *did not include* farmers whose land and labor were earning them nothing.) That figure is appalling enough without speculating on the insecurity that terrified the three out of four workers who still managed to cling to their jobs.

Numbers are one thing, individual lives another. What was happening to individual people out there who composed these numbers?

We learned of families in Oakland, California, who had set up "homes" in freshly cast sewer pipes that the manufacturer could not sell. In Connellsville, Pennsylvania, unemployed steelworkers kept warm in the big ovens they formerly had been paid to coke. Every big city had a slapped-together shantytown called a "Hooverville." (I do not intend a personal gibe by using that term; it was a word that had entered the common vocabulary.) Fathers and children haunted loading docks in produce markets for spoiled vegetables that had been thrown away. These were Americans—our neighbors!

In Chicago, teachers were instructed to ask a child what he had had to eat before punishing him for crankiness or sleeping in class. Those Chicago teachers—who, by the way, had not been paid for months— fed eleven thousand pupils out of their own pockets in 1931. In June the city's superintendent of schools publicly implored the governor, "For God's sake, help us feed these children during the summer." Relief was a responsibility of cities and states, not the federal government, and the cities and states were broke. New York City schoolteachers contributed $260,000 in a single month to feed their hungry pupils. Other New York City employees contributed 1 per cent of their salaries—a kind of voluntary, secular tithe—so the police could buy food for families they found actually starving. In a sense, this was an early suggestion of government responsibility. But, interestingly, it didn't come from the top; it came from low-paid civil servants who were neighbors of the people in need.

The most poignant act of charity coming to my attention was that natives of the West African Cameroons put together $3.77 to send to New York for "relief of the starving."

Who can measure the damage that hunger and beggary does to souls, especially to those of children? My wife, who had seen much of poverty during many years of volunteer social work, took a trip to the coal-mining towns of West Virginia. She came upon a little boy fearfully trying to hide his pet rabbit. The boy's sister told my wife secretly, "He thinks we are not going to eat it, but we are."

Poverty became so widespread that people began making distinctions between the "lazy" poor and the "deserving" poor. The "lazy" poor were generally those who had realized little of the American dream even in better times. The "deserving" poor, of course, were those who once had had property, sometimes professions to practice.

And there were many of those. I refer to them specially not because they were more "deserving" but to convey the extent of our collapse. There was a little girl in Philadelphia who could not get free milk at school under a program for needy children because her father—who was on relief—"owned property." This led to an investigation. They found that many impoverished tenants were sharing their relief food baskets with their landlords, who were just as hungry but ineligible.[2]

In New York a Committee on Unemployment and Relief for Chemists and Chemical Engineers was organized. Some of its members who had worked for years with our large companies were now spending their nights sleeping in subway trains. Another new group, the Association of Unemployed College Alumni, estimated that ten thousand college graduates were walking the streets jobless in New York City alone. That group's membership included alumni of Harvard and Columbia Law School, both of which I attended. Someone surveyed the Harvard class of 1911, men just seven years younger than I. One out of three of those men were frankly hard up, and one out of eight were on relief or dependent on relatives.[3]

Among some people I knew who lived in great comfort—and who had hardly ever met a wage earner face to face except their own butlers—there was constant talk of revolution. Fearful talk. It is human nature to fear the unknown, and to these men the American people were certainly unknown. On the other hand, while the common people of America had clearly lost confidence in their leaders, they had not lost faith in their system. They were not about to tear asunder their accustomed ways of growing crops and selling them, working machines and collecting wages, opening small businesses and seeking profits, until someone proposed a better way. Communism was proposed as a "better way," but this did not appeal to most Americans. In the election of 1932, held during the depth of our despair, the Communists could muster only 120,000 votes. A milder group of radicals, the Socialists, led by Norman Thomas, polled proportionately fewer than they had in 1912 or 1920.

Yet I frankly admit that I, too, at times wondered why the people had not revolted—not so much to institute a new system, but out of sheer rage. In fact, while revolution seemed remote, isolated, angry insurrections were indeed happening. Our accustomed respect for law and order was clearly falling victim to a spreading desperation.

In Seattle, less than a month before my inauguration, angry citizens seized the county-city building to demand food. In Detroit, unemployed workers roaming in angry bands invaded self-service grocery stores, filled their baskets, and walked out—without paying! Many items like this appeared in the newspapers across the country, inducing a contagion of "hunger riots."

This desperate kind of lawlessness began taking grander forms. In Iowa, unemployed utility workers tapped gas and electric lines so their fellow unemployed could continue to get services they could not pay for. Jobless miners sank their own shafts in closed mines, "bootlegging" as much as one hundred thousand dollars' worth of coal a day. Some they kept to keep their own families warm, some they sold. When mineowners brought them to court, juries of their peers refused to convict.[4]

A different kind of "lawlessness" had begun breaking out among our conservative citizens, the farmers. I say a different kind—and put lawlessness in quotation marks—because it raises the question as to what law may take away a man's farm after he has fertilized it with the labor of a lifetime. One of the early incidents took place in Logan, Iowa, when a farm owned by Ernest Ganzhorn was to be put up for sale for unpaid taxes. Five hundred neighboring farmers appeared at the courthouse. To bid up the sale price? Indeed no. They came to prevent the sale—and succeeded. In Bucks County, Pennsylvania, three hundred neighbors showed up at a tax auction of John Hanzel's farm. This was one of the great price fixes of all time. The bidding went up to all of $1.18—no one would offer a penny more. The bewildered auctioneer declared "Sold!" The crowd passed a hat to raise the handsome sum, then leased the land back to Farmer Hanzel.

These demonstrations were dramatic, of course, and here and there they saved a good man's property, but in thousands upon thousands of cases not appearing in the papers, farms were lost. Loss of land, however, was not the only issue that brought on rural lawlessness. What farmers wanted—forcibly demanded—was a price for their produce that would at least meet expenses. The only way they saw to do this was to shorten supply—regardless of hungry stomachs in the cities. Western ranchers slit the throats of their animals and hurled their carcasses into canyons. Wisconsin dairymen fought pitched battles with deputy sheriffs and hijacked tank trucks, dumping milk along the roadsides. A Farm Holiday Association in Iowa blockaded the highways around Sioux City for thirty days, refusing to ship or let food through until they could get the "cost of production."[5] These efforts, of course, all failed. But they convey the mood of our farmers —and the terrible economic crisis of agriculture—that my administration had to face up to as we entered office.

A father of hungry children thinks only of today—providing a meal for their bellies and his own *now*. He is too preoccupied with the present to think very much about the future. Yet our national collapse lit a long-fuse time bomb that could one day blow up in the faces of his children. I was terribly worried about what was happening to our schools.

By the end of March, the month of my inauguration, nearly one third of a million children were out of school because their communities were too broke to keep schools open. In Georgia, my "second home," 1,318 schools, with an enrollment of 170,790 pupils, shut down. In Ohio, the city of Akron owed its teachers $330,000 by the first week of May, Youngstown a half million dollars. Dayton schools were opening only three days a week.

The great farm states, in some ways, were in the worst trouble of all. In Iowa, for example, 95 per cent of the cost of public schools came from the property tax. With farm prices down almost to nothing, farmers weren't paying their taxes. They simply couldn't. Iowa closed junior colleges and many county high schools. Oklahoma "economized" in an even more interesting way: The legislature ordered that textbooks be used for ten years before replacement.[6] So in the interests of economy a whole generation of young Oklahomans might grow up without knowing, at least from their textbooks, that Lindbergh had crossed the Atlantic, that Hitler had overturned the government in Germany—or that Franklin D. Roosevelt was in the process of overthrowing the government of the United States!

This has been a long review of the ways in which our national economic and social collapse translated into personal anguish and desperation. Long, but necessary. It provides an essential background for several chapters that follow, describing many battles we fought, many laws we saw through to enactment and execution. These laws were designed to reform the functions of American government and to bring, once and forever, a certain minimum of security to American families.

Not long after President Wilson took office, he said to me, "It is only once in a generation that a people can be lifted above material things. That is why conservative government is in the saddle two thirds of the time." I entered office fully convinced that the cycle had swung to that "once in a generation."

Wilson's formulations often were touchstones of political wisdom. As for his political deeds, however, I think that after my seven years of service to Wilson I may have learned more from his mistakes than his successes. What I have in mind particularly is the poor use that Wilson made of the "honeymoon period" which every incoming President has with his Congress. He had a long agenda of progressive acts he hoped to accomplish, but squandered his "honeymoon" by spending most of his precious first year pushing a single measure, the Federal Reserve Act. He finally got it at the cost of almost all his political credit—and he got almost nothing else.

Wilson was a man of high principle. He also was one who lived by a great error made by many men, particularly those in the intellectual world from which he came, who consider that high principle is in conflict with politics. They are unable to reconcile the word "principle" with the idea of compromise. While "principle" is a high-minded idea, "compromise" connotes evil and lack of principle.

That is a great mistake. I see no principle in clinging to principle merely for the sake of doing so. When a man seeks to keep the purity of his principle intact and loses his battle to establish it as a living thing, what has he gained? What he gains is a private feeling of personal purity, a rather selfish victory. But he has gained nothing for others and may have lost them a great deal. On the other hand, the true believer in principle—the man of politics truly concerned with the welfare of others—believes in it enough to battle for the establishment of as much of his principle as the realities permit. Thus at least partly victorious, if his principle proves sound, he has gone a long way toward establishing the rest of it. And of course there is always the possibility—which too many men of rigid principle are often unwilling even to consider—that the principle may not have been so perfect in the first place.

If Wilson's progressive agenda was based on important principles, which I happen to think it was, he weakened it early in an uncompromising battle of principle over a relatively unimportant matter. The issue was the matter of making appointments to the civil service —patronage. Wilson had won the Democratic nomination over Speaker Champ Clark after a bitter convention fight. Clark was a party organization man. Wilson was not. (While serving as president of Princeton University, Wilson was so aloof from party affairs that few knew he was a Democrat, and he was known even to boast that he avoided voting.) The defeated Clark men were not overly interested one way or another in Wilson's progressive agenda. What they wanted more than anything else was for Wilson to redeem himself in their eyes by placing a loyal party man in charge of federal appointments. Wilson should have seen, for the sake of winning as much of his program as he could during his "honeymoon," that his first job was to unify his party, regaining the support of Clark's disappointed followers.

Instead of compromising on the tactical point of patronage, however, Wilson continued to fight them. He insisted on strict merit standards—entirely commendable, but politically premature. He lost. With it, he lost the potential unity of his party and the friendship of fellow Democrats in Congress by whom political patronage had always been considered an important survival weapon.

There was also something else he could have done. All he had to do was get word quietly around that available jobs would be filled *after* the passage of his legislation, that congressmen loyal to Wilson's program would be rewarded with patronage. Then, instead of losing all, he would have won his laws—embodying his principles—and converted party enemies into happy allies for the next go-round.

That is exactly what I did in 1933. We used patronage as a teaser. Thanking Democrats for their good work during the election, we merely added an additional hoop for congressmen to jump through before dispensing jobs: good work in passing necessary laws. This decision, of course, had certain costs. It meant we were surrounded for a while by holdover Republican jobholders, many of whom were hardly the most enthusiastic administrators of our cause. But what we got in return for this temporary cost was added Congressional support for the greatest collection of reforms ever voted in the history of the Republic. It was a worth-while bargain. And a principled one in the highest—by which I mean the most practical—sense.[7]

Congress had been called into special session for the single purpose of passing the emergency banking bill. Before the week was out, however, we decided to hold them in session for further action on the whole national emergency. They did not adjourn until June 15, exactly one hundred days after they had convened. There had never been such a one hundred days in all the seventy-two Congresses that preceded this one and there may never be again.

We obtained the enactment of fifteen major laws which, taken in all, represented a revolution in the relationship between the United States Government and the American people. For the first time the minimum welfare of every American became the common concern of all—and the business of their government.

On March 9, as I have already related, came the Emergency Banking Act, followed up on June 16 by the more permanent Glass-Steagall Banking Act, which insured bank depositors against loss through failing banks, as well as divorcing commercial from investment banking. Never again could bankers with an eye on financial speculation play fast and loose with the savings of innocent depositors.

On March 20 the Economy Act was passed. This helped satisfy a widespread demand to cut federal operating costs. It reduced federal salaries, which I think was quite justified in the emergency. Far more important, it revised the system of pensions to war veterans for a saving of $400 million.

Among the fifteen bills were a group that profoundly affected the natural resources of our country—the land, the trees, the waterways and power—as well as the lives of the people who cultivate these resources. These acts were the establishment of a Civilian Conservation Corps (passed March 31); abandonment of the gold standard, which affected farm prices (April 19); the Agricultural Adjustment Act, establishing a national agriculture policy (May 12); the Emergency Farm Mortgage Act (May 12); the Tennessee Valley Authority Act (May 18); the abrogation of the gold clause in public and private contracts (June 5); the Home Owners Loan Act (June 13); and the Farm Credit Act (June 16). The importance of these acts went far beyond farms and farmers, deeply changing the future of city dwellers as well.

The ravages of hunger and unemployment were attacked by two additional acts that were to have a central place in our determined march toward economic recovery. These were the Federal Emergency Relief Act, setting up for the first time a national relief system (May 12), and the National Industrial Recovery Act, a two-pronged action setting up a system of industrial self-regulation to promote recovery and a multibillion-dollar public-works program to provide useful jobs in public improvements (June 16). Both these experiments and their later modifications brought relief and hope to millions of people.

Also, the Congress passed a Truth-in-Securities Act, protecting investors, the little man as well as the big fellow, against fakery and unsupported claims of securities merchants (May 27); and the Railroad Co-ordination Act, creating the post of a federal co-ordinator to help save railroads from bankruptcy (June 16).

There was a sixteenth act as well, which some people felt overshadowed all the rest, from a standpoint of reviving not only the economy but their spirits as well. That was the act permitting the manufacture and sale, despite the Prohibition Amendment, of 3.2 beer.

These acts, later augmented by others, formed what came to be known as the "New Deal," a phrase I first used in my nomination acceptance speech. As author of that phrase, I suppose I ought to know something about what it is supposed to mean. But I often came to wonder what it *did* mean when I saw how it was defined and redefined by the press, by my enemies, and by some of my best friends. To some it was a peculiar combination of fascism and communism. To others it was a theology that, when brought to full fruition, would transplant Heaven to earth. To almost everyone who wrote of it, the New Deal seemed to connote some visionary philosophy that no one ever quite put his finger on.

That was all a very interesting surprise to me. I never regarded the New Deal as a theology or a philosophy, but simply a practical way of doing things. The New Deal was a conglomerate of economic experiments that appeared most promising under the political realities. We thought—and hoped—that some of them might work. If any philosophy lay behind them, it was this simple one: "Try something. If it fails, try something else." Fully a year before my inauguration—long before even my nomination—this is what I promised and nothing more: "bold, persistent experimentation."

Both enemies and friends kept expecting some master plan and, failing to get it, they would invent one—and attribute it to me. As early as April 19, 1933, reporters at a press conference around my desk pressed me to tell what would come next, as though a blueprint were all laid out. The philosophers either weren't listening or didn't want to hear my reply:

"It is a little bit like a football game that has a general plan of game against the other side [the other side, of course, being unemployment, low farm prices, and depression]. Now the captain and the quarterback of the team know pretty well what the next play is going to be and they know the general strategy of the team. But they cannot tell you what the play after the next play is going to be until the next play is run off. If the play makes ten yards, the succeeding play will be different from what it would have been if they had been thrown for a loss. I think that is the easiest way to explain it."

Felix Frankfurter, then a law professor at Harvard, sent me a little quotation that nicely states my "try it" philosophy: "The science of government is the most abstruse of all the sciences; if, indeed, that can be called a science, which has but few fixed principles. . . . *It is the science of experiment.*"

The source is as ironic as the quotation is apt. It was contained in an opinion of the United States Supreme Court—not the nine men who were soon to come near wrecking our experiments before they could bear results, but their predecessors by more than a century. The opinion was written by the very considerable Mr. Justice William Johnson in 1821.

Experiments should always bring learning, but cannot be expected always to bring success. As I once had to advise one of my young advisers, Rex Tugwell, who was sometimes a little more sure of his economic theories than of his politics: "You'll have to learn that public life takes a lot of sweat. You won't always be right, but you mustn't suffer from being wrong. If a truck driver were doing your job, he would probably be right fifty percent of the time. But you aren't a truck driver. You've had some preparation. Your percentage is bound to be higher." In the business of experimenting, that is the most you can expect.[8]

If the New Deal of those early days was not in itself a philosophy, it certainly was not lacking in philosophers. The White House became—I encouraged it to become—a battleground of free-for-all contenders, each pounding at the other with the conviction of having *the* world-saving idea. I stood in the middle of them all, as referee, which apparently convinced a number of the contenders (not to mention some distinguished columnists) that I was the only man around with a lack of conviction.

That, of course, gets us back to the difference between economics and politics. Each of these contenders, representing not only himself but a substantial body of public opinion, battled for the adoption of *his* world-saving idea and for the defeat of all the rest. My job as national leader—or national referee—was to keep them all in the ring, somehow hold them all together inside the ropes of a single administration, not drive them out to join an opposition, which would make our efforts hopeless.

The complexity of this political task can be appreciated only by understanding the diversity of these philosopher-battlers. Here is the briefest review of how they grouped:

1. There were some traditionalists, whose support and participation we needed. Basically, they clung to the old economic belief that capitalism is a self-correcting system; if the most painful symptoms of disease (such as bank failures) are alleviated, you can then sit back and wait until natural cycles bring us back to a period of boom. Their remedies seldom went further than reducing costs of government, collecting international debts, and, as far as banks were concerned, picking them up, dusting them off, and turning them loose to go on as before. Any stronger medicine, according to this group, would worsen the disease. Of those around me, I would roughly place in this group Lewis Douglas, my director of the Budget Bureau; Jesse Jones, my director of the RFC; and Bernard Baruch, a wealthy and influential Democrat.

2. Next were the currency tinkerers, who had a great free-for-all going among themselves. The trouble with these theorists was that they were not always theoretical. Too often, their prescriptions for restoring national prosperity were ideas for relieving the pinch in their own states while solving hardly anything anywhere else. Some were for printing dollar bills, a carry-over of nineteenth-century Populism, which might help a distressed farmer pay off his mortgage more easily but hardly help the tenant farmer in the cottonfields or the unem-

ployed worker or the frightened investor. Others put their faith in reducing the gold content of the dollar and raising the monetary importance of silver. Champions of this view were certain western senators led by Key Pittman of Nevada and Burton K. Wheeler of Montana, both from states whose prosperity is based largely on the mining of silver.

3. Then there were the "trust busters," who believed that economic stagnation was the result almost purely of overcentralization of wealth. To preserve the benefits of competition, the tendencies toward monopoly had to be curbed. This, of course, had already become an important part of accepted governmental function, and, clearly, more had to be done to control predatory financiers and manipulators. But with one quarter of our people out of work and facing starvation, the theory of trust busting would scarcely provide a man's next meal. The patron saint of the trust busters was Supreme Court Justice Louis D. Brandeis. Some people have all too facilely placed Felix Frankfurter in this cubbyhole, along with the many young protégés of Frankfurter, mainly because of his profound respect for Brandeis' great legal mind and works. I don't go along with that one.

4. An important new group, with growing support among the universities and the intellectual journals, were the believers in comprehensive economic planning by government. This was to find an important place in some of the things we tried—for example, the TVA. But the idea as a major philosophy was far from ready to sit well with the thinking habits of most Americans. And I am not at all sure that large-scale planning by government might not wind up as harmful in stifling the benefits of competition as unbridled growth of private monopolies. Frankly, I paid close attention to Rex Tugwell and Adolf Berle, the resident "planners" of the New Deal group (also, to some extent, Henry A. Wallace, my Secretary of Agriculture, and Hugh S. Johnson, soon to become NRA administrator) and their effective arguments that competition breeds as many hazards as benefits. But I was not about to swallow the canary whole.

5. Another distinct group, which included some very important individuals, might be called the "government in business" crowd. They were not socialists. They believed in private enterprise, but greatly distrusted it, especially utilities, whose services were essential to everyone, yet almost had to be monopolistic. Some of these men leaned toward the "planners" in sympathy, but by personality they

seemed too impatient really to plan. Thus Senator George Norris of Nebraska, a truly great man, had been pushing for years for the electrification possibilities of TVA but never fully saw its real potential for comprehensively improving the lives of the people of the great river valleys. Harold L. Ickes, my Secretary of the Interior, had great vision in believing in vast public works as a creator of useful jobs but was shortsighted in seeing the need for emergency projects to provide immediate relief from unemployment and hunger.

6. There was a large, powerful group of farm leaders concerned almost purely with getting rid of surplus crops to raise farm prices, but they disagreed widely among themselves as to how to do it— whether to "dump" them overseas, just dump them in our own rivers, or limit production.

7. Finally, there was organized labor, sometimes more concerned with higher wages and shorter hours of its dues-paying members than of the broader problem of getting all people to work and reviving the economy.[9]

These may seem an irreconcilable crowd of men and ideas to be living under one tent. But they were not. First of all, they were all *good* men, devoted to getting our country out of trouble and back into prosperity. Second, while each pressed his specialized point of view sometimes in opposition to others, each *knew more* than the others about some important aspect of the nation's sickness. Some simple-head is bound to ask—and we had plenty of them in 1933— "Yes, but where do *you* stand, Mr. President? Which group did you support? A President must take a stand."

I stood with them all. Not as a courtroom judge who listens sympathetically to adversary lawyers until he makes up his mind which has the stronger argument. I was not interested in a battle of words. I was interested in converting these ideas, even conflicting ones, into action—and finding out which ones worked. If I was not to be a courtroom judge, I was fully prepared to let real economic results be the jury.

There was still another pressure group in addition to the seven I have sketched out. This group encompassed the Congress and virtually all the American people. They wanted, demanded, *expected* action. To recapture the mood of this expectation, let me quote from one of the wisest of political observers and journalists, Anne O'Hare McCormick, writing in the New York *Times* of May 7, 1933. She speaks of a presidential power I did not seek but that was thrust upon me, and that had to be used both actively and wisely:

"Something far more positive than acquiescence vests the President with the authority of a dictator. This authority is a free gift, a sort of unanimous power of attorney. There is a country-wide dumping of responsibility on the Federal Government. If Mr. Roosevelt goes on collecting mandates, one after another, until their sum is startling, it is because all the other powers—industry, commerce, finance, labor, farmer and householder, state and city—virtually abdicate in his favor. America today literally asks for orders. . . .

"In his present temper the American is not in the least afraid of experiments. He is not thinking of the remote consequences of his emergency demands. In general he does not like dictators; he would not endure the strong-arm methods of Mussolini; he would destroy with laughter the shrill hysteria of Hitler; a Stalin shut up in a Kremlin would be a very unpopular Czar out in Iowa. But he wants action, the immediate action promised by Mr. Roosevelt in his inaugural address, and no lobby ever exerted so much pressure on Congress as the people now bring to bear to induce the President to use all the executive authority he can command.

"I suppose we have never had a President as powerful as Mr. Roosevelt is at this moment. In a century of growth and change we have not found it necessary to enlarge the frame of government as much as it has been extended in the past sixty days."

The necessary experimental action that the people rightfully demanded was precisely what they got in the First Hundred Days of the new administration. I recall a moment on June 17, the day after an exhausted Congress finally adjourned. Several of its leading members stood around my desk as I was signing a final sheaf of bills passed just before adjournment, including the National Industrial Recovery Act, with $3.3 billion for public works, the largest appropriation ever passed in peacetime. I remarked, "More history is being made today than in any one day of our national life." And Oklahoma's Senator Thomas Gore added: "During all time."

Perhaps the most surprised people were some politically expert columnists who, in the recent campaign, while intoxicated with their own expertness, revealed that they understood neither the national mood nor the nature of the craft of politics—or even the candidate they were supposedly exposing to public understanding. There was

Walter Lippmann, for example, who, to the great worriment of my campaign associates, had written in the New York *Herald Tribune:*

"Franklin D. Roosevelt is a highly impressionable person, without a firm grasp of public affairs, and without very strong convictions . . . an amiable man with many philanthropic impulses, but he is not a dangerous enemy of anything. [Methinks I hear my enemies choking at that, along with the laughter of my friends.] . . . He is a pleasant man . . . without any important qualifications for the office."

How these columnists later were quick to shout with glee that *I* had changed—not that they had been misleading their readers all along. Take J. Fred Essary in the *Literary Digest:* "Roosevelt the Candidate and Roosevelt the President are two different men. . . . The oath of office seems suddenly to have transfigured him from a man of mere charm and buoyancy to one of dynamic aggressiveness."

To be fair, one—and only one that I know of—admitted that perhaps *he* was mistaken, but this he did in private. In a letter to Harold Ickes, the famous editor William Allen White wrote: "How do you account for him? Was I just fooled in him before the election, or has he developed? . . . I have been a voracious feeder in the course of a long and happy life and have eaten many things, but I have never had to eat my words before."[10]

The reason I bring up these quotations is to reveal how naive our most "expert" columnists can be about the vast difference between running a campaign and running a government—between being a candidate and being President. In failing to comprehend these differences, they miss the main point that must be understood by anyone seriously engaged in American politics. It is a point that every politician understands in his bones but seldom talks about, at least in public.

During my campaign I discussed these political facts of life in some detail with Rex Tugwell, who kept careful diary notes of our conversations. (Had I known he was doing so, I might have kept my mouth shut! But now that I have these notes to refer to, and in the hope that progressives of the future will learn to be better politicians than they have been in the past, I am grateful for them.)

Rex would often tell me, after one of our private political talks, that I was a good teacher. Coming from a very good college professor, that was a pleasing compliment. But then he would try to turn his compliment around and say, in effect, "Why don't you teach the peo-

ple this way?" Persistently, this young man would urge me to give
campaign speeches explaining the roots of the depression and laying
out, step by step, what was necessary to cure it. Rex, a loyal and imaginative supporter, was an educator at heart. He knew I believed
in the "right" things—and kept wanting me to *say* them.

So the first thing I had to teach him was that a campaign is not a
program of adult education, but a fight for office. And that means a
fight. It requires all the timing, all the husbanding of potential
strength, all the cunning of any serious fight. A campaign is short. No
leader in a few weeks can change the deep opinions and prejudices
of a whole people—or of wholly diverse *peoples* that compose the
polyglot of the American electorate. What prejudices there are must
be accepted by a candidate and used by him if he would later turn
his election to good use.

The objective in an election campaign is to get elected.

If that statement seems too bald and simple, it does indeed have its
complications: It means that nothing should be said that will lose
more votes than it will gain. Nothing, absolutely nothing, if that is
at all possible. It also implies for an honest politician, however, that
nothing should be said in the interest of getting votes that will later
hamper the candidate's full freedom to govern rightly after his election.

What did this mean in the campaign of 1932? I was the challenger
against an incumbent President who was saddled with the burden of
our national trouble. For three years he had frozen himself into positions—all words and almost no action—that he now had to defend
and in which the people had lost faith. So he had lost his two greatest
advantages: the campaign advantage of incumbency and that of
representing the nation's majority party. We knew that at least a
third of registered Republicans were ready to vote for an acceptable
Democratic candidate. All we had to do was not drive them away. Independent voters would be overwhelmingly ours. All we had to do
was not drive *them* away.

Yet drive them away was precisely what some of my best friends—
Tugwell among them, and Walter Lippmann, too, if you want to call
him a friend—pressed me to do. They would have had me speechify
about the necessity of unbalancing the budget, driving away all those
supporters to whom a balanced budget was next to godliness. They
would have had me specify the details of a federal relief program and

its clear implication of higher taxes, driving away all those who wanted "something done"—but nothing that would hurt. They would have had me denounce this ideology or that, or the bankers and speculators and shortsighted industrialists, driving away a million here, two million there, gaining nothing but intellectual satisfaction.

The single most important fact of American politics, which self-righteous and self-centered intellectuals refuse to understand, is the diversity of America. That diversity makes us distinct from all countries of the world. Therefore it makes our politics distinct. No group among us can wield power against the will of most of the rest, at least not for long. The rich have power through their wealth, but so do the poor through their votes. The North has power through superior numbers, but so does the South through senior positions in Congress and makeshift alliances with other regions. Protestants have a majority, but are divided through a diversity of economic and regional interests; Catholics and Jews, each a minority, have great power, because their representation is concentrated in the political machines of the great cities. And all these groupings divide and subdivide: rural and urban, artisans and shopkeepers, immigrants and native Americans, union workers and non-union workers, employed and unemployed, ranchers and dairy farmers, cotton pickers and fruitgrowers, homeowners and renters, those who by nature seek constructive solutions to problems and those who merely want someone to be angry at. Each of these groups, every last one of them, has some justice on its side, some cause that is threatened by the cause of another group, something it wants. Also, each has its political spokesmen.

Now, a man may win office purely as a spokesman for dairy farmers—and against all other interests—if the district he runs in is composed predominantly of dairy farmers. But let that same man run for governor or senator in a diversified state—such as Illinois or California or New York—and he had better change his ways. Let him run for President and he had better forget all local interests, the special needs of one group over another. He must learn to think of a whole America, and that is a very difficult thing to do.

If he gets elected it may be more difficult. With every act he performs he will be accused of betraying some group—perhaps several groups—of his supporters. *We* elected you, they will cry. But the fact is—and this is a hard fact to grasp in American politics—that *no* group elects a President. He is not truly elected by a majority, but by an alliance of many minorities. They cheer together during a campaign, then fight each other tooth and nail after they've won it.

Voters love candidates and despise officeholders. Upon the speeches of candidates—usually vague speeches and necessarily so—voters can build dreams. Dreams of having everything *their* way. But in the actions of officeholders they are bound to find disillusionment. For the voter does not have to contend with the conflicting demands of many voices in a city, a state, a nation. He can keep shouting *his* demands, his idea of what is right, and shout down all the rest. A mayor, governor, President, must live with them, balance them, arbitrate among them, hold them together no matter how unhappily.

The presidency, it has often been said by my predecessors, does not look the same after entering the office as it did before. Nor did the governorship I served in New York; nor, I am sure, any mayoralty of a large city. These positions hold no durable power except to mediate among political powers. On the other hand, a President can wield great power—produce enormous change—when he can hold together a majority among the minorities that surround him. This he can do if these minorities are wise enough, politically mature enough to suppress their differences and settle for what they agree on.

Of course, there is another way. A ruling monarch or dictator can rule by suppression of a majority in behalf of one group, one class, one minority. His power to do this is backed by armed strength and the Machiavellian principle of divide and rule. Our Constitution has most fortunately guarded against this in America. The President is delimited by the Congress. Both are delimited by the frequency of popular elections. Yet there are advocates among us, humanitarian men and women, who in the name of democracy constantly call for suppression. I do not mean only our native fascists, but "progressives" as well: those who would nationalize banks or industries—because it would be "good" for the people—even though a majority desire no such thing; those who would unreasonably subsidize farmers with no care for the cost to city consumers; those who would protect union wages regardless of the effect on the economic machine that feeds us all. All these would be plain and simple suppression, advocated by well-meaning people who refuse to understand how big, diverse, complicated America is. They have not learned to respect the rights—the political power—of others who live in other places, of other means, other opinions, whom they do not see. And so they demand of their President, "You now have the power. Do what *I* think is right." The unwise politician sometimes tries. He loses not only his office but his cause. The wise officeholder knows he cannot. And so some of the minorities who joined so enthusiastically to elect him now desert him—and then charge that *he* deserted *them.*

They do not understand how the presidency looks—must look—to the President.

And too often they do not understand how a campaign looks to the candidate. To build the support of a majority of minorities, a candidate must choose as issues those problems that deeply stir us all. If he possibly can, he must weld his majority by raising an appealing issue—but not its solution. The reason is simple. More people will agree on a problem than on how to solve it. Of course, the candidate must go further. He must show a *quality* of concern. He must show a *resolution* to solve it. And he must convey an *ability* to solve it. And that is all. To go one step beyond is to invite the loss of votes.

Some people, often well educated, never understand this. On Herbert Hoover's side of the fence, there were ideological purists who believed that even giving the most paltry sums to states for emergency relief brought us to the brink of communism. On my side, I had to contend with the Walter Lippmanns and the small but vociferous crowd that edits, reads, and parrots *The Nation* and the *New Republic.*

Why do these people constantly demand what is politically impossible? Why do they never allow a candidate, whom they know inclines to be a friend, enough room to breathe in and survive? Why do they tear potential majorities apart with constant criticism of their friends? Why do they so dread being caught in an attitude of approval? Why do they insist that candidates be always "right"—and always losing?

Well, I did not take the advice of *The Nation* or the *New Republic,* or of Walter Lippmann or John Dewey or Paul H. Douglas (author of a high-minded and politically silly book called *The Coming of a New Party*). I did not specify precisely what I would do about every national problem. I did not promise to nationalize the banks and utilities or regiment private industry to guarantee jobs for everyone and cure the depression overnight. Perhaps I was too "amiable" and soft-headed to be as sure as they of the solutions to problems that the world had never before faced. Furthermore, I was "unprincipled" enough to take into account that whatever solutions I found had to pass through the high hurdles of Congress: Southerners and Northerners, men from cities and farm districts, elected officials who in their private lives are lawyers, shopkeepers, and landowners. My proposals had to become law and I had to be satisfied with what I could get.

So I conducted a campaign of "compromise." I said I would ask a lot, but said almost nothing of what I intended to ask. During that campaign, I detected no notable increase in the circulation of *The Nation* and the *New Republic*, the subscribers of which would have trouble electing a mayor of Poughkeepsie. But in my own election I did not do badly at all. And as for the progressive accomplishments that resulted from it, I will be happy to compare my "compromising" record against their "principled" one.[11]

BACKGROUND MEMORANDUM TO PART III

Emil Ludwig, the German biographer, describes sitting in Roosevelt's office one day as the President was signing his approval of a bill: "He signed . . . then lifted his clear open eyes to me, laughed out loud, and said, 'Now it's a law.' I have seen many gloomy foreheads bent over such desks. . . . I have seen ministers of state, bank directors, industrialists, some of them calm, others nervous, append their signatures. . . . Here for the first time I saw in action a man in whom the possession of power had not diminished his joy of life, but rather augmented it."

Grace Tully, the President's secretary: "The trait which I believe Roosevelt possessed in a more generous degree than most people . . . was a *will* to assume primary responsibility for events, and a *will* to make decisions regarding them. . . . In the White House years I heard the Boss say again and again to one or another of his top administrators who may have been buckling under attack, 'All right, send it over to me. My shoulders are broad. I can carry the load.' "

Eleanor Roosevelt describes her husband's zest for "the mechanics of politics, for politics as a science and as a game which included understanding the mass reaction of people and gambling on one's own judgment. . . . I never heard him say there was a problem that he thought it was impossible for human beings to solve. . . . He was completely confident that there was an answer."[1]

In politics "as a science and as a game" Franklin Roosevelt was as sophisticated as any man of his era. By the force of his political personality he brought a minority party into majority power to dominate the nation's affairs for more than a quarter century. He overhauled a 150-year-old

tradition of the role of the federal government, changing its policy of
laissez faire to economic activism, establishing government as a major
agent of economic regulation.

He came to be called "the architect of an era." Yet, in a sense, he was
not an architect at all, but a tinkerer—dealing with a crisis here and a
problem there, replacing this and reshaping that, denying a philosophy, yet
displaying a consistency of style and decision until a nation, a world, was
remade.

How did Roosevelt go about defining his problems and finding solutions
for them? How did he learn? How did he think? What was—the term
would offend him—his intellectual style?

Frances Perkins: "I never was able to make out that even during the
days of his illness [recovering from infantile paralysis] he had read substantially in the field of economics. He rarely mentioned a book on economics. He read Elsie Clews Parsons' book entitled *The Family* because
he knew Elsie Parsons, and he used to refer to it laughingly as 'a lot of
words,' saying that he knew what a family was and didn't have to read a
long book about it."

Raymond Moley: "During all the time I was associated with him I never
knew him to read a serious book. That is a pattern quite common among
politicians. Reading is a personal experience between the reader and the
author, and Roosevelt was too restless to enjoy that. . . . When Roosevelt
outlined to me his idea of what became the Civilian Conservation Corps,
I asked him whether he had ever taken a course with [William] James at
Harvard, for the idea he was expressing had a distinct likeness to what
James had said in his essay *The Moral Equivalent of War*. He answered
that he had never studied with James, but remembered him in the Yard as
the famous professor who had such abundant whiskers. . . . Roosevelt's
knowledge of economics was . . . like Sam Weller's knowledge of London,
'extensive but peculiar.' "[2]

Yet Roosevelt *was* a reader. He devoured newspapers "like a combine
eating up grain," in the words of one friend—not just clippings selected by
a staff assistant, but whole papers, six or eight before breakfast. And he
seemed to retain everything he had read. Early in life he displayed, if anything, a compulsion to read. At age nine, his favorite magazine was *Scien-
tific American*. One rainy day his mother found him going through—
reading, page by page—a dictionary. "He had an amazing ability," says
Eleanor Roosevelt, "to skim through any kind of book and get everything
out of it. When I gave him *Gone With the Wind* to read, he handed it back
to me in a very short time. He couldn't possibly have read it so quickly, I
was sure, and I told him so—but I couldn't catch him out on a single
point."

A little touchy about his avoidance of serious background reading, Roosevelt once remarked, "At Harvard I read some Kant, and a little of Rousseau, but in neither of these thinkers did I find the decisive leader. I would dip into my father's good library, taking a book here and there. I studied the five-volume encyclopedia from end to end." But then he added: "Even today I still find experience to be my best teacher."[3]

Frances Perkins: "Roosevelt could 'get' a problem infinitely better when he had a vicarious experience. . . . Proceeding 'from the book,' no matter how logical, never seemed solid to him. . . . When the problems of unemployment became more pressing, he heard many theoretical economic discussions, but he never felt certain about the theory until he saw a sweater mill located in a small village outside of Poughkeepsie which had employed no more than one hundred and fifty people. Roosevelt talked with the employer, who was in despair. He talked to the workers, who were frightened and confused. In this way he got the economic and human problem all at once. He had a basis of judging whether a program would be practical by thinking of how it would apply to the sweater mill. . . . To get wages back to a point where people could buy something and prices back to where a little businessman could make something on his investment and effort—this was the problem. He grasped the concrete and could make the application to an industry on a general basis."

In a remarkable letter to his sister, hardly a month after the inauguration, Raymond Moley wrote of his boss: "I've been amazed with his interest in things. It skips and bounces through seemingly intricate subjects and maybe it is my academic training that makes me feel that no one could possibly learn much in such a hit or miss fashion. . . . What he gets is from talking to people and when he stores away the net of conversation he never knows what part of what he has kept is what he said himself or what his visitor said. There is a lot of autointoxication of the intelligence that we shall have to watch. But he gets a lot from talking with people who come in. A typical approach to a big problem is 'so and so was telling me yesterday.' Another is 'now we found in dealing with the *state* so-and-so that we had to deal with such-and-such.' . . . The frightening aspect of his methods is F.D.R.'s great receptivity. So far as I know he makes no effort to check up on anything that I or anyone else has told him."

Bernard Baruch: "His fascination with new ideas was almost legendary. Ray Moley loved to tell the story of the crackpot who began to propound some very esoteric monetary ideas to F.D.R. The President seemed rapt as the man droned on and on. Finally F.D.R. sent him off in a blaze of enthusiasm. When someone asked why he had given this eccentric so much time, the President looked ingenuous and said, 'Well, he might have had something, you know.'"

Newton Baker observed the tendency early. "Young Roosevelt is very promising," he remarked before the days of F.D.R.'s governorship, "but I should think he'd wear himself out in the promiscuous and extended contacts he maintains with people. But . . . he seems to clarify his ideas and teach himself as he goes along by that very conversational method."

If reading and conversation could be joined—ah! then reading becomes another matter entirely. Madame Perkins recalls, "He once said to me, 'You know, I like to read aloud—I would almost rather read to somebody than read to myself.' Those words stuck in my mind because they illustrated his capacity to learn while he was taking part in an experience. . . . There was something incurably sociable about this man. His sociability was not only for purposes of pleasure and recreation. He was sociable in his intellectual as well as his playful moods."[4]

This "conversational method" was directly employed "to clarify his ideas and teach himself" in preparation for the 1932 campaign and the First Hundred Days of 1933. Once committed to the campaign for the nomination, Governor Roosevelt authorized Samuel Rosenman, then his staff counsel, and Raymond Moley, then a Columbia professor of public law and government, to organize a series of frequent and secret "seminars" for his personal education on national issues. The participants in these meetings came to be known as "the brains trust"—a term later formalized by the press, after word of the group got out, as the Brain Trust. Regular participants were Rosenman, Moley, and Tugwell (at that time a professor of economics at Columbia); Adolf A. Berle, Jr., a Columbia Law School professor; and Basil ("Doc") O'Connor, Roosevelt's former law partner. As Moley describes the role and work of the Brain Trust:

"The amount of intellectual ransacking that Roosevelt could crowd into one evening was a source of constant astonishment to me. The routine was simple enough. Sam, 'Doc,' and I would take one or two men [usually economists] on the late-afternoon train to Albany, arriving in time for dinner. . . . Roosevelt, Sam, or I would throw a question at the visitor, and we were off at an exciting and exhausting clip. The Governor was at once a student, a cross-examiner, and a judge. He would listen with rapt attention for a few minutes and then break in with a question whose sharpness was characteristically blurred by an anecdotal introduction or an air of sympathetic agreement with the speaker. . . . The intervals between them would grow shorter. The questions themselves would become meatier, more informed—the infallible index to the amount he was picking up in the evening's course. . . . By midnight, when the time came to dash for the train to New York, Sam, 'Doc,' and I would be done in; the visitor (who would not realize for some days, in most cases, that he had been squeezed dry) would look a trifle wilted; and the Governor, scorning further questions, would be making vigorous pronouncements on the subject we had been discussing, waving his cigarette holder to emphasize his points."[5]

This "hit or miss" way of learning misled many into an impression that Roosevelt was a superficial learner. James P. Warburg, the financier, observed that Roosevelt was "undeniably and shockingly superficial about anything that relates to economics and particularly anything that relates to finance. This is not, I think, because he is incapable of grasping these subjects, but because he does not like them and therefore refuses to make any great effort to understand them. . . . Ask him something about ships and see if you find him 'superficial.' Or ask him something about party politics." Roosevelt's capacity to retain minuscule political details, Mayor La Guardia of New York once remarked, was "aldermanic."

His fascination with ships, with uses of land, and with the exotic lore compressed in the pages of his postage-stamp collection all contributed to an astonishingly broad mastery of geography. John Gunther collected a few illustrations:

"A ship had been sunk off Scotland, either by a torpedo or by hitting a rock; Roosevelt said it must have been a rock, and at once guessed the height of the tide at the time, out of his knowledge of when that particular rock would be submerged. One story [has it] that if you drew a line in any direction across the United States, F.D.R. could name in order every county it traversed. Once Anne O'Hare McCormick saw him just after a visit to the Carpatho-Ukraine; whereupon F.D.R. proceeded to tell *her* all about the Carpatho-Ukraine. Once he asked Sumner Welles to prepare a report on Angola; the State Department worked a fortnight on it, and then found that he knew more about Angola than their experts did. . . . Eisenhower was astonished, after the Casablanca Conference, at the President's memory for historical facts and figures; he knew the Tunisia terrain better than some of the generals did. The artist Walter Tittle records that F.D.R. remembered particular buildings and streets in towns in Italy that he hadn't seen for forty years."

Yet these mountainous stockpiles of facts seem to have fed Roosevelt's thinking—without cluttering it.

Moley: "He had the successful executive's ability to keep his mind clear of 'details' once he had decided on a 'principle of action' together with a perfect faith that, somehow, someone would always be around to take care of 'details' satisfactorily. ('Details' included such questions as whether the CCC should recruit 250,000 or half a million men, whether $180 million or $385 million was cut from the budget, etc.)" And, according to Rosenman, F.D.R. was always ready to accept "that a good compromise bill today—so long as it did not sacrifice principle—was better than the hazy prospect of a perfect bill in the indefinite future. This willingness to compromise on small matters was a part of his general distaste for details—and his inefficiency in dealing with them. He was fond of looking at what he liked to call the 'whole picture,' and if its composition was good and its general effect was what he wanted, he did not worry about two or three badly executed lines in the painting."[6]

For all this patchwork learning, junk-piling of facts, and carelessness with detail, Roosevelt was a decision maker, a creator, the builder of a government wholly new in form and function. His associates were fond of saying that Roosevelt "didn't like to *think*"—but thinking he most certainly did, in some pattern less visible than the ordinary, a pattern less recognizable to the academically and politically trained men around him. His thinking, more intuitive and less analytical, was perhaps more like what is said to be a woman's. And it was a woman, Secretary Perkins, who alone has ventured to describe what that style of decision making—of creating, of *thinking*—really was:

"In the use of his faculties Roosevelt had almost the quality of a creative artist. One would say that it is the quality of the modern artist as distinct from the classical artist. The name for it in the graphic arts is automatism. It describes an artist who begins his picture without a clear idea of what he intends to paint or how it shall be laid out upon the canvas, but begins anyhow, and then, as he paints, his plan evolves out of the material he is painting. So Roosevelt worked with the materials and problems at hand. As he worked one phase, the next evolved.

"Roosevelt's plans were never thoroughly thought out. They were burgeoning plans; they were next steps; they were something to do next week or next year. One plan grew out of another. Gradually they fitted together and supplemented one another. . . . Roosevelt's mentality was not intellectual in the sense in which that word is ordinarily used. He was a man of high intelligence, but he used *all* his faculties when he was thinking about a subject. He did not enjoy the intellectual process for its own sake as many educated, perhaps overeducated, men do. . . . This was not the way his mind operated. He had to have feeling as well as thought. His emotions, his intuitive understanding, his imagination, his moral and traditional bias, his sense of right and wrong—all entered into his thinking, and unless these flowed freely through his mind as he considered a subject, he was unlikely to come to any clear conclusion or even to a clear understanding."[7]

Part IV

Trees, Crops, Water and Power

The Trees

Whether the social system known as the United States of America could survive as it was or whether it would collapse and turn fascist or communist was, in my opinion, the *second* most important question that faced us in the early days of my first term. The *most* important question was whether the United States was to be a permanent country—*physically,* as a piece of geography. An awful thing was happening of which all my life I had been painfully aware. It concerned me more than anything else.

The United States of America was slowly blowing and floating away. Literally.

We had long, long neglected our most precious possession—the soil that feeds us, that binds us together as a nation. A hundred years earlier our pioneers had trekked through the passes of the Appalachians to settle the vast spread of the Louisiana Purchase and beyond. They shaved the mid-continent of its forests and protective grasses, and what marvelous virgin soil they discovered underneath! Rich and brown and moist in their hands, limitless in both its yield and its breadth. When the rain was good, the abundance of God's gifts encouraged these settlers to plant even more the next year. Only when dry years came was there a hint that this land, too, could parch and go hungry, grow exhausted. But again rains would come, and men would forget.

What the settlers did not know was that the land was disappearing beneath them. When they cleared it of woods and grasses, they exposed the rich soil to erosion by wind, invited the ravages of floods, loosened it to the washing of rivers—and, all the time, they were drawing upon life-giving chemicals in the soil, taking but not giving back.

In 1932 the bill came due. A drought struck, thirsting the land with a "dry death" that pounded year after year until 1936. In a vast bowl of scorched pastures and cornfields stretching from Texas to the Dakotas, from Arkansas to Colorado, cattle fell in their tracks and died, and plowed land bleached into sand dunes. With no snow to melt and in spring no rain, the April breezes picked up the dead land and carried it away. The world had never seen such storms of dust.

Bewildered farmers fled west while the land they abandoned, borne by the prevailing winds, blew east. As though the depression were not enough, the tragedy of the dead land rose like a black cloud— literally—and struck us all. In Memphis, people walked the streets with handkerchiefs over their faces. A dust cloud more than a mile high darkened the city of Cleveland. Red snow fell on New England. Three hundred miles out in the Atlantic, astonished sailors discovered traces of dust on their decks—particles of the Great Plains coming to rest.

Soon after becoming President I ordered a thorough and specific study by the best government specialists in soil erosion to determine just what was happening to our land. What they came back with was a horror. They found that one hundred million acres of precious top-soil—equal to the combined surface of Illinois, Ohio, Maryland, and North Carolina—had been peeled off by the winds and rivers, and blown or washed away. Another one hundred twenty-five million acres were seriously damaged, still another hundred million under immediate threat—all of it once the most richly fertile lands of America. If a great fire were to sweep our factories and office buildings, causing damage in the thousands of millions of dollars, it would be awful; but men could go to work and replace them. Loss of land, however, is something else. Topsoil is irreplaceable, except by nature, in a work that requires centuries.

Many years earlier, in 1911, shortly after I was elected to the state senate of New York, I began to work for passage of what was known as the Top Lopping Law. This was mainly concerned with conserving soil by caring for trees. I arranged a visit by the Chief

Forester of the United States, Gifford Pinchot, to a meeting in our Assembly Chamber in Albany and drummed up attendance by senators and assemblymen. Many came, and it turned out to be a meeting I was never to forget.

Pinchot projected a picture on a screen of an old Chinese painting, done in about 1510, of some place in North China. It showed a populous, thriving town, walled in a beautiful valley. Along the mountainsides were crops and spruce-pine forests. Down the slopes and through the valley ran a beautiful stream. But up one mountainside there was a gash, and if you examined it closely, you found it was a logging chute. Those old Chinese had never heard of conservation. For a hundred years the people of that valley sheared the trees from the mountains, giving no thought to replenishing what they took from the land.

Then Pinchot showed a second picture, a photograph he had taken himself at the identical spot of the four-hundred-year-old painting. It showed a desert. Naked mountainsides, no grass, no trees, just rocks. Plundering of the trees had permitted that beautiful river to wash the Good Earth from those mountains and out of the valley for all time. What had not washed away, blew away. Nothing grew. Now the river, with no good soil to embrace it, had become a flood stream. The old, walled town was a ruin. There were, as I recall, only three hundred people left, eking out a bare existence. A great civilization of four centuries ago was wrecked, leaving ruins and rocks and a few hungry souls.

As chairman of the Forest, Fish and Game Committee of the state senate, I began to perceive conservation as the heart of progressivism. There were times when I felt alone in this cause. I was a rural Democrat, almost a contradiction in terms. The Democratic Party stood chiefly on the foundation of New York's Tammany Hall and the machines of other sizable cities. As the party of wage earners, it was alert to profiteers and plunderers, but hardly sensitive to the subtleties of the balance of nature. The Republican Party, on the other hand, with its large rural base, was also the party of non-interference with business, of a sometimes unthinking worship of profit seeking.

Neither party fully realized it, but true conservationism embraces the interests—the vital interests—of farmer and wage earner, tree grower and carpenter, pulp-mill owner and electric company, and, as much as anyone, the propertyless city dweller who rents an apartment and pays a light bill. The greatest mistake one can make in considering the issues of conservation is to see these interests in conflict. Conflict there certainly is. But all these interests are best served when—*only* when—they are served in harmony.

Nature, the great conserver of itself, when left alone, provides for the future while yielding for the present. God's greatest creation, Man, must learn to do likewise. A man may not starve his land while feeding from it and expect it to yield tomorrow's crop. He may not poison his water, yet have it to drink. He may not recklessly cut down his trees, yet have their beauty to enrich his eye and have their moisture-holding roots and their shelter against wind to protect his farmland. It is all a circle—a vicious circle when violated, a divine circle when conserved.

The conflict of conservation—which all my life I have tried to resolve into a harmony—is the conflict between private property and the public interest. Resolving that conflict is a profound issue of a populous democracy.

In 1907, before I entered New York State government, Governor Charles Evans Hughes, a progressive Republican (who, a quarter century later, was Chief Justice of the United States when I was elected President), advocated protecting the circle of nature by establishing a state monopoly of all streams and reservoirs on public lands, state construction of hydroelectric plants that would "feed" on that water, prevention of power plants and power lines endangering the timber and wildlife of forest preserves, and, finally, the distribution of state-produced power at fair prices. Chiefly because of that last item, the city-based Democrats supported Governor Hughes; his own Republican Party, interested more in the private right to plunder, opposed him. I shall be forever proud that my earliest education in practical politics was gained in helping Governor Hughes win much of his battle.

In 1912, twenty-one years and a day before my inauguration, I advanced the idea before an audience in Troy, New York, that our long struggle to establish the liberty of the individual was pretty well won. The new fight was for "liberty of the community," the right of all to require community responsibility of each of us:

"Why, let me ask, are so many of the farms in the State of New York abandoned? The answer is easy. Their owners 50 or 100 years ago took from the soil without returning any equivalent to the soil. In other words they got something for nothing. Their land was rich and the work was easy. They prospered for a while until the deluge came, and when it came they discovered that their lands would not produce. They had taken the richness away and did not pay for it with fertilizers and other methods of soil regeneration.

"Today the people in the cities and the people on the farms are suffering because these early farmers gave no thought to the liberty of the community. To have suggested to a New York State farmer one hundred years ago that the government would compel him to put so much lime or so much fertilizer on every acre he cultivated would have been an impossibility. He would have stared and muttered something about taking care of his own land in his own way. . . . I have taken the conservation of our natural resources as the first lesson that points to the necessity for seeking *community* freedom, because I believe it to be the most important of all our lessons."[1]

All the foregoing has to do with conserving the balance of nature. Another kind of erosion was simultaneously taking place, disturbing the balance of our social organization: the erosion of our rural population, leading to an unhealthful enlargement and overcrowding of our cities. Like neglect of the soil, this could lead only to disaster. Of this, too, I spoke early and constantly, saying before the Berkshire Bankers Association, at Lenox, Massachusetts, in June 1921:

"One of the great facts most significant to our national future has been almost wholly overlooked. That is the announcement by the census of 1920 that for the first time in our history more than fifty percent of our population is now living in cities, and less than half dwell in small villages or on the farms. At the time of the Revolution less than ten percent of the nation's people were gathered in urban communities, but since that day every decade has shown an increase in the proportionate ratio of the cities' growth. Today we must ask ourselves 'Where will it stop?' and more important, 'How shall we proceed to stop it?'

"For the growth of cities, while the country population stands still, will eventually bring disaster to the United States as it has to the life of nations in days gone by. Industrial manufactures are good. They should be encouraged to the point of rounding out the production of this great expanse of territory and population so that we may utilize to the full the wonderful gifts that the God of Nature has given us. Yet the nice balance must be maintained. . . . We have passed the halfway mark and are still headed towards that abyss. It is time to stop.

". . . I believe in killing two birds with one stone. We can help Nature to give us more and at the same time we can lessen the dangers to our civilization which have come with the growth of the cities."[2]

The idea of killing these two birds with one stone came to fruition under circumstances that in those days I hadn't dreamed—as President of the United States proposing my first major positive program to (1) conserve our natural gifts and (2) provide the chance for unemployed young men in crowded cities to work at wholesome, remunerative jobs in the country.

The creation of the Civilian Conservation Corps is a story of enriching the lives of more than one and a half million young men. It is also a story, at least in its beginnings, of how a President must manipulate members of Congress and his Cabinet to get something done, while they are all busy manipulating him.

At 9 P.M. on Friday, March 10, our seventh day in office, I met with Secretary of Agriculture Henry Wallace, Secretary of War George Dern, and Secretary of the Interior Harold Ickes to outline, in rough terms, a plan that had been forming in my mind to enlist five hundred thousand unemployed young men to work in the nation's forests. I pointed out that the plan was a fulfillment of a promise I had made to the nation, first in my acceptance speech at the Democratic Convention the previous summer and again in my inaugural address when I said:

"We must frankly recognize the overbalance of population in our industrial centers and, by engaging on a national scale in a redistribution, endeavor to provide a better use of land for those best fitted for the land."

The politicking and manipulating soon began. The following Tuesday morning Ray Moley arrived in my bedroom for our daily day-planning chat. He started right out telling me that a number of important people—Secretary of Labor Frances Perkins and Senators Wagner, Costigan, and La Follette—had been cooking up a bill for granting large sums of money to states for creating jobs.

They had in mind immediate "work relief," which I favored, too, and large-scale public-works construction, about which I had some strong reservations. We'll go into that later.

I responded by telling Moley of my plan for what I then called the Civilian Reclamation Corps. Moley remarked that he found the idea "stunning." Then he said that something like it had been suggested by a former Harvard professor of my day, William James, in his famous essay *The Moral Equivalent of War*, and asked whether I hadn't been influenced by it. Frankly, the query annoyed me. This was not the first time Moley had tried to hang one of my better ideas on that blessed essay. One of the dangers of reading too much is that you start thinking that books are the source of original ideas, when the obvious fact is that original ideas are the source of books.

Moley said, "Suppose we draft a memorandum on your Civilian Reclamation Corps, get it to the appropriate cabinet officers at once, and find out what they think about it." Of course, I had already spoken with the "appropriate" cabinet officers. I would have pointed that out to Moley, except that Ray was not really saying what he appeared to be saying. In a roundabout way, he was displaying good political sense, a shrewd understanding that presidential power does not really exist except by organizing and directing the power of others. He wanted, quite correctly, to avoid risking that my plan would be regarded as competition to the Perkins-Wagner-Costigan-La Follette plan for work relief. Why not show my plan around, let the others come back to me with their plan, and after a little give-and-take, work up something based on both plans that we could all support? What he was suggesting was a little bartering of enthusiasms.

That day, March 14, I sent a memorandum describing what I now called the Civilian Conservation Corps to Wallace, Dern, and Ickes—and this time added Frances Perkins to the group. The harmonizing strategy worked. They replied the very next day, saying, ". . . the undersigned have considered not only the draft of the bill with regard to the Civilian Conservation Corps, but also the whole program of relief for industrial unemployment. We are of the opinion that there are three items to be considered in this program." They listed work relief, public works, and the CCC.

These three programs became the basis of a presidential message to Congress on unemployment relief. Many people wondered why three such distinct undertakings were embraced by a single message and, as usual, the press invented imaginative theories to explain it. The reason was simply the politics of building support for each of the undertakings by binding them all together.

Meanwhile, the idea of the CCC, a simple but radical idea, had to be explained to the public. An opportunity came at my March 15 press conference when a reporter asked what kind of work CCC boys would do. I said:

"The easiest way to explain it is this: All through the East, where, of course, unemployment is relatively the worst . . . nearly all of the so-called forest land owned by the Government is second-, third-, or fourth-growth land—what we call 'scrub-growth'—which has grown up on it. What does that consist of? There are probably four or five thousand trees to the average acre—little bits of trees, saplings and so forth. . . . You will never get a marketable timber growth on that kind of land. . . . We are rapidly coming to an end of the natural lumber resources. The end is within sight and, unless something is done about it, we will have to become a very large lumber-importing nation within from twenty to forty years.

". . . Say there are five thousand of these saplings to the acre. Go in and cut out four thousand and leave one thousand. The men go in there and take out the crooked trees, the dead trees, the bushes, all of which have no value as lumber. . . . That means that the trees are sufficiently spaced to get plenty of light and air, and that there is not too much of a strain on the soil. Those trees then eventually will become a very valuable lumber crop.

"In addition to that, one of our great difficulties all over the country is with fire. These men will be put to work in building fire breaks. A fire break is merely an operation of cutting a thirty- or forty-foot swath through the forest, and plowing it up, raking all the leaves and everything possible away from that strip and keeping it clear."

Then Ernest K. Lindley, one of the reporters, raised an objection I was glad to have raised: "Even at a dollar a day pay for a year for these men, the cost is enormous. . . . I figure where you would need a half a billion or one billion and spend it on this one item."

I replied: "Just for background. . . . These people would be people who are today on the dole. They are today performing no useful work, earning no money. . . . It will help to relieve their own families. If a family man is taken, he will send a large part of [his wages] back home, and that relieves the community too."

Another asked, "How soon do you think you can get them to work?" Coming after three years of depression, inactivity, and hopelessness, my reply, I believe, startled them:

"Three or four weeks—that is, start getting them to work."

Mind you, this was the day I received the memo from my cabinet members—before the message was sent to Congress, before the bill was drafted, was passed by Congress, before a single physical arrangement was made to recruit, transport, and house a single boy and put him to work. Actually, it took four weeks and five days to accomplish all that and open the first CCC camp.

But that does not mean it was all clear sailing. There was more politicking and manipulating to be done. We had trouble with some senators—sad to say, the "progressive" ones upon whom I most hoped to rely. Elbert Thomas of Utah, for example, raised a false alarm that the CCC might become "concentration camps" of rebels marching against the government. That term "concentration camps" came up again at a press conference and I had to implore the reporter not to use it because it "sounds too much like that which some of us older people remember as used in the Cuban episode of 1907 and 1908." Of course, the term was soon to acquire an even more repugnant meaning.

Then my good ally William Green, president of the American Federation of Labor, raised a cry that the emergency wage levels of the CCC (about a dollar a day) would undermine the labor movement, that it was dangerous to organize gangs of the restless unemployed, and that the Corps smacked of "fascism, of Hitlerism, of a form of Sovietism." How much better I could deal with my enemies if only I could be spared contending with the fertile—but oh so gloomy—imaginations of my friends. Well, Green's fears were easily disposed of. I decided to appoint one of his labor officials, Robert Fechner, as Director of the Corps. Not another word of criticism ever came from labor—and Fechner did an excellent job.

Next I had to contend with my own official family, who had a whole government newly at their disposal, yet who asked, "How can we ever do this? How can we ever do that?" The Forestry Service of the Department of Agriculture wanted to plan and supervise the work, and rightly so. But, they complained, they had no facilities or experience in housing, feeding, clothing, transporting, and doctoring hundreds of thousands of men, or for keeping order among them. Yet they and the Labor Department people squirmed when I pointed out that that's why I had brought the War Department into the picture. (Liberals always squirm at any friendly mention of the War or the Navy Department.) The Army had tents, trucks, cots, blankets, shoes, underwear, soap, pots and pans—and officers skilled in organizing orderly camps.

Secretary Perkins wanted the Labor Department to be in charge of recruiting the men, an excellent idea, but she then complained that there was no staff to get it done. I said, "Do it through your United States Employment Service." She pointed out that the Service had been reduced to little more than a letterhead. I instructed her, "Resurrect it right away," assuring her we would get funds.

Someone complained that this multidepartment setup was very complicated, indeed not very efficient. Solutions to governmental problems are often neither efficient nor logical; they are political, designed to accommodate human feelings. I waved the objection away: "The Secretary of Labor will select the men and make the rules. The Army and the Forestry Service will run the show. Fechner will 'go along' and give everybody satisfaction and confidence."

I am perfectly aware that some of these "official family" members felt I had a way of making light of their great problems, setting goals that seemed beyond reason, then turning my back on details. And they were quite right. That's what a President *should* do. My job was to design ends; theirs, to work out the details of means. Later in my presidency, the sensible men who never believed in going "beyond reason" spoke of me as a man gone mad when I said America had to produce sixty thousand airplanes a year to save the free world. It wasn't my job to know *how* to do it. It was my job to know we *had* to do it. I set—in fact, announced—the goal. We did it. People who are so critical of these administrative methods of mine probably lacked an educational advantage I had, that of teaching four sons to swim. At first, I told my boys how to do it, *showed* them how, had them show each other how—and none of it ever worked. Then I took to tossing a boy off a raft and having him swim to shore any way he could get there. That worked.[3]

On March 31 Congress enacted the CCC Law, and on April 3, I put out the first call, for twenty-five thousand men of an authorized

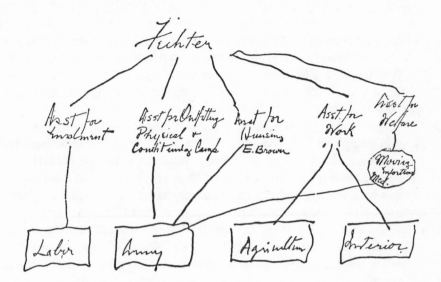

At a meeting early in April 1933 I sketched out this organization chart to show how the various government departments would share responsibility for running the Civilian Conservation Corps. My apologies to Robert Fechner for misspelling his name.

enrollment of 250,000. Enrollments were to be for six months and pay thirty dollars per month, of which most—usually twenty-five dollars—was to be sent home as a family allotment. By early July, 250,000 enrollees plus leadership contingents of twenty-five thousand war veterans and twenty-five thousand experienced woodsmen were settled in 1,468 forest and park camps of about two hundred men each, in every state of the nation. It was the most rapid large-scale, peacetime mobilization of men in our history.

On August 12 Secretaries Ickes and Wallace and I paid visits to several camps in Virginia, mainly along the beautiful new Skyline Drive of the Blue Ridge Mountains. Americans will be forever indebted to the boys of the CCC for that incomparable scenic highway. Somewhere in the archives of the Department of the Interior there still lies a plan I developed for an "Appalachian Parkway," of which the Blue Ridge drive would be the nucleus. It would start at the Canada line and run down through the Green Mountains and Berkshires, cross the Hudson River at Bear Mountain, skip along the ridges of northern New Jersey, Pennsylvania, and Maryland to join the Skyline Drive south of Washington, then continue south of the Smoky Mountains National Park to Stone Mountain, Georgia, where the Appalachian range tapers off into the cottonfields. I hope that someday it is built.

At one of those Skyline Drive camps we shared lunch with a couple of hundred healthy, eager boys whose ages averaged about nineteen. The meal, which the general in charge told us was typical, was steak, mashed potatoes, green beans, salad, iced tea, and something they called apple pie (made of dough and apples all right, but it wasn't a pie). No wonder that in three months the average youngster gained fifteen pounds. Yet these wholesome meals cost the government only thirty-five cents a day for each boy.

Harold Ickes told me that some of the boys were studying trigonometry and French under the tutelage of army officers. Harold learned this from a pompous commanding general who boasted to him, "There won't *none* of these boys leave these camps illiterate." I told Harold to be sure to put that in his memoirs—I couldn't.

No man can measure what the CCC contributed to the mental and physical health of more than 1,500,000 young men at an age when they might have formed habits of idleness, harming their entire lives. We can measure, however, that CCC funds were used to add 65,511 acres of wildlife refuge, 199,214 acres to our national parks, and 7,436,321 acres to our system of national forests. In national, state, and local parks, the CCC built lodges, museums, and cabins, and developed trails, lakes, and campgrounds that will be enjoyed for generations. It improved streams and ponds, restocked them with fish, built dams for flood control, and provided drainage.

The CCC was a way of insuring the health of the land while, at the same time, promoting the health of the men who worked on it. There is no accomplishment of my administration of which I am more proud. Were it not for the outbreak of war in less than a decade, the CCC might well have become a permanent part of American life.[4]

The Crops

We turn now to the tragedy of the farmer and his family. Unless he could work his way out of trouble, it was impossible to conceive of America working its way out of the depression. Poverty was not only ruining the farmer but was driving him to ruin his land.

In 1933 the land and the farmer were starving one another. Since 1929, farm prices had dropped 55 per cent. In farm families, annual cash income per capita had collapsed from $162 to $48.

What is a man to do when his cash income goes down and his mortgage stays high, when he must sell three bushels of wheat or three little pigs to buy an item at the general store that used to cost two bushels or two little pigs? (This was the actual disparity between 1929 and 1933.)

What he does, in desperation, is plant more and more, forcing more out of the tired land, further cluttering a depressed market, further collapsing prices, digging himself deeper and deeper into poverty, leaving his bills unpaid in town, breaking the owner of the general store. In turn, factories that supply the general store cut their payrolls, and unemployed workers find themselves penniless to buy what the penniless farmer works harder and harder to grow more of.

From a short-range economic standpoint, the farmer had to *grow less*. This would bring his supply into balance with the needs of city consumers. Automatically, prices would rise to cover the farmer's costs and a fair profit. The farmer would be saved.

From a long-range conservation standpoint, also, the farmer had to *grow less*. This would enable him to reciprocate the gifts of nature by giving large pieces of his land a year or two of well-earned rest and nourishment—by fertilizing and rotating to a less profitable, but land-enriching crop—thus rejuvenating the land to feed us another year, feed our children, and sustain the farmer's grandchildren.

So again we see that prosperity and conservation are a divine circle. But the individual farmer could not pursue this circle alone. Left alone, he is forced into the vicious circle of unbridled competition: producing as much as the land will yield, overfilling the market, fighting depressed prices by forcing still more from the land, ruining himself while threatening to ruin us all.

When the disease was viewed in this way, the medicine was easy to prescribe—but not so easy for many Americans to swallow. It required creating a partnership between private rights and community rights, between the laws of economics and the laws of nature.

We designed such a partnership, the most far-reaching piece of farm legislation ever devised in time of peace. In sending it to Congress on March 16, 1933, I said:

"I tell you frankly that it is a new and untrod path, but I tell you with equal frankness that an unprecedented condition calls for the trial of new means to rescue agriculture. If a fair administrative trial of it is made and it does not produce the hoped-for results I shall be the first to acknowledge it and advise you."[5]

I had listened to all sorts of doctors with all sorts of prescriptions for curing the farm problem: men who would get the farmer out of debt by printing paper money and passing it out; others who would declare all debts null and void, thus getting debtors out of bankruptcy by bankrupting creditors (surprisingly, Herbert Hoover, after leaving the White House, said he wished he had done this); who would take us off the gold standard as a way of devaluating the dollar (which, indeed, I was soon to try, without bringing on the disaster predicted by some, but also without helping the farmer as much as we had hoped); who would raise domestic farm prices by dumping surpluses at any old price overseas; who would raise farm prices by having government seize dictatorial control of farm production, slashing it and creating artificial shortages. All these are what a good doctor would recognize as treating symptoms, not the disease itself. Treating the disease required an understanding of the partnership between prosperity and land conservation.

The heart of the Agricultural Adjustment Act of 1933 was a "domestic allotment plan" under which *farmers themselves*—in local county committees, co-ordinated by a national committee working with the Department of Agriculture—would determine how many acres of each crop ought to be planted to keep a nice balance between supply and demand. Each cotton county, for example, would then be given an allotment of the national cotton-production quota, each wheat county the same, and so forth. In turn, county committees—chosen by their neighbors—would tell each co-operating farmer how many acres he might allot to each crop in the plan. If, say, a cotton farmer had been planting five hundred acres of cotton in previous years and now was given an allotment of only three hundred acres, the Department of Agriculture would pay him a kind of "rent" for the two hundred acres not planted in cotton. He was free, of course, to plant these acres in some unallotted crop—tomatoes or trees, or he could put it into clover—and county agents of the Department of Agriculture educated small farmers as to which new crops would be both money-making and refreshing to the soil.

I used the phrase "co-operating farmer." No one was forced to join the plan but, as in joining any club, you get the benefits only by signing your card and agreeing to the rules. The benefits of this "club" were considerable. In addition to receiving "rent" payments for taking land out of certain kinds of production, "club members" were eligible to receive loans from a new agency we created, the Commodity Credit Corporation. In 1934, say, a wheat farmer could borrow the anticipated value of his 1935 crop—based on an optimistic price set by the government. If he realized that price, fine—he repaid his loan. If he did not, he surrendered his crop to the government, which would resell it or store it and take the loss. Built into this scheme was another major social advance, which we established formally a year later, called the "ever-normal granary." In bounteous years the government could put away surpluses of wheat and cotton and other storable crops to prevent them from flooding the market and driving prices down. Then, in drought years, the surpluses were there to prevent shortages and hunger, and at the same time keep prices from getting abnormally high.

Of course, some people opposed the allotment plan before it was even tried. Considering what their interests were, I was not surprised. The cotton-ginning people didn't like it. The more cotton they ginned, the more money they made. They couldn't profit by reduced production. Similarly, the transportation people and the warehousers and exporters. They were not interested in the price of commodities, but merely in their quantity. So those interests raised a not-unexpected cry: "This is all a big handout."

The family farmer is the most independent citizen we have. No one is more repulsed by the idea of a subsidy or a handout than he. Our programs to help him—experimental programs all—were designed strictly for providing an economic incentive for (1) conservation of the land and (2) creating a fair and stable price structure that would carry the farmer more evenly through the fertile years and the dry ones.

While we felt sure that our daring program was economically sound, it also required a tremendous investment. How were we to raise the money for payments to millions of farmers? The AAA provided for a tax to be levied against the "first processor": the mill that ground the wheat into flour, the plant that converted the cotton into thread, the stockyard that butchered the hogs. Of course, we realized that this tax would raise the price to consumers. But once the declining economy had been reversed into an upward cycle, this price rise would be quite tolerable.[6]

Unlike the Civilian Conservation Corps, which cracked through Congress like a bolt of lightning, the AAA ran into a wall of words, a mire of questioning and haggling. Anticipating this possibility, I warned Congress in my March 16 message, "The spring crops will soon be planted, and if we wait another month or six weeks the effect on the prices of this year's crops will be wholly lost." Congress took fifty-seven days before sending me the bill—and that forced us into some very unpleasant emergency measures.

Since it was too late to reduce planting, we had no choice but to destroy the surplus of crops. We paid farmers $100 million to plow under ten million acres of cotton. This was a heartbreaking task for farmers who, after spending their lives training mules not to tread on a growing cotton stalk, now had to reteach those confused animals to trample baby stalks into the ground.

The worst came when we had to slaughter more than six million baby pigs and more than two hundred thousand sows about to farrow. The country was horrified at newspaper pictures of piglets overrunning the stockyards, scampering and squealing through the streets of Chicago and Omaha, doomed to slaughter. The public reaction almost ruined our program. People got the idea that AAA was synonymous with killing little pigs. Although slaughter was an emergency measure we undertook only in 1933, we had to keep convincing people in 1934 and 1935 that no more baby pigs were being killed. We had to convince people that not a single acre of food crops was being destroyed under the AAA and that the emergency killing of piglets in 1933 was not wasteful, that it provided a hundred million pounds of salt pork for hungry families on relief.

Poor Henry Wallace carried most of the burden of trying to quiet the public wrath. He chided critics for feeling that "every little pig has the right to attain before slaughter the full pigginess of his pigness. To hear them talk, you would have thought that pigs were raised for pets."[7]

By the fall of 1933, the first harvest during our administration, AAA justified its existence. In the South, cotton growers got nine to ten cents a pound, compared with only four and a half to five cents the previous year. Ten-cent cotton was not enough, but was a remarkable improvement for a single year. I even got Sears Roebuck and Montgomery Ward to agree on that. General Robert Wood of Sears Roebuck came to see me and said that in Georgia, for instance, Sears mail-order sales had increased 120 per cent over those of a year earlier. Sewell Avery, head of Montgomery Ward (an extreme conservative who I have reason to believe was not among my ardent campaigners), conceded publicly that AAA had been the single greatest cause of a sharp rise in Ward's business.

The price of tobacco doubled, and 97 per cent of tobacco farmers signed up for acreage reduction in 1934. In contrast, cattle, left out of the AAA because congressmen from the cattle country distrusted the idea, hardly budged a penny in price, leaving ranchers in very great trouble.

Wheat nearly doubled, too, but we must share some of the credit with nature. The drought of 1934, particularly hard on wheat, was an effective crop-reduction program of its own. I'll leave it to the economists to split hairs arguing how much credit should be given to the drought, how much to general industrial recovery, and how much to the AAA, but the facts are that cash income for all farmers rose steadily as follows[8]:

1932	$4,377,000,000
1933	5,409,000,000
1934	6,267,000,000
1935	6,900,000,000

On January 6, 1936, the farmers of America—all the people of America—were struck a great blow. Not by drought or storm, not by the fury of nature or economics, but by the United States Supreme Court. By a margin of a single vote, the aging majority of that Court, their thoughts still mired in the back roads of the horse-and-buggy era, declared the AAA unconstitutional. Specifically, what they found not to their liking was the processing-tax provision, calling it "coercion." In a later chapter I will go into detail about the crisis created by the Supreme Court by striking down measure after measure, thus frustrating the will of Congress, the American people, and their President—and how the people's will finally prevailed. Suffice it to say for now that the Court had wielded its ax and we had to find ways of living with the debris.

I wouldn't have said it then, but I'll say now that the Court's slaughter of the AAA, while legally unjustified, was a blessing in disguise. Since we had to write a new law leaving out the articles challenged by the Court, we were able to study our two years of experience to help make the new law a better one. The old one had done a good job in raising farm prices, but I was not satisfied that it was helping enough to conserve and enrich the land.

The new law, the Soil Conservation and Domestic Allotment Act of 1936, was designed to promote land conservation first and farm income second. Instead of addressing itself to commodities on a national scale—to corn or wheat or cotton or hogs—it addressed itself to the individual farmer and the way he worked his land. Like the old law, it paid the farmer to limit his planting of soil-depleting crops that were in surplus. But the new law *required* additional land-enriching practices: rotating his crops, putting some acres into pasture or woodlands, using fertilizers as advised by his local agent of the Department of Agriculture. The law said to the individual farmer, "If you will forgo the immediate cash income of dangerous, one-crop farming, we the people of the United States will share your sacrifice. We will pay you to protect *our* future by protecting your land."

Protection of land is an intricate, subtle, and technical business. It involves chemistry as well as saving the physical topsoil itself, and we had to make sure that the new law promoted *total* conservation. I realize that most city folk are not interested in these technical matters, but bear with me and I'll try to show you how fascinating this can be. I had to give the same lesson to my news-reporter friends in January of 1936:

"The purpose of this [new bill] is to prevent the loss of soil fertility. Now, of course, very few of you know anything about farming. . . . Let us bring it down to a field, where there isn't erosion in the sense that the soil is running off the field into the creek. . . . Soil erosion, when you come down to a matter of actual fact, may be in one of two forms, the tangible thing that you can pick up in your hand, such as a handful of mud, or it may be the chemicals that are being washed out of the land. For instance, Hyde Park is an entirely different proposition from down in Georgia. In Warm Springs, Georgia, the soil itself actually washes off the cultivated fields and eventually you get these great furrows, gullies. At Hyde Park we don't get any gullies except on some of the higher hills. But if I don't rotate crops at Hyde Park, if I keep on planting corn year after year in the same field, after a while I don't get any corn crop. There are two causes, the first being that the corn itself takes the minerals out of the soil. The second is that when that land is never put back into pasture, the chemicals in that particular field run off with the rains. That does not make a gully, because chemicals are almost intangible. You cannot pick them up in your hand.

"That is one of the questions in respect to this bill—whether it clearly enough states that soil erosion is not limited to the physical running off of the soil in the form of ground. Is that clear?"

It wasn't quite clear. One of the reporters voiced a frequent misconception about what we were trying to do: "Have you any estimate of the number of acres of crop land which will be taken out of commercial production?"

"Probably *not any*. As I said before, if you have a hundred acres all planted to one thing and if you take twenty-five acres and devote them to something else, that does not take them out of production. If you put a field into pasture, that does not take it out of commercial production."

To take the lesson a little further, you may roughly say that there are two kinds of crops: soil-depleting crops and soil-building crops. The soil-depleting crops are the intensive, cultivated row crops such as corn, cotton, tobacco, and the small grains such as wheat and oats. Soil-building crops are grasses, legumes, and green manure crops, which prevent rapid runoff of water and hold the soil in place, lessening the damage of floods. What our new law did was to pay a farmer for the combined acts of (1) shifting some of his acreage from soil-depleting crops to soil-conserving crops and (2) rotating them and fertilizing them year after year.

The results were immediate and dramatic. As under the old AAA, surpluses were reduced, prices rose, and farmers were more secure. That was important, but our secondary aim. The primary accomplishment was that cotton disappeared from the hillsides, where it never should have been grown. In the Great Plains, fields of grain flourished alongside great squares of soil-replenishing greenery and grasses. The dust storms ended, and I predict with confidence they will never return to plague us again.

The cost of this permanent soil-conservation plan, now that the processing tax is gone, must be paid from the general treasury. It is a big cost and may be with us for a long time, perhaps forever. But it is small, measured even in actual dollars, compared to the dollar value of the good soil we were losing every year. Let us bear that in mind when the dust storms are long forgotten and all we remember is last year's tax bill. If this law makes a success over the long haul, as it has in the short, of keeping our land forever young, its work is priceless.

I can foresee a day when prosperity is fully restored to farmer and city dweller alike and the city dweller asks, "Must I keep subsidizing that farmer for taking proper care of his land? Nobody pays me for taking proper care of my home or business." My answer to him would be that a farm is a very special kind of business. A man who owns a factory may milk the profits from his business, neglecting to plow some back for his future. If he does, *he* is the loser. A competitor will come along to build a factory and run it more wisely. But the farmer who, driven by hard circumstances or just plain foolishness, ruins his land, deprives us all. The land, while privately claimed, is a public treasure. We must employ every means short of compulsion—for, alas, if those means do not work, compulsion will be the only means left—to ensure that the farmer finds it profitable to protect and constantly enrich *our* land.[9]

Have I made all this appear a glorious and flawless success? Preventing surpluses, especially in cotton, was not a bed of roses (to mix my gardening terms). It did harm as well as good, and the harm was not so easy to deal with. The AAA provided direct benefits to landowners. But it also brought terrible threats to hundreds of thousands who *worked* the land: I refer particularly to sharecroppers and tenant farmers.

Tenant farming is widespread in the United States, and not necessarily a bad system when operated fairly. Under it, one man owns the land (as a landlord may own a store) and another man pays him rent to work it (like a storekeeper). In fact, my neighbor Moses Smith, to whom I previously referred, is a tenant farmer on land I own in Hyde Park.

A special form of tenant farming, however, is sharecropping, particularly widespread in the cottonfields of the South. Under this system the tenant works the owner's land and, instead of paying a cash rent as a fixed cost, he receives a share of the proceeds of his crop from his landlord—usually fifty-fifty. It is a system of guaranteed and interminable poverty for the sharecropper. Often the landlord— "the man," as he is usually called by his sharecroppers in the South— chooses to make only one contribution to the work of the farm he owns. He reserves to himself the chore of taking the cotton to market and collecting its price. Sometimes nobody knows but himself and God whether he gives his "cropper" an honest report of what the cotton sold for.

We are speaking here of a sizable human problem—as well as a threat to conservation. Back in 1880, shortly before I was born, 25 per cent of all American farmers were tenants. By 1935, tenancy had grown to 42 per cent—2,865,000 tenants and sharecroppers, hardworking folk who worked the land but did not own it, two thirds of whom were in the South. Since an aim of the AAA was to cut cotton production, it threatened to throw thousands upon thousands of sharecroppers off the plantation and into uselessness.

What a terrible dilemma this meant for us! To help the land, we had to hurt people. Yet sharecropping had to be reduced. Sharecropping is a poison to the land. When a cotton picker is desperately poor and does not know from one year to the next that he will stay on a certain piece of land (average tenancy in fact is less than two years), his sole object is to get as big and as quick a crop as possible. It must be a cash crop. He cannot afford, nor does he care, to fertilize the land except to help him get a bigger immediate return. He cannot afford, nor does he care, to improve the house, the barn, the shed, or the wood lot.

As sharecropping ruins the land, so does it ruin the men, women, and children entrapped in it. Expecting to move from one depleted patch to another, year after year, these poor souls develop no community, no local social order. Large families live in two- or three-room shacks, unscreened, leaky. In these shacks children are born and spend their living days and nights, sometimes hungry and diseased, no sense of permanent home, no semblance of hope, with schooling that is at best sporadic and inadequate. Under these conditions we are breeding a crop of young Americans! Driven from the land, where are these people to go? To the cities, for Heaven's sake, which are already overcrowded with desperate souls? What would become of them? What would become of our cities?

Here we have an example of a pressing humanitarian need that simply had to be held in abeyance in favor of the larger aim of getting the AAA passed. To tamper now with the relationships, no matter how unjust, between plantation owners and sharecroppers was to attack the whole social structure of the Cotton Belt. Consider that the Democratic Majority Leader of the United States Senate was Joseph T. Robinson—from the cotton state of Arkansas. Without his support and that of senators and congressmen throughout the South, there would be no AAA at all.

A group of zealously humanitarian lawyers in AAA—among them Jerome Frank, Lee Pressman, and Alger Hiss—with no experience in farming and little in practical politics, pressed us to protect the immediate security of sharecroppers over all other interests. This would have torn asunder our Congressional coalition in support of AAA. With the personal approval of Henry Wallace and me, AAA director Chester Davis got rid of this whole crowd of young lawyers by abolishing the office of AAA General Counsel. Calling this a "purge," some journals of the left were no wiser than the impatient lawyers in understanding the practical importance of holding on to southern support. One journal claimed that the "purge" was the end of an era of a "social outlook in agricultural policy."

Of course it was no such thing. For everything there is a proper time. The proper time—although it may have seemed an eternity to reformers who were so impatient in 1933—came four years later, when the AAA had proved itself to farmers and Congress, and its replacement, the Soil Conservation Act, had been safely passed. Now I was able to tell Congress in a special message: "The tenancy problem is the accumulated result of generations of unthinking exploitation of our agricultural resources, both land and people. We can no longer postpone action."

What was the action to be? If the plantation owners (and many of their friends in Congress) had their way, our national policy would be that sharecroppers driven from the land would be left with their "free and independent American right" to shift for themselves, into starvation or into the cities, anywhere, as long as they and their problem disappeared from sight. If the impatient reformers—typified by those lawyers in 1933—had *their* way, the policy would be, surprisingly, just as reactionary, while parading as humanitarian. They wanted us to require cotton planters to retain their sharecroppers— the same individuals—regardless of reduction in cotton planting. What could this do in the long run except freeze them into the sharecropping system—and protect the system of sharecropping itself?

My aim was to free sharecroppers from that system and to protect both them and the land by giving them an economic stake in the land. We carefully developed a Farm Tenant Act of sufficiently broad appeal to attract Senator John Bankhead of Alabama as its sponsor. The Act, passed in July of 1937, authorized federal loans to farm tenants, sharecroppers, and farm wage laborers so they could buy their own farms. It was not a perfect law, but the best one we could get. As a compromise with conservatives, we had to allow preference to families that could make some initial down payment or that owned livestock and farm implements. Granted, this meant that loans would not reach the poorest of the poor, but you don't get to second steps before taking first steps.

To anyone who underestimates our problem in establishing the principle of this Act, I would refer him to the miserly dollar support Congress gave it. For the first year, 1937–38, Congress appropriated a mere $10 million. The irony was that our opposition claimed that

I and my plan were "socialistic." The whole idea was to bring more people into the system of private property, to give them a greater stake in capitalism. The appropriation was so small that we had to restrict applications to 331 selected counties, about one tenth of all counties in the United States. Within six weeks, thirty-eight thousand sharecroppers and tenants seized at the opportunity by applying for loans. There were twenty applications for every loan we could give.

Loans averaged about five thousand dollars, repayable over forty years at 3 per cent interest. The following year, Congress voted twenty-five million dollars to cover seven hundred counties. This time there were twenty-five applications for every loan. By 1939, over twenty thousand farm families had obtained loans, bought farms—and rolled up a record of 97.4 per cent success in keeping up with their payments.

The lives of these families were forever changed. Their soil was made more secure because they had a stake in its conservation. These newly self-respecting and self-sustaining farmers, both Negro and white, became stable members of a community life. It was a fine, constructive, humanitarian, problem-solving program. But, unfortunately, it was a mere drop in the bucket compared to the need.[10]

Water and Power

Each year when I cast my vote at Hyde Park and am asked to identify myself by name and occupation, it is a proud moment for me. I always say, "Franklin D. Roosevelt, tree farmer." Being governor or President is a passing responsibility. But planting fine trees on my land, caring for them, weeding out the scrub growth, cutting down some carefully selected ones at their maturity, and selling them to bring shelter and Christmas joy to my neighbors—that was carried on long before me and I trust will continue after I am gone. That chain of responsibility, of which I am a single link, must go on. It is an obligation to my father and to my sons.

No man can have a more sacred calling than to cultivate and develop the earth in its most appropriate way, make its riches available to his fellow man, and preserve it for those who come afterward. Our land at Hyde Park was particularly suited for trees, so trees we grew. But not trees alone. A few yards from my house, behind a rose garden, there lies a great square surrounded by a high hedge. One day my wife and I will lie buried there. For most of my life and before I came, my mother and, before her, my father planted this square in rows of vegetables to be served at our family table. For many years in a meadow across from our house we kept cows. When I was at school and in Albany—and later when my sons were at school or in business—my mother insisted on sending us fresh cream, butter, and eggs. For a time I tried to persuade her that this was going too far. My son James, who went into business in Boston, called it the most costly milk route in existence. But she insisted and, frankly, there was something about it I considered precious.

The land is to use. It asks not only for man's labor, but for his ingenuity as well. God makes us this gift, but without a manual of instruction. It is for man to study and design how he will use it. If he plunders it, the punishment is sure. But if he studies wisely, the more he partakes of it the more he will leave to his descendants. I repeat: this calling is our most sacred.

If the land at Hyde Park is my homestead, the hills of northwest Georgia are my adopted second home. From a high mountain there, you may see across into Alabama. I believe that if you climb the highest treetop on the highest hill, you would catch a glimpse of Tennessee. I have come to deeply love those hills. They are peaceful, yet wild; abundant, yet unyielding. It has long been a harsh place to live. Its people are kind and devoted and hard-working, but no one has led them in a proper study of the gifts that lie in their wild hills. These gifts have lain there like untapped precious ores, while its good folk suffered.

Of the many opportunities I have been given to be of service to my neighbors, if God had given me the choice of only one I believe I would choose the work we have done in the Tennessee Valley. It is a tangible and permanent work. Up to my time, it is the greatest planned cultivation of a whole natural territory—and therefore of its people—in the history of mankind.

If the Civilian Conservation Corps was a way of killing two birds with one stone, the Tennessee Valley Authority was a carefully aimed boulder that shook a whole flock of birds out of the trees.

Efforts to make the land serve man better had heretofore been directed in many separate, often conflicting, ways: by preventing the land from blowing away or disappearing down the rivers; controlling floods; improving the growth of trees; fertilizing crops; restoring minerals to the soil while extracting food. The TVA *brought them all together* in one bold, integrated plan. Instead of gaining one human benefit at the cost of another, each rode on the others, piggyback. The TVA not only harmonized the needs of man with those of his earthly environment, but also harmonized private initiative and democratic government in *planning* for the betterment of all.

I know that the word "planning"—especially *government* planning or *social* planning—is a red flag in the eyes of some. That is just plain foolish. Everybody plans—every individual, every family, every civic group, every corporation. We plan when we put away a dollar for a rainy day, when we buy an insurance policy, when we weatherproof a house, when a corporation creates a sinking fund. Planning is vital to civilized life. A community or a nation that does not plan is a community or a nation that squanders its future, that is doomed.

No matter how the phrase may rile up some unthinking people, "social planning" is planning on a broad scale when a narrow scale won't do. The dust storms, the agricultural surpluses, our oversized cities, our poisoned rivers and disappearing timber, these are a few examples of the price of not planning cohesively on problems that planning separately cannot solve. If the words "social planning" blind your eyes, call it whatever you like. But for a people of a common geography, having reached a certain level of civilized progress and determined to keep progressing, it is a proper, necessary, ultimately unavoidable function of their government. It does not mean socialism or anti-capitalism. In fact it strengthens capitalism at the point of its greatest weakness.

The main trouble with the capitalistic system is that, while providing big rewards for big planners, it does not always encourage planning that is big enough—which, regardless of private profit, is best for the whole society. Capitalism rewards entrepreneurial *specialists:* the man who finds a vein of coal and hires others to dig it out; the man who extracts power from a rushing river and sells it to another who fires steel to bend it into motor cars; the man who fells a forest of trees to slice into lumber; still another who cuts a path through the countryside to lay a railroad.

These are ventures—big ventures—of private profit that benefit society. But they also hurt society. Their entrepreneurs, competitive specialists caught in a system of every man for himself, leave behind them a rubble of exploited resources and lost social opportunities.

On the other hand the main trouble with a socialistic or communistic system is that, while seeking to manage the whole society, it fails to encourage private initiative—its most valuable human resource—to create social inventions for bringing man and nature into their most profitable partnership.

Between these two extreme alternatives of unregulated capitalism and the single entrepreneurship of a socialist state, there is a middle way: preserving the strengths of private initiative within a framework of social planning. The time for it was long overdue.[11]

Five weeks after taking office, on April 10, 1933, I asked Congress to create a new form of government. Not for the whole country, but a part of it, spreading over several states. Not really a government, but a corporation with flexible powers, almost like those of a private business, to protect and promote certain specific interests for the common good of all the people living there.

That was the Tennessee Valley Authority.

In the short history of the TVA, I have seen it create a beneficial revolution in the lives of ten million people, helping just about everyone including the most successful profit makers of the region, and hurting no one that I can see. That is what good planning can do. I hope one day to see the same idea spread everywhere. Not the TVA as such, but other regional authorities designed according to the special needs of each region as the people of that region see their needs. So, as you read here of the TVA, read it as an account of a single, large-scale undertaking suited for a single, large place.

Great plans do not begin with theories spun from dreams of how the world *should* have been made, of some perfect future that disregards the past. They begin with the earth as it is, people as they are. They begin with what is real. The TVA story starts with the harsh reality of a place called Muscle Shoals, a wild, rapid-running section of the meandering Tennessee River. God put it there. So there man begins.

Muscle Shoals was a barrier to river navigation. The Army Corps of Engineers is in the business of making rivers navigable. If they had had their way, they would have built a dam with locks to make the river navigable and the devil take the rest. During World War I someone got the brighter idea of building a double-purpose dam. The region happens to be rich in certain minerals that can be made into nitrates, which, in turn, are important to the manufacture of explosives. Making nitrates requires a great deal of electric power. (Nitrates also make valuable fertilizers, but, at the time, hardly anyone gave much thought to that.) The bright idea was for a dam that would raise the river for navigation and at the same time put the rapids to work generating electricity. The dam, named after President Wilson, was built. But before the power and nitrate plants went into operation, the war ended. For years they stood unused, a white elephant, a waste.

The potential of Wilson Dam was not entirely forgotten. In the early 1920s Henry Ford, realizing the profits that might be drawn from the electricity and chemicals, dickered with the government to take over the whole Muscle Shoals project for a paltry five million dollars. It had cost American taxpayers thirty times that sum. Later the Alabama Power Company in conjunction with a large chemical firm tried to bring off a similar piracy.

Each time, the sellouts were blocked in Congress by the zeal and leadership skill of a single man, Senator George Norris. He was driven by a practical vision, although a limited one, of government development and distribution of electric power. He had seen the great change that cheap power could make in the life of his home state of Nebraska. Norris was the main force in getting his state to take over a private power company that had held back the spread of electrification by keeping prices high. After the state reduced prices, Norris watched electrification spread among his farm neighbors while the public operation paid for itself.

Six times in the 1920s Senator Norris, a Republican, introduced bills for federal operation of Muscle Shoals power, but a Republican Congress blocked them. The seventh time, his bill passed but was vetoed by President Coolidge. The eighth time, it was vetoed by President Hoover.

More than a month before taking office, I visited Muscle Shoals in the company of Senator Norris. The great plant, lying in idleness, was twice as big as I had imagined. That night, in a speech at Montgomery, Alabama, I pledged to put Muscle Shoals to work; in fact, to make it part of a far greater development: "We have an opportunity of setting an example of planning, . . . tying in industry and agriculture and forestry and flood prevention, tying them all into a unified whole over a distance of a thousand miles."

Reporters, forever skeptical of politicians, later asked Norris, "Is he really with you?" Norris, who had broken into tears upon at last seeing his life's work supported by a President-to-be, responded, "He is more than with me, because he plans to go even farther than I did."

Of course, that was true. With due credit to that great man, Norris' vision did not extend beyond electric power. On the other hand, southern farm organizations were mainly interested in cheap, effective fertilizers. Their spokesman, Senator Hugo Black of Alabama, said, "I care nothing for the power." Still others cared only about flood protection, and even they couldn't agree on what was most important. I had clipped a New York *Times* editorial that pointed out the conflicts raging around the single issue of flood control. Whenever there is a flood, it correctly pointed out, a group of people downstream rush to the government for money to build more and better levees. A group upstream wants dams; another group farther up wants to plant trees around the headwaters; still another says all the money and efforts should go into preventing soil erosion. Each group has its own pet theory.

My idea was to do all these things, but primarily to make the Tennessee Valley a different kind of place, give its citizens an opportunity to live a wholly different kind of life.

On my trip to Muscle Shoals I saw farm families—if you want to call their scrubby homesteads "farms"—in ramshackle, unpainted dwellings living like thirteenth-century serfs. I remember one farm wife, prematurely aged by excessive childbearing and manual labor, cooking a rabbit over a wood fire. She cooked and washed with water that she hauled in pails from a hand-operated well while her husband hunted the next meal. She sewed by light of a kerosene lamp by which her children studied—if they sustained the will to study at all.

None of them had ever heard a radio. There were whole families among their neighbors who had never visited the nearest community that might be called a town—which was less than twenty miles away.

The impoverished people of this valley, about two million spread over seven states, were of old English stock, descendants of pioneers whom we glorify. Yet they had been left out of the American story of progress. The power to save them, daily rushing by in the rapid river, imperiled them instead. Raging, cruel floods, one upon another, threatened constantly to wash all a man's worldly goods downstream, and perhaps some of his family with them.

On June 8, 1933, less then two months after I requested passage of TVA (and quickly got it), I issued an executive order to start construction of the mighty Norris Dam, on the Clinch River, a principal tributary of the Tennessee. It was designed for both flood control and power production, which generally had been considered conflicting aims. Prevention of floods requires a high dam; its reservoir must be kept relatively empty to receive and retain rising flood waters. Power production, however, requires a full reservoir, so that a constant heavy flow through the sluices of a dam whirls its generators.

This conflict was quite possible to resolve, as TVA engineers proved. The Norris is really one dam built upon another, soaring to a superheight. The lower portion is a power-producing dam containing an ever-full reservoir. Then, atop its sluices, the dam rises still higher, its "upper" reservoir empty in normal times, ready to catch the deluge and hold it back.

This plan had its penalty, too—or really an added blessing disguised as a penalty. The mammoth lake created by such a superdam inundates some of the most level and fertile acreage in the region. But in exchange for that sacrifice, the potential of a far more valuable industry is created—a recreation industry inviting hundreds of thousands to come fishing, boating, bathing, and camping, thus creating a great many jobs for which local people are well suited.

Upon authorizing the construction of Norris Dam, I also learned that the Army Engineers were about to ask for bids for another giant storage project on the Tennessee, Wheeler Dam. Their plan would have been a disaster of specialization. Concerned only with river navigation, they contemplated no production of electricity. One of my first acts in office was to cancel their request for bids. The dam was redesigned for production of electricity and was placed in full operation on March 4, 1936.

Before long, four additional great dams—Pickwick Landing, Guntersville, and Chickamauga, all on the Tennessee, and Hiwassee Dam, on the Hiwassee River—rose to change life forever in the Tennessee Valley.

Prevention of disaster never appears as dramatic as disaster itself. Few were excited on March 30, 1936, when Norris Dam, simply by standing there, saved the great city of Chattanooga from catastrophe. Had it not been for that mighty structure holding back the torrents, the Tennessee would have reached a flood stage at Chattanooga of forty-one feet, tearing through a thousand downtown acres. In two months, between December 18, 1936, and February 15, 1937, when torrential rains wreaked tragedy along the banks of the neighboring Ohio River, Norris Dam saved Chattanooga again—four times. Neighboring rivers are like any neighbors, bad or good; they can add to one another's burdens, or bail each other out. During a fifteen-day period when the Ohio River at faraway Cairo, Illinois, crested treacherously at fifty-eight feet, Norris and Wheeler reservoirs, hundreds of miles away, pitched in to store 964,000 acre-feet of water, probably reducing the flood stage at Cairo by a critical half foot.

Flood control is only a beginning of good land use. It saves the land from destruction but does not improve it. It saves farm families from ruination but does not teach them to become better farmers. If comprehensive cultivation of a region starts with what is at hand, what did the Tennessee Valley offer us? We had the nitrate plants. Beating swords into plowshares, we turned the factories for explosives into factories for fertilizers. That was one step. The other, equally important step—an integral part of the TVA plan—was an education program for farmers.

Immediately a cry arose from the National Fertilizer Association: "Is the government going into the fertilizer business?" Not at all. We were going into the business of educating industry as well as farmers. Our sole aim was to produce experimental quantities of fertilizers, show them to be effective, show farmers how to use them—and provide industry with a "yardstick" for measuring the size of a potential market and costs of production and for setting a reasonable price that would yield a fair profit. Creation of such a yardstick is a new concept in the function of government. If industry will really think about it, they will see it as an invaluable contribution to their own growth. As I told my newspaper friends one morning at Warm Springs in 1934:

"Now, if those gentlemen fail to avail themselves of this magnificent opportunity to conduct a sound business and make a profit, well, it is just too bad. Then somebody will get up in Congress and say, 'These fellows are not meeting their opportunities and the farmers will have to have the fertilizer and of course we shall have to provide it.' But I, for one, hope that that day will never come. Now, that is not holding a big stick over them at all. It is saying to them, 'Here is your opportunity. We go down on our knees to you, asking you to take it.'"

By 1937, 61,400 tons of TVA fertilizers had been demonstrated on 23,751 farms covering 3,278,665 acres. To promote erosion control, the TVA helped organize County Soil Conservation Clubs to purchase mechanical terracing equipment. These clubs rented the machines by the day to individual farmers. Before long almost three hundred thousand acres had been terraced.

What was another resource we had at hand? We had the CCC. A large force of CCC boys in more than twenty encampments was put under the direct control of TVA. They built check dams across gullies, dug diversion ditching, laid brush matting for riverbank protection, and planted Bermuda grass and other protective cover. They also planted more than fifty million trees.[12]

A few sentences back, I described the "yardstick" principle, whereby the government goes into the fertilizer business *experimentally*. Its aim is to find out how high production can go and *how low the price can go* so that the greatest number of farmers can benefit —and the enterprise still show a profit.

Keep that principle in mind as we now take a look at electricity and its spectacular effect on changing the lives of people in the valley —and beyond that, its immense implications for the entire nation. This subject, which has absorbed me all my life, can fascinate anyone if he translates dry terms such as "kilowatt-hours" into the joys of modern life: turning on a light to illuminate the pages of a book, substituting an electric washing machine for a scrub board, enjoying music and drama on the radio, saving a child from dreaded pellagra by serving him fresh fruit out of a refrigerator.

Commonplace as these benefits of modern life may be to city dwellers, they have been almost unknown to the twentieth-century American farmer. In 1933 nine out of ten farm families lived without electricity. At the rate farm homes were being hooked to electric lines, it would take half a century to electrify only half of our farms. What a penalty to pay for living on the land! It is morally inexcusable, because it is utterly unnecessary, technically or economically. And the blame for it lies squarely on the timidity, shortsightedness, and negativeness of private power companies.

Charles Steinmetz, the genius of electricity, once observed—and anyone can understand this, with the possible exception of a power-company official—that electrical power is expensive because it is not widely used, and, at the same time, it is not widely used because it is expensive.

The people of Corinth, Mississippi, whom I visited on November 17, 1934, understood that perfectly well. Some of those people couldn't read or write, but they taught the Mississippi Power Company how to make more money selling electricity.

Very few people in Corinth could afford electricity—the businesses and better homes downtown, and that was about all. I'm not sure what they paid for it. If their bills were anything like mine for my little house at Warm Springs, Georgia, they were paying up to eighteen cents a kilowatt-hour. That was four times as much as I paid at Hyde Park, New York, where almost everyone used electricity—and, therefore, rates were lower.

Then the local TVA people stepped in to put into effect a theory I had always believed in. They negotiated an agreement with the Mississippi Power Company to buy wholesale—far more juice at much less cost. What did the TVA people expect to do with all that extra power? Very simple. They offered to lend money at very low interest to other homeowners in town so they could wire their homes. By doing that, they found they could distribute household power at something like *two cents* a kilowatt-hour.

But the people of Corinth didn't stop there. They called a meeting of all the people in the county to discuss an interesting proposition: They explained that they could run electric lines out to the neighboring farms and sell electricity to these distant homes for three cents. But was that fair to the farmer? The people of Corinth decided it wasn't. Voluntarily, the people in town agreed to pay two and a half cents for power so that farmers could get theirs at an equal price.

There was no reason in God's world why the Mississippi Power Company could not have done exactly the same thing—and made money at it. But the TVA was first to try it, and, as a result, consumption of power almost doubled around Corinth. The TVA went ahead and did something else the power company should have done: They organized the citizens into a co-operative association to buy refrigerators and electric cookstoves and so forth at wholesale. With lower prices for these gadgets, electric consumption went up even more.

When I told that story of Corinth to reporters one day, one of them asked the critically important question: "Isn't there a considerable change in the company's cost by having to step up its power production to meet a demand like that?"

The answer: *"Very little.* The only overhead is when you get an extension of rural lines. There you have a larger inspection force to watch the lines. That is about all. . . . I hope that the proper power-company officials will accept this free education that the government is giving them. It is a fine offer and a grand chance. If they come in and do it right with a reasonable profit on their actual cost, that is all we are asking. . . . What we are after primarily is to improve the standard of living for the country as a whole."

Another reporter: "Do you think it is necessary to go ahead with the Tennessee Valley experiment on a national scale?"

"Not the same kind of government power development *if the other fellows will do it.* They have every chance in the world to do it."

It is important to point out here that TVA does not sell electricity directly to consumers. It is not a competitor of private companies. It is a wholesale producer and distributor of electricity. By law, priority is given to furnishing TVA power to public agencies that sell to consumers: cities, counties, and co-operatives. By 1937 TVA had contracts to furnish wholesale power to twenty-six municipalities (including Memphis, Chattanooga, and Knoxville) and sixteen co-operative power associations. By that time also, one private power company as well as twelve large industrial plants had become customers of TVA.

Don't think, however, that these big private interests didn't kick and scream before settling down to accept the benefits—to them—of TVA. The utilities argued, on the one hand, that there would be no market for the immense power that TVA dams would produce, and, on the other hand, that TVA would destroy the private utility industry. Wendell L. Willkie, head of the Commonwealth & Southern Corporation, a holding company that controls the big private companies in the TVA area, hired some of the highest-priced legal talent in the country to stop TVA in the courts, which he failed to do. In Congress, Representative Joe Martin, the Massachusetts Republican, tried to kill TVA by claiming it was "patterned closely after one of the Soviet dreams." The New York *Times* (soon to become one of TVA's stanchest defenders) editorialized: "Enactment of any such bill at this time would mark the 'low' of Congressional folly."

In the wake of these gloomy predictions, what really happened? The yardstick principle worked like a charm—for the balance sheets of the private utilities and, more important, for lifting the lives of the people of the valley. As more people used more electricity, private companies made more money while the average residential rates per kilowatt-hour were reduced as follows:

	1933	1935
Alabama Power Company	4.63	3.54
Georgia Power Company	5.16	3.63
Tennessee Electric Power Company	5.77	3.63
National average	5.49	5.03

The supreme irony was that private companies, spurred by the example of TVA, discovered the vast profit advantages in making it easy for consumers to buy electrical appliances. It had never occurred to them that the real profit lay in the years of sale of electricity that followed the sale of the appliances. How they suddenly went to work! Wendell Willkie's Commonwealth & Southern led the entire country in appliance sales in 1934 and 1935. In 1934 the Tennessee Electric Power Company won a prize from the Edison Electric Institute as "the outstanding company of 1934" for "one of the most, if not the most, remarkable sales increases in residential, commercial, and industrial power in the history of the electrical industry." So pleased was the Tennessee Company with "its" discovery of how to make money that in 1936 it opened the way to still more profits by reducing its rates again.

Try to imagine what an awesome thing the coming of electricity is to some poor hill farmer and his children who, never having left their home town, have never in their lives seen an electric light. I was told of one hillside hamlet to which a transmission line had just been strung. The people kept talking about the coming miracle. Finally a power-association office opened for business, the local TVA agent confident of a rush of customers. The first day passed without a single application. Next day the clever fellow, a true country psychologist, connected an electric bulb to a power line outside the office. Applicants flooded in. One old farmer told the TVA man:

"I reckon none of us knowed light come through paltry wires like those 'til we seen it with our own eyes."

While electricity spread like lightning through the Tennessee Valley, still the vast stretches of the rest of America's farmlands remained in almost total darkness. This deprivation had to end—and end quickly. About that, I was absolutely determined.

In my message to Congress of January 3, 1935, I urged Congress to include, as a small part of that year's emergency-relief work program, the creation of the Rural Electrification Administration. The legal justification was that many jobs would be created by the vast work of stringing long lines, of wiring houses, and of manufacturing electrical products. They gave me the authorization. On May 11, 1935, one of the happiest days of my life, in my cottage at Warm Springs, surrounded by old friends and neighbors, I signed an executive order that was the beginning of the end of twentieth-century darkness on the American farm. The aim of REA was to bring electricity to every forlorn byway of America within ten years—a mammoth, awesome undertaking, yes, but one we were perfectly capable of accomplishing once we made up our minds to do it.

The cost to the government would be next to nil. REA built no lines, installed no wiring. Instead it offered to lend the entire cost of these lines to private or public entrepreneurs at extremely liberal terms of 3 per cent interest to be repaid over twenty years.

The going was far from easy, thanks to our obstructionist friends in the power companies. Most of them refused to go along, refused to learn from what they had seen with their own eyes in the Tennessee Valley. Again they argued on the one hand that it was "socialism," on the other that farmers wouldn't buy the juice. City-owned power plants might willingly have jumped into the breach but were legally prevented from extending their lines beyond their own municipal boundaries. So the REA seized the initiative, where private profit makers refused it, and helped farmers organize electric co-operatives. Then—and only then—some power companies strung "spite lines" into some co-operatives' territory, but they had missed their boat. Farmers stuck by their co-operatives, which they could control. In place after place, on a slope of the Rockies, in a woodland of Upper Michigan, farmers and their wives and children would gather on the eagerly awaited night. At the pull of a switch to start a giant generator, they would see their homes, schools, churches, and town hall burst forth in dazzling light.

Six years later, in 1941, four out of ten American farms had electricity, when the war forced a halt to the rapid spread of light. There is no question in my mind that at the war's victorious end, we will resume the ten-year schedule of this great work.[13]

There is one more thing I want to say about electricity, a terribly important thing that I have tried to propagate; yet those who can most profit by it resist understanding it.

When some great invention comes along, inertia causes people to try to fit it into old ways of doing things rather than seeing it as an opportunity for creating new ways. For example, in an earlier chapter I described the old-fashioned ways that public leaders used radio. Instead of seeing it as a way to make a new kind of intimate contact with individual citizens, they used it as a grandiose public-address system for orating at crowds. It was a very ineffective use. Take the printing press. When Gutenberg invented movable type, the first book printed was the Bible, for distribution to priests. That was understandable and fine. But many years passed before there was a general realization that printing could change the world by spreading *new* knowledge to *all* people, that it opened the hope of making every human being literate.

So it is with a major aspect of electricity. Before we knew how to control electrical energy, the steam engine brought about an industrial revolution. It remade the world by concentrating production in large factories, inducing peasants and their families to leave their land and crowd into larger and larger cities. Steam energy could not be divided into parts to be shipped where the potential workers lived. Workers had to go where the steam engine was. That is what started the present dangerous trend, which shows no sign of abatement, of cities growing ever larger, more unhealthy, and more impersonal.

Electricity can reverse that trend while continuing to advance the cause of industrial progress. Unlike steam, electricity can be *divided* and *transported* in "packages" of any size and for long distances. The "package" can be small enough to light a bed lamp or large enough to run a mighty factory. Yet, through sheer inertia, we are continuing the old forms of overcentralization of industry—we are still slaves to "steam engine" thinking—long after we are technically able to promote decentralization of industry.

When I was governor of New York, I asked the head of the General Electric Company to develop a plan whereby units of a big manufacturing company might be detached and profitably operated in small, rural communities. Electricity made it possible. Granted, for many marginal farmers an industrial job might offer a better living, more security. But why must he abandon his land to take the job? Why couldn't manufacturing jobs be brought to him and his neighbors—through transportable electricity—so he could continue living on the old family place, growing his own vegetables, raising his children to develop a practical appreciation of animals and crops, which are the source of human life?

Nothing much came of it. As President, I talked up this idea with businessmen all the time. In 1934 I sounded out friends on a plan to call together the 265 executives who control 70 per cent of American industry to ask their co-operation in scattering new factory units over as wide an area as practicable. At the same time, I would ask them to budget production in such a way that a rural factory worker would feel guaranteed of a certain amount of employment each year. Perhaps it was that latter idea that scared them off, but I could generate little interest.

The day will come. In the Tennessee Valley we already see it coming. I deeply hope, for the sake of preserving the qualities of American life that we have most treasured, that that day will come soon all over America. A proper understanding of electrical energy makes it possible today.[14]

BACKGROUND MEMORANDUM TO PART IV

"He remains an enigma," the biographers keep saying ritually. The "enigma," as they see it, comes down to this: How did this sheltered patrician, born and raised on a lordly estate, unrebellious son of a railroad magnate, ever transform into the champion of the "forgotten man"? When did it happen? What is the source of his instinct for democracy?

The "enigma" persists because its inventors look to the wrong source for explanation. Roosevelt's presidency was at a time of labor upheaval, when liberals and intellectuals most closely identified democracy with the rights of working men to find security in industrial unions. By joining forces, for political reasons, with this movement, and by denouncing "economic royalists," Roosevelt became labor's hero. So his interpreters look to explain his transformation by some enlightening contact with workers and labor leaders, even by his wife's early, superficial contacts with the urban poor. Finding no adequate cause and effect, they invent the "enigma."

To get at the source we must look elsewhere. We have to get out of town.

Ernest K. Lindley, the journalist who had covered Roosevelt in Albany as well as Washington, saw the error of casting him as marshal of the proletarian cause:

"However the Marxists may classify him, Mr. Roosevelt seems to prefer to think of himself as a country squire or landed gentleman. . . . He has to an extraordinary degree Jefferson's distrust or dislike of urban life. He was brought up in a spacious country atmosphere and is distinctly an outdoor man. He has had too much first-hand contact with the Southern tenant and sharecropper situation and with sub-marginal farms in the Northeast to have the romantic notion, which some writers have attributed to him, that all country life is like life on the Roosevelt manor in Hyde Park. But he has revealed consistently and in countless ways that he thinks living in the country is preferable to living in the city. . . . I have never heard Mr. Roosevelt make a complimentary remark about skyscrapers. I have heard him praise beautiful scenery and rather plain countryside from one end of the nation to the other, but I cannot recall any speech in which he has congratulated a large city on its growth or its skyline."

There is no understanding the democratic passion that developed in F.D.R. without looking to his lifelong affair with the countryside—with land, water, and trees. That was the affair that touched the nerve center of our man, intertwined as it was with a most personal struggle to realize his own independence, his sense of manhood.

For fully the first four decades of his life, the land he knew best was indeed Hyde Park, which, one day, according to his father's will, he would inherit from his mother. He craved to manage this land not as an estate but as an enterprise.

Daughter Anna recalled for me: "As a little girl I'd ride horseback with him, in the saddle in front of him. He liked to talk to me about his trees. How did you *use* trees? These were things that were very *personal* to him."

Before turning thirty he successfully ran for the state senate as a "farmer," choosing as his main campaign issue the standardization of the size of apple barrels. Rapidly becoming chairman of what was, in effect, the senate agriculture committee, he relished displaying his expertness on all of New York State's agricultural problems, even the nation's.

Yet he chafed to exercise control over the "agricultural problems" of the beloved "farm" at Hyde Park. The fact is, however, that he *never owned* it. His mother, who owned it, ran it. Mama's refusal to let her boy be a proper farmer was recorded with amusement by Tugwell, his White House adviser on agriculture:

"His efforts to make a dairy pay were unhappy ones, but he did not seem certain whether this was because dairying was a losing business or because his mother would not let him run it as he wanted. She had told him firmly that a sizeable herd of milkers had been favored by his father for family reasons, not for profit; if money was lost, she would gladly make up the deficits. . . . The ventures into apples and Christmas trees, and his own reforestation project, were no more profitable. . . . His assumption that the experiences at Hyde Park meant anything to an average farmer must have caused skeptical smiles."

The lifelong undercurrent of tension over his non-ownership showed as late as 1938 in a strange incident of self-delusion. F.D.R. decided to erect a library on the estate for his presidential records, which required turning the land over to the government as a historic site. Mama being alive, he *still* didn't own it, and now never would. The Department of the Interior drew up the papers. He signed them. A government attorney made a routine title search. With extreme embarrassment, the attorney paid a secret visit to the President—himself a lawyer—to inform him that his signature could not authorize the transfer. The nation's most powerful citizen, his irritation scarcely concealed, shipped the papers to his mother. When *she* signed them, the transfer was legal.

Yet despite (perhaps because of) not being free to manage the land his way, all through his public life, in speeches, at press conferences, in interminable conversation about the vast complex of American agriculture, he injected "for instances" and "for examples," citing his inventiveness and successes as a Hyde Park "farmer." Just one illustration: In 1937 Eleanor Roosevelt passed on to the President the text of a radio speech on food and conservation delivered by their old acquaintance Hendrik Willem van Loon. The head of state took time to fire off a letter:

Dear Hendrik:
   The "Missis" showed me that gem of a broadcast. . . .
   . . . I am no great naturalist like T.R. but . . . let me tell you the tale of a part of my farm at Hyde Park. . . . As late as 1840 that farm grew prize corn. But the toll had been taken and from then down to 1910, when I took hold of it, went from bad to worse. While it did not lie on steep land, the topsoil grew thinner and thinner each year through snow-melting floods and later torrents. In 1910 it grew only about one half the crops that it could have grown in its earlier days. I can lime it, cross-plough it, manure it and treat it with every art known to science but it has just plain run out—and now I am putting it into trees in the hope that my great-grandchildren will be able to try raising corn again—just one century from now.
   That is the story of raising food supplies in America. At least one hundred million acres of land now under the plough ought not to be cultivated again for a whole hundred years. . . .[1]

The long struggle to get loose of Mama's reins and be an independent farmer was not to be resolved at Hyde Park and was certainly not a struggle that democratized him. It only charged him with a drive to prove—to himself, to Mama, to anyone he could engage—that a farmer and farm expert he was. He was soon led, by misfortune, to the proving ground.

If the transition from aristocrat to democrat can be identified with a place and time, it begins at Warm Springs in 1924—at age forty-two. He has been a state senator, carried on his battles for state conservation laws, for "liberty of the community"—but hardly for the "forgotten man."

Thanks to an early political commitment to the presidential candidacy of Woodrow Wilson, he has been elevated to wartime Assistant Secretary of the Navy, where he showed far more concern for bigger and better battleships than the wages of men who built them. Then he becomes a youthful candidate (in 1920) for Vice-President, his chief qualification being that he brought the name of a popular Republican President to the Democratic Party banner. Then, a year after that unsuccessful campaign, he is struck down by infantile paralysis, presumably ending a promising public career.

In one of life's accidents, he is introduced to the warm, buoyant, reputedly healing springs of the Georgia hamlet. From a rich New York friend, George Foster Peabody, who first brought him there, he buys an option at a stiff price—sinking $250,000 into the property before he is through—for a run-down winter resort. This property is *his*. An Atlanta newspaper runs a Sunday feature about the national celebrity seeking a revival of lost health. From distant places, other polio victims come. The townsfolk see the prospect of a new prosperity arising from the initiative of the smiling New Yorker. They call him "Doctor" Roosevelt, vaguely aware that his uncle or father or some relative had been President a while back. He becomes a newspaper columnist for the Macon *Daily Telegraph*. He makes friends. One is Tom Bradshaw, the blacksmith, who rigs up an old Model-T Ford with ropes and pullies so this new neighbor with the useless legs can drive it completely by hand.

Roosevelt drives around and sops up local lore—almost hungrily— which flatters his country neighbors, endearing him to them. They take him on rides to "Magic Mountain," a mile stretch of road creating an illusion so rattling that few local residents would dare go there at night. The road climbs the hill steeply, then suddenly seems to level off and turn downward while actually it is still headed gently up. The neighbors teach Roosevelt to put his gears in neutral and experience the shock of watching his car roll back "uphill." Roosevelt would laugh uproariously and try the prank on the nationally famous politicians who came to see him, to the great amusement of his Warm Springs neighbors. (Only one visitor, Harold Ickes, unable to understand the illusion, went away angry.)

That crazy little car (later supplanted by more modern versions) becomes a critically important tool, a turning, in the education and democratization of Franklin Roosevelt. He drives to "the Cove," a secret and hallowed gathering place of men during Prohibition, where good fellowship pours freely along with an illicit and formidable peach brandy. According to son Jimmy, Cove old-timers "swear they have seen Pa . . . drinking right out of a fruit jar along with everyone else." Returning from one of his rides, Roosevelt would swing by the home of Mrs. Jeanie Rowe, who sells him buttermilk and "chickens on the hoof." Mrs. Roosevelt—who increasingly detested Warm Springs and seldom went there—would distastefully describe to her children how the live chicken, with legs tied, would be tossed into the back seat of the car and how Daisy Bonner, Roosevelt's cook, would, after his return home, wring its neck and toss it into the stewpot.

Those were the gayer sidelights of life in Warm Springs. But there was a more important side. As Rex Tugwell describes it:

"He seemed to know dozens of local people, politicians and farmers; moreover, he knew the countryside with an intimacy that must have been gained by close and repeated investigation. . . . [He] spent part of nearly every day, sometimes whole days, exploring the back roads, visiting with farmers—simply driving into yards, pulling up under the inevitable chinaberry tree, and hailing whomever he could see. In these casual conversations, he had learned more about farmers' grievances than he would ever have discovered in New York, where they were filtered to him through professionals, or could have learned in Hyde Park on what was not a farm but an estate. . . . There were no barriers, or anyway none such as existed wherever else he went. He learned something real about life down the dirt roads and in the farmyards of Meriwether County, and he learned it for good."

A dramatic observation, made especially popular by the play *Sunrise at Campobello,* was that the misfortune of polio was what strengthened F.D.R. to become truly great. This is engaging because it is so close to the mark, at least in pinpointing the time of the turning. But it misses the point by not accounting for the nature of the turning. The new F.D.R. did not grow from the despair and enforced patience of having to learn to wiggle his big toe, a theory that some biographers seriously put forth. The new F.D.R. emerged from a new exposure—a democratic exposure—to the common people of Warm Springs. This was more than a political learning. It was also a satisfaction at last of a lifetime hunger. From a Hyde Park childhood of loneliness there had lurked the feeling of being outside and different, separated from the "common" children of the town, from the boys who came to Groton two years before him. Now he moved among the "commoners." Freely. Still the very special boy from the big estate, still the center of every conversation, as he had been among his mother's friends, yet an accepted and beloved member of a real community. It was exhilarating.

While providing him with an education, his country neighbors sought one from him, too, giving him a certain feeling of importance he had not felt as a New York legislator, as a national candidate, even when accompanying President Wilson to a postwar peace conference. He reveled in being guest speaker at a banquet of the Warm Springs Chamber of Commerce at the Tuscawilla Hotel, enthralling his audience on the subject "My Three Trips to the White House." (The first was as a boy of ten, accompanying his father to see President Grover Cleveland; the second at nineteen to visit his cousin T.R.; the "third" a composite of his visits with Wilson.) Roosevelt, flushed with satisfaction, remarked to a friend sitting beside him:

"I am *somebody* down here."

He certainly was. The Meriwether *Vindicator,* a weekly paper published in nearby Greenville, was the first paper in the United States to suggest in print the name of Franklin D. Roosevelt for President.[2]

On still another level in those early days at Warm Springs something was happening to Franklin Roosevelt. Making friends of plain country folk, yes; enjoying their close-at-hand adoration, yes; learning the grievances of southern farmers, yes. But beyond all this he had time—a rarity for a politician—to *think.* Nothing in his past had required that he really tangle with the kind of poverty—during a great national economic boom—faced by his Georgia neighbors. Tugwell notes: "His inquisitive mind gathered from what they had to say a full knowledge of the calamity they were struggling to survive. Running over their situation again and again, he speculated on what might help. . . . These were not his responsibilities, at least not yet; but he could think about them."

One sees again and again how Roosevelt the New Yorker insisted, against all kinds of criticism, upon concentrating—disproportionately— the expenditure of government relief money in the Southland. Critics to his right charged he was buying southern votes with northern tax money. Critics to his left charged he was subsidizing a system of oppression that barred Negroes from the polls through a poll tax, that encouraged lynchings of Negroes by letting white lynchers go unpunished, and that segregated Negroes as a device to bar them from justice and economic opportunity.

Whatever Roosevelt may have felt about these injustices, he carefully refrained from vigorously addressing them. The southern people he had come to know best were white people. Some of them poor whites. What few "colored folks" he knew—his cook, his valet (a former Atlanta barber), a sharecropper here or there—lived not much differently from the poor whites he came to know. Nothing in his past inclined him to do battle with *social* traditions. But economic traditions—especially those based on unthinking and wasteful use of the land—were something else entirely.

All around him in Georgia he saw proud, friendly, hard-working people who were hungry. They did not have to be. If race relations disturbed him at all, his answer lay in lifting the economic welfare of *all* his neighbors in the South. His eye was not on how the pie was to be cut between blacks and whites, but how to bake a richer pie. Again and again he was to say that the place to attack America's economic sickness was where it was sickest: among the rural poor of the South.

In his early state-senatorial days he expounded an abstract philosophy: the "liberty of the community." Now he begins to talk about people, real people he knows. Of course, when Roosevelt talks about his conversations with people, it is hard to separate apocrypha from true anecdote. He'll say, "Now, a man who runs a small general store came to see me the other day, . . ." never explaining how a storekeeper got in to see the President. But these anecdotes were drawn from some kind of human contact, some learning experience that stuck.

He spun one of those, four years after becoming President, in a speech dedicating a schoolhouse at Warm Springs:

It was way back in 1924 that I began to learn economics at Warm Springs. Here is how it happened: One day while I was sitting on the porch of the little cottage in which I lived, a very young man came up to the porch and said, "May I speak with you, Mr. Roosevelt?" and I said, "Yes."

He came up to the porch; and he asked if I would come over to such and such a town—not very far from here—and deliver the diplomas at the Commencement exercises of the school.

I said, "Yes"; and then I asked, "Are you the president of the graduating class?" He said, "No, I am principal of the school."

I said, "How old are you?" He said, "Nineteen years."

I said, "Have you been to college?" He answered, "I had my freshman year at the University of Georgia."

I said, "Do you figure on going through and getting a degree?" He said, "Yes, sir, I will be teaching school every other year and going to college every other year on the proceeds."

I said, "How much are they paying you?" And the principal of that school said, "They are very generous; they are paying me three hundred dollars a year."

Well, that started me thinking. Three hundred dollars a year for the principal of the school. That meant that the three ladies who were teaching under him, were getting less than three hundred dollars a year. I said to myself, "Why do they have to pay that low scale of wages?"

At that particular time one of the banks in Warm Springs closed its doors. At the same time one of the stores in Warm Springs folded up. I began realizing that the community did not have any purchasing power. There were a good many reasons for that. One reason was five cent cotton. You know what five cent cotton, six cent cotton, seven cent cotton meant to the South. Here was a very large part of the Nation that was completely at the mercy of people outside of the South, who were dependent on national conditions and on world conditions over which they had absolutely no control. The South was starving on five and six and seven cent cotton. It could not build schools and could not pay teachers; and the younger generation was growing up without an adequate education. You and I know that that simple fact is very, very true.

So I began expanding my economic philosophy. I started in the next year, as some of you will remember, and let a contract to build the golf course. The contractor, who was an honest and efficient contractor, got his labor, partly white and partly colored, from around Warm Springs. He paid them seventy cents a day and eighty cents a day—when the weather was good. Figure out the purchasing power of the families of these workers in the course of a year. Could they with such wages buy anything at the local store? Could the local store sell enough to keep the wheels of the factories in the North running?

By that process of reasoning, we saw that the prices paid to labor down here in Warm Springs, the prices that we people got for our cotton, all were tied in together with the prosperity of the factories of the industrial cities of the North and East. And so a number of years ago—and I was not the only one, for a lot of people were thinking along the same lines—we began trying to think of the picture as a national picture. We began to realize that here in this wonderful Southland there was a great opportunity, an economic opportunity, an educational opportunity, if we could only do something to stabilize the wages and prices people got for their work and for their cotton at a higher level, a level which would be more nearly the level in other parts of the country.

Two years later, in 1939, he spread this theme more broadly. Again it was an extemporaneous speech, this time to students of Alabama Polytechnic Institute, in which he decided to relate "my first experience with the agriculture of the South":

The first year I went to Warm Springs, fifteen, nearly sixteen years ago, I had a little cottage that was about a thousand feet from the old A.B.&A. tracks. The first night, the second night and the third night I was awakened out of a deep sleep by the sound of a very heavy train going through at pretty high speed and, as it went through town, the whistle blew and woke everybody up. So I went down to the station and said to the stationmaster, "What is that train that makes so much noise and why does it have to whistle at half past one in the morning?" "Oh," he said, "the fireman has a girl in town."

I asked him what that train was and he said, "That is the milk train for Florida." Well, I assumed of course, knowing that the climate of Florida, especially South Florida, is not very conducive to dairy purposes, that this train on the A.B.&A. contained milk and cream from Alabama and Georgia. I was wrong. That milk and cream for Florida came from Wisconsin, Minnesota, Iowa and Illinois and was taken through all the intervening States of Indiana, Ohio, Kentucky, Tennessee, Alabama and Georgia in order to supply milk and cream and butter for Florida.

That gave me a feeling that something was wrong with the agricultural economy of these States of the lower South, because you and I know from what we have been taught and from the experiments that have been made that these States can produce perfectly good milk and cream.

A little while later I went down to the village to buy some apples. . . . I knew of the magnificent apples raised at the southern end of the Appalachian System. I had tasted them; no apples in the world were better. Yet the apples in Meriwether County, Georgia, the only ones I could find, came from Washington and Oregon.

I went to buy meat—and I know that we can make pastures in these States—and the only meat that I could buy came via Omaha and Kansas City and Chicago.

I wanted to buy a pair of shoes and the only shoes I could buy had been made in Boston or Binghamton, New York, or St. Louis.

Well, that was fifteen years ago, and there wasn't very much change in that system of economy until about six years ago. It was then we began to ask ourselves, "Why is all this necessary?" I think that we have done more in those six years than in the previous sixty years all through these southern States to make them self-supporting and to give them a balanced economy that will spell a higher wage scale, a greater purchasing power and a more abundant life than they have had in all their history.

It means a lot of work. It means, incidentally, getting the South "out of hock" to the North.

To borrow a phrase from a blues song of the cottonfields, he put his money where his mouth is. To Roosevelt's purchase of 1,200 acres of Warm Springs resort property, he soon added 1,750 acres for farming and cattle grazing, determined to prove to his Warm Springs neighbors—the whole South if he could—that they must break out of their slavery to the single cash crop of cotton. His hired farmer-in-charge, Otis Moore, planted soybean hay and oats and fed them to 130 cows, two bulls, and some calves. One day Moore, a man of tradition as well as fiscal caution, asked permission to plant just a little bit of cotton "to help take care of the cost of labor." Roosevelt boomed, "No! We'll grow no cotton."

Roosevelt talked proudly and constantly of his "Pine Mountain farm"— even after its losses grew so painful he had to give up its operation. What he could not prove by himself on 1,750 acres, he was soon to try to prove—and substantially succeed—in the multibillion-dollar TVA demonstration spread across seven states.

And still another great change was to come in Roosevelt's life while at Warm Springs. One evening in 1928 he was called away from a poker game in his cottage to receive an urgent call on the town's single telephone, in a booth at the hotel. It was from Governor Alfred E. Smith of New York, who had decided to run for President. He wanted Roosevelt to run for governor. Roosevelt resisted. The warm-water therapy, he felt, was doing his legs good, and he wanted to keep it up for at least another year. At least that's what he said—to Smith, to Bronx Democratic leader Ed Flynn, to Eleanor Roosevelt, all of whose voices reached that country phone over the next twenty-four hours. A considerable reason may also have been that Roosevelt doubted that a Democratic candidate for governor could win New York while a Catholic headed the national ticket against as popular a humanitarian as Herbert Hoover, who was to lead the Republicans. (He was almost right. Smith was to lose New York by a hundred thousand votes, Roosevelt carrying it by barely twenty-five thousand.) Pressed by the argument of duty to party, Roosevelt gave in.

Less than a year after he became his state's chief executive, the roof fell in on Wall Street and Main Street. No one had ever seen such turmoil, such desperation, so many so hungry. Every village in once-prosperous New York State was suddenly Warm Springs. While Washington did next to nothing, the governor in Albany did at least something. He reached back to an idea that had been burning in his mind for two decades: his old thoughts, born of a concern for trees, about "liberty of the community." To his state legislature, on August 28, 1931, he made a memorable pronouncement on the role of the state, concluding with the then-radical request for creation of a State Relief Administration. Thus he enlarged "liberty of the community" from a public obligation to conserve trees to one of conserving human beings. The message rings with the authority of long, well-formed thought and commitment. It begins:

What is the State? It is the duly constituted representative of an organized society of human beings, created by them for their mutual protection and well-being. "The State" or "The Government" is but the machinery through which such mutual aid and protection are achieved. The cave man fought for existence unaided or even opposed by his fellow man, but today the humblest citizen of our State stands protected by all the power and strength of his Government. Our Government is not the master but the creature of the people. The duty of the State toward the citizens is the duty of the servant to its master. . . . One of these duties of the State is that of caring for those of its citizens who find themselves the victims of such adverse circumstance as makes them unable to obtain even the necessities for mere existence without the aid of others. . . . In broad terms I assert that modern society, acting through its Government, owes the definite obligation to prevent the starvation or the dire want of any of its fellow men and women who try to maintain themselves but cannot.

For 1931 that was a thunderbolt. No other governor among his fellow forty-seven appeared ready to assert any such thing, and certainly not the head of the federal government in Washington.

The following year, Roosevelt's activism in rescuing the suddenly poor was a major element in his winning nomination and election as President. He entered the White House with no clear, specific plans (although claiming in public to have them) for saving the banks, for harnessing industry and labor into an NRA partnership, even for putting millions of unemployed on a government work-projects payroll. For these plans he relied upon picking and choosing, modifying and compromising, among an array of conflicting ideas turned in by others.

But the CCC and TVA were something else. Ray Moley, in charge of filtering and siphoning to the President all policy ideas from every source, says he was "stunned" to hear F.D.R. spring full-blown the plan for the CCC. Ernest Lindley, equally surprised, was soon to write:

"The sureness with which Mr. Roosevelt outlined the Tennessee Valley experiment in its full scope at the very outset of his administration was the result of many years of thought. Not even Senator Norris, the stanch defender of the public's interest in Muscle Shoals and a great conservationist by any standard, envisioned the unified and harmonious development of an entire watershed with Mr. Roosevelt's imagination and completeness. TVA and the Civilian Conservation Corps are among Mr. Roosevelt's peculiarly personal contributions to the array of New Deal enterprises."[4]

Part V

The Ethics and Politics
of Work

Americans are a self-reliant people, who do not want to get anything for nothing. Our way of life is built on work. A man's pride and dignity stand on his work. He wants to take care of his family, make them secure, by work.

I believe in work. My consistent aim in the New Deal was to create work, spread the opportunity for work, guarantee the right to work. If America ever forsakes its traditional ethic of self-support through work, we will not be the same people, the same country. I don't think I would like it.

The greatest falsehood my opposition has tried to pin on me is the lie that I would undermine our traditional ethic of work by substituting "handouts" and "giveaways." That is the exact opposite of the truth. The truth is that my opposition—Republicans in Congress allied with certain outdated Democrats who worshipped "economy" and cheap labor above preservation of the American character—fought me every step of the way. *They* were the champions of "handouts" and "giveaways." They insisted on keeping destitute families alive through a humiliating dole, which might indeed sustain bodies but was bound to destroy souls. They believed in the dole because they thought it cheaper.

The record will show this to be true. That is the record I want to set down plain as day in this chapter.

I know a little about "handouts"—the old name was charity—from my very young days. While still a student at Harvard I used to call upon a young lady, Eleanor Roosevelt, a distant cousin who was soon to become my wife. I would meet her at day's end at the Rivington Street Settlement House among the slums of New York's Lower East Side, where she did charity work with other young ladies of the newly formed Junior League. She conducted dancing classes and taught manners and "grace" to children of the very poor. When the ladies learned of a family in particular trouble, they filled a food basket and brought it to the family's door. This work, I am sure, did the families good. But I am now convinced that that way of being "helped" was demeaning and humiliating to the poor. Humiliation is bound to teach contempt of oneself, and self-contempt turns to hatred of others. Getting something for nothing is no good.

My problem as President—our problem as a people—in 1933 was not to create government charity but to get money passing from hand to hand, in wages or as payments for goods bought and sold. How were we to do this? Let me begin by telling how *not* to end a depression.

The Bonus Marchers

Many of the unemployed were national heroes, veterans, who only fifteen years earlier had put their lives on the line for their country during the First World War. It happens that in 1924 the Congress had voted to pay bonuses to war veterans twenty-one years later—in 1945. In the worst year of the depression, 1932, Representative Wright Patman of Texas, a believer in freely created dollars, introduced a bill to pay the bonuses immediately. While many Congressmen favored it for vote-getting reasons, this was not a wise thing to do. For one thing, almost all (more than three million out of 3,500,000) veterans had already borrowed from the government against their bonus certificates, which the Bonus Law permitted. Therefore, those most in need would probably receive least. Secondly, we undertook a survey which showed that many veterans would use their bonus payments to retire overdue debts on land, homes, and businesses. Thus the money would not go into new purchases at the corner store or new investments in capital equipment that would create jobs. If the government were to go into debt for the sake of an emergency distribution of money, it must be put into the hands of those we could pinpoint as needing the money most, needing it immediately, needing it to spend on groceries and shoes, the purchase of which in turn would create new jobs.

In May 1933, during the opening weeks of my presidency, several thousand unemployed veterans descended upon Washington to demand their bonuses *now*. The immediate reaction of some panicky people, in government and out, was fear that this "mob"—war heroes and family men—might storm the White House, burn down the Capitol, start a revolution.

The Bonus March of 1933 was indeed an extremely serious matter, because of the still-open wound of a much larger Bonus March less than a year earlier. That one had come to a terrible end, which the country managed to survive—but would not survive a second time. It is important to look back at that notorious episode.

The 1932 march had started small. An ex-sergeant, Walter W. Waters, collected three hundred veterans in Portland, Oregon, who hopped freight trains to Washington, camping along the way and collecting other followers. Many brought their wives and children. On June 8, 1932, eight thousand veterans paraded down Pennsylvania Avenue. There was no violence, no disorder. Naturally the cry went up that the veterans were Communists, or led or influenced by Communists. President Hoover, mesmerized by this fantasy, denounced the marchers, refused to see them, and many years later continued to reminisce that the march was "promoted by the Communists and included a large number of hoodlums and ex-convicts . . . frequently addressed by Democratic Congressmen seeking to inflame them against me. . . ."

A President, who must listen to advisers, also must decide for himself what advice to heed. Hoover chose to heed the fears of his friends in big business and his Secretary of War, Patrick Hurley. In doing so, he chose to reject the firsthand information about the marchers gathered by his own Secret Service. Here is the personal account by Ed Starling, chief of the White House Secret Service detail, of what he reported to the President:

"Our agents were among them, keeping us informed of the number of radicals in every group, and checking on the influence they had with the men. Generally speaking, there were few Communists, and they had little effect on the men's thinking. The veterans were Americans, down on their luck but by no means ready to overthrow their government. . . . It was our opinion that camps should be provided for them, in isolated spots where adequate living facilities were available. They should be fed and housed, we thought, and separated into small groups so that no concerted action could be planned and carried out. Instead, they were allowed to camp between the White House and the Capitol, on Pennsylvania Avenue—the most conspicuous spot in America. Others were just across the Potomac River, on the Anacostia flats. They built themselves shanty towns, of the type that was springing up all over the country under the general name of Hooverville."

Far from revolutionaries with a plot, they seemed to be confused patriots with no plan at all. When the defeat of the Patman bill was announced, no one knew what would happen. The angry men gathered at the Capitol. An alert newspaper columnist, Elsie Robinson, whispered to Sergeant Waters—their leader in supposed "Red revolution"—to tell the men to sing "America." He did—and they did.

Having no place to go and nothing to do, the marchers hung around Washington in their Hoovervilles and an empty building on Pennsylvania Avenue. The President, never once agreeing to talk eye to eye, finally had his say. He ordered the Army to run the veterans out of town.

The Army Chief of Staff, General Douglas MacArthur, personally led cavalry, infantry, and tanks down Pennsylvania Avenue. At his order, our young men in uniform unslung bayoneted rifles and threw tear-gas bombs at peaceful citizens who themselves had been the army of their country in war.

I cannot forget my amazement the next morning. I was at Hyde Park preparing for my campaign after receiving the presidential nomination a month earlier. At about 7:30 that morning, while I was still in bed, someone brought me the New York *Times* with a full page of pictures that seemed like scenes from a nightmare: women and children choking from gas, their husbands and fathers being carried into police wagons, and an unforgettable picture of the general himself, standing by a fence, nonchalant, imperious, and self-satisfied, drinking from a cup.

Rex Tugwell was a house guest and I called him from across the hall. I told him that I ought to apologize for having suggested Herbert Hoover as the Democratic candidate for President in 1920 to succeed Woodrow Wilson (a nomination that went to James M. Cox, with me as his running mate). After Hoover's massive work of bringing food relief to the war-shredded countries of Europe, he had become regarded as the world's greatest humanitarian. Now look at him. Imagining a few thousand patriotic indigents as revolutionaries, this man—a Quaker, dedicated to the renunciation of violence—had ordered his palace guards into violence and suppression. And all that the "revolutionaries" wanted was to talk with him. I told Rex there was nothing left inside this man but jelly—if there ever *had* been anything. The people of the country would not like what they saw.

MacArthur in a single hour had done a perfectly effective job of preventing Hoover's re-election. My own political problem was now smaller than I would have believed twenty-four hours earlier.

When I said that, Rex looked skeptical. He pointed out that Republicans were pretty traditional people. Wouldn't they vote the party ticket anyway?

I said no. This went deep. Look at the most traditional of Republicans, landowning farmers of the Midwest, who at that very moment were rebelling against tradition by preventing foreclosures, by spilling milk, and by killing cattle. Anybody could sense this went deep —anybody except those insensitive fat cats, the same men who had urged me as governor to call out the National Guard when the worsening depression led to demonstrations in New York for food and relief. I never once called out the guard. Suppression was never good enough as an answer.

I said I might feel sorry for Hoover if I didn't feel even sorrier for those thousands of people driven out of their nation's capital. The cruel rout turned into more than a week of tragic headlines, which an idle country absorbed itself in following. The state of Maryland stationed troopers along its boundaries, herding the bonus refugees into trucks and passing them like hot potatoes to Pennsylvania. A single compassionate public official, the mayor of Johnstown, a veteran himself, invited the refugees to camp and rest in his city's public parks. But his city council vetoed the offer, and Pennsylvania state trucks hustled the veterans and their families, many now starving, farther westward. The story came out telling of a colored man—a resident of Washington, D.C., who happened to be walking by the veterans' camp when MacArthur attacked—who was trucked all the way to Indianapolis.

A little later in the campaign, when Rex and I were talking about politics and politicians, I remarked that Senator Huey Long was the second most dangerous man in the country. The *first,* I told him, was Doug MacArthur. I have known Doug for years. In his strong, silent way he is as much a demagogue as Huey was, but has a far greater potential as an American Mussolini. He never doubts, never argues or suggests; he makes pronouncements. His voice seems to come from an oracle's cave. He has complete faith in his infallibility and feels that all people need do is take his orders. It's prefectly true that his is precisely the kind of personality that Americans are inclined to distrust. But let things get disorderly enough, drum up enough anxiety in enough good citizens, and they may indeed turn to a strong man who happens to be at the head of the Army.

Obviously, President Hoover did not share my fear. In a campaign speech in St. Paul, Hoover said, "Thank God, we still have a government in Washington that knows how to deal with a mob."

I say, Thank God, we soon had a government in Washington that knew how to deal with a MacArthur. MacArthur was politicking all over the War Department to get me to appoint as his successor as Chief of Staff one of his own men, Major General George S. Simonds. Not about to do any such thing, but also not wanting to get into a clash with the generals, I checked up on General Simonds. I discovered that he had just about four years to go until his scheduled retirement. A Chief of Staff's term is four years. I then prevailed upon MacArthur to serve a few months beyond *his* term (it didn't take much prevailing) on the pretext that I needed him to help formulate some legislation regarding the War Department. After six months went by, I eliminated Simonds as a candidate on the ground that he couldn't serve a four-year term since he would be retiring in three and a half years. Then I sent MacArthur on a trip to Hawaii accompanied by Secretary of War George Dern. While they were away I appointed MacArthur's successor as Chief, General Malin Craig, who could be depended upon to tend to his Army knitting and leave civilian affairs to civilians.[2]

Of course, years later, when we were forced into World War II, our survival depended upon expert military leadership, and no one would question MacArthur's training and skill as a soldier. I gave him the Pacific Theater of Operations, relying on faith that his potential as a political force would be kept under control after military victory was achieved.

I began this sordid tale as an illustration of how *not* to end a depression. I mean that in two ways: First, paying a soldiers' bonus, politically appealing as it may have been, was not a way to cure our economic disease. The right way was creation of work. But moreover, turning the armed might of the United States against our own needy citizens, whose demand was not unreasonable even if it may have been economically unwise, was certainly not a way to solve any problem. My job as President was not to turn government against people or people against government. It was to weld us together. It was to show concern where there was legitimate need, to make all the American people feel that the distress claimed us all.

So again, in the spring of 1933, the veterans, although a smaller band, were hitchhiking and hopping freights to Washington to plead their cause, and this time it was my turn to handle a Bonus March.

A group called the Veterans Liaison Committee got a letter into my hands on April 29 telling me that "large groups" were on their way to Washington, that they would be orderly and disciplined, and that they "should be treated as any other group holding a Congress or Conference at the capital of the nation." Fine. Then the letter "respectfully" requested that this "conference" be treated differently. They wanted the government to house and feed the visitors. My assistant, Louis Howe, tried to persuade them to send a delegation of only two hundred to represent the veterans back home. This did no good. So I ordered the head of the Veterans Administration, General Frank Hines, to set up a camp for six thousand men at Fort Hunt, Virginia, just across the Potomac, and issued an executive order to cover expenses. The Committee assured us that the men would guarantee their own discipline and cleanliness—in fact, they insisted on it, demanding that they not be "molested or harassed" by the police or the Army. Again, fine.

In a way, I had a more difficult situation than President Hoover. Not only did I oppose the Patman bill for immediate payment of the bonus, as Hoover did, but I had just asked Congress in a message on government economy, which included a request to reduce government salaries, to reduce pensions of partially disabled veterans by a total of $400 million. This was a painful but necessary thing to do. The demand was great to cut government costs, particularly since there was a popular feeling that Hoover, who never balanced a budget, had been an "expensive President." On the other hand, I knew that the government had to go into debt to finance mass relief. I resolved this dilemma by cutting expenses—*operating* expenses—of government by a full 25 per cent, then requesting large *special* appropriations to take care of the unemployed.

Sometimes the right symbolic gesture can have a greater effect than an act of substance. Following through a plan I cooked up with him, Louis Howe one day asked my wife to go out for a drive. They were close friends of many years, frequently plotting together—I suspect much of the time to outwit me—and this invitation did not surprise her. She was greatly surprised, however, when they headed for the veterans' camp. Then Louis announced he was going to sit in the car and take a nap, but that she was to "walk around among the veterans and see just how things were." As she related it to me later, she was terrified, but after a few minutes found herself in easy conversation with the very courteous men standing in a chow line. In a big dining hall, the men asked her to say a few words. Thoroughly unprepared, she reminisced about her visits to the battlefronts in 1919. Now, *there* is sound political instinct for you. Delighted, the men sang old songs of the war and took her on a tour of their barracks and an impromptu hospital. After she left, one of the men made a remark that was soon quoted widely:

"Hoover sent the Army. Roosevelt sent his wife."

Effective as this was, it was merely a gesture. What act of substance could we provide? Relief money back home for the most needy? Yes, but that would be some time in coming. Passage of the Federal Emergency Relief Act was still a few days ahead. These men wanted action now, not promises for later. Well, we had made room in the CCC for twenty-five thousand veterans of World War I. That was the plan we devised for breaking the log jam of the Bonus March, for giving the men some kind of positive answer instead of tear-gassing them out of town. We offered them work. Fort Hunt was turned into a CCC camp to accommodate 1,200 enlistees. Many signed up on the spot and others returned home satisfied that their government was trying to respond to their urgent needs. In all, 2,663 of the marchers joined the CCC. Their records showed that not one of these men created trouble.[3]

Emergency Relief

Sam Rosenman used to remark that I have been "blessed politically with unintelligent opposition."

When President Hoover proclaimed in the summer of 1930, ". . . the depression is over," I believe he honestly thought so. In 1931, when the suffering in my state of New York had become unbearable, I went in person to the state legislature to ask for $20 million to provide the most needy with useful work. I offered to let Republican legislators introduce the bill. Let them take the credit, as long as we got the money. They refused. (The bill was passed over their heads, in which connection Sam made his remark.)

Through two terrible winters the people of America suffered and there rose a tide of demands, even in Congress, that the government directly create jobs. Hoover's "advisory" committees of Republican businessmen, who saw the world exactly as he did, nodded vigorously as he answered the demands with homilies, homilies, homilies. To one such committee, meeting at the White House to lead a "national charity drive," the President said:

"Our tasks are definite.

"The first is to see that no man, woman or child shall go hungry or unsheltered through the approaching winter.

"The second is to see that our great benevolent agencies for character building, for hospitalization, for care of children and all their vast number of agencies of voluntary solicitude are maintained in full strength.

"The third is to maintain the bedrock principle of our liberties by the full mobilization of individual and local resources and responsibilities.

"The fourth is that we may maintain the spiritual impulses in our people for generous giving and generous service—in the spirit that each is his brother's keeper."

Words, words, words while children shivered and their empty bellies ached. In New York, bankers, moved by "spiritual impulses" of "voluntary solicitude," made a *loan* of all of one million dollars to the New York City Department of Welfare. They set a seemingly charitable condition that every penny had to go to needy families, none for "bureaucratic" administration. As a result, the checks were greatly delayed in going out because the city had no money for postage stamps. That's how much those Republican bankers knew about the disastrous state of local governments. Local governments had been so unprepared for mass destitution that not a single state had a department of welfare until I organized one for New York in 1929.

Finally, in the election year of 1932, the factual truths that he could no longer avoid came crashing down on Mr. Hoover. He asked Congress for RFC money—*loans*—to bail out the states crying desperately for cash relief: all of $300 million, which hardly scratched the surface of a full year's need.

Thus Hoover trapped himself into creating a government dole. Repugnant as this idea was to him, his only alternative was to create public jobs, which offended him even more. For two years, he and committee after committee of his businessmen produced excuse after excuse for not creating jobs ("an increase in Government expenses," "only a few limited undertakings of this nature available," "possible Government works were not always near centers of unemployment," and so on and on—all Hoover's words).

What all these slogans added up to was his fear that emergency creation of jobs smacked of state socialism. So he chose the dole. In a typically Republican way, he justified it by looking backward, by relying on tradition instead of reaching for a new way to meet a new need. After all, the dole drew some respectability from the British "poor laws" established during the reign of Queen Elizabeth. So the President, who had been elected on the euphoric slogan of "two cars in every garage and a chicken in every pot," now gave in to treating his countrymen like sixteenth-century paupers—because he could justify it by tradition.

Although reluctantly surrendering to the dole, Republicans could not get out of their heads that it was a disgrace to be broke. Anybody down-and-out offended these Republicans as unsightly evidence that the world was not the way a tidy world *ought* to be. So the luckless had to be punished. As late as 1938 an opinion poll showed that one out of three Republicans still thought that people on relief should be denied the right to vote. And, in fact, the constitutions of several states, thanks to their backward legislatures, had done just that.

Horrifying? Yes. Vicious? No. These honest Republicans were not bad people. Merely righteous, inflexible, and boneheaded.

I took office promising action, and people rightfully expected it. My desk was soon cluttered with two thousand separate plans and suggestions for federal action on unemployment. Where does one begin? Everyone and his unemployed brother wanted to see me to push his particular plan, while my appointments secretary, Marvin McIntyre, was frantic trying to arrange my schedule of seeing politicians, congressmen, job seekers. An urgent request came from Secretary of Labor Frances Perkins for me to see my former lieutenant in New York, Harry L. Hopkins, chairman of my New York State Temporary Emergency Relief Administration, and William Hodson, Director of the Welfare Council of New York City. They, too, had a plan, but, unlike most of the others, theirs was based on experience. That was what we needed. It was a plan for immediate grants to states, one federal dollar for every three dollars from local public sources. Hopkins and Hodson were practical, not theoretical, men. They brought me state-by-state information showing that in some states funds were so depleted that local money would not be available. Therefore, half the federal appropriation would be placed in a "discretionary" fund that would not have to be matched locally.

We knew we would have to resist the pressures of congressmen and governors, perhaps even my own Democratic National Chairman, James Farley, who were already urging that we take care of "deserving Democrats" first. I insisted that we "never ask whether a person needing relief is a Republican, Democrat, Socialist or anything else."

I called in Senators Wagner, La Follette, and Costigan, who immediately drew up a bill to establish the Federal Emergency Relief

Administration with a working capital of $500 million. It passed and I signed it on May 12, 1933.

Yes, this, too, provided a dole, but I was determined that it would not last long. It was a short-term way of keeping people alive. Hungry people who need meals three times every day cannot eat philosophies or long-drawn-out debates. The people needed money in the fastest, most direct way we could get it to them.

On May 22 I appointed Harry Hopkins to run the Federal Emergency Relief Administration. As good a job as he had done as my relief administrator in New York, nothing there hinted at the explosive energy with which this baggy-suited, sallow, former Iowa farm boy took up his new task. Before nightfall of his first full day in federal office, Hopkins made grants to Colorado, Illinois, Iowa, Michigan, Mississippi, Ohio, and Texas. Nothing could have pleased me more than the astonished report of action—tangible *action*—in next morning's Washington *Post*. Under the headline "Money Flies," it said: "The half-billion dollars for direct relief of States won't last a month if Harry L. Hopkins, new relief administrator, maintains the pace he set yesterday in disbursing more than $5,000,-000 during his first two hours in office."

In fact, the half billion dollars lasted far less than the year it theoretically was intended for. Before long, I asked for an additional $850 million. Part of this was to pay for our first step away from the dole, our first major undertaking of federal creation of useful and dignified work under the Civil Works Administration. That, however, gets us a little ahead of our story.

Let me just say, before laying aside this thread of our fight against the dole, that from the very first day of FERA, Hopkins and his assistants and I constantly heard touching stories of how relief recipients, although grateful, felt degraded and humiliated at having to take handouts when they wanted, above everything, to work and contribute. One story I especially remember was of an elderly man with a large family who was getting fifteen dollars a week on relief. Without being asked, he went out every day to sweep the streets of his village, explaining, "I want to do something in return for what I get."

And you can be sure that Hopkins and I and everyone we could enlist repeated stories such as that to every congressman and newspaperman we could get to listen. We were determined to create a climate that made possible the federal creation of emergency employment to replace the dole. That proud and courageous man who took up a broom in his village represents something of the American spirit.[4]

The Flight of the Blue Eagle

At least one citizen (there were many, many) really caught the spirit of what the New Deal was all about. In West Orange, New Jersey, at the headquarters of Thomas A. Edison, Inc., the company president, Charles Edison, posted a notice for his employees and callers to see:

> President Roosevelt has done his part: now you do something.
>
> Buy something—buy anything, anywhere; paint your kitchen, send a telegram, give a party, get a car, pay a bill, rent a flat, fix your roof, get a haircut, see a show, build a house, take a trip, sing a song, get married.
>
> It does not matter what you do—but get going and keep going. This old world is starting to move.

That gay spirit was perfectly sound. We must remember that our goal of emergency creation of work by government was a means, not an end. The end was industrial recovery, the return to a norm of *private* buying and selling, hiring and paying wages, building houses, profitable harvesting, of people supporting themselves by serving one another. So, before detailing our direct creation of jobs by government, a complex political story in itself, we ought to go into our direct effort to revive and reform private industry.

The effort was called the National Industrial Recovery Act. Perhaps it will be better remembered by the initials of the agency the Act created—NRA, for the National Recovery Administration—and by its symbol, a blue silhouette of the American eagle. To me, and I think to many, the image of the Blue Eagle calls up a happy memory of unity under adversity, of hope, of pulling together, of national courage and determination. There was a *spirit* about the time of the NRA that I hope will not be lost under the description of its day-to-day stresses.

The idea of the NRA evolved, one might say, in response to something I was against. That something was a bill pending in Congress introduced by a fine gentleman, Senator Hugo L. Black of Alabama. He was a first-rate lawyer (whom I later appointed to the Supreme Court), but he did not have a realistic understanding of economics—how industry creates jobs and jobs create industry. The bill was inflexible and certain to retard recovery. Furthermore, I was convinced it was unconstitutional. Most dangerous of all, it seemed to have enough support to pass.

Simply stated, the Black bill would establish as law that every wage worker engaged in production for interstate commerce would be limited to working thirty hours per week.

The premises of the bill were entirely wrong—but surprisingly popular. There had been a flood of books and magazine articles by a certain brand of professors and intellectuals, many of whom had assembled in a vigorous movement called the technocrats. The way the technocrats saw it, there was a limit to what America could usefully produce, and that limit had been reached and passed; unemployment was the direct result of our having produced more than we could consume, and this overproduction had been caused by the unbridled introduction of labor-saving machines. The answer to the machines— so the technocrats thought—was to cease increasing, even to cut back, production by decreasing the contribution of human labor. Since the machines left less work for humans to do, the way to end unemployment was to spread the remaining work around, not to have some people working forty-eight hours a week and others none, but to share the work at thirty hours per worker.

The idea was all wrong. It pictured the market place of men, machines, and the materials they produce as something static. It assumed a fixed limit on what we could consume; therefore, on what we should produce; therefore, on the number of potential jobs and the size of a potential payroll. That was Senator Black's big mistake. If there is such a limit—and I cannot accept it—we certainly had not reached it in 1933. A limit is not yet anywhere in sight.

Aside from that basic objection to the bill, I felt it was unrealistically inflexible in applying the same rule to all industries, as though all industries were alike. What would people do in the dairy industry, the fruit- and vegetable-canning industries, where the work must be done when the produce becomes available? As I argued at cabinet meetings and in conferences with congressmen, you have to adapt working hours to what I called "the rhythm of the cow."

The answer to unemployment lay in a dynamic, expanding economy —enriching people's lives by producing more, thus creating jobs enabling people to buy what they produce. Perhaps at some time in the future, the people—the society as a whole—may decide to sacrifice some added material wealth in favor of more leisure time. To some extent this has already taken place and may continue. Organized labor had worked hard to establish an 8-hour day and a 6-day week. By the mid-1930s a few business organizations were putting in a 5½-day week and there was a growing sentiment for a 5-day week. This may work out very well. But at some point, people will say, "No. We do not want more idle time. We want the material goods and comforts more—as well as the feeling of purpose that work itself brings."

Yet I could not openly oppose the Black bill. A powerful alliance of the American Legion and the American Federation of Labor was for it. A. F. of L. president William Green praised the Black bill for striking "at the root of the problem—technological unemployment," going so far as to threaten a general strike in support of the 30-hour week. Stampeded by this pressure, the Senate, on April 6, 1933, surprised almost everyone, perhaps even itself, by passing the Black bill, 50 to 30.

I tried to stem the tide in the House by sending Secretary of Labor Perkins to testify that, while we considered the bill impossible to administer, at least it might become workable if certain economic safeguards were built in. (To lend a subtle hint of official "weight" to Madame Perkins' testimony, I sent my wife to sit in on the House committee hearings as an "interested spectator.") The main safeguard would be to regulate hours, industry by industry, after hearing advice from employers and workingmen's committees—and by accompanying such control of hours with a plan for *minimum wages*. Thus, at least, we could forestall the reduction of the wages of a man who was presently working a full week. Matthew Woll of the A. F. of L. balked at this, fearing that minimum wages would become maximum wages.

Meanwhile, some employer groups flew into a tizzy over the thought of minimum wages set by law. The result was that the unified support of the bill became disorganized, and the bill died in the House. That did not at all displease me, for some of my people already were secretly at work on alternative, far more comprehensive plans, which were soon to be born as the NRA.[5]

As I sit here trying to trace and reconstruct the genesis of the NRA from the detailed recollections of Ray Moley, Frances Perkins, and others—how so many little creeks of ideas trickled into streams and ultimately flowed into great rivers—I have to suppress the temptation to laugh uproariously at those who picture me as having walked into the White House with a bundle of radical philosophies tucked under my arm to thrust upon an unwilling public. The fact is that all we knew was that we had to make some sense out of the mess industry was in. Industry knew it, too, and its most responsible members were as anxious as I.

For example, I had personally talked several times during 1932 with Henry I. Harriman, president of the United States Chamber of Commerce, and at my request on February 10, 1933, he gave me a document entitled "An Economic Program," a plan of self-regulation by industry that wound up as an important part of the NRA. This plan and many others collected by Moley were turned over to James Warburg, the young financier, to sort through and synthesize.

Unfortunately, Warburg botched the job. In his "summation" he proposed that government encourage industry to hire more employees, whether they presently needed them or not, by *guaranteeing industries against losses* for a stipulated period, in return for which the *government would share in any profits.* Coming from a man of big business, how's that for a socialistic idea? Warburg further suggested that we subsidize purchases of manufacturing machinery (capital goods) instead of trying to distribute money to the penniless, which would stimulate the purchase of consumer goods. That might indeed be a sound way of creating jobs and new purchasing power over the long run. But how many millions would starve while they waited? These economists go off the track when they dwell, as they so often do, on the rhythms of industry and forget the rhythms of three meals a day for living human beings.

I don't mean to deride the well-intended efforts of Mr. Warburg. But as an illustration of how confused and panicky some big businessmen were, how they themselves invented some of the monstrosities they later would try to attribute to me, Warburg drafted a "Message to Congress"—for my signature—with which he thought I should forward his plan to the Hill. It said (the italics are mine): "I shall submit to the Congress a bill for the *regimentation of industry* and ask of Congress its immediate passage." That was about all I needed.

Meanwhile John Dickinson, Assistant Secretary of Commerce, apprehensive that I would throw administration support behind the Black bill, volunteered a different set of proposals. These were far more precise in focusing on industrial injustices and excesses that contributed to unemployment of heads of families. He proposed that a new government law:

1. Prohibit from interstate commerce the products of night work by women or children, or of "sweated labor." One definition of sweated labor would be labor employed more than fifty-four hours a week. (Obviously it made better economic, political, and humanitarian sense to curb an excess of working hours than to set an impractical maximum of thirty hours.)

2. Call for the members of an industry, meeting in conference, to agree voluntarily upon a *code* of labor standards covering maximum hours and minimum wages. When such a code was approved by the Secretary of Labor, it would have the effect of law, and the violation of it would constitute an unfair practice.

3. If an industry could not agree on such a code, the Secretary could promulgate one.

Henry Harriman's "Economic Program" was somewhat different but dovetailed with Dickinson's in a most interesting way. He suggested that we amend—or suspend—certain provisions of the Clayton Act and Sherman Anti-Trust Act that were designed to prevent collusion and price fixing by competitive companies that might hurt the public interest. The amendments would permit trade associations to discuss and make agreements—in effect, *codes*—to eliminate certain kinds of competition that were destructive, such as harshly competitive undercutting of prices and wages as well as unfairly long hours of work. As a safeguard, Harriman suggested that 60 or 70 per cent of an industry's members would be required to label a practice "unfair," in addition to approval by a proper government agency.

Even though coming from conservative men of commerce and finance these were radical ideas. But they had a precedent. In an earlier national emergency, World War I, the country had willingly submitted to self-regulation under the War Industries Board, headed by Bernard M. Baruch. That gave us an idea. Moley "borrowed" Baruch's long-time right-hand man, General Hugh S. Johnson, a personage of energy and charm, to take the ideas of Harriman, Dickinson, and others and write them into a workable bill. I sent Rex Tugwell to work with him.

That was one great river, but meanwhile an entirely separate one was in full flow. A man named Meyer Jacobstein, a Brookings Institution economist and former New York congressman, was at work with Senator Robert Wagner in developing a bill to launch a multi-billion-dollar program of public works. Their theory—about which, as I have said, I had reservations—was that the way to recovery was to build bridges and tunnels, schools and hospitals, dams and reservoirs, not only to create direct employment in constructing them, but to stimulate the vast private industries that would supply these government projects with lumber and concrete, girders and derricks, thus "indirectly" creating hundreds of thousands of additional jobs. (My objection, in a word, was that I did not believe that such ambitious projects, requiring immense surveying, planning, and land acquisition, could get started quickly enough for the three-meal-a-day need of the hungry. Later events, I believe, bore me out.)

From both these rivers, and from many streams feeding them, the crosscurrents and confusion threatened to drown the possibility of a unified plan. So I brought all the big planners together—Johnson and Dickinson, Madame Perkins and Lew Douglas, Senator Wagner and a lawyer named Donald Richberg—and Ray Moley and I listened and listened while they argued and argued.

Finally I told the whole crowd to lock themselves in a room, argue to their hearts' content—and not come out until they were all agreed on a bill. Well, you should have seen the jaws tighten and the jowls drop. I guess this struck them as the height of evasiveness and irresponsibility. They imagined themselves engaged in a cataclysmic clash of opposing, irreconcilable philosophies. They felt a choice had to be made. And they wanted Papa to choose.

What I wanted was a bill. These were all good people doing good thinking. Who was to say that one faction was right and another wrong? We were about to try things that no one had ever tried before.

Until these good people were ready to reconcile—by compromise—their good thinking into a single national experiment, we were not ready to try anything. On the other hand, when they found the proper compromise, we would know we had a plan that all sections of Americans might find a way to support.

I know that some individuals in that group thought—still think—that this method of mine, locking them all in a room together until they agreed, which I have used more than once, is not their idea of "strong" presidential leadership. I happen to think it is sound presidential politics.

Days later (I suppose the men and lady went home to sleep and shower, but I made it my business not to check), they arrived at not one bill but two, one primarily by Johnson, the other by Dickinson. They begged Moley to come in and mediate. He sat with them, but said hardly a word. His silence forced them into further compromise, and they finally emerged with a National Industrial Recovery Act.

A fairly complete plan, except for one thing. After I approved their draft in principle, Secretary Perkins came to me with a worried look. "This is very drastic," she said. "The wages and hours of labor are involved. I think I ought to get the president of the American Federation of Labor to go over it."

She sent for William Green, who approved it on the whole but raised the objection that its code-making provisions could put labor unions out of business unless there were some recognition of the right to collective bargaining.

The next few hours produced a greater change in American history than any of us, including Bill Green, then suspected. Hugh Johnson, aiming merely to put Green's fears to rest, scribbled out a sentence which became Section 7a:

"Employees shall have the right to organize and bargain collectively through representatives of their own choosing, and shall be free from the interference, restraint, or coercion of employers of labor, or their agents, in the designation of such representatives."

It was a set of words that no one seemed to take very seriously—until after the bill passed. The A. F. of L. was soon to call Section 7a "labor's Magna Charta." John L. Lewis compared it to the Emancipation Proclamation. He soon hoisted banners in mining towns declaring, "The President Wants You to Organize!" Within a few months his membership doubled. Unwittingly we had established the principle that later was to be embodied in the National Labor Relations Act.

The final bill, which I signed into law on June 16, 1933, was divided into two parts: Title I declared a national emergency, thus justifying partial suspension of the anti-trust laws, and set up machinery for creating voluntary industrial codes, pretty much as Harriman and Dickinson had conceived them. Title II authorized a $3.3 billion public-works program.

Public works could easily have been a separate bill. But that would have invited separate battles over public works and the industrial recovery codes, and no one could be sure which one—if either—might have won Congressional approval. By combining them into a unified recovery program, we eliminated effective opposition. So, while the economists continued to argue over their pet theories, the practical politicians won the day.[6]

Days before the bill was passed, I informed Hugh Johnson that he would be appointed administrator of this wholly new kind of government undertaking. Everyone agreed he seemed to be the right man —impeccably honest, personally dramatic, and popular. These were the qualities needed by a man administering a law so dependent on getting the co-operation of business competitors, of employers, workers, and consumers. And he had the experience of the industrial control effort of World War I.

If I had known then what I know now, that appointment would not have been made. Today, after depression and war have brought enormous growth to the size of government, we have developed systematic ways of checking up on the private lives as well as public abilities of important prospective appointees. In those last days of small government, the tradition was still to accept the recommendations of friends, and of friends of friends. Johnson looked just right.

The first hint of trouble arose at a cabinet meeting on June 6, ten days before I signed the NRA into law. It seems that Johnson, feeling secure in his impending appointment, was already rounding up a staff, not exactly quietly. Some of his rumored selections raised the hairs of a couple of cabinet members—and when I heard about them, some of mine, too.

Why not let him appoint whomever he wants? Why not leave a man free to accomplish a job in his own way? This is an argument that often accompanies government appointments, usually presented by people who don't fully understand the presidency and the Executive Branch. The entire Executive Branch—all the departments headed by cabinet officers, all the executive agencies and all their tens of thousands of employees—is an extension of a single man, the President. The President is the only executive elected by all the people of all the states. The people hold him responsible.

Congressmen and senators are in a different position. Each is elected by his own constituency and, in a sense, is in business for himself. He can say and do anything he pleases, subject only to the approval of his constituency on the next election day. No senator or congressman speaks for the Government of the United States (a fact that foreign governments do not always understand). On the other hand, no cabinet officer or major appointee may say or do anything without involving the President.

I am amused sometimes when political writers or ideologists criticize a cabinet officer for not fighting in public for this or that, as though he were in business for himself. Fighting within the Cabinet, yes; in private meetings with the President, yes; out in public, no. Of course, from time to time I would ask Harold Ickes or Henry Wallace to make a speech on this or that, setting forth a position that was not yet mine. This is sometimes a useful way to test public reaction to a position we might be considering. If the reaction is bad, the President can disclaim that position. It is then the cabinet officer's duty to advocate the position no further and fall into line with established policy. He must never forget that he is an extension of the President.

I told Secretary of Commerce Dan Roper to instruct Johnson not to promise any major job to anyone without conferring first with me. Roper then pointed out that Johnson's duties, which had no precedent in government, would overlap the domains of several departments, among them Commerce, Labor, Agriculture, and Interior. He thought a committee of these departments ought to pass upon General Johnson's work as well as his personnel.

Harold Ickes thought that would be too cumbersome and suggested that Johnson and the NRA ought to be attached somehow to Commerce. Coming from the head of Interior, that seemed an unselfish suggestion. I said it might be the right one. Then Labor Secretary Perkins said she doubted whether Johnson, with his "temperament," would be able to work under a Secretary, whereupon Ickes asked how Johnson could work for four Secretaries if he couldn't work with one. Frankly, that was all a bit unsettling.

Next Madame Perkins reported to me that Baruch had called upon her at home "socially" and made a point of discussing Johnson. She quoted him as saying, "He's been my number-three man for years. I think he's a good number-three man, maybe a number-two man, but he's not a number-one man. He's dangerous and unstable. He gets nervous and sometimes goes away for days without notice." That euphemism had an ominous ring. Just about every family (even the Roosevelts) has had a member who "goes away for days without notice," until returning home repentant—and dry. Baruch warned Madame Perkins: "I'm fond of him, but do tell the President to be careful. Hugh needs a firm hand."

Johnson had already become so conspicuously activated by his promised appointment, it was too late to reconsider it now without public explanation that we would not care to make. Well, not entirely too late. On June 16 I brought the bill, as passed by Congress, to the Cabinet, to honor its members by signing it right there and announcing Johnson's appointment. I gave the Cabinet a little speech about the difficulties of administering Title I—the industry and labor provisions—and the hazards of cartelization that could arise from the suspension of the anti-trust provisions. This would require the unremitting vigilance of a great administrator. Then I brought up the multibillion-dollar public-works section:

"What do you think about the administration of Title II? As the bill is written it seems to be taken for granted that it will be administered by the administrator of Title I, but I suppose it could be separated. I have read the bill, and I see no reason why I should not appoint, under the law, another administrator. What do you think of it as a matter of policy?"

One member after another agreed that was a highly desirable plan. If public works did not have someone's closest attention, one member pointed out, it could become a pork barrel to waste the people's money. We all quickly agreed that Harold Ickes would be in charge of Title II. Then I sent for Johnson, who had been waiting outside the Cabinet Room. When I told him I was about to sign the bill and appoint him administrator, he made a fine statement promising to devote his life to the great project. Then I told him how the Cabinet concluded that to ask one man to adminster both Title I and Title II

was to put an inhuman burden upon him. We had decided to make
the burden bearable by separating the difficult, time-consuming, and
more pedestrian job of managing public works, and assigning it to
Ickes.

I knew he wouldn't like it, but I hoped for a less pronounced reaction than I saw. Johnson's first flush of pleasure turned to a blush
of dismay. As I talked he seemed to turn purple. When I finished he
said in almost a growl, "I don't see why. I don't see why." I pre-
tended not to notice.

I dismissed the Cabinet and whispered to Madame Perkins, "Stick
with Hugh. Keep him sweet. Don't let him explode."

Some situations require a woman's touch, and Madame Perkins is
a great lady. She linked arms with Johnson, who seemed dazed, and
led him out a side door—where the press couldn't get to him—and
they left in her car. As Frances described it all to me later, she told
her chauffeur to drive to the Tidal Basin, then to another park and
another, to some of them twice. Hugh kept muttering, "He's ruined
me. I've got to get out. I can't stay. It's terrible." Finally her praise
of his great job in planning NRA, her urgings that he be a good
soldier, that the President needed him, took hold.

Next day I began saying around, "Frances Perkins is the best man
in the Cabinet." In another day or so I called Johnson in for a pep
talk and we got along fine.[7]

Development of codes for every major industry had to be a long
process of argument and reconciliation—among employers, between
employers and labor—with no peacetime precedent in American life.
On July 24, 1933, I went on the air for my third Fireside Chat:

"The proposition is simply this: If all employers will act together
to shorten hours and raise wages we can put people back to work. No
employer will suffer, because the relative level of competitive cost
will advance by the same amount for all. But if any considerable
group should lag or shirk, this great opportunity will pass us by and
we shall go into another desperate winter. This must not happen.

"We have sent out to all employers an agreement which is the result
of weeks of consultation. . . . It is a plan—deliberate, reasonable
and just—intended to put into effect at once the most important of
the broad principles which are being established, industry by industry, through codes. Naturally, it takes a good deal of organizing
and a great many hearings and many months, to get these codes per-

fected and signed, and we cannot wait for all of them to go through.
The blanket agreements, however, which I am sending to every employer will start the wheels turning now, and not six months from
now."

In absence of finished codes, these temporary "re-employment"
agreements, of course, had to be entirely voluntary. But as any
army sergeant knows, there are ways to "encourage" volunteers. Hugh
Johnson one day came up with the happy idea of the Blue Eagle,
which we printed up by the millions in every size from large window
posters to small stickers. Any employer signing the agreement was
entitled to display this emblem. They were emblazoned on billboards,
in newspaper ads, even in the windows of the corner grocery store
and barber shop. All Americans were urged to patronize businesses
showing the emblem—and, in effect, to boycott those not showing it.
In my Fireside Chat, I explained:

"In war, in the gloom of night attack, soldiers wear a bright badge
on their shoulders to be sure that comrades do not fire on comrades.
On that principle, those who co-operate in this program must know
each other at a glance. That is why we have provided a badge of
honor for this purpose, a simple design with a legend, 'We do our
part,' and I ask that all those who join with me shall display that
badge prominently. . . . And it is my purpose to keep posted in the
post office of every town a Roll of Honor of all those who join with
me."

To further the recovery spirit, I personally sketched a three-cent
NRA postage stamp showing a farmer, a businessman, a worker,
and a woman marching together, with the legend, "In a Common
Determination." Upon receiving the first stamp I wrote to Postmaster
General Farley:

Dear Jim:

Thank you for the N.R.A. postage stamp and cover. The honest
farmer, who looks like me; the honest businessman, who looks like
Grover T. Whalen; and the honest blacksmith, who looks like Lionel
Barrymore, are magnificent. But Oh Heavens what a girl! She is wearing
a No. 11 shoe, also a bustle, and if recovery is dependent on women
like that I am agin recovery.

In spite of the above, it is a grand stamp, gotten out in record time,
and will do worlds of good.

Frances Perkins, whose dainty feet could fit many a man's No. 11 shoe, decided to visit some steel towns to hear directly from working-men what they wanted in the steel code. We wanted to make sure that workers did not view NRA codes as cozy contracts between employers and government. She wanted to visit, among other places, Homestead, Pennsylvania, which had a sorry record of labor relations, often violent. She asked my permission to go without the usual battery of advisers and publicists, accompanied only by a Catholic priest, Father Francis Haas, well known as a friend of labor. Not many cabinet officers would feel her instinct for getting close to people. I told her (and here I rely on her notes):

"You and I have the instinct for freedom of association. Unfor-tunately, I can't practice it any more, what with the Secret Service and the politicians. . . . You know, that is one of the great things about Eleanor. She has already thrown off the Secret Service. They can't keep up with her. The result is that she goes where she wants to, talks to everybody, and does she learn something!"

As Frances related her adventure to me, it seems that the Burgess of Homestead, as the local "mayor" was archaically called, arranged a public hearing for her in the Hall of Burgesses. A few workers asked questions and stated some mild complaints, surprisingly mild. At the end of the meeting, she became aware of a disturbance down-stairs. A newspaperman whispered to her that a lot of men were gathered outside, because the Burgess had barred them. Frances sug-gested to the Burgess that those men be let in to have their say, that she had plenty of time. The Burgess grew red in the face: "No, no, you've had enough. These men are undesirable Reds. I know them well. They just want to make trouble."

Perhaps so, Frances thought, but if she didn't hear them they might make more trouble. She said good-by to the Burgess and went downstairs and out the front door, right into the midst of a couple of hundred angry men, where she made a little speech: "My friends, I am so sorry that you were not able to get into the hall. It was very crowded, but perhaps we can hear what you have to say right here."

The Burgess, flanked by police, fumed: "You can't talk here! There is a rule against making a speech here." Frances offered to move to a park across the street. That wouldn't do either: "There is an or-dinance against meetings in a public park."

Good old Frances. Her eye caught sight of the American flag across the square. Surely a federal official could not be barred from conducting a meeting in a federal post office. There, in a long corridor lined with postal cages, Frances stood upon a chair, made a brief speech about the steel code, and listened to twenty or thirty of the men express their fears and grievances. She wound up inviting the most vocal and obstreperous of the speakers to Washington to appear at a more formal hearing. It all ended with much handshaking and general rejoicing that the New Deal wasn't afraid of the steel trust.

When I read next morning about the "nervous Burgess of Homestead," I telephoned Frances to say, "You did just the right thing and you gave the post office free advertising. You know, the post office in every community ought to be the people's contact with the government."

Secretary Perkins soon brought me another tale to illustrate not only the code-making difficulties in steel, but how the NRA was affecting social manners. When the code negotiations dragged on and on, she invited the heads of major steel companies to her office. There was no steelworkers' union at the time, so she invited William Green, president of the A. F. of L., as a general representative of labor. Green was sitting there as the steel operators filed in—Eugene Grace, Myron Taylor, William Irwin, Ernest Weir, Thomas Girdler, and others. Frances experienced what she described to me as "the most embarrassing social experience of my life" when she started the introductions. Most of these company presidents and board chairmen would not permit themselves to be introduced to Mr. Green, backing away like frightened boys. Frances could not believe that grown men could be so timid. They explained to her privately that if it became known that they had shaken hands with William Green— talked with him!—"it would ruin their long-time position against labor organizations in their industry." For three quarters of an hour they huddled in a corner, refusing—except for William Irwin—to sit down with Green, until Green, a most mild and polite man, finally left in a huff. Poor Frances, terribly upset, began to see how funny it all was when she came to the White House to tell me about it: "I felt as though I had entertained eleven-year-old boys at their first party rather than men in charge of the most important industry in the United States."

Years later, after Myron Taylor had become a good friend of mine (in fact, I was later to appoint him as my personal representative to the Vatican), I remarked to Frances one day, "You know, Myron has learned a lot from us. He is a better man than he was that day . . . and I think he is happier."[8]

Hugh Johnson pitched into code making so noisily, somehow stirring fresh headlines in every newspaper edition, ordering cabinet members around like office boys, that I sometimes wondered whether he was chief of state or I. He was doing a remarkable job of getting codes signed, but also succeeding in raising the blood pressure of cabinet members. Their irritation was released in hilarity at a cabinet meeting on July 28, 1933, when Dan Roper, usually the quietest fellow around, had us in stitches telling how Johnson had "taken over" Dan's Commerce Department. I added my bit: Three days earlier, Johnson had burst into my office, coattails flying, to lay three codes on my desk for signature. He ordered me to sign them at once, looking at his watch, because he had just five minutes to catch an airplane. He fled with the signed codes for Lord knows where and I hadn't seen him since.

Johnson was unparalleled at arousing enthusiasm and the ballyhoo required to whip opposing parties into line to sign codes and root for recovery. But when it came to the tough administrative work that followed, of getting the signers to live up, day by day, to what they had agreed to, Johnson was out of his depth. He seemed driven to win his battles by reaching for headlines, each one infuriating somebody new. Then I kept hearing about a problem with his administrative assistant, a very forceful lady. She attended all his conferences and acted like a meddling wife. People found him more and more difficult to deal with, he became increasingly defensive and suspicious, and he disappeared "for days without notice."

I must confess that I have never been very good at firing anybody, especially as loyal a man as Hugh Johnson, who had contributed so much. For months I wished he would see the light and resign. I hinted at it and asked others to hint at it. At the mere suggestion, Johnson would turn theatrical and promise anything—except a resignation. On September 10, 1934, I had him up to Hyde Park and treated him as coolly as I could an old friend. This man was too emotional—and publicity-minded—to fire outright. We had enough problems without the storm he would raise. Finally—almost a month later—Johnson gingerly asked if I wanted him to leave. I accepted his offer before he could back off.[9]

In fairness to Johnson, not all the troubles of NRA could be blamed on him. The fact is that the country was not ready for the kind of broad co-operation—the whole nation playing like a team— that the NRA required. When a baseball team is out to win, sometimes the batter who would just love to swing for a home run has to bunt into a sacrifice play to get his teammate home.

But too many men were unwilling to make that sacrifice. The men of big business *talked* about a team win, and I took them at their word. At the annual meeting of the United States Chamber of Commerce in May 1933, more than half of the forty-nine speakers advocated greater control by government over industry. Only nine opposed it. But when they came down to writing codes and living with them, big businessmen sang a different tune. In agreeing to raise wages and create more jobs, industrialists insisted on raising prices so high and so rapidly as to wipe out the gains in purchasing power. We asked them to hold back increases as long as possible and to seek profits in the larger sales volume that was sure to come. Not all, but many, refused to hold to the team effort. Many employers tried to suppress workers—sometimes violently through local police forces they controlled—when these workers exercised their right, made legal by Section 7a, to organize unions. They chased organizers out of town and broke up meetings and picket lines, sometimes resulting in bodily harm.

And there were subtler kinds of sabotage of team interests. One kind was reported to me in a confidential memorandum from Harry Hopkins, who made a tour of all the states of the South, talking to every governor, every NRA board, to bankers, farmers, and labor leaders. He told me he "found enormous enthusiasm for the NRA." Yet how were some employers meeting the NRA requirement that they raise wages? "There is a tendency, which is growing, to discharge negroes and replace them with white labor," Hopkins told me. Of course, one way to protect the jobs of Negroes would have been to write into the codes the traditional differential between the wages of southern Negroes and whites. Although this might have been "realistic," it would have been morally wrong. So employers went along—on paper—with the "principle" of equal pay for equal work, but abrogated it in the reality.

The one time in the history of the New Deal that I called upon industrial and business leadership was in designing the NRA. I sought their advice and heeded it. It turned out to be a costly error that I did not make again until World War II forced an entire change in national attitudes.

Meanwhile the team spirit of my left-of-center "allies" was not always better. Even necessary price increases were denounced as exploitive "plots to milk the workers," a constant barrage of criticism that undermined support for the NRA. Unions were unrestrained in calling strikes all over the landscape, further weakening the economy and postponing recovery. The most dramatic of these was a general strike in San Francisco in 1934, which certainly did not contribute to a national team spirit. I am not saying that these strikes were not justified in terms of short-run grievances that no doubt were painful and pressing. Nor am I saying that employers were always unjustified in raising prices or resisting wage demands that might threaten the survival of their businesses. But there is a proper time for achieving short-range goals, and another for longer-range goals. This was a time when all of us should have made a greater effort to give up something short-range in the interest of national recovery that would save us all.[10]

Yet I did not speak lightly when often I referred to the NRA as a magnificent success. Even if we didn't find all the answers, the NRA forced us to do some hard thinking on economic freedom versus industrial control, the rights of labor versus the rights of the employer, the liberty of the individual versus the liberty of the community. It brought us face to face with some of the long-neglected but central problems of modern life.

Some successes were tangible, too. The downward spiral of wages was reversed. From June 1933 to June 1934 average hourly earnings in manufacturing rose 31 per cent. Weekly earnings per capita increased 14 per cent. Meanwhile, during that period, the cost of living increased less than 7 per cent. So we did succeed in keeping the income rise ahead of the price rise. It is important to note that, while coded industries enjoyed the greatest direct gains, the whole economy was lifted. A report to me by the Research and Planning Division of NRA on January 1, 1935—an 18-month progress report—showed a 30 per cent increase in the wage rates of coded industries and a 10 per cent increase in non-coded industries. Everyone got a lift.

While we may never know the exact contribution of NRA to recovery, we know that it produced historic, permanent reform in the human conditions of modern industry. Child labor in factories was virtually eliminated from American life. The sweatshop began to be a thing of the past. The principles of a maximum-length work week and a minimum hourly wage enforced by government were established. These reforms forever changed life for the American laboring man and woman.

If these dry statistics leave anyone unimpressed, I could not remain unmoved by the letters that came to me every day from ordinary working people, for some reason particularly from women. A lady in the Southwest wrote me:

> If the poor people could only express themselves like the rich there would be no question as to whether NRA had been a benefit to the working classes or not. Before NRA some of the girls in the factories here had to work as long as 12 hours a day for about $7 a week. Never before have the working-people here enjoyed their work as in the past two years under NRA.

A midwestern woman wrote to me:

> Those who don't like the NRA never worked in a sweat-shop 80 hours a week and received $3.50 for pay such as I have or they would not take this attitude.

Another:

> Before the New Deal came into effect we was compelled to work 15 hours of each day during the rush and no overtime and fired if you get a [union] card. Now we got our union and we got our decent work-week and we got more girls working here and we got better wages. Where I used to never get more than $8 a week now I don't never get under $13.50. Our life is no bed of roses because that aint the way it is for the workers yet but it's better for us than ever I seen it and I been in a factory 9 years since I was 15.

Employers wrote to me, too, letters such as this one, which I received in April 1935 from a man in the West:

> In my own plant I paid 25 percent more wages for 1934 than I did for 1933. . . . I also paid an income tax for 1934, the first since 1930.[11]

That, in brief, is the tale of the short, exciting life of the NRA. Now it's time to tell of its untimely death. The Supreme Court killed the NRA on May 27, 1935, as they were soon to do with the Agricultural Adjustment Act (which I have already described). The day of the fateful NRA decision was to become known as the "Black Monday" of the New Deal.

It is important to take a close look at that court decision because it was a critical point in the development of constitutional law—and of the New Deal. From the beginning, we New Dealers knew we were playing a risky game with the Supreme Court. The extreme emergency of the depression gave us no choice. There was no precedent for our problems. Yet we did feel we had legal precedents for justifying our unprecedented remedies. Do you recall my pointing out that the Act declared a national emergency? We felt that justified the government's right to promulgate codes when industry and labor representatives could not agree on them. In a 1932 opinion written by Justice Louis Brandeis, the depression was described as "an emergency more serious than war." Later, in January 1934, a majority opinion written by Chief Justice Hughes upheld a Minnesota moratorium on mortgages, saying, "While emergency does not create power, emergency may furnish the occasion for the exercise of power." Two months later another majority opinion, written by Justice Owen Roberts, upholding New York's power to set minimum and maximum prices for milk, declared, "Neither property rights nor contract rights are absolute." These opinions certainly seemed to sustain the intentions of the Act in establishing industry codes for the emergency.

Naturally we expected that some free-wheeling businessman somewhere, depression or no, would refuse to be bound by the industry-government partnership for recovery, and would sue the government to test the legality of the NRA. Sure enough, such a case came along when the owner of a southern lumber mill, W. E. Belcher, challenged the lumber code. To our dismay, a federal judge in Alabama ruled that the Act was unconstitutional and, therefore, Belcher did not have to observe the code. Donald Richberg, a lawyer and Hugh Johnson's successor as head of the NRA, moved immediately to appeal this decision to the Supreme Court. But Stanley Reed, the solicitor general, and Felix Frankfurter, my good friend at Harvard, convinced me to withdraw this appeal. Frankly we didn't trust the jury— the nine aging justices with old-fashioned views. (Those earlier decisions I referred to a few sentences ago had been 5–4 decisions, too close for comfort.)

To my non-lawyer friends, let me point out that when that Alabama judge called the NRA "unconstitutional," his opinion did not strike down the law. He opened the way to permitting people to ignore the law, but only in his district, which we did not think most patriotic businessmen in that district would choose to do. Only the Supreme Court could kill the law.

The Belcher affair came up when I was about to leave on the SS *Nourmahal* for a fishing trip around the Bahamas. No sooner did I leave than some newspaper editorialists, who apparently had run out of constructive thoughts, unloosed a cry that the government was shrinking from a Supreme Court test of the NRA. Attorney General Cummings decided to meet this criticism by taking directly to the Supreme Court another case, brought in New York by two brothers named Schechter, who were in the poultry business. They had been found guilty of violating the Live Poultry Code by their treatment of employees as well as by selling kosher chickens that were unfit for human consumption. It became known as the "sick chicken case." After discussion with Felix Frankfurter, Thomas Corcoran radioed me:

Washington, D.C., April 4, 1935

F.F. CALLED. HAS LEARNED VERY VERY CONFIDENTIALLY CUMMINGS . . . INTENDS ANNOUNCING TO PRESS THIS AFTERNOON THAT GOVERNMENT WILL IMMEDIATELY EXPEDITE TO SUPREME COURT A NEW NRA CASE FROM SECOND CIRCUIT IN NEW YORK INVOLVING POULTRY CODE. F.F. SUGGESTS MOST IMPOLITIC AND DANGEROUS TO YIELD TO ANTAGONISTIC PRESS CLAMOR NOW BECAUSE FUNDAMENTAL SITUATION ON COURT NOT CHANGED. FURTHER SUGGESTS YOU WIRE CUMMINGS NOT TO TAKE HASTY ACTION AND HOLD SITUATION ON NRA APPEALS IN ABEYANCE UNTIL YOU RETURN. SUGGEST AT THAT TIME THOROUGH DISCUSSION IN PRESENCE OF ALL CONCERNED.

That is exactly what I radioed Cummings to do, but somewhere along the line this message was delayed in getting to him. He had already requested that the Supreme Court take up the Schechter case immediately, forcing a constitutionality test of the NRA. I do not know who held up my message or whether it was a purposeful act by one of Cummings' men who was overly eager to force the test. It doesn't really matter, because the Schechter case was surely headed for the Supreme Court anyway. Once Cummings forced the issue, I could not again decide to delay it without fueling the editorial criticism.

What stunned us most when the Supreme Court a few days later struck down the NRA was the vote. It was unanimous, 9–0. My heart was sore to think that even Justices Brandeis and Ben Cardozo had turned their backs on progressivism.

Clearly, Teacher had to take the nation to school again, and again I chose as my classroom the device of a press conference, the reporters all gathered around my desk. Even Mrs. Roosevelt was there, knitting a blue sock. Those sturdy boys of the press, already up to their ears in my cram course to make farmers out of them, now found themselves enrolled in the Roosevelt School of Law. After all, to one of these trades I was born, and in the other I was trained.

"The implications of this decision," I told them, "are much more important than almost certainly any decision of my lifetime or yours, more important than any decision probably since the Dred Scott case."

The grounds for killing the NRA were two: First, the Court said, Congress could not delegate its legislative authority to the President, and the Court said Congress had done so by permitting the President to impose a code upon an industry when its representatives had failed to agree on one. The Court's opinion, written by Chief Justice Hughes himself, stated: "Extraordinary conditions do not create or enlarge constitutional power. . . . Such a delegation of legislative power is unknown to our law and utterly inconsistent with the constitutional prerogatives and duties of Congress." Justice Cardozo wrote a separate, concurring opinion in which he condemned the law as "delegation running riot. No such plenitude of power is susceptible of transfer." Now, that's a fine point. He seemed not to be objecting to the delegation of powers as such, but to the *quantity* of it.

Well, that wasn't all too serious. As I told the reporters, "The Supreme Court has at least intimated that in so far as the delegation of power was concerned, the language of the Act could have been so improved as to give *definite directions* to administrative or quasi-judicial bodies and in that respect it refers to the methods already used in the case of the Federal Trade Commission and cites that with approval. In other words . . . an Act could be written which would in general conform to this opinion of the Supreme Court as to delegated powers."

The second ground was the really important one, the one that could cripple almost any kind of federal effort to solve the present emergency—or almost any major national problem. It challenged the fundamental idea I was trying to bring to government, the idea that in time of trouble, when the states could not provide remedies, the federal government must work *actively* to guarantee minimum protection for all Americans. The Court declared that the NRA could be enforced only in interstate commerce, defining "interstate" so narrowly as to make the federal government impotent.

Specifically, the Court ruled that the "sick chickens" were killed in New York for probable sale in New York, therefore were to be considered *intra*state commerce. The Court didn't stop there but reached back to a decision of 1885 limiting the definition of interstate commerce to *goods in transit*—nothing else! What a monstrosity for this day and age! As I pointed out to the reporters, our nation has five major economic activities—transportation, construction, mining, manufacturing, and agriculture. The Court was saying that the federal government has no right to regulate the last four of these. If I couldn't argue with the Court, at least I could give a proper lesson in constitutional history to my friends of the press:

"The country was in the horse-and-buggy age when that [interstate] clause was written and if you go back to the debates on the Federal Constitution you will find in 1787 that one of the impelling motives for putting in that clause was this: There wasn't much interstate commerce at all—probably 80 or 90 percent of the human beings in the thirteen original States were completely self-supporting within their own communities.

"They got their own food, their own clothes; they swapped or bought with any old kind of currency, because we had thirteen different kinds of currency. . . . They had in those days no problems relating to employment. . . . Nobody had ever thought of what the wages were or the buying capacity in the slave-holding States of the South. There were no social questions in those days. The question of health on a national basis had never been discussed. The question of fair business practices had never been discussed. The word was unknown in the vocabulary of the Founding Fathers. . . . If one man could skin a fellow and get away with it, why, that was all right. . . .

"The prosperity of the farmer *does* have an effect today on the manufacturer in Pittsburgh. The prosperity of the clothing worker in the city of New York has an effect on the prosperity of the farmer in Wisconsin, and so it goes. We are interdependent—we are tied in together. And the hope has been that we could, through a period of years, interpret the interstate clause of the Constitution in the light of these new things that have come to the country. . . .

"The big issue is this: Does this decision mean that the United States Government has no control over any national economic problem? . . . . If we accept the [Court's] point of view . . . the Federal Government must abandon any legislation. . . .

"We have got to decide one way or the other. I don't mean this summer or winter or next fall, but over a period, perhaps, of five years or ten years we have got to decide: whether we are going to relegate to the forty-eight States practically all control over economic conditions—not only State economic conditions but national economic conditions. . . . That actually is the biggest question that has come before this country outside of time of war, and it has to be decided. And, as I say, it may take five years or ten years. . . .

"Don't call it right or left. That is just first-year high-school language, just about. It is not right or left—it is a question for national decision on a very important problem of Government. We are the only Nation in the world that has not solved that problem. We thought we were solving it, and now it has been thrown right straight in our faces. We have been relegated to the horse-and-buggy definition of interstate commerce."[12]

That little class in law turned out to be an uninterrupted monologue—without notes, I might say as an aside to some of my former law professors—of one hour and twenty-five minutes. Months and years later, I read secondhand historical accounts of that press conference describing me as "intemperate" and "angry." That just shows what may happen when news ages into legend. I certainly was neither. The very next morning's New York *Times* reported—through a man who was there—that my tone was "courteous and serious . . . outward good humor but only slightly masked irony." Arthur Krock wrote, "By the time the President had finished his public examination . . . he had changed the viewpoint of many who first thought the decision wholly constructive. . . . The President once more had turned what seemed a retreat into a firm advance against a more important salient."

The impact of the court decision was immediate and painful. An A. F. of L. survey showed that, within six business days after the Court had its say, a million wage earners suffered wage cuts and had their work weeks stretched.

Another result was that I became convinced we were not prepared to swallow the medicine of central economic planning. To the sorrow of some of my most devoted advisers, I dropped the word "planning" from my vocabulary. Too many Americans shrink from it. I did not push for repassage of NRA in some modified form, nor would I again give peacetime support to such a planning scheme. We had to find other ways to take the medicine, in smaller spoonfuls—and did.

Section 7a was soon to be born again as the National Labor Relations Act (also known as the Wagner Act). An end to child labor and establishment of minimum wages and maximum working hours were to be realized through the Fair Labor Standards Act. The Guffey Act was to replace the NRA code in bringing sanity to the coal industry.[13]

Relief by Handout, or Work?

The Supreme Court decision, while killing the industrial codes (Title I), left intact the huge authorization to create jobs through public works (Title II).

This was more of a blessing than I desired. The controversy over this $3.3 billion appropriation had been fierce. Those who favored it —Senators Wagner, La Follette, and Costigan, my own Frances Perkins and Rex Tugwell, as well as the Hearst press—had the right sentiments but the wrong means. Many against it, Director of the Budget Lewis Douglas and his fellow conservatives in Congress and private business, had other reasons—equally wrong.

The progressives had fought for $5 billion. They somehow imagined that a huge sum of money could automatically be turned into jobs—the more money the more jobs. If I had been a legislator, I might have thought so, too. There is a difference between the legislative mind and the executive mind. A legislator expresses his *wishes* —sometimes his pipe dreams—through passing a law, making an appropriation. The Chief Executive has to live with it, not only execute the law, but try to accomplish its intended results. Instead of asking, *"Ought* these results be accomplished?" he must ask, *"Can* this law accomplish them?"

That is why Presidents sometimes disillusion their supporters by opposing laws that seem to be just the kind they would favor. A congressman, a placard bearer, a political speechmaker, may make political hay confusing purposes with methods, but a President is answerable if the methods don't work.

Like the progressives, I was all for spending money to create jobs. But I was convinced that public works, as defined in the law, would not permit me to spend the money *fast enough*. What kind of projects did the progressives imagine? Two of Senator Wagner's favorites, for his own state of New York, were a Triborough Bridge to connect Manhattan with the Bronx and Queens, and a Midtown Tunnel under the Hudson River. Fine! But how long would the architects and engineers have to plan before even a thousand laborers could bring home their first pay checks? For all the good intentions of the large public-works fund, its results would be another long winter, perhaps even two, of maintaining cold and hungry families on the dole.

The conservatives opposed public works, because it meant an unbalanced budget and because they felt the government should not actively enter economic life—by building buildings, employing men, affecting wage rates, and so forth. Their position was as confused as it was anxious. They wanted the government to do something, yet not do anything. If it had to step in to help, they wanted the government to help not the poor but the rich. A Chicago banker visited me to express his fears about the cost of public works, yet asked me to "do something" to stimulate the durable industries—steel, construction, and so forth. I asked him:

"What will *you* do? Will your bank lend $10 million to put up a 60-story building on Michigan Avenue?"

"Certainly not," he told me. "Office space is in surplus now. It will be ten years before it will be economically sound to construct big buildings."

I had to find a practical program between the do-something-but-do-nothing of the conservatives and the plan-too-much-and-do-too-late of my public-works friends in Congress. It had to create quicker, smaller-scale projects than public works, yet larger-scale than the existing FERA. Wherever possible, FERA relief grants to the states were being used to create small, local work projects. But that law specifically forbade use of federal funds to purchase materials—bricks, steel, machinery, and so forth. Only hand tools, such as rakes and shovels, were permitted, our idea being that practically all the money should go into relief wages. This limitation turned out to be crippling. The relief jobs created were hardly jobs at all: gathering leaves, picking up pieces of paper in the park. Isn't such made-work as destructive to a man's pride as the dole itself?[14]

Harry Hopkins and I decided we needed to employ millions in dignified, useful jobs before winter. These had to be, in the main, construction jobs that could be planned and started quickly—road building and repair, park landscaping, improvement of public buildings, something on the scale of CCC work but not restricted to forests. It had to employ the skilled as well as unskilled. To do this, we needed the right to buy materials and heavier tools. Could the huge public-works appropriation legally be used, at least in part, for small-scale projects? I was willing to risk it.

But again we ran into opposition from my "friends" in organized labor. They were firmly opposed to jobs at low emergency wages, fearing a reduction of wage standards in private industry. For four months after passage of the NRA, that opposition immobilized us. Then Harry found a clever way out. He sent his deputy, Aubrey Williams, to see Dr. John R. Commons at the University of Wisconsin, known to know almost everything about the history and affairs of organized labor. Commons dug up an old newspaper clipping—from 1898!—in which Samuel Gompers, the father of organized labor, had advocated putting the unemployed of his time to work in what he called a "Day Labor Plan." It was precisely the kind of thing we had in mind. Harry took it to the A. F. of L. Since that plan was from one of "their boys," not from "our boys," labor decided our plan was orthodox after all.

Harry brought this news to me at lunch in October 1933. I asked how many jobs he could create in a hurry. He said four million. The figure seemed impossible, which is what I liked most about it. Harry has courage.

On November 8, 1933, I established the Civil Works Administration (CWA), with Harry Hopkins at its head. Rather than go to Congress, I did this by executive order, taking $400 million from Ickes' public-works fund. Was this in keeping with the intent of Congress? I felt it was. At the cabinet meeting where I made the announcement, Ickes flushed, then grumbled that it "ought to be done."

My executive order stated that the CWA "is designed to remove from relief all employable persons." At a CWA conference in Washington on November 15, speaking extemporaneously (which I hasten to point out to explain my faulty syntax), I said: ". . . of those four millions of people, two million are today on what we might just as well call, frankly, a dole. When any man or woman goes on a dole, something happens to them mentally—and the quicker they are taken off the dole the better it is for them during the rest of their lives."

Thirty days later Harry had created jobs for 2,610,451, in another month well over four million—almost as many as all those who had served in the armed forces in World War I. This he did with no formal planning staff, no shelf of job ideas, with a central office of only 121 people paid a total of $22,000 a month. That wonderful man!

In the next hundred days CWA workers, engaged in 180,000 projects, were improving or building five hundred thousand miles of roads, forty thousand schools, one thousand airports. They developed parks, cleared waterways, fought insects and pests, dug swimming pools and sewers. In Detroit, CWA workers restored a city-wide system of trolley tracks and modernized and painted the cars. In Key West, which was so broke it could not collect garbage, CWA workers cleaned up the littered streets and beaches.

Such physical labor was only one kind of CWA work. Unemployed teachers were hired to reopen rural schools for farm children; they also began teaching more than a million and a half adults to read and write. Doctors, broke because of uncollected bills, were sustained by emergency wages while immunizing a million children against disease. Unemployed rabbis compiled a Hebrew dictionary.

To check on the effectiveness of Hopkins' work, I sent Frank Walker, an old political friend, around the country. From his home state of Montana, he wrote to me:

"I saw old friends of mine—men I had been to school with—digging ditches and laying sewer pipes. They were wearing their regular business suits as they worked because they couldn't afford overalls and rubber boots. If I ever thought, 'There, but for the grace of God —' it was right then."

To nobody's surprise, the Republican National Committee called CWA "gross waste" and "downright corruption." Soon, however, influential men such as Winthrop Aldrich of the Chase National Bank, financier James Warburg, my own Budget Director Lewis Douglas, and an expanding corps of Republicans and southern Democrats in Congress began to look back nostalgically at the FERA dole, which they had also protested, for over the winter I found I had to divert an additional $533,000,000 from public works to sustain CWA.

These people argued that the expenditure could be cut in half by killing the costly business of creating jobs—and resuming a direct dole for the needy. They called for an end not only to CWA, but to the Public Works Administration (PWA) and the CCC. They deplored the "moral consequences" of work relief while calling for the morally destructive dole.

I'm glad to say that at least one conservative took my side, which he may have regretted two years later. Governor Alfred M. Landon of Kansas, who was to run against me in 1936, wrote to me in 1934: "This civil-works program is one of the soundest, most constructive policies of your administration, and I cannot urge too strongly its continuance."

Still, the opposition was becoming more vocal. A Congressional election was coming in November. If the sentiment against CWA became strong enough, it could jeopardize the Congressional majority that was essential to the whole New Deal. In March 1934 I ordered Hopkins to close down CWA.

This meant returning to the old FERA dole again until we had assurance of popular support for a back-to-work substitute. I know the order to end CWA broke Harry's heart. Instead of threatening to resign—as Harold Ickes would have done—Harry cracked the whip with his associates to quit complaining and get on with the job of taking care of the needy. That is the kind of loyalty a President needs—and rarely gets.[15]

Handouts or Work—Phase Two

The people rallied behind the New Deal in November with a force that surprised even me. Little wonder! By mid-1934 almost five million workers were on payrolls again who had been out of work the month I took office. In manufacturing, jobs were up by 40 per cent; factory payrolls, a heartening 80 per cent. Nobody can fool working people, farmers, and merchants about facts like that. On June 28, the Congressional campaign about to begin, I anticipated and answered Republican propaganda, saying on the radio:

"The simplest way for each of you to judge recovery lies in the plain facts of your individual situation. Are you better off than you were last year? . . . Have you as an individual paid too high a price for these gains? . . . Have you lost any of your rights or liberties or constitutional freedom of action and choice? Turn to the Bill of Rights of the Constitution, which I have solemnly sworn to maintain. . . . Read each provision of the Bill of Rights and ask yourself whether you personally have suffered the impairment of a single jot of these great assurances. I have no question in my mind as to what your answer will be."

The answer was a House of Representatives—which generally swings away from the President in an off-year election—of 322 Democrats and ten Progressives and Farmer-Laborites. The Republican minority was reduced from 117 to 102, the lowest in that party's history. Their Senate rout was even more humiliating, falling from 35 to 25. Republicans were left with only seven governors and no real national leader. The party had paid heavily for its neglect and negativism.

This tremendous national victory showed that I had paid too much heed to the cranky men who had no vision beyond a dole. I wrote my January 1935 annual message to Congress as a direct attack on the dole, the essence of Hooverism—and as an opening volley of a renewed campaign to create work:

"The lessons of history . . . show conclusively that continued dependence upon relief induces a spiritual and moral disintegration fundamentally destructive to the national fibre. To dole out relief in this way is to administer a narcotic, a subtle destroyer of the human spirit. . . . It is in violation of the traditions of America. . . .

"The Federal Government must and shall quit this business of relief.

"I am not willing that the vitality of our people be further sapped by the giving of cash, of market baskets, of a few hours of weekly work cutting grass, raking leaves or picking up papers in the public parks. We must preserve not only the bodies of the unemployed from destitution but also their self-respect, their self-reliance and courage and determination."[16]

That is what the Democratic Party believes in, and I hope will always believe in. I asked Congress to replace FERA with a new, enlarged program of work creation to be governed by these practical principles:

1. All work should be useful, that is, contributing to improvement of community life and creating new wealth for the nation.

2. Compensation, in the form of "security payments," should be "larger than the amount now received as a relief dole, but at the same time not so large as to encourage the rejection of opportunities for private employment."

3. Work projects should require a large percentage of direct labor, not overly dependent upon machinery or a disproportionate expenditure for materials.

4. Preference should be given to self-liquidating projects, those which might produce income to the government and thus eventually pay for themselves, such as toll bridges and electricity-producing dams.

5. In order not to go overboard on large-scale, long-term projects,

work should be planned that can be tapered off as the demand for workers by private employers increases.

6. Projects should be located where the need for jobs is most intense, not necessarily where the need for physical improvement is greatest, "our ultimate objective being the enrichment of human lives."

In this back-to-work crusade, one of the great objects I had in mind was saving children from the spiritual and moral deterioration induced by dependence. We learned that families on relief included about 7.4 million children under sixteen. Was the temporary disaster of the depression, coming as it did in the most impressionable years of these young lives, to leave lifelong scars? The growing field of social workers worried about this, as I did. A report on "Unemployment and Relief," published by the Family Service Association of America in May 1935, pointed out that "deprivation and want are nurturing soil for the criminal. . . . The resulting feelings of inferiority and jealousy express themselves in striking out against society. For long years to come we shall be dealing with the social costs . . . of stunted children, embittered and crushed men, women worn and aged before their time, seared and abraded personalities."

I can imagine no worse fate for a child than to spend his early years seeing his parents reliant on some public or institutional benevolence that can never be sufficient. It can only be resented by both giver and receiver. Whatever short-run favor a dole may be, in the longer runs it robs a child of the essential experience of seeing his father and mother making their way with self-reliance and pride. If direct relief were permitted to continue another year—if it threatened to become a "national habit," as Harry Hopkins and others around me feared—I dreaded to think of the number of children whose lives might be ravaged beyond saving.[17]

The election was a clear signal that the time was right for boldness. Again breaking a record for a peacetime bill, I asked Congress for $4.8 billion to launch this new kind of simpler, more practical public-works program.

How were we to justify spending far more money than we had, with no certainty as to how and when the debt would be repaid? That question would have defeated us if I had relied on the economists of the time. The traditional economic theory, personified by

President Hoover and my recently resigned Budget Director, Lew Douglas, was that economic cycles were automatically controlled by "natural forces." Just leave everything alone, keep the federal budget neatly balanced, which (in some manner never explained) restores business "confidence," and everything rises back to "normal" again. That had been an unquestioned belief, approaching a theology. But clearly, these "natural forces" were not at work.

A second conventional idea, held mainly by labor leaders and technocrats, was to spread out available jobs by shortening the work week. As we have already discussed, this remedy is static and defeatist, leading nowhere.

Those two theories were the sum total of our most respected economic thinking. There were no other reputable ideas around.

We had to invent a new kind of economic thinking, with no experience to guide us. By going into government debt—for relief, for CWA, for CCC, for payments to farmers—we saw the economy begin to well up again, modestly but definitely. While businessmen and Republican ideologists raised their voices louder about "loss of confidence," we saw confidence rising. The people as a whole were more confident. More of them were eating wholesome meals again, working again, some even saving. Even the stock market began to rise. The rise in debt did not bring disaster, but indeed seemed to lessen its probability.

Here I must give some credit to a very interesting man in England, an economist named John Maynard Keynes. The experiments in economics that we were developing in practice closely resembled some new ideas he was developing in theory. In brief, he was daring to say that at a time of economic stagnation, government debt is a *good thing*. It is a stimulant, an investment, to get the wheels going again. When the wheels are turning full speed, the debt may be repaid. In fact, his interesting theory goes a bit further: the debt may repay itself. If government investment helps produce an expanding economy (the exact opposite of the static economy of the technocrats), the debt would be retired by the increased taxes paid by thriving industry and full pay envelopes.

Despite the shudders of some friends, I invited Professor Keynes to the White House several times. He does have a way, like most economists, of going off into an abstract world of mathematical equations and charts and graphs. But when you bring him down to earth,

he is a practical fellow. On his first visit to me, in June 1934, after I
got him to put away his equations and graphs—to his disappointment,
I think—he stated plainly what our experience was already teaching
us: that a dollar spent on relief was a dollar passed to the grocer, by
the grocer to his wholesaler, and by the wholesaler to a farmer. So
with one dollar of borrowed government expenditure, you have created four dollars in national income. Taxable income.

Through Felix Frankfurter a group of Oxford University economists, disciples of Keynes, sent me a lengthy memorandum commenting on what we in the New Deal were doing. I called a confidential
little gathering—Secretary Morgenthau, Attorney General Cummings,
Eugene Black and George Harrison of the Federal Reserve, and some
others—and read it to them. A paragraph that especially interested
me (which would have brought on an epidemic of apoplexy had I
read the memo before Congress) was one that made a virtue of financing public works by going into debt. The italics are mine:

"It is essential that these schemes should *not be financed by taxation.* If they are, the income that is put into one pocket is taken out
of another, and there is no net increase of purchasing power nor tendency for prices to rise. We therefore recommend a great drive for relieving distress through the agencies of the federal, state or municipal
administrations on *borrowed money.*"

Lew Douglas had resigned because he could not bear hearing members of my Cabinet and staff—or me—uttering similar blasphemies.
I wonder what he would have thought if he were still around to attend a certain cabinet meeting during my second term when another
of our resident conservatives, Jesse Jones, head of the Reconstruction
Finance Corporation, began thinking out loud:

"Mr. President, at the depths of the depression the national income
was $42 billion. In 1934 it was $49 billion. In 1937, $71 billion. If
we can get the national income up to $90 billion in the next year or
two, and I see no reason why we shouldn't, we don't have to give
another thought to the budget. It will balance without the slightest
difficulty. Mr. President, what we have discovered is that the national
income grows by economic movement. . . . If nothing unforeseen
happens"—he was referring to the possibility of war—"we shall be
out of the woods."

(Of course, the foreseen "unforeseen" was soon to happen. The
outbreak of war has shown us how deeply into borrowing our govern-

ment can go when we need to. Instead of going broke, we have put every available hand to work at good wages, the wartime "prosperity" producing such inflationary strain that we have had to put a ceiling on wages and prices. What the economic effects are to be afterward remain to be seen. Some of our economists now predict that an outcome of all this wartime spending by government will be the longest, most uplifting prosperity we have ever known. If that turns out to be so, all of us will have to revise some old and cherished ideas about the sins of public debt.)[18]

When I asked Congress for the $4.8 billion, a great battle ensued between Congress and the Executive. Not a battle so much over ideology or economy, but over the relative powers of the two branches of government.

Commentators seem to enjoy saying that during those early New Deal days I built up the power of the presidency, some going so far as to say I usurped for myself and future Presidents many of the powers that had previously resided in Congress. The first part of that may be true, but hardly the second. A President cannot *usurp* Congressional authority. The Constitution won't permit it. But he may *borrow* certain powers—if he can persuade Congress to lend them. He does not get them, as one gets money from a bank, by telling what he is going to do with what he borrows. He gets them by telling as little as possible.

I needed a sum that was very large, at the same time one I could use with maximum flexibility. I needed money for large public works where they would do the most good, but also for quick-and-simple work projects where *they* would do the most good. I needed freedom to start projects and terminate them as dictated by a changing employment picture. I also had in mind launching whole new relief ventures that I preferred not to submit to Congressional haggling: the Rural Electrification Administration (whose grand work I have already described), a National Youth Administration to provide basic sustenance for students, a Resettlement Administration to help unemployed city workers build low-cost homes in the country, and expansion or contraction of the CCC as the need might warrant.

What persuasion could I use with Congress to lend me these powers of decision? First and foremost, there was the pressing need itself, which the majority of Congress felt as urgently as I. They could not dally long without being blamed for inaction by their impatient constituents.

My second weapon was simply the use of silence. In asking for the money I specified as little as possible as to its uses, except for the broad principles clearly stated in my January message. This brought on some great howls at the Capitol. The complainers found a voice in columnist Walter Lippmann:

> The Senators were not told who was going to administer the program. They were not given definite information about the scope or character of the program. They were not even furnished a thorough, cogent, and considered argument in favor of the Bill. . . . The Senate was confronted not with a policy but a mystery. . . . It was the opportunity of Senators who for partisan reasons were glad to frustrate the President, of Senators who wished to get at the pork barrel.

That last sentence was certainly correct. If I were to specify how and where the money was to be spent, I would surrender to Congressional debate all the flexibility a successful works program would need. Instead of going to where families were most in need of work, the money would go to enrich the districts of congressmen who held the most power in committees.

Some members of Congress demanded to know who would be in charge of spending this tremendous sum of money. I replied that *I* would. There were good reasons for keeping my own counsel. Everyone assumed there were only two likely candidates for administering this broadly defined works program. One was Harry Hopkins, the other Harold Ickes. To many congressmen these two men symbolized different philosophies. Hopkins represented imagination and flair, as well as fast distribution of purchasing power. As a social worker, he was known for putting human needs ahead of achievements in steel and concrete. This had made him many friends, especially in the freshly elected House, but a number of enemies in the more conservative and slow-moving Senate. Senators, on the other hand, were more inclined to admire Ickes for his very real qualities as a cautious planner and administrator who leaned toward adorning the various states with great permanent monuments, such as dams and public buildings.

The last thing I intended to do was to open a Pandora's box of

Congressional debate over these two personalities. Only by my silence could I hope to keep this box closed. The truth was that I did not yet know myself which of these two men—if either—I would put in charge.

Still another potential debate needed to be kept as low-key as possible. I had indicated that I planned to set men to work at roughly fifty dollars a month, about twice what a dole would provide in most states. We found a nice name for this sum—a "security wage"—to distinguish it from a fair wage in private employment. But, sure enough, the A. F. of L. rang an alarm again, demanding that work-reliefers receive the "prevailing wage" for each area. That, of course, would never do. A worker on a "security wage" had to have an incentive for leaving public employment just as soon as he could find private employment.

The "prevailing wage" argument presented a devastating threat. While our right flank in Congress opposed work projects altogether, preferring the cheaper dole, the "prevailing wage" people threatened to crumble our left flank. Good men who should have known better, such as Senators Robert Wagner and Hugo Black, joined forces with the likes of Senator Huey Long, an opportunist who would promise anything at any public cost as long as it brought him closer to the White House; Senator Pat McCarran, who would have us print dollar bills promiscuously, backing them with as much silver as his Nevada constituents could dig; and Father Charles Coughlin, a Catholic priest in Michigan who was building a sizable radio following by fanning people's justified economic fears into flames of religious bigotry, a dangerously tempting alternative to practical solutions. These opportunists didn't surprise me, but good men such as Wagner and Black did. Why do such humanitarians so easily fall for quick-cure medicines—like the "prevailing wage"—when the medicine itself was sure to intensify the disease?

This pressure became even more threatening when a noisy left-wing group called the Unemployed Councils enlisted a Minnesota Farmer-Labor congressman, Ernest Lundeen, to introduce a thoroughly impractical bill providing "unemployment benefits"—handouts without work—to all unemployed workers *at prevailing wages*. These "benefits" would be dispensed by local committees of "rank and file" members of "workers' and farmers' organizations." At a Congressional committee hearing, a leading Communist official, Israel Amter, boasted that "the original writer of the workers' [Lundeen] bill was the Communist Party." Whether that was true or not, the Lundeen bill became a principal rallying point of radical activity and showed signs of gathering considerable Congressional support. (As things turned out, in 1936 we had to give way to the "prevailing wage" sentiment, but with a saving compromise. Work projects began to pay a prevailing daily wage, but for a reduced work week, usually three days. Thus we maintained the "security wage" principle, preserving a worker's incentive to find a full-time private job.)

While this battle was approaching its climax in the Senate, I put myself out of easy reach by going fishing in the Bahamas. The "strategy of silence" worked slowly but well. Congress was forced to lend me the decision-making powers along with giving me the $4.8 billion. On April 8, 1935, the passed bill was flown to Jacksonville and brought to me aboard the SS *Nourmahal*, where I happily signed it into law.[19]

On May 6, 1935, by executive order, I created the Works Progress Administration (WPA). To this day, Ickes has never stopped grousing about its name, resenting the easy confusion of WPA with his PWA. Well, if the confusion helped create a feeling of a unified back-to-work program, all to the good.

Now I did have to face choosing a head man. Ickes' fine record of keeping the PWA free of graft would be a reassuring asset. To leave him out would affront him. On the other hand, Hopkins' more daring style was what we needed.

The executive order established an Allotments Committee, with the all-important power of approving work projects. To the chairmanship of this key committee I appointed Ickes. But to make sure he would not hamstring it with too much caution, I decided to sit regularly with this committee myself. I gave Hopkins the title of WPA Administrator, assigning to him the seemingly less influential duty of seeing that work progressed according to schedule.

But my real plan was tucked away in the fine print of the executive order. Hopkins, as WPA Administrator, was empowered to "carry on small useful projects" to assure a maximum spread of jobs. Not even Ickes objected. And that was what changed the entire nature of our back-to-work effort.

While Ickes plodded away planning fine, but ever-so-slow, undertakings such as the Triborough Bridge and Boulder Dam, Hopkins shoveled out money on "small useful projects" in every direction.

As I expected, Ickes soon cried "thief!" Hopkins, he felt, was making off with projects that ought to come under Ickes' PWA. What was a "small useful project"? I got them to agree on a dividing line of $25,000. Hopkins then encouraged cities to subdivide their large projects into little pieces, each of $25,000 or less. At one overheated meeting, in August 1935, Hopkins blithely stated that "what was or wasn't a PWA project was a matter of opinion." Ickes insisted it was a "matter of fact," and grew impatient with me for not seeing the justice of his view. I stayed out of it. My concern was not "justice," but jobs. Hopkins was creating them.

The stormiest case in point was a sewer system for Atlanta, Georgia, obviously a multimillion-dollar project. Hopkins had accepted applications for it, divided almost block by block into $25,000 pieces. We decided to transfer that one to Ickes.

I stayed "neutral" in their feud—as long as Hopkins won most of the time. What Ickes had trouble getting through his head was that our main objective was not impressive construction but to get almost four million able-bodied men off relief and back to work in less than a year. Hopkins had a rule that a WPA worker had to be recruited from the relief rolls. Thus every WPA job reduced the relief rolls by one. I could not require the same of Ickes. Skilled workers, needed for many PWA projects, could not always be found on relief. Ickes' main counterargument was that big PWA projects produced "secondary" employment—private jobs in manufacturing and shipping of steel and concrete and so on. This was not good enough. I wanted direct evidence that each new job took a man directly off relief.

When, by the end of September, the rivalry between Harry the Hop and Harold the Ick grew a little too intense, I took them both with me on a long fishing cruise in the Pacific. There's nothing like salt water and sea air and the lively tug of a line to cool good men down.[20]

The "laziness" of WPA workers now became the target for New Deal opponents, as expressed by a new brand of jokes. Have you heard of the doctor who announced the discovery of a new medicine for cancer, but nobody can get any? The medicine is sweat from a WPA worker. Another was one I tried on Harry when he visited me at Warm Springs. Greeting him with a very long face, I told him I heard there had been a terrible accident on a WPA project up at Greenville—a worker had broken his hip. He had been leaning on a shovel so long that termites had eaten through its handle. So the stories went.

Let me tell you what several million lazy reliefers accomplished leaning on their shovels. By October 1937 they had built 1,634 schools and improved 16,421 others; built or improved more than twenty thousand gyms, stadiums, firehouses, hangars, courthouses, hospitals, and other public buildings. I could bore you with statistics of roads paved, bridges built, culverts dug, curbs laid, street signs hoisted, of runways, swimming pools, tennis courts, sewers, mosquito control, levees, fire alarms, and fish hatcheries. While I won't slow this long story with these statistics, I urge the reader to take at least a glance at the accomplishments of WPA included in Appendix II. The story of WPA—of men and women in trouble who wanted to give generously for what they got—is a story of accomplishment that changed the physical face of America.

But physical change is only part of the story. After construction workers built rural community centers, unemployed doctors and nurses and teachers gathered mothers in the centers and taught them child hygiene and nutrition. They organized rural visiting-nurse services and almost two thousand nursery schools. WPA workers collected books and magazines in the cities, then brought them to back-country districts, establishing what became known as bookmobiles; where passable roads ended, libraries were carried by pack horses.

The WPA conducted research into what was happening to "depression youth." Many youngsters had virtually become hoboes, wandering aimlessly from town to town, hitchhiking, riding freight trains. On one sample day in May 1935, fifty-four thousand young people were registered at transient camps and shelters for homeless youngsters operated by the WPA. How many hundreds of thousands were not registered?

On June 26, 1935, I established the National Youth Administration, with a first-year allocation of $41.2 million and $68 million the following year. Over several years, this tiny fraction of our relief fund went far in rescuing the lives of almost five million young people. For more than two million it provided a subsistence stipend of fifteen dollars a month for staying in college or high school while doing work in a school library or office or laboratory, or helping maintain school grounds and buildings. For a greater number, not in school, NYA provided work to introduce them to the simple disciplines of regular jobs.[21]

All this took some stretching of a "public works" law. Where I stretched it most, and in some ways most happily, was in authorizing the WPA Federal Arts Projects. Artists—musicians, actors, and writers, as well as painters and sculptors—have to eat and want to work, like everyone else. Why shouldn't they do what they do best, bringing enjoyment to others? So the WPA put artists to work at their art. They taught painting and clay modeling at night in schools and churches. Then we got another idea. As long as we were building schools, hospitals, and post offices, why not have professional artists on WPA paint murals and carve statues for their lobbies?

I hung some WPA paintings in my office and around the White House that, frankly, were more to my taste than many I saw in public lobbies. I think a good painting should be an inspiring and clear picture of something real, not an impressionistic distortion. The pictures I chose were mostly of ships, and I turned down several that, although beautiful, had incorrect rigging and construction details. Personally I cannot excuse such carelessness in the name of art. But I recognize that that is a matter of personal taste and many critics disagree with me.

The arts project that stirred up the most fuss in Congress, yet directly benefited most people, was the Federal Theater. It gave jobs to several thousands of actors and singers and jugglers who brought plays and operas and puppet shows and even a circus to more than thirty million children and adults, many of whom would not, even in the best of times, have had a chance to see live performances. Besides bringing Gilbert and Sullivan to the Ozarks, the Federal Theater produced current plays such as It Can't Happen Here, based on Sinclair Lewis' novel, with translations in Yiddish and Spanish. The English version became a hit on Broadway at low prices that a school student could afford. The Federal Theater got itself into trouble by putting on plays of leftish comment. Some congressmen used that to try to discredit the whole WPA. I could never understand how grown-up congressmen could get so riled up over play-acting, but we finally had to close down the Federal Theater.

My favorite arts undertaking was the Federal Writers Project. It was the least criticized, although it did some questionable things that caused us grief, such as a research project into the history of safety pins. (Poor Harry Hopkins had to defend that against needling by the press: "You may be interested in washing machines, somebody else in safety pins. Every one of those projects are worked out by technical people. . . .")

The biggest and finest undertaking of the writers was the American Guide Series, a guidebook for every state, many cities, and several of our major highways. These were no ordinary chamber-of-commerce guides. Local boasts were weeded out (335 cities had claimed to be "the crossroads of America") and many skeletons in the closet were thrown in (a former governor of Massachusetts wanted us to burn all the copies of his state's guide because forty-one lines of a 675-page book dared to recall the Sacco-Vanzetti case).

These books were a joy to thumb through. Where else would you find a nineteenth-century fisherman in Massachusetts, descendant of the Puritans, quoted: "Our ancestors came here not for religion. Their main end was to catch fish." Or read of a New England farmer who made a deal to board a 94-year-old Yankee for the rest of his life for a cash payment of $120, only to watch the boarder live to 116? Or of the two Maine paupers who escaped from the Bangor almshouse and, before being caught the next day, made $1,800 each by "selling" fictitious timberlands? How could one safely visit Missouri without first learning in the WPA guidebook that in the Ozarks it is a bad omen to encounter a cross-eyed person, especially at the fork of two pathways?

These guides were issued by a dozen private publishing houses at no cost to the government. One book, *The New England Hurricane,* about the 1938 disaster, became a best seller. I agree with Lewis Mumford, who called these books "the finest contribution to American patriotism that has been made in our generation."[22]

In 1937 *Fortune* magazine conducted a broad survey of individuals on relief and WPA in a cross section of cities. Contradicting many popular myths, *Fortune* summarized its findings, in part, as follows:

> Are the reliefers bums? No.
> Have they had much education? No.
> Did industry fire them because they could not do their jobs? No.
> Do they ask for too much help? No.
> Has industry taken many of them back since 1935? Yes, almost half.

Are those remaining on relief "marginal men" in that they are unfit for employment by lack of skill, age, or disability? Yes.

Are these "marginal men" unemployable? The unskilled, no; the aged and disabled, probably yes.

Is the WPA "spoiling" them and wasting the taxpayers' money? No.

Are the local communities doing as good a job of giving direct relief to these unemployables as the federal government did two years ago? No. . . .

A great proportion of the people left on WPA rolls did need kindly prodding, the constant help of a social worker, close work supervision. For some of these people WPA jobs were the best they had ever had. WPA supervisers sometimes had to teach the simplest forms of personal reliability and cleanliness, how to wash hair and clothes, how to clean house, how to tell time.

Some reactionary editorialists cited this as "proof" that WPA workers were worthless. I offer it as proof that the WPA helped provide an important human service. I do not know what will become of these people who have been left behind in our most ordinary ways of learning to do ordinary things. They require understanding and patience. But surely their salvation is not in keeping them dependent. Perhaps we will need a generation or two of something like the WPA, not to cure a depression but to provide simple jobs and simple life instruction to those at the end of the line, people who have been somehow left out of our common experience. They must be offered a proper way to live. The proper way is through some appropriate work, not deepening the dark holes of their lives by consigning them to a permanent dole.

Every step of the way, I had to keep fighting for that idea. As late as November 29, 1935, I had to scold businessmen for their growing opposition to work relief. At Atlanta, Georgia, I sounded my old theme:

"I can realize that gentlemen in well-warmed and well-stocked clubs will discourse on the expense of Government and the suffering they are going through. . . . Some of these same gentlemen tell me that a dole would be more economical than work relief. That is true. But the men who tell me that have, unfortunately, too little contact with the true America to realize that in this business of relief we are dealing with properly self-respecting Americans to whom a mere dole outrages every instinct of individual independence. Most Americans want to give something for what they get. That something, which in this case is honest work, is the saving barrier between them and moral disintegration. I propose to build that barrier high and keep it high."[23]

The constant assaults sustained by the WPA never seemed to harm the good reputation of the PWA. That was in great part due to Harold Ickes, who, although cantankerous, was a peerless public servant. He supervised construction contracts amounting to billions of dollars, yet not the slightest suggestion of impropriety or scandal ever touched the PWA.

Every state and almost every county had a PWA project, more than twenty-five thousand in all. These included about 70 per cent of all school-building construction, 62 per cent of hospitals and 65 per cent of courthouses, city halls, and sewage-disposal plants. PWA created the port of Brownsville, Texas, gave Kansas City a municipal auditorium, Denver a water system. After the earthquake of 1933, it rebuilt the schools of Los Angeles. It connected Key West to the mainland with roads and bridges. Besides financing the great dams of the TVA, PWA tamed the Columbia River with the Grand Coulee and Bonneville, the Colorado with Boulder, and the upper Missouri with the Fort Peck Dam. To the Triborough Bridge and the Lincoln Tunnel in New York, PWA also added the Queens Midtown Tunnel under the East River.

Some of these more spectacular projects wound up costing the Treasury nothing, for they were to pay for themselves in motorist tolls or sales of electric power. Self-liquidating projects were very popular—even with Republicans and newspaper publishers. And, oh, we could have had many more "self-liquidating" projects if we had taken all comers. One city wanted a "self-liquidating" maternity hospital. Our investigation showed it would pay for itself if every woman in town became pregnant within two decades, which the city fathers were not prepared to guarantee. One application for a "self-liquidating" graveyard would have required the death of everyone in its town within seventeen years. The most lunatic proposition of all came from a mathematician who suggested we spend one hundred million dollars to finance a round-trip passenger-carrying rocket to the moon. Our recovery program, however, was national, not interplanetary. And for every idea too big there was always one too small. A middle-western mayor wanted the PWA to redecorate his office. A Kansas preacher asked for funds to buy new Bibles for his church. We had to disappoint both.

In one instance we had trouble getting rid of money. We had to twist the arm of the Pennsylvania Railroad before it would consent to borrow eighty million dollars of the PWA fund to hire unemployed men to electrify its line between New York and Washington and complete the 30th Street Station in Philadelphia. Their reluctance reminded me of the boneheadedness of the southern power companies. It turned out to be one of the most profitable investments the railroad ever made.

One of the first PWA undertakings, very close to my heart because of my experience in the Great War, was to start rebuilding the Navy. PWA built the aircraft carriers *Yorktown* and *Enterprise,* as well as four heavy cruisers, four light cruisers, many destroyers, submarines, airplanes, and military airports. This came to an end in 1935, however; Senator Borah, a pacifist, let his nice sentiments overcome his good sense when he pushed through a rule forbidding military work by the PWA. I think that was a foolish mistake, but I had to go along.

Our practical goal of recovery required constant attention to practical politics. Harold Ickes argued with me not to approve building the Fort Peck Dam in Montana, claiming that other places were more in need of the seventy-five million dollars. Perhaps true. But I could not overlook the political fact that Senator Burton K. Wheeler of Montana wanted the dam—and Senator Wheeler was chairman of the very powerful Senate Interstate Commerce Committee. The best way I could help unemployed workers in Tennessee and California was to keep Senator Wheeler, like Senator Borah, securely on our side. By the same reasoning, I don't hesitate now to affirm that one major factor in my approving the great Columbia River dams, Grand Coulee and Bonneville, was to oblige—and obligate—the Senate Republican leader, Charles McNary of Oregon, whose support at some critical moment I might need to call upon.

There was one additional way in which I was determined to use public works. PWA was putting up well over a billion dollars for hundreds of sewage-disposal projects; still-additional sums were being spent by WPA. In 1937 I ordered the following:

MEMORANDUM FOR HON. HARRY L. HOPKINS:

Will you please tell all your Regional Directors that as a matter of administration policy no further WPA projects will be approved for improving or repairing or adding to sewers which dump into any creek or river? . . . The same order has gone out to the PWA Administrator.

This is of the utmost importance.

F.D.R.

Toward the same end I tried to work my personal influence among my own neighbors, but less successfully. On a visit to Hyde Park I raised a complaint to the press:

"For twenty-five years I have been talking to the people of Poughkeepsie about two subjects. The first was to quit dumping raw sewage into the Hudson River and, second, to get a decent supply of pure drinking water—not out of the Hudson River . . . but nobody has done it. . . . Perhaps it will be another twenty-five years before something is done."[24]

BACKGROUND MEMORANDUM TO PART V

"He lived his own life exactly as he wanted it."—Eleanor Roosevelt

Now to break through the more difficult part of the "enigma," not that of political philosophy (how he became a small-d democrat) but of personal character.

On a mass scale he inspired faith, from a few associates extreme loyalty. Yet some who worked with him at close range were imbued with less than trust of their leader.

He was a sayer of bold political truths, yes, but also of half-truths. At times, lest truth get out, he could infuriate by saying nothing. And he could deceive. Tell lies? A clever man seldom has to lie. He circles around the truth, conveying an impression that he will do *this,* never explicitly saying he will—then doing *that.* And how adeptly he could evade the statement of a painful truth to a man's face. Examples: sending MacArthur and Dern to the Pacific to avoid the discomfort of their being around when he appoints Malin Craig Army Chief of Staff; giving the impression of support to public works in order to buy support for his NRA, all the time calculating ways to divert the public-works fund to unspecified purposes; giving the "top job" in WPA to Ickes, yet through the "fine print" delivering the significant power to Hopkins.

Evasiveness, duplicity, underhandedness are generally taken as imperfections of character. Perhaps so, but they may also be regarded—especially in the case of F.D.R.—as skills of a high order in the fine art of ambiguity.

Ambiguity, no matter how else it may be regarded, can be an invaluable tool of politics. Used for the public good, it is a tool for getting a great deal done while losing as few friends as possible for the next stage of accomplishment. It is what enables a national leader to line up mutually antagonistic constituencies behind him, emphasizing one part of his program to farmers, another to union workers, this part to shopkeepers, that part to manufacturers, trying to lose none while appealing to the others. It is a technique for assembling a majority out of contending minorities.

Ambiguity enables a man like F.D.R. to tell *this* part of the truth to one senator or cabinet member, *that* part to another, yet tell the whole truth as he sees it to nobody. It is the art of keeping one's own counsel while giving others the exhilarating impression they are "on the inside." In this art F.D.R. was peerless.

When a man plays a game of concealment, his technique must itself remain concealed. One of the extremely rare times F.D.R. openly acknowledged that a technique existed was at a lunch in 1936 with Henry Morgenthau during Roosevelt's opposition to the Patman soldier-bonus bill. While in 1935 Roosevelt's opposition had been adamant, in 1936 it was less so. Although planning to veto the bill again, he was not unwilling for it to be passed over his veto, because, according to Raymond Moley, the bonus might "stimulate the economy so that it would be very good by election time." Morgenthau, who did not know of this change of heart, told what he was doing to shore up Congressional opposition to the bill, later noting in his diary, "I was rather surprised to find a sort of coolness." Roosevelt told Morgenthau:

"You know we may have to compromise."

"What do you mean?"

"Well, we might have to pay the present bonus."

"Mr. President, there is nothing like that in your speech. You say definitely that you are against the bonus."

"Why, yes, but how can I tell what kind of bill they may pass? Patman asked me point-blank this morning if I was against all bonus legislation or whether I had an open mind and I told him that I had an open mind because how could I know what they might pass."

Morgenthau, among cabinet members not the most attuned to political pliability, says he "had a sort of sinking feeling and found myself sort of gradually crumpling up." He responded:

"If you want me to go on, please do not talk that way to me, because I am building a bonfire of support for you."

Roosevelt, with a smile, replied:

"Let's agree that I will not talk to you about any compromise if you will not talk to me about any bonfire." Roosevelt wasn't asking Morgenthau to desist. The bonfire was all right—as long as F.D.R. could pretend not to *know* about it. "In other words," the President explained benignly, "never let your left hand know what your right is doing."

"Which hand am I, Mr. President?"

"My right hand," Roosevelt assured him. Then he added, "But I keep my left hand under the table."

Morgenthau, with a trace of exasperation, wrote in his diary that this was "the most frank expression of the real F.D.R. that I ever listened to and the real way that he works."

What stirred Roosevelt to start perfecting this art of ambiguity, which was later, in the crosscurrents of Washington, to serve him so well? To probe its source we must go into the making of fundamental personality. Ambiguity is a deeply implanted configuration of behavior learned early in simple form which becomes a matrix of the complex behavior of an adult.

We can perceive the boy learning the art of ambiguity in the torrent of schoolboy letters to Mama. Twice a week, year after year, he writes, full of chatter and newsiness. He tells Mama *everything*. Everything except real thoughts, feelings, yearnings, fears, and self-doubts of a lively adolescent, emotions he is to live out his life without discussing with anyone. What exudes from the letters is a portrait of a boy in the act of creating a deep privacy, a loneliness, a kind of separate life beneath the show-all-and-tell-all of his letters. This becomes most strikingly apparent as we trace, through the letters, the manner in which young Franklin experiences the emergence, overwhelming to any adolescent boy, of sexuality. The pattern we find in this most tender of areas is one that continues to govern, with modifications, his relations with the women of his life through all his days—and is a guide to the way he dealt publicly with men.

Approaching his seventeenth birthday Franklin, at Groton School, has written fully 166 letters over more than two years to "Dearest Mama and Papa" (or some other close relative) before his first mention of a male-female relationship as such. This first reference is hardly noteworthy, except that it is so late to be the first:

> Groton School
> Nov. 30, 1898
>
> . . . By the way, last Monday Mr. Sturgis [a master at Groton and Franklin's half-uncle] came back after an absence of over a week and announced his engagement—! to Miss Barnes of N.Y. He was covered with rice by the V and VI Forms and we compelled him to make a speech! He was awfully bashful, but he soon got over it, especially after he was again raided by the rest of the school! I suppose the dirty squaws will be pleased to hear of it! . . .

Well, perhaps there is one small thing worth noting: the nervous exclamation points. Occasionally, one of his letters from school might contain one or two, but not in such a breathless series of sentences since he was six years old ("we coasted! yesterday   nothing dangerous yet, look out for tomorrow!!").

Less than a week later, December 4, he refers again to the tense subject of girls—this time, girls for himself. This is the first appearance of what is to become a remarkably consistent pattern. He makes an elaborate display of indifference. Too bored to be bothered, he asks Mama to think up partners—and, in fact, soon begins asking her to make the arrangements with them. Invariably when he refers to a girl who is not a relative or Hyde Park neighbor, not someone well known to Mama, she is an "ice-cart," a "pill," or a "brat." This might not be at all unusual for a nervous boy making his first dates. But in Franklin's case, he continues—and expands—the pattern without letup through his years at Groton and well into his days at Harvard.

What we are witnessing is the unfolding of a subtle and complex game with Mama. It is a game of power. Sensing her wish to exercise power over his social life and not wishing to challenge it, he learns to keep reassuring her that everything will be exactly as she wants. By allowing her to manipulate him he is learning to manipulate her. One day she is to find that he has everything exactly as *he* wants—but that gets us ahead of our story.

The quotations from his letters that follow are not chosen selectively to verify this theme. They are *all* his references to girls and dances and teas in his remaining days at Groton and Harvard. To begin, the portions of his letters regarding his first socially active Christmas season of 1898, starting with the first one, of December 4, read:

> I have not yet had an answer from Laura [Delano, a cousin] about the Orange dance, but I suppose she can do it. I wish you would think up some decent partner for me for the N.Y. dance, to which I suppose I will be invited, so that I can get somebody early, and not get palmed off on some ice-cart like the [name deleted]* girl!! Who do you think it would be nice to have at Hyde Park with the crowd? You had better send me a list first and I will try to add to it if necessary.

> Dec. 6, 1898
> Just a line to say that I am all mixed up. I got a letter this morning from Cousin May Soley (enclosed) inviting me to dinner the *28th*

* Deletion of names here and in subsequent letters is by Elliott Roosevelt, editor of his father's collected correspondence.

the *date of the Dodworth dance.* . . . Now your letter of Sunday says the Orange dance is the *28th also!*

Laura has accepted for the Orange shindy—What is to be done??! please let me know if I am to accept the Soley invite. . . .

Dec. 8, 1898

Just a line to thank you for yours of the 6th explaining about the holidays. I promptly answered Mrs. Soleys invitation accepting it, but as I was in a quandary as to whom to ask for the N.Y. dance, and not caring at all, I drew lots and and [sic] the fateful die fell on Mary Newbold [his Hyde Park neighbor since childhood], so I wrote at once. . . .

Dec. 11, 1898

Dearest Mama and Papa,

More shindies to attend to! The enclosed came last night, and what is to be done about it? If it is the date of the Orange dance (27th) of course I cannot go, but otherwise I might as well. I wish you could either decline or accept it as you think best. If you accept and there is to be a German at it, I think it would be a good idea for you to ask Helen [Roosevelt, daughter of his half-brother] for me, for the German. It will save time and it is only two weeks off. [Name deleted] cannot dance at the Dodworth thing, (just as well); so I have written asking Muriel [Delano Robbins, a cousin]. I don't want to get left with the [name deleted] girl as I did two years ago to my great and everlasting regret! . . . I am so glad Aunt Jennie's dear lambs are to be allowed to come and hope Muriel can come too. I cannot think of anyone to get up here, as most of the boys are already engaged that I would like to have, so I hope you will be able to find someone else. How about Teddy Robinson and Eleanor Roosevelt [both distant cousins]? They would go well and help to fill out chinks.

Dec. 14, 1898

. . . Yours from N.Y. just come [sic], and you say nothing about the Street dance, only that you have declined the Appleton one on the 27th. I also got a letter from the [name deleted] brat (!!!) accepting with thanks ! for the 28th & one from Muriel declining with thanks for the 28th. So you see I am all clear for the Dodworth dance but quite in the dark about the Streets'.

So in his first season of active "dating," he has assured and reassured Mama of his preference for girls approved (indeed chosen) by her; all eligible young ladies not in the immediate clan of relatives and neighbors being pills and brats. Soon after Christmas—on January 20, 1899, ten days before his seventeenth birthday—the ultimate reassurance to Mama when he requests: ". . . could you send the little picture of yourself in the little silver heart-shaped frame on my bureau, as I want it to put on my desk here."

For most of the ensuing year at Groton his stream of letters returns to schoolwork; sports; requests for clothing, toiletries, and medicines; and his enthusiasm for bird watching. (Biographer Frank Freidel comments: "Even in his final term there he was far more excited about birds than about girls.") Yet girls, for all his studied indifference, are an explosive topic. It is safe to explode if the girl is someone else's. Comes this bursting letter of October 4, 1899:

> . . . What do you think is the latest news?
> ### Mr. Griswold is engaged
> !!!!!!!!!!!!!!!!!
> It came out this morning and there was a celebration!!!!!! He was carried round by the VI form and cheered, etc. Tell Helen & tell her to break the news gently to Taddy & Miss Fromont. I feel that this is quite enough excitement for one letter so will write you the name of "she" tomorrow. . . .

> Oct. 6, 1899
> . . . The future Mrs. Griswolds name is Miss Brewer, of New Haven, & her father is a Yale prof. He (Push) met her abroad & with a large party travelled thro' Palestine together. Push broke the news to Mr. Billings first by holding up her photo and saying laconically "She's mine"!!!!!!!!! . . .

> Dec. 10, 1899
> . . . Dont you think we had better ask up one or two girls for the 2nd? A Draper girl or anyone, I don't know any so will trust to you entirely. Only not the [name deleted] brat! please!! . . .

He is turning eighteen when we find that not every encounter with the subject of girls brings tension. At an all-male school a theatrical production may require that boys be cast as girls. To some boys this might bring discomfiture, but that can be overridden by a large display of embarrassment or by burlesquing the part. Not so for Franklin, in whom the opportunity evokes sincere eagerness—followed by frankly stated disappointment:

Jan. 16, 1900

. . . I have tried another part in the play, a women's, but shall not have it, as it is being saved for Kerr Rainsford, who will be back from the operation the first week in February! I think it rather hard as there are so few girls and I am sure I could do as well as Kerr. As it is now I doubt if I get a good part at all, and Mr. Cushing is being bullied by his Boston friends (!) to give *them* all the best parts! . . .

Before filing that letter away, Mama corrected "women's" to "woman's."

The following October, Franklin is a freshman at Harvard. One of his letters home has had three sentences deleted by his family from the version available to researchers. Son Elliott describes the deletion as "a reference to his half-nephew, who had just contracted an alliance judged unfortunate by the society of the time." Elliott permits a partial quotation of Franklin's comment. It is a haughty censure that befits his new collegiate manliness—and sure to please Mama: "It will be well for him . . . to go to parts unknown . . . and begin life anew."

As Christmas approaches, he resumes the annual bother of the dance season. One might expect that a young man of nineteen is vastly different from himself at seventeen, especially where girls are concerned. But not so for Franklin. The game played in the previous letters, of making sure of Mama's approval of his girls, thus insuring her approval of himself, is an established arrangement:

December 3, 1900

My dearest Mama & Papa,

. . . It is very good of you to bother so about my dances, I am writing Ellen & Laura, and as I dont like the awful [name deleted] pill & don't know the [name deleted] pill I shall ask either Alice Draper or Jean Reid for the Metropolitan. Please answer the enclosed or keep it, I dont know what it means. . . .

For the first time, he favorably mentions two girls not related to him. Knowing Mama will find them highly acceptable, he submits their names to her anyhow to reassure her of his good judgment. Alice Draper is the sister of a Groton schoolmate; Jean Reid, the daughter of Whitelaw Reid, editor of the New York *Tribune*. The final sentence, however, is the annual echo that this business of social invitations is a bore.

That season's dances were not to be attended. Five days after the writing of the December 3 letter, Papa James died at seventy-two in New York. "In the immediate and ensuing years," Elliott notes in the collected letters, Sara "turned more than ever toward her son for a replacing com-

panionship." Ten months later, Franklin mentions a resumption of his social life. The pattern is as ever in this P.S. to Mama:

Oct. 16, 1901

What do you think of my taking M.D.R. [Muriel Delano Robbins]
Helen [Roosevelt] & Mary Newbold to see the Harvard-West Point
game at West Point Saturday afternoon. . . . If you approve make
arrangements as to trains. . . .

If you approve? These are two relatives and a neighbor with whom he
shared a tutor as a child. He is almost twenty years old, away from home
for four school years. Does there churn, in that chamber of the mind
where thoughts are suppressed, the faintest yearning for sexual independence? If it's there, young Franklin D. Roosevelt is getting a lot of exercise
in what is to become the style of his presidency, a virtuoso skill at "keeping his own counsel."

The established pattern of unreproachable dates and reporting each
one to Mama makes its final appearance with a single sentence during the
following year: ". . . I am asking Mary Newbold to go to the Yale game
if she is in Boston then. . . ." Not that he suddenly seizes independence.
Instead, Mama's influence is about to be exercised at closer range. Heart-
broken by her husband's death and lonely in the memory-laden Hyde
Park mansion, Mama, who didn't like sending her only son away to school
in the first place, now decides to follow him there. She takes a small house
in Cambridge for the winter of 1902, and again in 1903. There is a hint
that Franklin is not overly taken by this turn of events. His letters, which
have always dripped with solicitude for her every concern, make no mention of this important step until the final sentence of the final letter before
her move:

Jan. 9, 1902

. . . I am sorry I can't see to anything about the house, but I shall be
otherwise engaged—Will drop a line tomorrow if I have time.[1]

Let's pause and take stock. What we have in the foregoing is the classic
story line of the mama's boy. It is of a man who may make occasional
tentative moves at acquiring a proper mate but, never finding one who
measures up to the womanly devotion he already knows, stays tied to
mama. If Franklin's letters were the true—the whole—expression of the
emerging man, that is what we might reasonably expect.

But beneath what he writes and says he is learning to keep that left hand
under the table. To get a portrait of the man that was emerging, we must

look at the man who emerged. As an adult political leader, when people come to him, friend or opponent, no matter what they say, he nods. If they come to press for a commitment he won't make, he starts talking first, keeps talking, evading the unwanted subject. In speeches, time and again, when he gets to the crux of an issue on which he is unsure of support— what he is trying to persuade his audience to—his favorite phrase is "You and I know. . . ."

The essence of Franklin Roosevelt's style—a style he learned in coping with Mama—is to sidestep personal confrontation. When you differ with an adversary, face to face, you do not state it; you state only the portion of the issue on which you can agree. You say that part of the truth that will dispel the apprehensions of your adversary; then, when you know what you want to do and the circumstances are right, you do it.

Mama taught this technique, unwittingly but assiduously. Confrontation with her was futile, pointless, hopeless. She does not hear what she does not want to hear. Not having heard it, she goes on believing—as every family member who describes her asserts—that Franklin "can do no wrong." (From her book: "He had shortcomings, as many as other youngsters of his age, I am certain, but errors of judgment just did not happen to be among them.") To press an "error of judgment"—any disagreement—is to challenge that unquestioned approval, its lovely comfort and warmth.

So the way to manage difference is to appear to agree. "Surrendering" to her manipulation, he devises a countermanipulation. You differ by agreeing, then doing what you have to do. Also, you learn to keep your own counsel until you make your move.

A classic mama's boy forever bound by her devotion? The letters alone give no hint of the underlife that the manipulation and countermanipulation are about to bring forth in young F.D.R. At least Mama has no hint of it, and its appearance is devastating.

In the spring of 1902, following Mama's first season at Cambridge, they are riding together in a parlor car up the Hudson from New York City to Hyde Park. A restless Franklin strolls through the train, comes upon his cousin Eleanor in a coach, and invites her to visit Mama in the parlor car. He doesn't know Eleanor very well. When he was about four, Mama noted in her diary, Franklin was enlisted at a party to carry two-year-old Eleanor piggyback. While they must have met later at family parties, Eleanor's first recollection of noticing him was at the Christmas party in 1898 to which she was invited to "help fill out chinks." He is said to have remarked to his mother at about that time, "Cousin Eleanor has a very good mind."

Her attractions are more than that. She is not at all the "ugly duckling" her mother convinced her she was, but a graceful, willowy eighteen-year-old trained in deportment at an English school. Furthermore, she is the openly declared "favorite niece" of the incumbent President of the United States, to whom Franklin, as a Harvard *Crimson* editorialist, has become supremely devoted. His attentions on that train ride are to be remembered by Eleanor all her life. To Sara, still in black with a veil that draped to the ground, the incident is merely pleasant.

Something is awakening in the young man, even if surprisingly late. On May 27, 1902, the first hint of a peacock emerges in a letter from Cambridge to Mama. A Boston dentist has repaired a chipped front tooth:

> . . . I feel like a new person and have already been proposed to by three girls. My best friends don't recognize me and say "Who *is* that handsome fellow?"

This new teasing of Mama may be cover for a more specific awakening. Eleanor's name begins to appear with increasing frequency in his sketchy Line-A-Day diary, especially beginning in the autumn of 1902, when he notes seeing her at the New York horse show, and two weeks later, following Christine Roosevelt's dance, the entry "Lunched with Eleanor." Before returning to Hyde Park for Christmas, he slips away after a shopping tour with Mama for "tea with Eleanor." In Washington for New Year's festivities, he attends a White House tea with Alice, the President's daughter— with whom Eleanor happens to be staying. At the New Year's Day reception he stands beside Eleanor in the "inner circle" as thousands file through to shake hands with the President. Then dinner with the President and "to theatre and sit near Eleanor. . . . Very interesting day." A month later, half-brother Rosy invites Eleanor among the celebrants of Franklin's twenty-first birthday—"very jolly!" That spring, Franklin takes a lively interest in visiting Groton for sporting events, seeing old friends. By coincidence, Eleanor also betakes herself there, to visit Hall, her younger brother. She is always accompanied, at her grandmother's insistence, by a maid.

Not all of Eleanor's hours are chaperoned and sheltered. In New York she is involved in the newly formed Junior League. She and Jean Reid are "teaching calisthenics and fancy dancing" to children of New York's Lower East Side at the Rivington Street Settlement House. As Eleanor was later to recall it, "Jean often came and went in her carriage, but I took the elevated railway or the Fourth Avenue street car and walked across from the Bowery. Needless to say, the streets filled with foreign looking people, crowded and dirty, filled me with a certain amount of terror." Sometime that spring, unbeknownst to Mama, there is a visit by Franklin to the alien, exciting world of the Lower East Side—and to Eleanor. The children gather around Eleanor, asking her "if he was my 'feller,' an expression which meant nothing to me at that time." She takes him on a visit to a child who is at home sick, later recalling, "He was absolutely shaken when he saw the cold-water tenement where the child lived, and kept saying he simply could not believe human beings lived that way." They are broadening each other's worlds; he hers by attentions she has never known; she his by an aura of worldly wisdom he never encountered at Hyde Park or Groton or Harvard Yard.

In April Mama offers Franklin a summer trip to Europe, a gift for his coming Harvard graduation. He is obviously torn, but over what is not easy to discern. Has the interest in Eleanor so blossomed that he doesn't want to leave? Yet he wants to go. Is his concern for leaving Mama as heart-rending as he would like it to appear? But he *does* want to go. What comes out is a solicitude, finely tuned by years of practice, that approaches double talk:

> April 27, 1903
> . . . I have been thinking over the month's trip abroad, and as I can't come to any decision myself, I really want you to tell what you would want me to do. I have told you what I feel about it: that it would in all probability be good for me, and a delightful experience; but that I don't want to be away from you for four weeks in the summer; also that I don't want to go unless you could make up your mind not to care at all. I feel that really it would be a very thoroughly selfish proceeding on my part. . . .

He lets himself be "persuaded" to go. At an end-of-school party at Hyde Park in June, Franklin's usual companions are augmented by Eleanor. Franklin notes that they all walked to the river "in the rain," played tennis and blind man's buff. There may have been other walks with Eleanor, perhaps even without her maid, for the weekend is long. She has arrived on Saturday and Franklin takes her to the train on Tuesday. Dashing back to Cambridge, Franklin picks up his diploma, earned in three years, returning for another house party. Eleanor is there (with maid), as well as those described in Sara's diary as "my six young people." A week later, Sara and Franklin have tea with Eleanor at Tivoli-on-Hudson, home of Eleanor's grandmother, with whom the parentless girl lives.

Before departing for Europe, Franklin invites Eleanor to visit Campobello immediately upon his return. There is no hint, in her diary or any letter or any known conversation, that Mama reads the slightest significance into this interest. Nor is Franklin showing the slightest diversion from his accustomed solicitude. On the day of sailing aboard the *Celtic,* he writes Mama not one, but two letters before the final mail pickup at Sandy Hook, even starting a third, to be mailed from England. The first of these says:

July 24, 1903

. . . Goodbye dear Mummy I am longing for Aug. 25. Dont worry about me—I always land on my feet—but wish so much you were with me. . . .

In his first letter from England, the peacock surfaces again, in a lavish display for Mama such as he has never put on. Writing about a "tea on a heavenly terrace" of British acquaintances, Franklin, at twenty-one, preens the feathers of some new-felt manhood:

. . . As I knew the uncivilized English custom of never introducing people I had about three fits when we arrived & got at once separated from Aline & her Father—but I walked up to the best looking dame in the bunch & said "howdy?" Things at once went like oil & I was soon having flirtations with three of the nobility at the same time. I had a walk with the hostesses' [sic] niece over the entire house which was really perfect in every way—I mean the house—although the walk wasn't bad—I will have to wait to tell you about it in person—again I mean the house. Then I inspected the gardens with another 'chawmer' & ended up by jollying the hostess herself all by her lonesome for ten minutes while a uniformed Lord stood by & never got in anything except an occasional "aw" or an "I sy." We stayed about an hour and I made about 15 bosom friends & got on so well with about 10 of these that I found out their names! . . .

Shades of the White House Franklin D. Roosevelt! He "chawmed" everybody, first one, then three, then ten. They are not participants, but audience; even the uniformed Lord "never got in anything." No longer fluffing off the girls as "ice-carts" and "pills," he teases Mama with their attractiveness—and with his—yet all the while careful to assure her, I charm them, but you and I know that it's merely a game.

While putting on this display for Mama, his far more private enterprise is coming off successfully and coolly. Next fall, he is back at Harvard for postgraduate courses:

Nov. 10, 1903

Dearest Ma—

. . . I will meet you at 10 West 43rd on Sat. at about 7.30 a.m. Eleanor is going to get four seats on the 3.38 up river so don't get any. . . .

By now, Franklin is sending Eleanor poetry—at a time when, as she later described it, "You knew a man very well before you wrote or received a letter from him . . . and to have signed oneself in any other way than 'Very sincerely yours,' would have been not only a breach of good manners but an admission of feeling which was entirely inadmissible. . . . And the idea that you would permit any man to kiss you before you were engaged to him never even crossed my mind."

The poem he sent is forever lost, for almost thirty-five years later Eleanor was to burn all of Franklin's love letters to her. Nor was the Library of Congress, at the request of Eleanor's biographer, able to identify the poem from a line she quotes, suggesting that it may be of Franklin's own composition. Calling the poem "splendid," she comments, "but what ideals you have to live up to! I like 'Fear nothing and be faithful unto death,' but I must say I wonder how many of 'we poor mortals' could act up to that!"

He invites her to the Harvard-Yale game at Cambridge on Saturday, November 21. They are chaperoned by Muriel Robbins' brother Warren, a Harvard student. Franklin writes in his diary:

> . . . Eleanor and I walk to the Library, see the pictures, and then walk up Beacon Hill. I out to lunch in Cambridge and lead the cheering of the Harvard-Yale game, 16-0, but our team does well. Show Eleanor my room and see them off to Groton.

Next morning he rejoins Eleanor at Groton, attending church, and then to lunch. That night, overcome with clandestine delight, the young man of almost twenty-two marks his diary with a secret code (cracked almost seventy years later by three Boston scholars). Deciphered, his entry says: "After lunch I have a never to be forgotten walk to the river with my darling."

On that walk, Franklin has asked Eleanor to marry him.[2]

Almost immediately, Eleanor, who returns to New York quivering with excitement, must cope with new countermanipulations—deceptions—of Mama. Eleanor writes him:

> . . . I have been thinking of many things which you and I must talk over on Sunday. Only one thing I want to tell you now. Please don't tell your Mother you have to come down to see Mr. Marvin on Sunday, because I never want her to feel that she has been deceived & if you have to tell her I would rather you said you were coming to see me for she need not know why. Don't be angry with me Franklin for saying this, & of course you must do as you think best. . . .

How deeply Franklin's passion ran beneath the prose and poetry of his letters we can never know. But Eleanor, in her autobiography, tells us of hers: "I had a great curiosity about life and a desire to participate in every experience that might be the lot of woman. There seemed to me to be a necessity for hurry; without rhyme or reason I felt the urge to be a part of the stream of life . . . though I was only nineteen, it seemed an entirely natural thing and I never even thought that we were both rather young and inexperienced. I came back from Groton . . . and asked Cousin Susie whether she thought I cared enough, and my grandmother, when I told her, asked me if I was sure I was really in love. I solemnly answered 'yes,' and yet I know now that it was years later before I understood what being in love was or what loving really meant."

Franklin, meanwhile, lost little time—a week—in visiting Mama to break the news. Her journal entry: "Franklin gave me quite a startling announcement."

Startling indeed. Bringing off this romance under her nose, he had kept his counsel so completely that even Lathrop Brown, his Harvard roommate, knew nothing about it. Was this a feat of his now-mastered skill, or merely a sign of Mama's capacity not to see what she did not want to know? Unquestionably both. Mama was later to write in *My Boy Franklin:* ". . . It probably surprised us only because he had never been in any sense a ladies' man. I don't believe I remember ever hearing him talk about girls or even a girl. . . ."

Some Roosevelt observers have speculated that Mama's shock and open opposition to the marriage grew from her disapproval of Eleanor's "flawed" heritage: an alcoholic father and her mother's two hard-drinking brothers. The more likely reason is expressed many years later by the couple's eldest son, James: "The basic trouble was that Granny, though she would have denied it indignantly had anyone accused her of it, never quite forgave Mother for marrying her boy, Franklin, right out of college at a time when Granny was looking forward to enjoying a few years with Franklin all to herself."

Having assumed that Franklin was back with his books at Harvard, Sara indignantly notes in her journal upon going to her Manhattan town house, "I find Franklin still in New York." She adds next day, after Franklin escorts Eleanor to an audience with her, "I had a long talk with the dear child." They consent to Mama's demand that no one else be informed of their plan to marry.

Franklin's next letter to Mama is as solicitous as ever—but with a new firmness. He is unfailingly sweet, but not giving an inch:

Dec. 4, 1903

Dearest Mama—

. . . Dearest Mama—I know what pain I must have caused you and you know I wouldn't do it if I really could have helped it—mais tu sais, me voilà! Thats all that could be said—I know my mind, have known it for a long time, and know that I could never think otherwise: Result: I am the happiest man just now in the world; likewise the luckiest— And for you, dear Mummy, you know that nothing can ever change what we have always been & always will be to each other—only now you have two children to love & to love you—and Eleanor as you know will always be a daughter to you in every true way— . . .

But sweetness won't do. Mama won't give an inch either. She insists that Franklin and Eleanor not be seen in New York together, apparently still hoping that the marriage plan will collapse before it is announced. She insists, in fact, that he betake himself to the shelter and influence of Hyde Park. This demand she conveys to a torn Eleanor, who relays it by letter to Franklin:

Boy darling,

I have rather a hard letter to write you tonight & I don't quite know how to say what I must say & I am afraid I am going to give you some trouble, however I don't see how I can help it.

I went to the apartment this morning & saw your Mother there for a few minutes & then we went out together & had a long talk. She is coming down next Friday to meet you & she wants us to lunch & dine with her & then she wants you to go to Hyde Park with her Sunday morning. Helen and Cousin Rosie [half-brother James] have been asking when you were coming home. She thinks they are sure to hear you are in New York & say that you are loafing & never coming home & she also says that if we go to church together we are sure to be seen. She also thinks that you ought to go home on account of the place, & your interest in it. She asked me to write you & tell you all this dear because I think it only fair. Of course it will be a terrible disappointment to me not to have you on Sunday as I have been looking forward to it & every moment with you is very precious as we have so little of each other but I don't want you to stay if you feel it is your duty to go up & I shall understand of course. I realize that we may be seen if we go to church together, but we will have to choose some small church. However, I suppose your Mother feels more strongly on the subject than I do & I am afraid I must leave the whole thing to you to decide. Whatever you do I shall know to be right but I don't think your Mother quite realizes what a very hard thing she was asking me to do for I am hungry for every moment of your time, but you mustn't let what I want interfere with what you feel to be right dearest.

Now for the second thing. Cousin Sally [Mama] said she did not think you would want to go on a trip now & she said she thought of taking a house in Boston for three months. She said she hoped I would come & stay once or twice during that time but if she took the house she did not want you to be coming to New York. I can understand how she feels but I'm afraid I can't promise not to want you more than twice in all that time. However I think you & she will have to talk it over next Saturday & decide that also. . . . These were the only two things she asked me to write about. . . .

Oh! boy dear, I want you so much. I'm worried & tired & cross & I don't know what I ought to do. . . .

Franklin's response, written directly to Mama, fends off demand with sweet reason, scarcely acknowledging that a difference of opinion exists. Already the F.D.R. to be, he doesn't lose his smile, he constructs close logic for his case, making allowances to the other side, but remaining assured he will have his way. Thoroughly practiced in not telling the whole story, he doesn't see why Mama has to tell the whole story:

Dec. 6, 1903

Dearest Mama—

. . . I am so glad, dear Mummy, that you are getting over the strangeness of it all—I knew you would and that you couldn't help feeling that not only I but you also are the luckiest & will always be the happiest people in the world in gaining anyone like E. to love & be loved by.

I confess that I think it would be poor policy for me to go to H.P. next Sunday—although, as you know and don't have to be told, I always love & try to be there all I can— I have been home twice already this term & I feel certain that J.R.R. [half-brother Rosy] & Helen w'd be sure to smell a rat if I went back for *part of a day* just a week before the holidays, for they would know I had been in N.Y. a whole day. *Also* if I am in N.Y. on Sunday *not a soul* need know I have been there at all as if we go to Church at all we can go to any old one at about 100th St. & the rest of the day w'd be in the house where none c'd see us. Of course I suppose you have told no one you w'd see me Saturday. Now if you really can't see the way clear to my staying in N.Y. of course I will go to H.P. with you—but you know how I feel—and also I think that E. will be terribly disappointed, as I will, if we can't have one of our first Sundays together— It seems a little hard & unnecessary on us both & I shall see you all day Saturday which I shouldn't have done had the great event not "happened."

Two stubborn people play their cards. Mama tells Rosy and Helen that he *is* coming to Hyde Park, trusting that will foreclose any alternative move on Franklin's part. But Franklin, saying no more about it, goes to New York and spends both days with Eleanor. In his next letter, he is the schoolboy again and all smiles:

Dec. 16, 1903

You will be relieved to hear that there aren't any more diphtheria cases—only 7 or 8 out of 4,000 students isn't bad exactly—I am very well and can't tell you how glad I am that I had Sunday in N.Y. It was rainy in the morning & we didn't see a soul except the Goodwin family in church. . . .

Mama has one last card to play, suggested in her long message transmitted through Eleanor. She could try keeping them apart by taking a house in Cambridge for a third successive winter, but Franklin's possible rebellion is more than she wishes to risk. So she urges upon him—as an obligation to her—that he "think the whole thing over" on a cruise to the West Indies with Lathrop Brown. To this Franklin consents. Instead of *sending* the young men, Mama *takes* them.

Recalling this episode years later in *My Boy Franklin,* Mama shows that she, too, can arrange—and rearrange—facts according to convenience. Reversing the order of events, she writes first of taking him on the cruise and then that "Franklin, unknown to any of us, had become engaged to his distant cousin, Anna Eleanor Roosevelt, a delightful child of nineteen, whom I had known and loved since babyhood."

The cruise did not change Franklin's mind or heart.[3]

Franklin enrolls at Columbia Law School, and the wedding date is set for St. Patrick's Day, March 17, 1905, when President Theodore Roosevelt is to be in New York for the parade, thus can be on hand to give the bride away. It is the major social event of the season, more because of the bride's social standing than the groom's. Postponing a wedding trip until completion of the school year, the couple entrains for Hyde Park to spend their "first honeymoon." Then they take a small apartment in a hotel in the West Forties in New York. "I knew less than nothing about even ordering meals," Eleanor writes. ". . . As soon as my mother-in-law moved to Hyde

Park for the summer we moved into her house, and were promptly taken care of by her caretaker, so I still did not have to display the depths of my ignorance as a housewife."

While that inadequacy can be overcome—if not a housekeeper, she turns out in later years to be a practiced manager of housekeepers—another failing, probably more disappointing to the young groom, is soon revealed. On the honeymoon crossing aboard the *Oceanic,* it becomes clear that there is a precious part of her husband's life she is never to share. "How terrible," she writes, "to be seasick with a husband . . . particularly one who seemed to think that sailing the ocean blue was a joy!"

Eleanor cannot separate boats and ships from the deepest of fears. At age two and a half she was enroute to Europe with her parents aboard the *Britannic* when the ship was rammed in a fog. The deck was an unforgettable scene of blood and terror: many died; a child was decapitated. Tiny Eleanor had to be dropped down the side of the ship into the outstretched arms of her father in a lifeboat. Weeks later she would tremble at the mention of the sea, refusing to go when her parents rescheduled their trip. They had to leave her with an aunt. Thus Eleanor, in whose memory the incident remained, associates water travel not only with physical threat but, perhaps even worse, with abandonment.

However disappointed he may be, Franklin writes cheerfully to Mama, "Eleanor has been a *wonderful* sailor."

And what other things of a more intimate kind are being discovered by this young woman who fears to think of herself as attractively feminine? And by this young man whose masculinity has been so long concealed beneath his assurances of devotion to Mother? We are not without glimpses behind the marriage curtain. Eleanor herself provides one many years later: "There were certain subjects never discussed by ladies of different ages, and the result was frequently very bewildered young people when they found themselves faced with some of life's normal situations!" She is one day to confide to her daughter, Anna, that sex "was an ordeal to be borne."

This is not an easy subject for a daughter to talk about, even to think closely about, a difficulty that shows up in Anna's conversation with me: "I'm not too interested in probing *the* most personal. . . . But it was obvious to me that Father was a much more openly affectionate person than Mother was. There was never any question that there were areas where these two, Eleanor and Franklin, were terribly, terribly close. And we all know that there are different levels of love, and whether theirs was less on the sexual side and more on these other sides, which may be so—which I would guess probably *is* so because of her inhibitions which he didn't have. And he added some, too."

Franklin, of course, would never think of discussing such matters with anyone. If only we could look into the unconscious of this man who held his feelings so privately he may not have known them fully himself. In a way, we can. We know of two dreams—only two, and only fragments at that—both guilelessly disclosed by Eleanor. After the marriage, Eleanor discovers that Franklin "suffered from nightmares." Aboard ship "he had started to walk out of the cabin in his sleep. He was very docile, however, when asleep, and at my suggestion returned quietly to bed."

Sleepwalking, which occurs more commonly in adolescents than adults, is no light matter. In *The Encyclopedia of Human Behavior,* Dr. Robert M. Goldenson calls it a "fugue state occurring during sleep," a fugue being "a more extreme form of escape than the more common types of amnesia" in which the subject "may perform wish-fulfilling activities." It is an extreme way of acting out "repressed impulses, anxieties or conflicts" by "immature, suggestible, dependent individuals." Of course, we cannot know, and it would be foolish to guess, what repressed but imperative wish the groom is acting out by leaving the cabin. Are the recesses of his mind leading him *toward* some compelling act—or *away from* some threatening one? Whatever the case, this affable, elegant, seemingly secure young man is harboring insistent, irrepressible conflicts beneath the serenity he is so practiced in displaying.

The second instance is a dream that, as Eleanor describes it, might be called a nightmare. Several nights after the shipboard sleepwalk, when the couple is staying with friends in an antiquated cottage in northern Scotland, "I was awakened by wild shrieks in the neighboring bed. . . . He pointed straight to the ceiling and remarked most irritably to me, 'Don't you see the revolving beam?' I assured him that no such thing was there, and had great difficulty in persuading him not to get out of bed and awaken the household."

However his nocturnal terror may tempt Freudian guessing games, the meaning of a single dream is interpreted with peril. The important thing here is that early next morning Franklin—at twenty-three, fully accomplished at showing only what he wishes to show, perhaps at knowing only what he wishes to know—is all composure, self-command, even righteousness. Eleanor gingerly inquires whether he remembers his dream. "He said he did, and that he remembered being very much annoyed with me because I insisted on remaining in the path of the beam which at any moment threatened to fall off in its gyrations."

A few days further into their honeymoon, in the mountains of Cortina, Italy, Franklin, again disappointed by what his bride cannot share, is perfectly "understanding"—then makes his own arrangements: "My husband climbed the mountains with a charming lady, Miss Kitty Gandy.

She was a few years his senior and he did not know her very well at that time, but she could climb, and I could not, and though I never said a word I was jealous beyond description."

Early in their courtship—it rings clear in Eleanor's letters—Franklin senses the lengths Eleanor would go to accommodate him. People accustomed to getting—or taking—their own way have sensors for this trait of accommodation and surround themselves with those who have the trait. The transaction serves both parties. For example, self-centered husbands often choose wives so accommodating they make room for their feminine rivals. This may also serve the wife who fears a test of her own femininity, making a virtue of her fears by taking the rival as a "friend." Eleanor now provides the first minor illustration of what is later to become a more pronounced pattern: "Perhaps I should add that Miss Gandy has since become one of my very good friends!"

The bride Eleanor churns with fears that she is not an adequate woman—in the most basic way. On the voyage home, hardly the "wonderful sailor" at all, she is sick constantly. The cause soon comes clear. On their honeymoon trip she became pregnant with Anna, later writing: "I will have to acknowledge that it was quite a relief—for, little idiot that I was, I had been seriously troubled for fear that I would never have any children and my husband would therefore be much disappointed. I wonder whether any girls today ever go through such foolish fears. . . ."

That proof of her womanhood, however, does not put the fears to rest. Throughout her marriage her writings are sprayed with self-abnegation, assertions of failure, guilt, ever-haunting doubt of her attractiveness as a wife, effectiveness as a mother, desirability as a companion. Around these self-rejections Franklin has to learn to live—and to find accommodation:

"My mother-in-law did everything for me. . . ."

"Blanche Spring [a nurse] took care of me and of the baby single-handed. . . . I had never had any interest in dolls or in little children and I knew absolutely nothing about handling or feeding a baby. . . ."

"As I look back [at entertaining], I realize that I was a very unsatisfactory person on these occasions. I was always worried. . . . I never was really carefree. . . ."

"I played no games, I could not swim. . . . After days of practice [at golf] I went out with my husband one day, and after watching me for a few minutes he remarked he thought I might just as well give it up. . . ."

"My husband enjoyed riding. . . . I tried riding Bobby, which had been Franklin's father's horse. . . . After a few efforts to ride Bobby alone, I decided that I preferred not to ride. . . ."

"I never again attempted anything but walking with my husband for many years to come. . . ."

"My husband had bought a little Ford car. . . . I ran into the gate-post. . . . I felt so terrible . . . at having spoiled everybody else's pleasure that I never again touched a car for many years. . . ."

"It used to annoy him that when he asked me what I would like for my birthday or Christmas I always wanted utilitarian things such as towels, sheets and pillowcases. . . ."

"I think one of my most maddening habits, which must infuriate all those who know me, is this habit, when my feelings are hurt or when I am annoyed, of simply shutting up like a clam, not telling anyone what is the matter and being much too obviously humble and meek, feeling like a martyr and acting like one. . . . What a tragedy it was if in any way my husband offended against these ideals of mine—and, amusingly enough, I do not think I ever told him what I expected! . . ."

"I was always more comfortable with older people, and when I found myself with groups of gay, young people I still felt inadequate to meet them on their own gay, light terms. I think I must have spoiled a good deal of the fun for Franklin because of this inability to feel at ease with a gay group, though I do not remember that I ever made much objection to his being with them as long as I was allowed to stay at home."[4]

True, no "objection." Just "shutting up like a clam, . . . feeling like a martyr," jotting her annoyance in a diary she keeps briefly in 1908, the third successive year she is pregnant. "Dined alone" with Sara, says an entry, while Franklin plays poker at the Knickerbocker Club and "returned home at 4 A.M." Two weeks later: "F. went to Harvard Club dinner & got home 3:30 A.M. Dined with Mama."

In the sense that wives are often disguised duplicates of their husbands' mothers, Eleanor in one important sense is an extension of Mama: Franklin knows he can manipulate either one with a kind word here, a deft oversight there, then go ahead and do as he pleases. In a further sense, she is easier: Eleanor is a Sara of whom he need not be terrified. Cousin Corinne Robinson tells of a party in 1907 at which Franklin had "a lovely time" after Eleanor had left with Sara after dinner. Corinne recalls: "It was an all-night affair and he could not have left before three or four in the morning." Upon arising, ". . . he was pale as a sheet and furious. His mother had upbraided him for staying out so late, especially with his wife unwell, and had forced him to come down for breakfast at eight A.M." That morning, Corinne and Franklin strolled out to the greenhouse. "Suddenly there was a clatter of pipes and Franklin literally jumped." Corinne couldn't resist teasing, "Are you afraid Mama is after you again?"

But, really, who is more terrified by whom? Whether or not Franklin is by Sara, Eleanor certainly is of both, and the whole family suffers. As Eleanor sees it, Sara was "determined to bend the marriage the way she wanted it to be. What she wanted was to hold onto Franklin and his children; she wanted them to grow up as she wished. As it turned out, Franklin's children were more my mother-in-law's children than they were mine." In an article, "I Remember Hyde Park," published post-humously by *McCall's,* Eleanor recalls that at the dining table Franklin sits at one end, Sara at the other, she along the side. In the living room, two large armchairs flanking the fireplace are occupied by Franklin and Mama, while Eleanor sits "anywhere."

Daughter Anna sees this differently: "I think that Mother overstressed this in her books. She says that Father and Granny couldn't be left alone because they got into these awful fights. I think this is overstressed. It's her own stress over Granny. I hate the way Granny is described in *Sunrise at Campobello*—and Dore Schary knows this. She is played as a harridan instead of a grande dame, which she definitely was. She could be one of the sweetest people. If Mother had had the self-assurance to stand up to Granny, what happened would never have happened. Granny would never have taken over bringing up the children and building a big house out of a medium-size house at Hyde Park. There would have been separate houses, but Mother didn't know how to stand up—at that period."

No matter how the evidence is turned for examination this way or that, F.D.R. the adult is no longer dominated by Mama. Shaped by her, yes. Ever concerned not to collide with her, yes. Financially beholden to her, yes, which at times chafes. But dominated? He can sweet-talk her out of almost anything, and when that doesn't work, he simply doesn't talk about it any more; he just goes ahead, doing what he wants.

His capacity for avoiding—not seeing—an outburst of personal emotion and conflict is enormous. (An exceedingly valuable trait for a politician, who lives by conflict, thrives on it, yet who does well not to feel it personally. To F.D.R. the politician, a conflict is a contest between gentlemen, like the Harvard-Yale game; a contest of loyalties and prin-ciples, yes, but nothing that need be personal.) His carefully learned blindness to inner emotional conflict strikes Eleanor in 1908, after Mama builds twin, side-by-side town houses in New York, which neither she nor Franklin consulted Eleanor about. Mama's constant presence, Eleanor's feeling not in command of her own children, feeling the drift away of her husband, feeling helpless to make herself the wife and mother she craves to be—all this descends upon Eleanor:

"That autumn I did not quite know what was the matter with me, but I remember that a few weeks after we moved into the new house in East 65th Street I sat in front of my dressing table and wept, and when my bewildered young husband asked me what on earth was the matter with me, I said I did not like to live in a house which was not in any way mine, one that I had done nothing about and which did not represent the way I wanted to live. Being an eminently reasonable person, he thought I was quite mad and told me so gently, and said I would feel different in a little while and left me alone until I should become calmer."

Daughter Anna points out how there is not necessarily a paradox in a man who detests conflict yet who would one day want to become President:

"Well, you know, this is personal conflict, and nothing could bother him more than to have one of the close females burst into tears, you see. Confrontation and fights and politics—being President—this is something entirely different. He could deal with it even in his secretarial staff. But if one of them took to becoming the emotional type, this he couldn't stand. If it's a personal thing—go somewhere else and settle it."

Too simple? One of the befuddling aspects of F.D.R.'s "complexity" is his capacity—on some things—to be simple, not unlike his mother. Religion is one of those things. Eleanor finds this out:

"I do remember once, when the children were still very young, asking him solemnly how much religion he felt we should teach them, or whether it was our duty to leave them free minds until they decided for themselves as they grew older. He looked at me with his amused and quizzical smile, and said that he thought they had better go to church and learn what he had learned. It would do them no harm. Heatedly, I replied: 'But are you sure that you believe in everything you learned?' He answered: 'I really never thought about it. I think it is just as well not to think about things like that too much.' "

If the young man, at the time of his wife's emotional outburst, seems preoccupied with thoughts of another order, he is. One of his fellow law clerks at a downtown firm, Grenville Clark, recalls a conversation in 1907 on an idle afternoon. Several young clerks are comparing ambitions. When Roosevelt's turn comes, Clark recalls, "I remember him saying with engaging frankness that he wasn't going to practice law forever, that he intended to run for office at the first opportunity, and that he wanted to be and thought he had a very real chance to be President." What he describes is precisely the route Cousin Teddy, then in the White House, followed: "I remember that he described very accurately the steps which he thought could lead to this goal. They were: first, a seat in the State Assembly, then an appointment as Assistant Secretary of the Navy, and finally the governorship of New York. 'Anyone who is governor of New York has a good chance to be President with any luck' are about his words that stick in my memory. . . . I do not recall that even then, in

1907, any of us deprecated his ambition or even smiled at it as we might perhaps have done. It seemed proper and sincere; and moreover, as he put it, entirely reasonable."

Only one hitch is to disturb young F.D.R.'s precise strategy. When, three years later, as though preordained, a committee of Dutchess County Democrats asks the handsome young squire to run for the state assembly, he can hardly consent fast enough. Then, unexpectedly, the Democratic incumbent, who is to vacate the seat to run for the state senate, decides that a try for the higher office would be suicide in rural New York.

So F.D.R. is asked to run for the senate, sacrificing himself to almost certain defeat. He accepts—and wins. Even though minor and local, the victory of a young Democrat bearing the Republican President's name draws national attention and helps him win a conspicuous place in the 1912 presidential nomination campaign of Woodrow Wilson. Sounded out on what reward he wishes, F.D.R. is soon—perhaps sooner than he might have dreamed—appointed Assistant Secretary of the Navy.[5]

In this new position of social as well as governmental importance, his wife plays her part dutifully, undertaking "a kind of social life I had never known before, dining out night after night and having people dine with us about once a week." Among her new Washington tasks, Eleanor spends tedious afternoon upon afternoon, loaded down by a carful of children, leaving calling cards at the homes of other official families: "I tried at first to do without a secretary, but found that it took me such endless hours to arrange my calling list, and answer and send invitations, that I finally engaged one for three mornings a week."

The part-time secretary is twenty-two-year-old Lucy Page Mercer, securely established in Washington and New York society. As Eleanor needs Lucy's assistance, Lucy needs Eleanor's pay. The Mercer family has come upon hard times. Lucy's duties are more than secretarial. In the spring of 1914, when Eleanor and the children are visiting Hyde Park, Franklin writes his wife upon returning to work in Washington—the first written mention of the young lady by the young father and husband:

Dearest Babs—
   Arrived safely and came to house and Albert [the chauffeur] tele-phoned Miss Mercer who later came and cleaned up. Then a long day at the office and dinner alone at 7:30. . . .

About Lucy Mercer it has been said that "every man who ever knew her" fell in love with her. While tall—five feet nine inches—she is sur-passingly graceful, with sympathetic yet mysterious blue eyes, a voice described as having "the quality of dark velvet," and light hair usually said to be blond although she describes it as brown. Her exquisite manners and aura of modest reserve make her a most agreeable listener, which contributes to a man's feeling of importance. Abundantly she is what Sara Roosevelt always believed a woman should be, one who strives to please a man, never to challenge him. And she is so competent at the tasks that inundate Eleanor. A friend of Lucy's, Aileen Tone, who has held a similar job for Henry Adams, tells how Lucy, whom she calls a "charmer," would plant herself on the living-room floor and spread bills, letters, and invitations about, making order of them in a twinkle. When Eleanor lacks a woman for a dinner party, she readily invites Lucy.

There are other, more subtle attractions that Roosevelt may find in the young lady. To a man whose inner life is sacrosanct, Lucy's elegant reserve, while alluring, gives assurance that intimate self-revelation will neither be offered nor asked. Her reserve comes naturally. The relationship between her parents appears to have emphasized a pursuit of proper and advantageous attachments rather than romantic intimacy. Both parents were supremely devoted to cultivating their social positions. Lucy's mother, Minnie Leigh Tunis, was described by *The Clubfellow and Washington Mirror* as "easily the most beautiful woman in Washington society for a number of years, and to be invited to one of her dinners was in itself a social distinction that qualified one for admission to any home." Her marriage was socially perfect, to Carroll Mercer, a retired Army major and descendant of the Carrolls of Carrollton. He was a founder of the Chevy Chase Club (where Franklin golfs) and prominent in the Metropolitan Club (Franklin's favorite dining and partying place). While an adornment to Minnie's beauty and standing, the marriage was a personal failure almost from the beginning. They lived separately through most of their marriage years. Mercer, a drunkard soon unable to support his wife and two daughters, was to die a pauper. Minnie went to work in New York as an "inside decorator," a field of self-support in which she was also to train Lucy.

Lucy's young life, a constant round of social events with proper companions, is not known to have included a romantic attachment with any eligible young man. Roosevelt's relationship with her during World War I is to become known almost fifty years later as a romance. There is evidence to support this. The romance is translated by some biographers and journalists, however, into an enduring love affair, a definitive and controlling influence over the rest of their emotional lives. This is based on pure surmise, which in this and in a subsequent memo we will have to examine.

Whatever they may seek from any brief indiscretion, we know what each eventually chooses. Roosevelt chooses to preserve his marriage, in a manner of speaking. Lucy soon undertakes a marriage that appears consistent with her search for security. Less than two years after World War I ends, she marries Winthrop Rutherfurd, a widower more than twice her age—she is twenty-eight, he fifty-eight—of impeccable position and wealth, who owns imposing homes in Aiken, South Carolina, and Allamuchy, New Jersey.[6]

What do we know of Franklin and Lucy's wartime romance? And what does it further tell us about the education of F.D.R.? To the first question the answer is: Very little.

Concerning the period between 1913, when Eleanor hires Lucy, and the spring of 1917, absolutely nothing has been turned up by the several biographers fascinated by this romance except the one time, early in her employment, when Lucy "came and cleaned up." During these years, dozens of summertime letters from Franklin in Washington to Eleanor at Campobello detail matters about the household and children, Franklin's wide travels in supervising internal affairs of the Navy, and his running battle with Secretary Josephus Daniels and President Wilson. Wilson is most eager to take no step that might bring America closer to war, while Roosevelt, with methods that sometimes approach insubordination, presses hard to build up the Navy. In the summer of 1916 he is out of Washington a great deal on Navy business and as a candidate in the New York Democratic primary for the United States Senate, an election he loses.

In the summer of 1917 we find the first clues that Franklin's awareness of Lucy is something beyond that of his wife's part-time employee. For one thing, she has joined the newly formed women's corps of the Navy as a yeoman third class and is assigned to Navy headquarters. Then, late in July, we learn, she is escorted by Nigel Law, a subordinate at the British Embassy and a favorite companion of F.D.R., on a weekend yachting trip, which Franklin not only also attends but has arranged. It is aboard the *Sylph,* the smaller of two presidential yachts frequently used by the Secretary and the Assistant Secretary of the Navy. In a letter to Eleanor, Franklin volunteers an account of this party. Is this a sign of innocence, or a duplication of his "cover" reports to Mama of his encounters with Eleanor while Mama had no idea they were courting? He writes:

> The trip on the Sylph was a joy and a real rest, though I got in a most satisfactory visit to the fleet. Such a funny party, but it worked out *wonderfully!* The Charlie Munns, the Cary Graysons, Lucy Mercer and Nigel Law, and they all got on splendidly. We swam about four times and Sunday afternoon went up the James to Richmond. We stopped at Lower and Upper Brandon, Westover and Shirley and

went all over them, getting drenched to the skin by several severe thunder storms. Those old houses are really wonderful but *not* comfy!

Once, earlier that summer, Nigel and Lucy were on the *Sylph;* that time, Eleanor also was along.

About a week before the weekend cruise, Eleanor left with the children for Campobello. Judging from a letter Franklin writes her the day after her departure, she is nervous about what may go on back in Washington. And so is he. He sweetly manipulates:

> . . . I really can't stand that house all alone without you, and you were a goosy girl to think or even pretend to think that I don't want you here *all* the summer, because you know I do! But honestly *you* ought to have six weeks straight at Campo, just as *I* ought to, only you can and I can't! I *know* what a whole summer here does to people's nerves and at the end of *this* summer I will be like a bear with a sore head until I get a change or some cold weather—in fact as you know I am unreasonable and touchy now—but I shall try to improve.

A month later, Lucy is a social companion again, this time lacking Nigel Law:

> Dearest Babs,
> I had a very occupied Sunday, starting off for golf at 9 . . . quick lunch at Chevy Chase, then in to town and off in car at 2:30 to the Horsey's place near Harper's Ferry. Lucy Mercer went and the Graysons and we got there at 5:30, walked over the farm—a very rich one and run by the two sisters—had supper with them and several neighbors, left at nine and got home at midnight! The day was magnificent, but the road more dusty and even more crowded than when we went to Gettysburg.

In the next sentence Lucy is still on his mind as he turns to a business-like report. Eleanor has helped organize a wool-and-sweater-collection drive for the Navy, enlisting Lucy to take her place for the summer—but insisting, over Lucy's protests, upon paying her. Franklin continues:

> By the way, they handed in a record amount of sweaters and other wooleys [sic] on Saturday. . . .

The business of payment, whatever it may mean to each member of the triangle, turns into a wrangle. Lucy declines to accept a check,

Eleanor insists, and Lucy apologizes. Then Franklin instructs that she return it again with the explanation that two wool collections were not made. Finally Eleanor writes Franklin, "I've written Miss Mercer and returned the check saying I knew she had done far more work than I could pay for. She is evidently quite cross with me!"

Early in September, Franklin, apparently with relief, reports the end of the "wooleys" drive: "*You* are entirely disconnected and Lucy Mercer and Mrs. Munn are closing up the loose ends."

There is some gossip, which may not reach Eleanor's ears, and at least one piece of contrived mischief, which does. A mischief-maker of the time, and for two generations to come, is Alice Roosevelt (later Long-worth), T.R.'s daughter. One summer evening while Eleanor is away, Alice invites Franklin to dinner. When he gets there he finds Lucy has been invited, too. Years later Alice is to say, "He deserved a good time. He was married to Eleanor." Of course, true mischief calls for more than that. One day Alice runs into Eleanor at the Capitol. Eleanor reports the encounter to Franklin with annoyance—supposedly at Alice: "She inquired if you had told me and I said no and that I did not believe in knowing things which your husband did not wish you to know so I think I will be spared any further mysterious secrets!"

She is not to be spared. While the foregoing was until recently the total record of known facts of the World War I relationship, hardly a strong case for a "romance" so sensationally publicized, one additional fact has come to light: In 1918, when Franklin returns from a battlefront tour of Europe ill with double pneumonia, Eleanor's first instinct is to find some practical way to help him. She leafs through his correspondence —presumably mail forwarded directly to him overseas—to see if she can help him catch up with replies. She is stunned to find letters from Lucy.

I first heard of this, secondhand, in April 1967 from a Hyde Park friend of Eleanor Roosevelt's who said she had once frankly told him about it. Later, Anna Roosevelt Halsted confirmed it to me. It is now further confirmed by Joseph Lash, who was told of the letters directly by Mrs. Roosevelt. Many of her confidences, like this one, turn out to be liberally distributed.

Eleanor confronts Franklin with the letters and offers him "his freedom" if he feels he can accept the consequences for the children.

The children are not the only consideration. If he actually contemplates divorce—and we don't know that he does—there is the obstacle of Lucy's Catholicism. Also, Lash reports that Mama, getting wind of the crisis, "applied pressure with the threat to cut him off if he did not give up Lucy." Perhaps the overriding consideration is that a divorce would end any thought of a national political career. Franklin agrees never to see Lucy again.[7]

Not having those secret letters—and having so little else to go by—we know next to nothing about the depth of Franklin's feeling for Lucy. All we know is Eleanor's reaction, that whatever she found, deeply and permanently hurt her. But we do have here an event that is unique in Franklin Roosevelt's life, inconsistent with a twenty-year history—since Groton—of most careful defense of his "underlife" and inconsistent with anything he is ever to do again. Even allowing that Eleanor, whose emotions are fragile, may have overreacted to what the letters said, Franklin has been caught in a devastating error: If he was sure the letters would not be found, he was wrong. If he thought of that possibility and assured himself he could explain them away, he has misjudged Eleanor's reaction. For the first time in his private life he has been forced to explain defensively something he has not chosen to explain. He has been forced to salvage a situation that has gone out of control.

This uncharacteristic error is the most telling evidence that something extraordinary and consuming took hold of Franklin. He went overboard in a way he never had—and will henceforth make sure it does not happen again.

F.D.R. is to have one more relationship with a woman—the most comfortable, devoted, and intimate (in so far as he could or would have) of any in his life. Far from a summer romance, it endures for two decades. Far from a surreptitious alliance, it becomes, over all those years, part of his daily working and private life. From 1921 to 1941 it makes Lucy—or whatever it is that Franklin briefly sought in her—no longer necessary. It remains "concealed" during its duration and in all the decades since, because it is so open. Of the many who see its daily evidence—with the possible exception of Eleanor, who accommodates herself to it—virtually all take care to convince themselves they are seeing something else.

Describing this relationship—which itself delineates the extraordinary composition of F.D.R., so social and yet so veiled—requires the stage setting of the terrible occurrence of August 1921.

In 1920 Roosevelt was the candidate for Vice-President on the losing, Democratic ticket. In a burst of postwar, postelection partisan vengeance, a Republican Senate subcommittee chairman accused the previous administration's Navy leadership of negligence in office, which threw Roosevelt's name across ugly headlines before the ex-Assistant Secretary had a chance to defend himself. His career in jeopardy and burning with indignation, Roosevelt, now running the New York office of an insurance firm, the Fidelity and Deposit Company, demanded and obtained an appearance before the committee. While he effectively refuted the accusations, the damage smarted.

Leaving steamy Washington, he keeps a commitment to visit a Boy Scout camp in upstate New York, then heads for Campobello Island to rejoin his family. During that week his body is incubating the virus of poliomyelitis.

Arriving at Campobello, Roosevelt immediately seeks the peace of mind he always finds in sailing and fishing. Preparing his tackle aboard the tiny sailboat *Vireo,* which he bought to teach his sons to sail, he slips and falls overboard. By Roosevelt's own account:

"I'd never felt anything so cold as the water. . . . It seemed paralyzing. . . . The next day we landed on the island. There was a blue haze over it, pungent with burning spruce. All that day we fought a forest fire. Late in the afternoon we brought it under control. Our eyes were bleary with smoke; we were begrimed, smarting with spark-burns, exhausted. We plunged into a fresh-water pool on the island to revive ourselves. We ran in our bathing suits along the hot, dusty roads to the house.

"I didn't feel the usual reaction, the glow I'd expected. Walking and running couldn't overcome the chill. When I reached the house the mail was in, with several newspapers I hadn't seen. I sat reading for a while, too tired even to dress. I'd never felt quite that way before.

"The next morning when I swung out of my bed my leg lagged, but I managed to move about and to shave. I tried to persuade myself that the trouble with my leg was muscular, that it would disappear as I used it. But presently it refused to work, and then the other. . . ."

Next day an elderly local physician, disregarding the patient's complaints of weakness in the legs, a dull ache in his back, and recurrent teeth-chattering chills, diagnoses the condition as a cold. The aching spreads, temperature rises to 102 degrees, and three days later, his body immobile from the chest down, Roosevelt learns he has the disease he always dreaded his children might contract, infantile paralysis.

Louis Howe, loyal to F.D.R. since 1912, has just accepted a lucrative job with an oil company. He drops it immediately to get to Roosevelt's side and takes charge of the delicate logistics of entraining Roosevelt for a New York hospital with minimum attention by the press. By the time reporters finally catch up with Roosevelt, in a New York rail depot where he is lifted through a window of the train painfully on a stretcher, Roosevelt is mentally set to give them a big smile and an impression of gay self-assurance. He has had some practice. At Campobello, to which Mama rushed, Roosevelt mustered all his strength to stage what has been called "a major act of cheery nonchalance for her benefit."

At New York's Presbyterian Hospital, an old school friend, Dr. George Draper, takes charge of the patient. Draper writes a Boston expert on polio, Dr. Robert W. Lovett:

> He is very cheerful and hopeful, and has made up his mind that he is going to go out of the hospital in the course of two or three weeks on crutches. What I fear more than anything else is . . . that when we attempt to sit him up he will be faced with the frightfully depressing knowledge that he cannot hold himself erect. . . . He has such courage, such ambition, and yet at the same time such an extraordinarily sensitive emotional mechanism that it will take all the skill which we can muster to lead him successfully to a recognition of what he really faces without crushing him.

Does Roosevelt recognize what really faces him? To a friend, he writes on September 16, barely a month after he is stricken: "I have renewed my youth in a rather unpleasant manner by contracting what was fortunately a rather mild case of infantile paralysis." Yet there are days in that hospital and afterward, he is to confess years later, when, unable to dissolve the waves of despair that overwhelm him, he is convinced that God has forsaken him.

The two women by his side, mother and wife, also recognize what faces him, but respond in opposite ways. According to Eleanor, Mama "made up her mind that Franklin was going to be an invalid for the rest of his life and that he would retire to Hyde Park and live there." Eleanor, on the other hand, insists—with Franklin's concurrence—that he go to the Sixty-fifth Street town house, that as soon as possible he engage himself—by receiving visitors, by letter, by telephone—in his familiar, talky, busy world of civic and political affairs. Anything else would be surrender to invalidism and lifelong despair. In what has been called "a battle to the finish between these two remarkable women for Franklin's soul," Eleanor shows a strength and decisiveness that her husband perhaps never knew she had. If he is not surprised, Sara certainly is. Eleanor wins.

Some of the strength for her victory is drawn from Louis Howe, in whom she discovers a new ally, leading to a melting of earlier suspicion and the beginning of a remarkable trust, partnership, and friendship between them directed toward restoring Franklin Roosevelt's fortune and destiny. In fact, in future years, until his death in 1936, Louis Howe is the only person whose trust is to be shared simultaneously and equally by Franklin and Eleanor.

The Louis-Eleanor relationship is a compact to serve converged purposes. Eleanor needs Louis—and values him—in her battle against Mama and to restore Franklin. Louis needs Eleanor, now more than ever, to serve the single purpose of his life—making Franklin President. Guilelessly, Eleanor describes his use of her: "Mr. Howe felt that one way to get my husband's interest aroused was to keep him as much as possible in contact with politics. . . . In order to accomplish his ends, Mr. Howe began to urge me to do some political work." Acquaintances lead her into the Women's Trade Union League, the League of Women Voters, and soon into the women's division of the Democratic State Committee, for the last of which she is surprised to find herself presiding over a fund-raising luncheon.[8]

Meanwhile she urges Franklin to take on a secretary, someone of sensitive judgment who will insure that he keep up a lively correspondence, yet who will know where to set a limit on activity so he won't neglect his daily rest and muscle-restoring exercises. They decide on Miss Marguerite A. LeHand, a bright, well-mannered twenty-three-year-old who has pleased him as an employee of his vice-presidential campaign headquarters, where she kept his speaking schedule in order, along with other chores.

Becoming a daily presence at Sixty-fifth Street, "Miss LeHand" is too much a name for the Roosevelt youngsters to pronounce. Anna begins calling her "Missy"—and Missy it remains for the rest of her days.

Missy is not a pretty girl but, like Eleanor, radiates a charm that gives her beauty. Five feet seven inches tall, she has large, candid, intensely dark-blue eyes and dark hair that already shows speckles of a premature turning to silver. As her hair begins to whiten against the radiant complexion of a young woman, she wears a bun that remains black, providing a striking contrast. Fulton Oursler, the author and editor, is taken with "the lovely throaty voice and quick upturn of her face . . . lips parted in that strange secret smile, compound of cunning and innocence forever baffling." Less lyrically, Grace Tully, for many years Missy's assistant, recalls her "rather large features—a large nose, and teeth a little protruding, but then everybody around Roosevelt had protruding teeth, including me."

In the early days of her employment by F.D.R.—or "F.D." as she (and she alone) is always to address him—Missy shares an apartment with a cousin and his wife, traveling daily to Roosevelt's Sixty-fifth Street house to work afternoons and evenings, sometimes spending weekends of work at Hyde Park.

Our knowledge of Missy's first three years with Roosevelt—what he may have seen in her or felt about her—is a blank, as it is of a similar period with Lucy. All we know is that the man is paralyzed, immobile, captive of the chair he sits in, the room that contains him, the people in his presence. He has long known how to make himself the center around whom the lives of others revolve. Now, however, this accustomed attention is transformed to *attending*.

Missy attends him.

In the winter of 1923, Roosevelt needs sunshine and exercise, craves the gentle exertion of swimming and fishing. And he needs to think about his life. Late that winter he rents a small houseboat, *Weona II,* to float around the warm waters of the Florida coast, accompanied by a series of visiting friends. Eleanor dutifully goes aboard for a few days, but it is not to her taste. She writes: "I had never considered holidays in winter or escape from cold weather an essential part of living, and I looked upon it now as a necessity and not a pleasure. I tried fishing but had no skill and no luck. When we anchored at night and the wind blew, it all seemed eerie and menacing to me."

For the following winter, he buys a run-down but larger houseboat, in partnership with a school friend, John S. Lawrence of Boston. They call it *Larooco* (pronounced La-roe-co) for Lawrence-Roosevelt Company.

During long cruises of two months—February to April—in each of three years, 1924 to 1926, Roosevelt suns, bathes, and fishes, leading a cheerful and loafing life.

Except for one brief visit in the last of the three winters, Eleanor avoids the *Larooco*. Missy, except for a couple of emergency absences, is always aboard.

The *Larooco*, seventy-one feet long, has, starting from the stern, a kind of "back porch," then crew quarters. One room is occupied by a captain and his wife who serves as cook and housekeeper, both employed on a single salary of $125 a month; the other room, an engine mechanic. Forward of these quarters is a large engine room and galley.

In the bow section, on the port side of a passageway, is a bathroom and large stateroom used by F.D.R. He gets rid of a brass double bed that came with the boat, replacing it with two single bunks. On the starboard side, two smaller staterooms contain two bunks each. Near the bow a short flight of steps leads from the passageway up to a vast, windowed living room. More steps rise to a top deck equipped with awnings. Roosevelt has the mattress of the brass double bed placed up there for sunning.

If the arrangement of Missy's constant presence, and not Eleanor's, for cruises of eight weeks in such close and isolated quarters seems odd, especially for a man of prominence, friends don't mention it—or they cover it over by stretching the truth. John Lawrence recalls some years later, "I spent about a month each year with him on *Larooco*. When neither [of us] had guests, Louis Howe and Miss LeHand were aboard." This is a gentleman's convenient failure of memory. Lawrence never

boards the craft until the final month of its third cruise, in 1926. Louis
Howe never saw it.

Mama openly objects to the arrangement, but Eleanor accepts it.
Eleanor explains in her book—and son James in his, and Elliott in the
notes of the collected letters—that Missy accompanies Roosevelt "to
handle his correspondence." The accommodation is more than that, of
course. As Lash puts it, Eleanor is "grateful to the young woman. . . . It
eased Eleanor's sense of guilt because she was unable to do more for him."
She is determined to fulfill her vow of devotion—which truly remains a
devotion—in any way she can, even though she is one day to tell friends,
according to Lash, that she has not been in love with Franklin "since her
discovery of the Lucy Mercer affair, but that she had given her husband
a service of love. . . ." Prodded by Louis Howe, Eleanor now devotes
herself to what she feels she can do—keeping alive the name of her
husband in civic affairs. The personal attending to Franklin, at which she
has never satisfactorily succeeded, she now settles for leaving to someone else, from whom it appears more welcome.[9]

On Saturday, February 2, 1924, Roosevelt and Missy arrive in Florida.
For the first three days, when the two are alone in the forward section of
the houseboat, Roosevelt, who faithfully keeps a daily log, does not
mention Missy, a gingerliness he is soon to drop. His log entry for the first
day:

Sat. Feb. 2.
    At Jacksonville, Florida. F.D.R. went on board and put Larooco in
commission. Sailing-master Robert S. Morris and Mrs. Morris spent the
day getting provisions, and the trunks etc. were duly unpacked, fishing
gear stowed and Library of the World's Worst Literature placed on
shelves.

On Tuesday, February 5, Maunsell S. Crosby (in the log as M.S.C.), a
Roosevelt neighbor from Rhinebeck, New York, comes on board at St.
Augustine for a three-week stay, which Mama has suggested. A good companion, he is a visitor for each of the three cruises. Next day: "M.S.C.,
M.A.L. [Missy] and F.D.R. went fishing in the inlet. Caught one sea
trout. M.S.C identified 33 different species of birds. . . . All hands
played solitaire. M.A.L. ate too much." The following day, while Crosby
and George Dyer, the engine mechanic, go off bird watching, "M.A.L.
and F.D.R. in launch fishing in p.m. No luck. . . . Painted ¾ of a chair—
booful blue."

And so it goes daily, Crosby a sharer of F.D.R.'s interests, Missy ever present, the crew not often mentioned in the log, except as pleasant servants tending to their business, held off at a servants' distance.

On February 10, the boat scarcely a week out, "M.S.C. ashore for telegrams and brought back sad news of death of M.A.L.'s father. Arranged for train berth etc." Next morning, "Our party broken up by M.A.L.'s departure for Boston at 7 a.m."

Missy returns on February 23. During the twelve days of her absence F.D.R., while enjoying high jinks with Crosby, is apparently lonely. He begins to write, in longhand on legal-size yellow sheets, of all things, "A History of the United States." He reaches the fourteenth page before Missy returns; the project is never to be resumed.

The "history" is itself a revelation of Roosevelt's development, perhaps drawn from reading during his early, most confining convalescence. It emphasizes causes and effects rather than historical accidents, and the importance of tensions between classes of society. Especially interesting, coming from F.D.R., it downgrades the importance of individual personages. The latter theme shows up early and emphatically. His first scripted page has been lost, but the second page begins:

> . . . for lack of general record. It is therefore more correct to say that the Columbus discovery was the first which became a part of the world's knowledge.
> Many other factors contribute to the thought that the period itself was the discoverer of America, and Columbus the agent of his time. . . . America was discovered by the era. It is perhaps not stretching the point to assert that definite knowledge of America to the European world was bound to come at the end of the 15th Century.*

Another interesting event during Missy's absence is the writing of one of his rare "Dearest Mama" letters from the *Larooco,* thanking her for the fun with Crosby—"for the happy thought of asking him you are responsible!"—but no mention of Missy's presence, of her departure, or, most surprising of all, of her father's death. Her presence having been a subject of some crossness between them, it is therefore—typically in dealing with Mama—made not to exist.

On February 23, Missy returns, on the twenty-fourth Crosby departs. For the next nine days F.D.R. and Missy are alone with the crew. Entries in the log turn unusually lazy and short, many of only two lines:

* The full length of this document, while not directly relevant to the presidential memoirs, merits inspection by the student of F.D.R. Therefore, I am including it as Appendix III.

"M.A.L. and Mrs. Morris ashore shopping. In the p.m. a drive to Miami Beach to call on J.C. Penney etc." "Tied up at dock all day because of engine repairs—too much wind to go down Biscayne Bay anyway." ". . . M.A.L. experienced the first pangs of Mal de Mer as it blew hard on the way down from the West and gave us a good roll. In late p.m. tied up inside Creek." "A lovely warm lazy day. Fished for angelfish, grunts, etc. and got enough for a meal."

On Wednesday, March 5, a friend of Missy's, Miss Eleanor Hennessy, arrives for a week. That afternoon, F.D.R. and Missy host a "tea party" on deck with "Mr. and Mrs. William H. Kelly of Syracuse—the Democratic leader,—and Mr. J. C. Penney, the chain store man who has a large farm near Hopewell Junction, Dutchess Co. Much discussion of cows, politics and boy-scouts." Roosevelt is anticipating the arrival of Livingston Davis, a schoolboy chum and, for a time, F.D.R.'s assistant at the Navy Department. On March 12 he notes: "Miss Hennessy left us at noon—very sad not to be able to wait to meet the attractions of Davis who comes next Sunday." Again, three days alone with Missy, and brief, uneventful entries. The first full day of Livie Davis' presence brings a startling—or at least startled—entry:

Mon. Mar. 17.
    Water too cold to swim and wind to [sic] high to go to reef. L.D. went to the R.R. bridge to fish and came back minus trousers—to the disgust of the two ladies [Missy and Mrs. Morris]. Earlier he had exercised on the top deck a la nature. Why do people who *must* take off their clothes go anywhere where the other sex is present? Capt. Morris remarked quietly that some men get shot for less.

That is a puzzling entry in a log that is not a private document, but one that Roosevelt makes a show of displaying to all who come aboard. Is it a poorly worded expression of amusement—or is F.D.R. as annoyed as the words make him appear?

Two days later: "L.D. went off to the stream alone . . . gone all day. . . . M.A.L. and F.D.R. went swimming." And the next day, ". . . a heavy storm was rapidly approaching from the West. . . . Hell to pay. Davis got the awning off but had to disrobe to do it as it was raining." While Davis' visit, which extends to April 5, appears to proceed merrily enough, he is not invited back to the *Larooco*. For the final week of the cruise F.D.R. and Missy are alone again with the crew until April 13, when the good ship is put out of commission until the following winter.

In one of the few intimate observations Missy ever relates about F.D.R., she is one day to tell Frances Perkins (who later tells it to Frank Freidel),

". . . there were days on the Larooco when it was noon before he could pull himself out of depression and greet his guests wearing his lighthearted façade." Missy knows the moods, the shifts, the façade, and the underlying "F.D." that the façade so actively conceals.

The next year's cruise goes much as the first. Before the *Larooco*'s third cruise—in 1926—Eleanor decides to swallow her distaste for houseboating. For the first time since the *Weona,* in 1923, she departs for Florida with Franklin—and Missy does not. After putting in a dutiful ten days—F.D.R. mentions her in the log only once in all that time, "A.E.R. took dory with Capt. Charlie to try to reach Miami before bank closes"—Eleanor leaves as Missy arrives.

After that third cruise F.D.R., as son James puts it, "had had enough" of the *Larooco:* "He learned that, while frivolity and aimlessness were enjoyable in small doses, he could not take the life of a dilettante as a steady diet." He decides with partner Lawrence to sell it when, in September 1926, a violent hurricane tears the boat from its boatyard berth two miles up the Ft. Lauderdale River, driving it upstream to settle finally and comfortably on a bed of pine needles at the edge of a forest four miles inland. Since salvage is impractical, Roosevelt has the ingenious idea of trying to sell it as a hunting lodge. No takers. In 1927 the *Larooco* is sold for junk, Roosevelt noting in the postscript of its log: "So ended a good old craft with a personality."[10]

The story of Franklin Roosevelt and Missy LeHand unfolds more fully at Warm Springs. We must shift back to 1924, to the end of the *Larooco*'s first cruise. Roosevelt returns to New York to assume management of Governor Alfred E. Smith's drive for the Democratic presidential nomination. Smith prevails upon him to make the nomination speech, a test of both courage and muscle in standing up (supported by leg braces) at Madison Square Garden for his first major appearance since his illness. (After a marathon of more than a hundred ballots over six days, Smith loses the nomination.)

During the convention an Atlanta newspaper publisher tells F.D.R. of a young man, a polio victim named Louis Joseph, who has learned to walk with canes after spending several summers swimming in a pool fed by natural warm springs at an old resort in Bullochville, Georgia (soon to be renamed Warm Springs). Accompanied by Eleanor and Missy, Roosevelt heads for the resort in October 1924 for a three-week visit. Finding its central building, Meriwether Inn, a run-down firetrap, Roosevelt rents a nearby cottage from a man named Hart.

After a few days Eleanor, who finds Georgia folkways no more to her liking than houseboating, departs. Missy stays. As word spreads of the famous man seeking to bathe his way back to health, Warm Springs soon becomes a colony of more than a dozen paralytics, most of them younger than Roosevelt, a few of them children. No medical man being present, Roosevelt takes charge of inventing and teaching daily warm-water exercises to the hopeful throng.

Their common misfortune and hope binds Roosevelt to this band of cripples, and them to him, in a kind of democratic, easy, purposeful, and unselfish friendship and trust such as he had never had or was ever again to have the opportunity to experience. During that first visit and in longer ones in years to follow, of all the members of his "family," only Missy is to share fully these good days at Warm Springs that bring forth Franklin Roosevelt's simplest and most direct humanity.

Roosevelt already has hints, soon to be confirmed, that both Mama and Eleanor are, at best, indulging his new enthusiasm. To Mama, who doesn't like Missy being there without Eleanor, he writes during his first visit: "It is too bad that Eleanor has to leave so soon, but she and I both feel it is important for her not to be away the end of the campaign as long as I have to be myself." And a few days later, ". . . and Missy spends most of her time keeping up a huge and constant local correspondence." To Eleanor, a somewhat franker story:

It is just a week since you left . . . life is just the same day after day and there is no variety to give landmarks. The mornings are as you know wholly taken up with the pool and four of the afternoons we have sat out on the lawn. . . . I have worked at stamps or cheques or accounts or have played rummy with Missy. The other three afternoons we have gone motoring with Mr. and Mrs. Loyless [he is the manager of the resort] and have seen the country pretty thoroughly. I like him ever so much and she is nice but not broad in her interests, but she chatters away to Missy on the back seat and I hear an occasional yes or no from Missy to prove she is not sleeping. . . .

On April 1, 1925, Roosevelt and Missy proceed directly from the *Larooco* to Warm Springs, staying until mid-May, a fifteen-week absence from Eleanor and home. Late that summer he takes a cottage for himself and Missy at Marion, Massachusetts. Not only is it near the Horseneck Beach cottage of Louis Howe but, more importantly, it is down the street from Dr. William McDonald, a neurologist who has devised an unorthodox treatment of exercise for rehabilitating polio victims. The exercises, though tedious and painful, seem so promising to F.D.R. that he and Missy extend their stay until December 5. Again, in early 1926, after the *Larooco* cruise, Missy and F.D.R. settle in at Warm Springs. That summer he returns to Marion, being joined by Missy as soon as she completes a

European vacation. From then on Roosevelt invests all his hope for re-covery in Warm Springs, going there with Missy for two long stays each year, departing only for the Christmas season and the hot summer months, until he re-enters political life in late 1928.

By early 1926 the possibilities of Warm Springs begin captivating Roose-velt not just as therapy but as a business venture. He persuades himself that the run-down hotel, refurbished, can be made to pay for itself—and subsidize a professionally run rehabilitation treatment for polio victims. By paying their way, the healthy resort guests would, so to speak, carry the polio patients on their backs. He begins negotiations to buy the shambles from George Foster Peabody, a New York banker, at a price double Peabody's original cost. Roosevelt agrees to put down twenty-five thousand dollars in cash, obligating himself to $170,000 in payments over the next ten years, to buy the inn, springs, cottages, and twelve hundred acres. This gets him into a tangle of pulls and counterpulls with Eleanor and Mama; he nods, "understanding" both their points of view, but goes on anyhow. Eleanor, taking a dim view of the enterprise, writes: ". . . I know you love creative work, my only feeling is that Georgia is somewhat distant for you to keep in touch with what is really a big undertaking. One cannot, it seems to me, have *vital* interests in widely divided places, but that may be because I'm old and rather overwhelmed by what there is to do in one place. . . ."

If he can't get moral support from Eleanor, perhaps he can get financial support from Mama. Invoking his old schoolboy ways of per-suasion, he writes to her: "I had a nice visit from Chas. Peabody [George Foster's brother] & it looks as if I had bought Warm Springs. If so I want you to take a great interest in it, for I feel you can help me with many suggestions and the place properly run will not only do a great deal of good but will prove *financially* successful."

Eleanor breaks in to warn Franklin: "Don't let yourself in for too much money and don't make Mama put in much for if she lost it she'd never get over it!"

Franklin, undaunted, invites his mother to Warm Springs for a two-week stay so she can see for herself. Immediately afterward, he pushes on with the game of "You and I know," writing Mama: "I miss you a lot and I don't have to tell you how I loved to have you here, and I know you were really interested in seeing what I think is a very practical good to which this place can be put and you needn't worry about my losing a fortune in it, for every step is being planned either to pay for itself or to make a profit on."[11]

Mama does worry. She goes so far as to invest the price of a new cottage to produce rental income, but no further. Roosevelt, meanwhile, builds a cottage for himself (not the more commodious one to become known one day as the Little White House, which he builds in 1932). Also he convinces Missy to put her modest savings into a cottage—not to occupy, but as an investment for income.

As on the houseboat, Roosevelt, who, as all his friends and relatives know, cannot bear being alone, requires Missy near him. She occupies a room in his cottage. The arrangement, having weathered Mama's disapproval of it aboard the *Larooco,* and with Eleanor's acceptance of it, is now a way of life. Family correspondence of the years 1925 through 1928 permits a reconstruction of just how established a way of life it becomes. In those four years—208 weeks in all—Roosevelt is away from home more than half the time, a total of 116 weeks, on the *Larooco,* at Marion, and at Warm Springs. Of those weeks away, Eleanor is with him for four, Mama for two. Missy is with him almost constantly, day and night, for 110 of the weeks away. Thus Missy is the sole adult "member of the family" to share an aggregate of more than two years of the most trying and self-searching four years of Roosevelt's life.

Their living arrangement at Warm Springs is known and seen by many. It is most closely seen—at times, virtually shared—by a young friend of Missy's, Miss Barbara Muller, whose older sister went to high school with Missy at Somerville, Massachusetts, and by Barbara's fiancé, Egbert T. Curtis. Curtis was trained in hotel management at Cornell, and on Missy's recommendation F.D.R. hires him to become manager of the Warm Springs property.

Mr. and Mrs. Curtis recall with vividness and fondness their days at Warm Springs when Barbara, paying extended visits to her husband-to-be, sometimes shares Missy's room in F.D.R.'s cottage. The following recollections are taken from several hours of taped conversation I had with them:

MRS. CURTIS: There was a big living room and three bedrooms, but they were very small. He had done a lot of the designing himself.

MR. CURTIS: In his bedroom, which he had designed, the only way you could open the closet door was by moving the bed.

MRS. C: Missy and I would have to go through his bedroom to get to the bath. I'd go through his bedroom the same as she would. Of course, anybody that has been an invalid for any length of time is used to seeing a lot of people in his bedroom—carrying on your business in your bedroom. We didn't think anything about it. There was always a lot of joking. They had a cook at Warm Springs, but she didn't sleep in.

MR. C: There were only two people in the cottage—him and Missy.

The conversation further reveals that apparently nobody "thinks anything about it." F.D.R. does nothing to conceal it. He has arranged what is, even for a disabled and dependent man, an extraordinary restructuring of his life. For at least half of each year, he has largely eased out of his ties with the woman to whom he is married, and substituted a young companion he employs, whose company he clearly prefers, who serves him not only as secretary and hostess, but shares his fun during all his waking hours, is privy to the dark moments he is so careful not to show anyone else, who gives up all opportunity for an alternative personal life of her own, who shares his homes away from home.

MR. C: There was never any indication of any kind that I can remember that this was in any way abnormal, any out-of-the-ordinary way of living.

MRS. C: He was always having people come down from New York and Chicago and other places, people of considerable means that he would like to interest in Warm Springs and have them give money, like Edsel Ford who was down there with his wife. Missy was hostess, taking the place of—like a wife would, in that sense. Since there wasn't much entertainment, there was more bridge playing than nowadays. We'd be a couple and she and Roosevelt would be the other couple.

MR. C: I'm quite sure they had one rule—that they never drove down together. They always went by train for the very simple reason that a man prominent in politics couldn't afford to be—even adjoining hotel rooms or whatever—if Roosevelt and Missy drove down together, even if there was any truth in it or not, it would be a scandal. Maybe this might have something to do with it: There might have been lots more talk about it if she had had a room at the Meriwether Inn and was over at the cottage in the evening and working with him or whatever. Then there could be whispering. But she was a member of the family. She was a business member, but also a personal member.

One thing Missy can do that Eleanor cannot do is to share Roosevelt's fun—what Grace Tully calls his "sense of nonsense." Tom Loyless tells of the time Roosevelt and Missy are holding a cocktail party—during Prohibition. Loyless and F.D.R. are engaged in their favorite sport, topping each other's stories. Loyless' sister and Missy are mixing cocktails in the kitchen when they hear a knock on the door. Missy runs to it gaily and finds herself facing an unexpected visitor, the local Baptist preacher. Shunting him over to F.D.R., she throws an apron across the cocktails and spirits them into the kitchen. According to Loyless, "F.D.R. sat there agonized with laughter."

MR. C: One day some visitor came by, someone who'd been driving in that part of the country. This fellow greeted Roosevelt like a long-lost friend. Roosevelt didn't have the vaguest idea of who the guy was. Before he left, Roosevelt was calling him by his first name, asking about his wife and children and so on. I asked Missy afterwards how the devil he did it. She said, "It's not as difficult as it seems. In the first part of the conversation he'll figure out where he met this man, and then by association he promotes clues for the recollection to come back." And the guy never suspected that Roosevelt didn't know him instantly when he walked into the room.

You know, Roosevelt had a very, very characteristic laugh. He was one of the relatively few people who could tell a story and laugh like hell at it himself and get the whole room laughing with him. The story could be lousy, but everyone laughed. I once made a remark to Missy about it, and she said, "That's his political laugh." Some time later I mentioned in her presence his "political laugh." She got madder than hell. I wasn't supposed to say that.

MRS. C: . . . He worked, as you probably know, a great deal of his work was done at night—without interruptions. He would work night after night through all hours of the night, and she was always right there working with him. He could take it, but I think her strength just didn't hold out to take all that.

MR. C: She said quietly one time that he had no idea of the demands he put upon people who were close to him. "Would you do this?" and "Would you do that?" And it went beyond some of their powers to keep up.

Roosevelt's daughter, Anna, in discussing the relationship with Missy, brings this up, too:

"I think this applied with Mother as well as with Father. The people who worked with them had to be just as if they had no lives of their own. I think both of them unwittingly and unknowingly even to themselves—it never occurred to them that these people lived their lives through them, and had nothing of their own. The same is true of Mother's Miss Thompson. She never—for years and years—had a life of her own. . . .

"I think Missy became utterly and completely devoted to this man. . . . You know, many years of illness had to change a relationship—which became a very, very close relationship, because she was with him all the time. . . . She *was* the office wife, quote, unquote. . . . Then, of course, it becomes more personal. And with him—you see, there's a great difficulty that people have to realize, because of his paralysis—many people saw this man in bed. Ordinarily, you'd never see the man you work for in bed.

And I think it was, without a doubt, it became—I know Father became interested. She told him all about her family. And I know he was very interested in her nieces. . . . And he became involved in her personal life."

Missy's early life in Somerville has resemblances to Lucy Mercer's, except for social class. It is the not unfamiliar story of a girl from an unraveled family, hardly a family at all, who thus has never learned by example how to make a conventional commitment to a life mate. Her father (who, she tells a writer during her White House years, was "in the real estate business") was a gardener and lawn tender for Somerville neighbors. He was a drinker and lived separately from his wife during much of Missy's childhood. Mrs. LeHand, with two older children to raise besides Missy, took in a couple of Harvard students for extra income. Upon finishing high school Missy left for New York to find a job and make a life for herself. Being Catholics, the parents never considered divorce, and shortly before he died, the father returned home.

MRS. C: Even as a high school girl, she had a certain class to her. I remember one time watching her go around the corner—our houses weren't too far apart—and my mother kind of looked out the window and called my attention to her. She said, "She certainly looks smart." She had a dark suit on to go to high school. She stood out for having a better appearance and being smarter than most.

MR. C: One thing we haven't said, there was nothing stuffy about her. She could get along with anybody. Of course, Missy picked up a lot of things from being close to the Roosevelt family. Without making a point of it, she just absorbed it, certain mannerisms and even the way she spoke.

Margaret Suckley, Roosevelt's Hyde Park cousin, one day comments that it's remarkable how Missy has become a person of such fine manners "without any background at all."

During the summer of 1926, when F.D.R. returns to Hyde Park between stays at Warm Springs, Barbara (soon to be Mrs. Curtis) and Missy go on a Mediterranean cruise, also a visit to Norway and Sweden.

MRS. C: Eleanor Roosevelt gave her a gift of extra spending money, and Missy was very pleased with that. She did a lot of shopping in Paris and got a lot of pretty things, négligées and so forth. We had a good time on the trip, and she enjoyed the attention she got. The cruise director used to keep his bottle of liquor down in our stateroom and he would come down there. Those were Prohibition days, you

know. It would be the three of us sometimes, and then there was one
man who was engaged and going back to get married, and we'd sometimes be two couples with him. He'd sometimes meet her early in the
morning on shipboard to watch the sunrise. It wasn't always the same
one, but it was enough for you to see that she certainly was attractive
to men. She enjoyed male companionship, but not enough to be interested in marrying. I talked about it at times with my older sister,
and we both came to the conclusion that she was just too devoted and
interested in F.D.R. She'd never meet anybody that would come up to
Roosevelt.

MR. C: You have to bear in mind that she and F.D.R. had a very
close relationship and F.D.R. was a man of surpassing charm when he
wanted to use it.

One charming gesture that especially touches Missy: Roosevelt spends
some idle hours at Warm Springs carving and fashioning a small hanging
bookcase for her. She prizes it enough that she will specify it in her will,
leaving it to her favorite niece and namesake, Marguerite Jane Farwell,
along with her mink coat, diamond wristwatch, and diamond ring.

But what is the nature of this "very close relationship" that binds them
to one another's presence, day and night, for year upon year? What can
its nature further teach us about the ways—personal and political—of
Franklin Roosevelt? Is it love? Is it being "in love"? About F.D.R. we
can only wonder. About Missy we can ask: Was Missy in love with
"F.D."?

MRS. C: I wouldn't be at all surprised. Would you?
MR. C: I wouldn't be surprised.[12]

If Missy's devotion to F.D.R. is to be called love, it cannot be known
to him. Of all his sensors, the keenest is for adoration, devotion, love.

The question probes a relationship between a partly paralyzed man
and a Catholic girl that developed in the 1920s, before speculation about
love inevitably opened speculation about sexual intimacy. Did this man's
illness preclude the possibility of a sexual relationship? The factual answer
is no. In 1932, to put an end to rumors that his health might stand in the
way of his serving as President, Roosevelt submits himself to a complete
examination by three eminent physicians, the summary of their findings
to be published. Among the then unpublished details, the last sentence of
their report reads: "No symptoms of *impotentia coeundi*." (No sign of
impotence—*coeundi?* The doctors appear to have invented a Latin term,

found in no medical dictionary, derived from the gerund *coeundum;* meaning: "of copulating.")[13]

The medical fact being established, there are two major reasons, beyond the moral restraints of the time and the man, to support doubt that he would be drawn into a sexual relationship. It is hard to imagine that this proud man, so resistant to intimacy to begin with and now crippled, would permit such vulnerability. Extreme fear of and abstention from sex is common among paralytics and the suddenly lamed, including those to whom sexual activity may previously have been important. Their physical self-confidence is so fragile, as studies on this subject have shown, that most decline this ultimate test of personhood. For Franklin Roosevelt in particular there is a second reason, implicit in the development of his personal drives. Everything we know about this man suggests conflict and, consequently, repression of sexual drive: his early emotions entwined inextricably with those of Mama, submission to her control of the choices of female companions, his early sensing that interest in "other girls" was in competition with Mama's devotion. To such a boy—this is common among "mama's boys"—lust is a betrayal of the primary source of love. Flirtatious he might become, eliciting and cultivating the attentions of attractive women, thus perhaps earning a reputation as a ladies' man. But sensual lust impinges upon the conflicts that are sealed off by repression. While a need for conquest may be the central force of his life, it is most likely to be exercised through charm and assertion of power and not through a more direct, sexual form. Such a man commonly chooses, as Franklin does, a sexually disinterested wife. But a devoted wife. One who clearly signals a will and a commitment to advance a destiny first envisioned and infused in him by his mother.

The sex lives of figures in the limelight are almost always a topic of speculation and banter by those around them, but not so for Roosevelt. Raymond Moley suggests why: "Everyone assumed he was indifferent to sex. I always attributed this to religion, his class upbringing and that sort of thing. But he was interested in a different kind of relationship with a woman, friendly and close without being sexually intimate. We're so obsessed today with sex that we can't understand a relationship that doesn't include it. But there's no doubt that Missy was as close to being a wife as he ever had—or could have."[14]

We already know that coincident with the period of his first sexual challenges as a bridegroom young Roosevelt experienced sleepwalks and a nightmare. If those occurrences indeed arose from sexual conflict, the stresses became resolved in an undemanding marriage and a disabling illness. Did new stresses—and new conflicts expressed through fantasy—take their place? There is a suggestion that new, unresolvable urges did have a certain hold on him. And they appear to involve those seemingly carefree days of the mid-1920s when Roosevelt and Missy are "away from it all" at their little Warm Springs cottage. To explore this, we must put ourselves forward to the evening of May 12, 1935, at a private dinner in the White House. Present are Missy, Mrs. Louis Howe (whose husband lies ill in a nearby room), Fulton Oursler (the editor of *Liberty* and other MacFadden magazines) and Mrs. Oursler. According to Oursler, who keeps meticulous notes of his White House visits, the talk turns to detective stories.

"A good detective story," the President, in an exuberant mood, proclaims, "is the answer to Lowell's question—'What is so rare as a day in June?' Hundreds of such novels are published every year but only a few are really worth the time and attention of intelligent readers. Even in the good ones there is often a sameness. Someone finds the corpse and then the detective tracks down the murderer. I do not believe that such stories have to follow an inevitable pattern or formula."

Oursler asks the President if he has ever felt moved to write one himself.

"To tell you the truth, I have often thought about it. In fact, I have carried the plot for a mystery story in my mind for years. But I can't find the solution to my own plot! And I've never found anyone else who could solve it either."

Oursler, always the editor, eggs him on.

"All right, you've brought it on yourself," declares Roosevelt. "Here in a nutshell is the idea. The principal character in my story is a man of considerable wealth. Perhaps he has six or seven million dollars tied up, as such fortunes naturally are, in a variety of investments—stocks, bonds, and real estate. My millionaire is not an old man—just over forty and wise enough to feel that his life is only beginning. Perhaps his wife, to whom he has been married for twenty years, now definitely bores him. Perhaps, too, the sameness of his middle-aged routine has begun to wear him down. Furthermore, he is disheartened at the hollowness of all the superficial friendship surrounding him. The men at the club smile and slap him on the back but they go away to do him in the eye. Finally, he has an ambition, a dream."

Oursler interjects: "He would like to get away from it all."

"Only in this case there is a difference. He would like also to get away *with* it all. First, he wants to find a new world for himself, one in which he will no longer be bored. He wants to start life fresh. He's finished with his present career and feels he has exhausted it. Second, and equally important, he would like to try out a certain experiment in public health and recreation in some small city where, in his new identity, he will not be recognized. To carry out this laboratory experiment—which, if successful, would become nationwide and benefit all the people—he will need five million dollars. The dream will cost money, you see. Moreover, he feels that he has a right to live well and enjoy in his new environment the fruits of his labors in the old. In other words, he wants to vanish, but he wants his money with him when he goes.

"Now, this man has an estate of six or seven million dollars. If he leaves a million or so behind him he has made ample provision for his wife and the others dependent on him. That ought to be easy. But it's not. The problem is not so simple as it seems.

"How can a man disappear with five million dollars in any negotiable form and not be traced?

"For years I have tried to find the answer to that problem. In every method suggested I have been able to find the flaw. The more you consider the question, the more difficult it becomes. Now—can you tell me how it can be done?"

Fiction, it is often said, is autobiographical in some transformed way. Roosevelt's own situation at Warm Springs is not quite the same as his character's; the resemblance is at best metaphorical. Roosevelt does not own six or seven million dollars.* His treasure is "tied up" in the will of his very-much-alive mother. And his most valuable asset, as impossible to "vanish" with as stocks and bonds, is the name of Roosevelt, a social position and a political reputation. Perhaps the most interesting thing about Roosevelt's "mystery story" is that he creates one he can't solve.

It's only a story meant for amusement, of course, not to be made too much of. But, on the other hand, it is a story that his mind chooses to dwell on for years.

Clever editor that he is, Oursler suggests that he engage six well-known mystery writers, each to invent a solution to "The President's Mystery Story." Roosevelt gladly gives him a go-ahead, and a six-part *Liberty* serial is born—but not before Roosevelt's vigilant press secretary, Stephen Early, subtracts the references to "public health and recreation" and the twenty-year marriage that has grown boring, explaining to Oursler that "it might be construed by some readers as the President's 'personal feelings.'"

Roosevelt spins another, more exotic story that night. It is of an innocent young girl sent on a sailing voyage in the care of a nun. The nun, a severe chaperone, keeps the girl locked up in their cabin. Then one day

* Mrs. Roosevelt, who is seldom amused by flights of fancy and who perhaps blocks some implications of this particular fancy, brushes it off in *This I Remember* (p. 125): "One of his favorite little games was trying to figure out ways you could disappear with $50,000."

the girl discovers the nun at the bathroom mirror—shaving. The "nun" turns out to be an escaped convict in disguise.

This story, too, in embellished form, Oursler publishes in *Liberty* under the title "Dark Masquerade," its proceeds going to the Warm Springs Foundation. Letters come to Oursler from "all over the country" that the story is a timeworn sailors' folk tale. Roosevelt holds his ground, however, insisting that he *knew* the girl and that he can "vouch for its authenticity."[15]

For all the fun and mischief Roosevelt finds in mystifying his friends with these two stories, he clearly has a deep-running fascination with the idea of shedding one's identity and masquerading in another.

So, even supposing that these fantasies arise from possibilities that tease his mind during those days and months and years of a reconstituted life in the Warm Springs cottage with Missy, Roosevelt can playfully discharge them by dinnertime storytelling. How about Missy? Something during that period of her life affects her deeply. In the spring of 1927, at the age of twenty-nine, her youth and marriageability having all but disappeared in the years of her commitment to F.D., this always pleasant, even-tempered, self-possessed young woman falls apart. It happens at Warm Springs. What immediately brings it on is not known. Dr. LeRoy Hubbard, a muscle-rehabilitation specialist whom Roosevelt has enticed to Warm Springs, orders her "hospitalized" in so far as the Warm Springs treatment center is a "hospital" (a designation Roosevelt does not like). The symptoms, while serious, are puzzling. Roosevelt soon writes Mama that "heart action" is "greatly improved, but since Wednesday p.m. she has had a *serious* attack of dysentery, or colitis and is rather low and very miserable. Another nurse comes from Atlanta today and I am writing for either her brother Dan or his wife."

The disease, as it turns out—in the words of Grace Tully—is "a little crack-up." Miss Tully recalls Missy's gratitude that Roosevelt "took care of her—paid her expenses and all that." Mrs. Curtis, who is at Warm Springs when the collapse occurs, recalls:

> It was a nervous breakdown. She was—much more to him than Grace Tully ever was. She was very ill for quite a while.
>
> MR. C: Dr. Hubbard was the only doctor at the place. He was called "surgeon-in-chief." They threw big titles around. Warm Springs was not organized for psychiatric care. She had to be treated there on a more or less emergency basis.
>
> MRS. C: I recall her wiring to her cousin in New York to send some silk nightgowns. And, of course, in the little Warm Springs railroad station where they sent the wire—they'd always use their own head

about adjusting the messages—they couldn't imagine a sick person wanting silk nightgowns. So they changed the wire to "sick" nightgowns. When her cousin got the wire, she didn't know whether she was supposed to send those hospital kind or Missy's silk nightgowns. Missy liked pretty things. After a while, she recovered from that illness.[16]

In the fall of 1928, Al Smith, this time victorious in his quest for the Democratic presidential nomination, puts tremendous pressure on Roosevelt to run, as his successor, for governor of New York. When Roosevelt pleads (over poor telephone connections from Warm Springs) that he wants another year to concentrate on his legs, Smith replies that he'd only have to be in Albany three months a year to sign legislative bills, that Lieutenant Governor Herbert H. Lehman would "mind the store" the rest of the time. Roosevelt does not press argument against this unacceptable suggestion. Instead he protests that he is up to his neck in financial commitments at Warm Springs. Smith puts John J. Raskob, the millionaire national chairman of the Democratic Party, on the phone, who assures Roosevelt that the debt will be "taken care of." Egbert Curtis, who has driven Roosevelt to the telephone, recalls: "He was in there for quite a while. When he came out, he was wringing wet and was very much disturbed. I said something like, 'Will you run?' He said, 'Curt, when you're in politics, you've got to play the game.' I knew he had made his decision. Those were exactly his words: 'When you're in politics, you've got to play the game.' "

Elected, Roosevelt moves into Albany's gingerbread governor's mansion with his family. With more than his family. The household arrangement now brings under one roof the two private lives of Franklin Roosevelt. He and Eleanor agree that Missy will live there, too. Mindful that her teen-age boys are sometimes resentful of Missy's closeness to their father— as Anna was toward Louis Howe when he occupied a preferred room in the Sixty-fifth Street house—Eleanor tentatively suggests giving Missy the smallest bedroom in the mansion, writing Franklin during his final days at Warm Springs, "We can talk that over."

If this new arrangement appears oddly triangular, one is hard put to determine who is the "other woman." Eleanor is gone at least half the time, tending to a furniture-crafting business she has started at Hyde Park with Nancy Cook and Marion Dickerman; teaching at the Todhunter School in Manhattan, which she has purchased in partnership with the same two women; and busy in her work for the women's division of the Democratic State Committee, where she first met these two friends.

In the eight years since her husband was stricken, a yearning for independence—from Mama certainly, and more ambivalently from Franklin—has seized her, releasing deep wells of energy and capacities for accomplishment she did not know she had. Again she is "grateful"—Lash's word—to Missy for living in the mansion, thus enabling her to continue these activities. Lash adds: "Yet it made her unhappy that Missy served as hostess . . . while she was in the city and that he accommodated himself so genially to her absences; she would have liked him to protest."

Some years later Eleanor expresses the nearest thing to her own protest. It is soon after the death of her husband, when "I had an almost impersonal feeling about everything that was happening. . . . Perhaps it was that much further back I had had to face certain difficulties until I decided to accept the fact that a man must be what he is, life must be lived as it is . . . and you cannot live at all if you do not learn to adapt yourself to your life as it happens to be.

". . . Before we went to Washington in 1933, I had frankly faced my own personal situation. . . . I felt sure that I would be able to use opportunities which came to me to help Franklin gain the objectives he cared about—but the work would be his work and the pattern his pattern. He might have been happier with a wife who was completely uncritical. That I was never able to be, and he had to find it in other people. Nevertheless, I think I sometimes acted as a spur, even though the spurring was not always wanted or welcome. I was one of those who served his purposes."

The growing separation between the lives of Franklin and Eleanor is not to be misread as the loss of a certain quality of affection. His "Dearest Babs" letters continue during his Warm Springs visits. While governor, he makes a trip to Europe during which she writes him:

> . . . I hate so to see you go. . . . We are really very dependent on each other though we do see so little of each other! I feel as lost as I did when I went abroad. . . !
> . . . Dear love to you. . . . I miss you & hate to feel you so far away. . . .
>
> Ever devotedly,
> E.R.

So little of each other—on the night of his landslide re-election as governor in 1930, while a jubilant Franklin is surrounded downstairs by politicians and Missy, Eleanor retires early to get to New York and her class next morning. She congratulates her husband by leaving a penciled note on his pillow: "Much love & a world of congratulations. It is a triumph in so many ways, dear & so well earned. Bless you & good luck these next two years.—E.R."

The following year Missy falls ill again. Eleanor, scheduled for a political trip to Maine as a fill-in for Roosevelt, takes Missy along, working in a stop at Newport with Eleanor's cousin Susie Parish. Eleanor writes to Franklin more about Missy's health than Maine politics: Missy "smoked less today and I thought seems more ready to sleep tonight. She is eating fairly well."

Lash reports: "Once a friend saw Eleanor go over and kiss Missy goodnight. 'I thought to myself—how could she?' It required great strength and self-control for Eleanor to treat Missy with such warmth and friendliness. It was difficult for Missy, too."

The fragile harmony of this trio requires that each member play his part exactly right. Missy, unlike other women fascinated by Roosevelt, instinctively understands her part. Anna recalls:

"You remember my brother Jimmy was married to Betsey Cushing? Mother felt Betsey was trying to usurp some sort of position with Father. She was perfectly open in saying, 'Betsey thinks she owns him, you know.' I mean, she'd—there was no—it was just *annoying* to her. Betsey would come and say, 'Pa says he wants so-and-so after dinner.' And Mother's feeling would be, Well, Pa should have asked me himself. And the same thing happened when Harry Hopkins and his wife Louise moved into the White House. Louise would arrange dinner parties and seat the table—my mother would be home. This would annoy the pants off her. This was her *position*. These weren't people whom she was jealous of as taking her place with Father, either of these two. But they were threatening her position.

"And I don't think Missy ever did this. You see, this is where Missy was a very, very astute little gal."

Even in a handwritten Christmas note to "Dear FD," Missy never forgets:

You should have a Merry Christmas without anyone wishing it for you, but with the whole country rising up to call you blessed—your cup *must* be full of happiness.

I guess I'm usually too flippant to tell you "Well done" but it sounds so inadequate somehow. However, you must know how proud I am every time you get something accomplished—which is *all* the time— just being with you is a joy I can't express.

I've had a happy year—for all the times I've misbehaved I hope both you and Mrs. Roosevelt will forgive me—that would be my nicest present—

Please let me do things for you—both of you—you are the ones who have my love and *only* real devotion—without that I would have little reason for taking up space, don't you think?

Merry Christmas—a very real one—

As ever—

Missy[17]

For Franklin Roosevelt this is a devotion exquisitely designed. It is a complete giving—on the terms available—unmarred by assertion of prerogative or hint of emotional demand or personal intrusion, any of which might cause this man to turn away.

The rearrangement of Franklin Roosevelt's life is a *tour de force* that finds its best parallel in—in fact, helps explain—the style of his politics. He accepts the limitations of his life as they are. Without confronting them, he turns them into their opposite. In a marriage grown arid, he channels his wife's continued devotion into what she freely offers, political service. The personal companionship he constantly craves he finds in the young woman who commits her life to attending him. Everyone is useful; everything is used. The severest limitation upon him, the crippled state of his body, provides the means for making the most of these other limitations. Using a limitation, he designs a contentment—a freedom. No confrontation, no demands; just simple adjustments—compromises—using what is at hand to win what he wants.

Victory through compromise. In his first days of presidential power, when he—and he alone—wants the CCC, and other powerful men want public works, he does not pit one against the other. He arranges their "marriage" in a single work-relief message—and wins the CCC. When he wants NRA and those same men press for funds for public works, he arranges for both, unmatched as they are, to live together under a single roof as Title I and Title II of the NIRA. And when it is important not to hurt Ickes, yet to accept Hopkins' opposite philosophy of job creation, he gives Ickes the most prominent title in WPA—and delivers the power to Hopkins through the "fine print." Taking the New Deal as a whole, he preserves the outward form of government while changing forever the character of government—in its obligation to its people.

The political limitations of the presidency? He relishes them, manipulates them, stretches them, uses them—and gets the essence of everything he asks for. In ways unsuspected by political reporters and columnists who estimate (and underestimate) him, Franklin Roosevelt comes to the office uniquely equipped—through the techniques of management perfected in his private life—to study and use the extralegal potentials of presidential power.

Everyone is useful; everything is used: As governor, Roosevelt finds that the state of New York owns a small boat suitable for river and canal trips. He decides to combine pleasure with inspections of state institutions. To him an inspection is not a formality to dignify some bureaucrat's report; it is a test of the bureaucrat's report against reality. He begins to teach Eleanor to serve as an extra set of eyes and ears. She writes:

"Walking was so difficult for him that he could not go inside an institution and get a real idea of how it was being run. . . . I would tell him what was on the menu for the day and he would ask: 'Did you look to see whether the inmates actually were getting that food?' I learned to look into the cooking pots on the stove and to find out if the contents corresponded to the menu; I learned to notice whether the beds were too close together, and whether they were folded up in closets or behind doors during the day, which would indicate that they filled the corridors at night; I learned to watch the patients' attitude toward the staff; and before the end of our years in Albany, I had become a fairly expert reporter on state institutions."

Later, traveling the nation as wife of the presidential candidate:

"From him I learned how to observe from train windows: he would watch the crops, notice how people dressed, how many cars there were and in what condition, and even look at the wash on the clotheslines. . . . Franklin saw geography clearly. . . . On the 1932 campaign trip, Franklin was impressed by the evidences of our wastefulness, our lack of conservation, our soil erosion; and on what he saw he based his plans for action."

Frances Perkins: "They had not been in Washington a month before the President asked her to go down into the southern Appalachian region, from which he had had pathetic letters, to see what the problems were and what could be done. . . . He said more than once, 'You know, Eleanor really does put it over. She's got great talent with people.' In cabinet meetings he would say, 'You know my Missus gets around a lot,' or 'my Missus says that they have typhoid fever in that district,' or 'my Missus says the people are leaving the dust bowl in droves because they haven't any chance there,' or 'my Missus says that people are working for wages way below the minimum set by NRA in the town she visited last week.'

"He had complete reliance in [sic] her observations. He often insisted on action that public officials thought unnecessary because Mrs. Roosevelt had seen with her own eyes and had reported so vividly that he too felt he had seen. They were partners."

Eleanor: "Always, when my husband and I met after a trip that either of us had taken, we tried to arrange for an uninterrupted meal so we could hear the whole story while it was fresh and not dulled by repetition. He had always asked me questions . . . but now his questions had a definite purpose.

"Franklin never told me I was a good reporter. . . . I realized, however, that he would not question me so closely if he were not interested, and I decided this was the only way I could help him. . . ."

In her first year as First Lady, Mrs. Roosevelt travels forty thousand miles. That first spring, *The New Yorker* runs a cartoon of a surprised coal miner nudging a pick-and-shovel partner: "For gosh sakes, here comes Mrs. Roosevelt!" In June 1935, the Washington *Star* society page carries a headline: "Mrs. Roosevelt Spends Night at White House."

Regarding these travels, I had this interesting bit of dialogue with daughter Anna:

Q: I must confess that her books make me wonder whether he didn't have a certain eagerness to have her go.

ANNA: Well listen, I always suspected this. Neither of them, obviously, would ever tell me whether they were reluctant or eager, but I think without a doubt that it was more peaceful. . . . So that this was—I don't know whether you want to call it an accommodation or what.

Q: It is serving each other in the best way that under the circumstances they could.

ANNA: That under the circumstances they possibly could. That's it. He knew she wanted very much to be needed—to be useful.

For all her traveling in behalf of the President, Eleanor is not entirely unchoosy. A few days before the inauguration, when the President-elect is carefully staging a dramatic descent upon Washington, he turns to Raymond Moley, a little put out, and says: "I have a funny wife. She doesn't want to go down on the train with me." Roosevelt does not insist, and she goes separately. Moley always remembers the comment, because a critical remark by Roosevelt about a member of his family to any outside person is rare.

Only once does Eleanor make an overture to Franklin, upon their moving into the White House, to get more involved in his daily work, perhaps taking over some of his mail: "He looked at me quizzically and said he did not think that would do, that Missy, who had been handling his mail for a long time, would feel I was interfering. I knew he was right and that it would not work, but it was a last effort to keep in close touch and to feel that I had a real job to do."

Roosevelt permits his First Lady almost as much personal freedom as he requires for himself. She accepts paid lectures, writes magazine articles, contracts for a series of radio broadcasts, and becomes editor of a Macfadden magazine on motherhood called *Babies—Just Babies*. When she is asked by a major newspaper syndicate to write a daily column, "My Day," describing her travels and activities, Roosevelt consents, trusting her ability to avoid political booby traps. Politically riskiest of all, when the *Ladies' Home Journal* asks her to write her serialized autobiography (later to be published as her first book, *This Is My Story*), he not only consents but permits considerable frankness. He does some blue-penciling. In her description of the onset of his polio, at his request she deletes a statement that "one night he was out of his head." In telling of her brother Hall's divorce after his alcoholic deterioration, she quotes a friend, "If you love a person, you can forgive the big things. Infidelity under certain circumstances need not ruin a relationship." Roosevelt deletes the remark about infidelity.

In 1938 Eleanor formalizes her independence as, long before, Franklin more or less formalized his. She creates a separate home for herself in the stone cottage, called Val-Kill, in which her now-defunct furniture factory was located, about a mile and a half from the "Big House" at Hyde Park. In it she creates a small apartment for Malvina Thompson—"Tommy"—her secretary and constant companion, mirroring Missy's occupancy of a room at Warm Springs and now of a third-floor apartment at the White House. When Franklin is at Hyde Park, usually receiving a stream of visitors, she temporarily transplants her residence to the Big House, although continuing to work at Val-Kill with Tommy.[18]

At the White House, "while the other secretaries keep office hours, the advisers come and go, Missy is there—always there." The observation is Doris Fleeson's in a *Saturday Evening Post* portrait of Missy. "No invitation is accepted by Missy if it means leaving the President alone. . . . Missy is attuned to his moods, knows how to keep him company both with conversation and with silence." A *Newsweek* piece on Missy in 1933: "She knows when he is bored before he realizes it himself . . . she can tell when he is really listening to an interlocutor and when he is merely being polite—which no one else can—and she sometimes even senses when he is beginning to disapprove of something that he still thinks he likes."

Grace Tully: "She'd sit with him in the evening when he was reading or playing with his stamps. Sometimes she'd sit with him while he was doing mail. He liked somebody around in case he wanted to say something. He didn't want to talk to the air. He liked to think out loud, and if he thought out loud he wanted somebody to listen. Sometimes she had things to do—she'd want to wash out some things or something like that in her own apartment. But she was there and if he wanted her, all he had to do was pick up the phone and tell her to come down. And she'd come down."

And from a unique authority, Lillian Rogers Parks, a White House maid: "Now that it is all over, and Missy and the President are both gone, I can say that Missy was more than a secretary—she was the warm-hearted listener, the boon companion and, yes, a sort of mother substitute for the President. She was the one who worried about drafts and got excited if he appeared to be catching cold. . . . She was the one who shared his private jokes; the one who first learned of his ideas, and the one who applauded them without reservation.

"She was always there. . . . She kept *his* hours, eating dinner with him in his office, when the First Lady was not around. . . . She even went swimming with him to keep him company, though it was common knowledge that she hated the water. . . . Missy gave him the companionship, the rapt attention, the ego-building boost that men sometimes find in their wives. Mrs. 'R' was not the kind of woman who would give blind praise or blanket approval. For that kind of warm support and recognition, no matter what he did, the President turned to Missy. There was definitely no question of anything improper. It was a spiritual attachment, although Missy built her whole life around him and never married. . . . Backstairs, we used to wonder if Mrs. 'R' wasn't a little jealous of Miss LeHand, but she never seemed to be."

Afternoons, when Roosevelt feels the need to get away, to go out for a drive, Missy goes along. During one of Harold Ickes' obstreperous periods, Missy directs the car to Ickes' front door and the President calls out from the car window to an astonished housekeeper, asking whether the man of the house is at home. "It is pretty hard," Ickes grumbles in his diary, "to keep a mad on with a man who makes such friendly gestures."

When the President expresses a wish one day for a quiet evening in the country that nobody would know about, Missy couples the wish with her knowledge that Ickes, needing to be pacified, is extremely susceptible to flattery. She arranges to have a party on his high-hedged lawn, with a small group that includes Tom Corcoran, the White House aide who possesses an accordion and a pleasant Irish tenor voice. "The President certainly carries his liquor well," Ickes scribbles later. After servings of cocktails, a dinner claret, champagne, and dessert liqueurs, "He must have had five highballs after dinner. He drank gin and ginger ale but he never showed the slightest effect. . . . Miss LeHand prodded him two or three times and insisted that he must go home and to bed."

A glimpse of the family flavor of relaxation at the White House is recorded in the journal of Fulton Oursler. Missy is about to serve the Ourslers a drink in the President's second-floor oval study just as Roosevelt returns from a Saturday afternoon of fishing.

"Why not let me mix it?" the President says heartily.

Missy replies, "Oh, but we are having Martini cocktails."

"Oh, no we're not." By phone he orders new fixings, gin and orange juice, meanwhile boasting of his day's catch. He mixes and serves the concoction, which Missy refuses. "She insisted on scotch and soda. There was a little tiff between them because she declined his cocktail and he at once offered to make her a Martini. She insisted that she would have the scotch and soda and nothing else."

Oursler compliments Missy on her light-blue evening dress, mentioning to her embarrassment that he has seen her in it before.

"She told us that she did have another dress but that it was at the cleaner's, and laughed very heartily and blushed a little, and the President did not seem to like the trend the conversation had taken.

"I could not help thinking, too, how odd was the whole arrangement. The President admitted that he did not know where Mrs. Roosevelt was that night. . . . His only companion was Marguerite LeHand." During a supper that followed, "not once was the name of Eleanor Roosevelt mentioned."

Some months later the Ourslers are invited again, for the annual reception for the Supreme Court, one of the starchiest of White House occasions. Roosevelt detests it, usually coming downstairs as late as possible, leaving as early as possible. Missy spirits the Ourslers to her third-floor apartment. She phones the President's study. As Oursler reports both ends of the conversation, she inquires:

"What are you doing?"

"Sitting at my desk."

"Would you like to talk to some friends?"

"Yes."

They slip downstairs to the second floor, through the President's bedroom, and into his study. He greets them:

"Well, children." And, as though in revolt against the main-floor formalities, he picks up the phone and orders beer.

Unexpectedly, "Mrs. R. rustles in. Beer comes. She's not having any." At Oursler's mention of the success of the new F.D.R. biography by Emil Ludwig, Mrs. Roosevelt comments that the book is interesting, "especially for its European point of view," but not accurate. Then (if we are to believe that Oursler hears and notes correctly) she comments "about her ideal being T.R. and not F.D.R.," adding, " 'I'm not picking any bones.' . . . President said the T.R. part was nonsense. . . . Mrs. R. then looks at beer. 'Are my other guests included in this?' President frowns. 'No.' . . . She is gone without a parting glance. . . . We feel we are part of a much darker quarrel which we can only guess about."

In memoir after memoir—Rosenman's, Ickes', Moley's, Ed Flynn's—references are made to the most intimate White House dinners on the most

delicate political matters, with Missy present as the President's dining partner. From James Farley, typical notations: "I had dinner at the White
House with the President, Ed Flynn, Vincent Dailey, and Missy LeHand
at which it was decided that Joseph V. McKee . . . should make the race"
for mayor of New York. In 1939, when Farley, opposed to a third term
and eager to run for President himself, is "summoned" to Hyde Park for a
man-to-man talk: "He came whirling down the lane in his hand-braked
Ford. Missy LeHand was at his side. . . . We had iced tea and cake on
the porch. Missy was with us almost continuously during an hour and a
half of conversation. Once or twice she was called to the phone."

In 1937 Ickes laments to Tom Corcoran that the President has scarcely
anyone "with whom he could really talk on matters that affected him most
deeply. Tom said that this was true and that he didn't think there had been
anyone whom he could really talk to except his son Jimmy [then on the
White House staff] and Miss LeHand." Later: "Apparently Harry [Hop-
kins] doesn't know what is moving in the President's mind, although he
has been living at the White House for at least two or three weeks and is
undoubtedly closer to the President than anyone else, except 'Missy'
LeHand."

In the first year at the White House, the year of Ray Moley's greatest
closeness to Roosevelt, Moley hears only one puzzled reference to the
peculiarity of the relationship with Missy. He is riding in a car from Hyde
Park with Marvin McIntyre, F.D.R.'s appointments secretary and a political lieutenant during the 1920 vice-presidential campaign. Mac, irritated
by F.D.R.'s having consulted Missy trustingly on some matter while holding Mac at arm's length, blurts out, "What goes on there anyway?"

In her personal record keeping, Missy is as circumspect as she is in her
daily behavior. Of the thousands of file boxes of White House papers at the
Roosevelt Library at Hyde Park, Missy's virtual anonymity is broken by
merely a single thin folder marked with her name: a letter to a department
store urging it to change her mailing address to the White House, her will,
copies of her reminders to F.D. of a Roosevelt child's birthday, her Christmas notes to her boss. There is, however, one touching personal item she
decides to file as a memento. It is a note scrawled in pencil by the President:

M.A.L.
    Can I dine with you or will you dine with me? 7:30

                                                                        FDR

Missy's interest is still courted by other men. "Even the most ardent
swain," says *Newsweek* in 1933, however, "is chilled at the thought that,

to invite her to a movie, he must call up the White House, which is her home. The bachelor Prime Minister of Canada, Richard Bennett, seemed quite taken with Missy when he visited Washington last spring." "Ambassador [William C.] Bullitt was very much in love with Missy at one time," says Barbara Curtis. "He used to telephone her lots and lots of times from Paris. When he'd come to Washington, he'd take her out. But after a while she'd get bored. She just didn't seem to be interested in anybody— enough to marry them." Tom Corcoran assiduously cultivates her friendship, some say out of personal interest, others say in exploitation of her unique standing with the President. Says Grace Tully: "She didn't like Tommy Corcoran, but he didn't exploit Missy or anybody else." Joseph P. Kennedy likes to have Missy to dinner at Marwood, his palatial Maryland place, sometimes along with Corcoran and Farley, all Irish Catholics with whom he feels comfortable. Felix Frankfurter always transmits his confidential memos through Missy, taking every opportunity to flatter her (example: upon the White House appointment of Corcoran, his protégé: "I know this arrangement is essentially due to you, and I have no doubt that events will prove that in bringing it to pass you have rendered another great service to the President and the Administration").

On all this, Eleanor, too, has something to say, perhaps born of slight envy as well as admiration for Missy's skill at serving Franklin's purposes:

"Some of the people who worked closely in the administration with my husband . . . were brought in through Missy LeHand's efforts. Stanley High and Thomas Corcoran came . . . as close advisers, and for a time William C. Bullitt was given important positions and was frequently consulted.

"I think none of them ever meant a great deal to Franklin. I also think they exploited Missy's friendship, believing her more interested in them personally than in what they could contribute to Franklin's work. In that they were mistaken; . . . though occasionally someone fooled her for a time, I always waited for enlightenment to come, with confidence borne of long experience."

Missy, says Sam Rosenman, is the "frankest of the President's associates, never hesitating to tell him unpleasant truths." Yet she never stirs the President to resentment as Eleanor does. For some reason, Missy's challenges bestir affectionate fun. One day she takes a noontime stroll in a park near the White House and comes upon a palmist who has set up shop under a tree. Submitting her hand to the fortuneteller, Missy is told, "My dear, you can have a future. You have ability, but you must also have confidence in yourself. You must learn to speak up." Carrying this revelation back to the office, Missy brings forth an uproarious laugh from the President. If she feeds him the awful truth in larger doses, he protests, he doesn't know that he could take it. Thereafter, there is a new running White House joke: "Speak up, Missy."

Her method? Something in her experience makes it as natural to her as Roosevelt's early life with Mama makes it necessary to him: avoidance of confrontation.

Rosenman: "She could read the President's mind correctly and anticipate his wishes. . . . She would suggest that certain people be invited to tea or dinner who she thought would have helpful ideas about problems he had on his mind. When the strain of the daily work and grinding routine became too tough, she would get his permission to ask some of his friends to come in for cocktail pleasantries or a game of poker in the evening. And when sometimes he would seek to put off some decision or some action, she would stand there firmly but pleasantly and keep reminding him to do it.

"She frequently would hold up a letter the President had written in anger, and beg him the next day not to send it. In most cases the President's anger had subsided overnight and the letter would be torn up. If he persisted, I have known her to put the letter away in her desk again and try once more in a day or two."

In a tribute to her in a 1944 column in *Newsweek,* Raymond Moley, whose emerging differences of philosophy made it impossible to continue with Roosevelt himself, writes:

"Marguerite LeHand would have been amused and startled, had anyone attributed statesmanship to her. She had little concern with ideologies. . . . Politics, public life and government, to her, were people in their relations with each other. . . . Her influence was vastly greater than that of most of those who believe they are statesmen.

"Hundreds of people kept their contacts with the President almost solely through 'Missy.' But this was not her major service. She knew by intuition that almost everybody favors reform, if the mood in which it is presented is calm and reasonable. . . . Her immense influence on those with whom she worked was in the direction of seeing that the 'lesson' was 'more kindly.' Her quiet observation to the President that a sharp passage 'doesn't sound like you' smoothed many a ruffled front."

Odd that this younger woman should be fated to occupy a place in history in a kind of juxtaposition to that of Eleanor, and for reasons, at least in part, named by Moley. After all, who more than Eleanor respects being "calm and reasonable," is "more kindly," more able to "smooth many a ruffled front"?

What makes them opposite, however, is not their qualities of manner but the quality of their personal expectations of Franklin. A woman who has witnessed more than her fair share of personal weakness and failure— a father, two uncles, and a brother destroyed by indulgence—Eleanor has learned to live by a rule of righteousness. It is a code that permits no compromise. Late in her life, trying to understand an interest by her friends in psychiatry, even befriending two psychiatrists, having long talks with them to plumb what they are about, she turns away from the idea. Why can't a person just *do* the right things? Why can't they live by the straightforward ideals she found in the courtship letters of twenty-year-old Franklin to which she responded: "But what ideals you have to live up to! . . . I must say I wonder how many of 'we poor mortals' could act up to that!"

It is this uncompromising righteousness, imposed upon herself, which, when projected upon her expectations of her husband, prevents her—blinds her—from comprehending the style of his life. At one time she discusses with Rex Tugwell what he calls "confusing traces of the young man remaining—in his quick smile . . . in the many other ways he seemed to admit people to his confidence." He *did* give people, Tugwell reports her as saying, false impressions, "but that this was a deliberate use of an early training in manners that had become 'second nature.'" Then she added ruefully that even she "was not quite certain about the 'first nature.'"

The difference is that Missy seeks and finds the interior Franklin, the "first nature," accepting the "second nature" as an essential outer form. She accepts his "political laugh," all the compromises of political life. What Eleanor and others read as weaknesses Missy accepts as necessities —to his person as well as to his politics.

"Perhaps, in the long run," Ray Moley observes, "fewer friends would have been lost by bluntness than by the misunderstandings that arose from engaging ambiguity."[19]

Perhaps. But ambiguity, for Franklin Roosevelt, is not a matter of choice among alternatives, the result of some sort of executive decision. It is the way of his life, the way the boy was shaped, the way the man has to be.

It is part of what must be loved if one is to love the man Franklin Roosevelt.

It is part of what must be understood and accepted and admired if one is to admire the political leader Franklin D. Roosevelt, who vaulted the limitations of the presidency to put a crippled nation back on its feet.

Part VI

Demagogues, Democrats, and Demography: A New Strategy for 1936

Two Demagogues and a Country Doctor

Having talked about building dams and tunnels and sewers, now let's talk about bridges. Not bridges of steel, but political bridges. If politics is the building of a majority out of minorities, a politician must know how to build and maintain bridges; also, when it is wise to burn a bridge behind him.

My dear mother, a discerning lady in many ways (but politics is not among them), provides a simple and amusing example of how, why, and when *not* to burn a bridge. During the campaign of 1932, shortly after I had said to Rex Tugwell that Huey Long was the second most dangerous man in the United States, I invited the senator from Louisiana to Hyde Park for lunch. Several old family friends were there that day, too, in addition to my mother and my wife. I had some important talking to do with Long, which I scarcely cared to mix with the general table conversation, so I asked my mother to seat him, rather than one of the ladies, at my right. My mother, at the other end of the table, couldn't take her eyes off the senator's mop of hair falling over his florid face, his checkered suit, orchid shirt, and watermelon-pink tie, not to mention his table manners. She asked her neighbor in the most pronounced stage whisper I have ever heard, "Who is that *awful* man sitting to my son's right?" Fortunately, Long was so engrossed in our conversation, I'm quite sure he didn't hear.

She was setting a match to a bridge I was trying to build. In politics, of course, you don't throw people away because you don't like their backgrounds or their clothes or their manners. You judge purely whether they can hurt or help your cause.

Put another way, in politics you often cross a bridge with the devil —until you reach the other side.[1]

Huey Long's deviltry had first become important to our cause a few weeks earlier, at a critical moment of the Democratic Convention. A deadlock over the presidential nomination seemed to be in the making. If one of the leading candidates, of whom I was one, did not win on an early ballot, we would probably all lose to a "dark horse" who would satisfy almost nobody.

Edward J. Flynn, the Bronx Democratic leader and my New York secretary of state, was going to bed in his Chicago hotel room at 2 A.M., dead tired, when he heard a banging on his door. There stood the senator from Louisiana, surrounded by his ever-present bodyguards, who pushed their way into Ed's room. As Ed has told it to me, Long simply announced that he was supporting Roosevelt. This was no slight piece of news. He not only controlled Louisiana absolutely, but had enormous influence in several neighboring states. Long had arrived in Chicago, he went on to say, with an "open mind," but after visiting each of the other candidates—Al Smith, Senator Byrd of Virginia, and Governor Ritchie of Maryland—he had found none to his liking. No, he didn't want to meet with me the next day, he told Ed, because he might find himself disappointed in me, too. Then he'd be left with no one to support! So he'd rather throw his votes to me "sight unseen."

That's the kind of impetuous, rambunctious, unpredictable fellow Huey Long was.

And what a devil he was on the convention floor! His personal popularity in neighboring states was a powerful bludgeon he would not hesitate to use in very unsenatorial ways. I know that two of our most distinguished and most powerful senators—Joseph T. Robinson of Arkansas, the Majority Leader, and Pat Harrison of Mississippi, chairman of the Senate Finance Committee—were at times terrified by him. Both their states, while in our camp for the first ballot, were in doubt for the second. We knew that Arkansas would go as Mississippi went. Mississippi had agreed to a "unit rule"—all delegates would vote with its majority—but Senator Harrison, a more conservative man than I, was threatening to bolt the rule. Long stalked up to

Harrison on the floor, shook a fist in his colleague's face, and bellowed, "If you break the rule, you so-and-so, I'll go into Mississippi and break you!"

Arkansas and Mississippi stayed with Louisiana in the Roosevelt column.

After the convention, Long proceeded to tell everybody—including me—that he had "given the nomination to Roosevelt" and that he expected to win the election for me. He demanded a special train to carry him from state to state spreading the promise of immediate payment of a soldier bonus. When Jim Farley refused, Huey threw a fit: "Jim, you're gonna get licked. . . . I tried to save you, but if you don't want to be saved, it's all right with me." My purpose in having him to lunch was to keep his enthusiasm up while keeping his promises down. We did let him do some speaking in a few states where we thought he would do a minimum of harm. Actually, his spellbinding theatrics and populist agitation made him as great a success elsewhere as he already was in Louisiana. One thing we learned was never to underestimate Huey Long.

The story of the long road leading to my second-term election, of 1936, is a story of keeping bridges in repair that connected us with several demagogic politicians, with some far more honest men who gave us troubles too, of some history made in guaranteeing the social security of the American people, of old bridges burned and new bridges built. The story best begins with that most difficult and frightening man of all, Huey Pierce Long.

Long, who had been governor of Louisiana before he decided to be its senator, proved that it is possible for Americans, at least of one state, to accept and adore an absolute dictator. The way to become one, he also showed, is to sound like a left-wing radical, spouting easy solutions to the problems of the frustrated and poor, whom he would control. Of brilliant mind and irresponsible tongue, Long, more colorfully than anyone else, railed against Wall Street, the banks, and utilities, as though to identify the "enemy" is to subdue him. How people do love to hear one of their own kind speak from a tree stump as they themselves would love to speak!

It was not all talk. As governor, Long built roads and bridges (the steel kind), provided free school buses and new schools, opened hospitals for whites and Negroes, benefits that Louisianans had never known. He built a great university, Louisiana State, where, as elsewhere, he put his friends into positions of importance. As for the utilities he railed against, he "punished" them for their excesses in most interesting ways. Long and his friends set up a private company called the Win Or Lose Corporation. His company acquired natural-gas fields from the state at very friendly prices, selling the lands to natural-gas companies at far less friendly prices, threatening to increase their taxes if they didn't buy. In one year, these resourceful sales methods produced a profit to his company of $350,-000.

I do not believe money interested Huey nearly as much as power; he was far more a politician than a thief. With the weapon of his personal popularity he browbeat his state legislature into laws that transferred almost all parish (county) powers into state power, and other laws that gave great state power to himself. What he could not control by law he controlled through threats against the people who administered the laws. Thus he turned a state bureaucracy into a private political army.

Long's corrupt radicalism had little in common with the New Deal's progressivism. As it turned out, he opposed the National Recovery Act, because it involved co-operation with "Wall Street." He fought us on the Government Economy Act. As the chasm between us deepened he traveled widely—not only through the South, but everywhere—luring friends to his "radicalism" and trying to turn them against the New Deal, denouncing us for being "dominated" by the "same old clique of bankers" who had controlled Hoover. This was an undermining of support we could little afford.

He was as likable as he was hatable. And I think he liked me as much as he hated me. A man who craves being loved as Huey did is most susceptible to persuasion on a personal, man-to-man basis. In June 1933 I asked Jim Farley to bring Huey to the White House for a little talk. The issue, ostensibly, was patronage. Senators generally have the privilege of controlling federal appointments from their states, a privilege I had withdrawn in Long's case, and of course he was hopping mad.

He plunged into my office and dropped himself into my deskside chair, wearing his straw hat throughout our whole talk, removing it only now and then to slap on my knee to emphasize his points. The astonishment on Jim Farley's face was more amusing than Huey's behavior.

After hearing out his colorful protests (with much hat slapping), I pointed out that my sole interest was in seeing that good men were named to public office; if Huey would start recommending good men, I would appoint them. Of course, he knew he couldn't get far arguing against that; and, of course, he also knew that the qualifications of some of his retainers would begin looking ever so much better if he, Senator Long, improved his political deportment.

I made a point, of course, of finding out his reactions. To Farley, Huey muttered upon leaving, "What the hell is the use of coming down to see this fellow? I can't win any decision over him." To a reporter he said, "I'm never goin' over there again." But when a group of reporters gathered around him in the lobby, Huey said, "The President and I are never going to fall out. I'll be satisfied whichever way matters go."

I admired that quick recovery, but not half as much as his characterization of me a short time later, in which he compared me with my predecessor. Hoover, Huey said, was a hoot owl, while Roosevelt is a scrootch owl. A hoot owl, Huey explained, catches a hen by banging on its roost, knocking the hen "clean off," then seizing her as she falls. "But a scrootch owl slips into the roost and scrootches up to the hen and talks softly to her. And the hen just falls in love with him, and the first thing you know, *there ain't no hen.*"

All this, of course, was sideshow. The real importance of Huey Long—his real threat to the enactment and popular support of the New Deal—was his alarming success at propagating his quick-cure, harebrained "Share Our Wealth" program. Long had proposed—actually introduced a bill—in 1932 that we solve our problems simply by confiscating through taxation *all* income over $1 million and all inheritances over $5 million. Next year he improved this scheme, proposing to reduce all existing fortunes to about $3 million, seizing the excess for the commonweal. By 1934 Long found an even more appealing panacea, emphasizing the cure more than the treatment, the result rather than the means. Every American family would be paid a "homestead allowance" of at least five thousand dollars and an annual income of at least two thousand dollars. Everyone over sixty would receive a $30-a-month pension. (This was soon changed to an "adequate" pension. As Long's director of the "Share Our Wealth" movement, Gerald L. K. Smith, explained, "We decided to put in the 'adequate' and let every man name his own figure.")

Youngsters meeting certain standards would receive a free college education.

Now, who would argue that those guarantees aren't all very attractive? But aside from moral questions raised by guaranteeing such benefits unrelated to work—none of Huey's proposals said anything about work—the simple arithmetic was pure fantasy. Huey would say—and millions of the desperately deprived eagerly believed—that "taxes off the big fortunes at the top will supply plenty of money without hurting anybody." He crazily overestimated what his plan for confiscation would produce. Unconscionably rich as some rich men were and are, their fortunes simply would not spread as thickly as Long imagined over the millions of wage earners and farmers earning less than two thousand dollars, over the unemployed and the indigent. In the 1930s Huey was still waving the same statistics in the air that he had begun waving in 1918.

But to the little man who has nothing but an unpaid mortgage and hungry children, who sees one or two families up on the hill with servants and motor cars and more money than they know how to spend, Long's simple "solution" seemed a miracle medicine; his medicine man's sideshow gathered a large audience.

In 1935 the Democratic National Committee learned through a secret poll that Huey Long, who was threatening to launch a third party, might win between three and four million votes, not only in the South but in northern farm and industrial areas. These votes would be drawn more from Democrats than Republicans. Even in New York, the poll showed, Long might draw off at least a hundred thousand votes, which could cost us that vital state. Through an irresponsible appeal, not answerable by reasonable and logical persuasion, he threatened to capture a national balance of power.

Louis Howe carefully monitored the Long movement, passing on to me, for example, a letter addressed to me from a Montana banker describing Long as "the man we thought you were when we voted for you." Daniel J. Tobin of the Teamsters Union also wrote me with concern: "I have several letters from our members, most of them decent and honest fellows inquiring about and asking me if they should proceed to organize clubs."

I do not hesitate to say that Huey Long was my most troublesome political worry as the 1936 election began coming into view. More than that: If we did not succeed during the following four years in

throwing off the depression, demagogues would have even more al-
lure for the frustrated. In 1940 Long would be only forty-six years
old.[2]

Long had at least one great rival for leadership of what we called
the "damaged souls" electorate, in the person of Reverend Charles E.
Coughlin, pastor of a Catholic church in Royal Oak, Michigan. Father Coughlin could not threaten Long—or the country—as a candidate for President. Americans were far from ready to consider
electing a Catholic priest, especially since religious grounds had been
important in their rejecting Al Smith, a Catholic layman. Besides,
Father Coughlin was of Canadian birth, foreclosing his legal candidacy. On the other hand, Father Coughlin's followers may have
exceeded Long's in number. His Sunday afternoon radio broadcasts
outdrew the most popular evening programs: "Amos 'n' Andy" and
Ed Wynn. He received more mail than anyone in America; more,
I regret to say, than we usually received at the White House.

Coughlin's stock in trade, like Long's, was to attack Wall Street
and the banks, but in language of the Bible, not of the tree stump,
impressing his generally unlearned audience by citing some obscure
"fact" or quotation, usually far removed from its context, to stir
up his listeners against some imagined Wall Street conspiracy. (At
White House dinners I enjoyed amusing my friends by imitating Father Coughlin's addiction to quotation: "And my friends, as Jesus
of Nazareth said, *quote,* Suffer little children to come unto me, *end
quote.*")

Coughlin's hold on Catholic people of the working classes (many
non-Catholics, too) was quite powerful in New York State when
I was governor, and I was careful to keep contact and a good relationship with him. In 1931, when the Columbia Broadcasting System, upset by his vague and emotional attacks on bankers, demanded
the right to see his scripts in advance of broadcast, I was one of
many who protested this as censorship. (The following fall, CBS
refused to sell Coughlin time, and he organized his own national
hookup of independent stations.) During the 1932 presidential campaign he propagated a slogan, "Roosevelt or Ruin." His whipped-up
followers, I suppose, identified my anti-Hooverism and anti-do-noth-
ingism with Coughlin's feverish anti-Wall Streetism. His sloganeering
was indeed helpful to us in the election. Later, Coughlin sermonized
favorably for the NRA, public works, and regulation of the stock

exchanges, all helpful. To keep the bridge in good repair I invited him to visit me at the White House. A short time later he said— and was quoted widely—"I will never change my philosophy that the New Deal is Christ's deal."

Coughlin opposed our farm program, but that was not where our break came; it was over the prevalent nonsense about silver. The over-all cure for the depression, according to Coughlin, would be a "religious crusade against the pagan god of gold. . . . Silver is the key to world prosperity—silver that was damned by the Morgans!" Over this, Coughlin did indeed change his philosophy that "the New Deal is Christ's deal." Henry Morgenthau at the Treasury drew up and released a list of silver speculators, and heading the list was Father Coughlin's secretary. Coughlin promptly sent up new psalms to what he called "gentile silver"—which I could only interpret as vengeance on Morgenthau, who happens to be of the Jewish faith. Religious bigotry became increasingly prominent in Coughlin's weekly tirades.

While becoming disgusted and alarmed with the tones of his crusade, I sometimes sent a mutual friend—Joseph P. Kennedy or Frank Murphy—to pat his hand and cool him down. He was very amenable to these attentions, and what came out was confusion and self-contradiction. Soon after slandering Morgenthau, Coughlin restated his faith "in the courage of our President and in the stalwart uprightness and integrity of his Secretary of the Treasury." As long as he retained the power of speech, he said, he would support the New Deal. Indeed! Then, suddenly, my effort to save capitalism was as hopeless as "removing in a sieve the water from the Atlantic Ocean to the swimming pool of the New York Athletic Club." After my message to Congress of January 1935 Coughlin switched again: "Today I believe in him as much as ever." By March another switch: my administration had "out-Hoovered Hoover. . . . I will not support a New Deal which protects plutocrats and comforts Communists."

Perhaps he was authentically confused; or perhaps his confusion was calculated as a means of appealing to diverse sections of his emotional followers. This confusion was most evident in his "uncompromising" opposition to capitalism. Uncompromising? He commented one day, "The sane people in this country have always lent their support and *will* always lend their support to that theory of economics." Like many radicals, he was for nationalizing power, light, oil, and natural gas, but (lest he be misunderstood) he once explained, "By nationalization of power, light, oil, and natural gas . . . I do not subscribe to the theory that we should nationalize public utilities." Capitalist production for profit, he argued, along with more intellectual Socialists, must be abolished in favor of "production for use." But lest he be misunderstood, he once made clear, his particular brand was "production for use at a profit."

Even if we could overlook the shrill crescendo of Coughlin's anti-Jewish divisiveness and his eventual vituperations against me as "the great betrayer and liar" and as "Franklin Doublecrossing Roosevelt," we had to take him seriously when he formalized his crusade into an organization, the National Union for Social Justice. He took pains to emphasize it was not a political party—and soon took further pains to negotiate with other demagogic organizations, among them Huey Long's Share-Our-Wealth movement, toward a third-party threat in the 1936 election.[3]

A third participant in that third-party threat was a force that one Republican senator, Bill Borah, without too much exaggeration, called "the most extraordinary social and political movement in recent years and perhaps in our entire history." This movement arose from a "plan" for old-age pensions invented by an aging country doctor, Francis E. Townsend. It seems that Dr. Townsend, a good and kindly man (with almost nothing in common with the likes of Huey Long or Father Coughlin), after retiring to Long Beach, California, and being down to his last hundred dollars in savings, looked out his bedroom window one day and saw two elderly ladies picking at garbage cans for food. The injustice of that awful scene inspired in a flash, he has said, his plan. Teaming up with Robert Clements, a far more worldly real estate promoter, Townsend propagated a scheme to pay a pension of two hundred dollars a month to every citizen over sixty on condition that the recipient (1) retire from gainful work and (2) spend the sum within thirty days in the United States, thus "guaranteeing" a whirlpool of cash circulation.

Townsend's idea was to raise the pension money through a retail sales tax. When someone pointed out that elderly people on fixed incomes are traditional opponents of sales taxes, the Townsendites invented a 2 per cent "transaction tax," to be paid upon sale of a commodity every time it changed hands from raw material to finished product. This, of course, would be a compounded sales tax, but the

Townsendites satisfied themselves that "most of the money" would come from stock and bond transactions—Wall Street again. Dr. Townsend also thought of giving his scheme a flying start by printing two billion dollars' worth of currency as well, but his advisers talked him out of that.

By Townsend's guess, eight million men and women would qualify, amounting to a disbursal of $1.6 billion *every month*. More expert and skeptical estimaters predicted that more than ten million would qualify. Their annual pensions of $24 billion would come to half the national income—not government income, but the combined incomes of every business and every working man and woman—and twice the current collection of all federal, state, and local taxes. Thus the Townsendites would restore prosperity and an "equitable" redistribution of wealth by channeling half the national income to less than one tenth of the population, those who had survived sixty years.

Well, didn't the true believers flock to Dr. Townsend! Townsend clubs spread like the measles, and by 1935 at least ten million well-meaning folk had signed his petitions. In 1934 the Townsend movement gave rise to a competitive offshoot, the candidacy of Upton Sinclair, the socialist author, for governor of California. He captured the Democratic primary and, for a time, we thought he might win the election. More directly, the Townsend movement found official expression in a Congressional bill introduced by a Californian, seventy-two-year-old Rep. John S. McGroarty.

True believers those people were. So sure were some Townsendites of their eventual deliverance, that they hounded stores, seeking to make purchases payable upon arrival of their Townsend checks. I heard of one elderly couple in San Diego who ordered a stove, refrigerator, kitchen cabinets, a radio, and twin beds, but the delivery man would not accept their promise of payment "next month," when the Townsend check arrived. It got so bad that in many stores, as soon as someone over sixty appeared at the door, the salesmen disappeared.

Something like that disappearing act happened in Congress, too—when the McGroarty bill finally managed to get to the floor. The debate was not long, its highlight being a speech by another Californian, John Tolan, about Mother: "She is the sweetest memory of my life, and the hands that used to feed me and cool my fevered brow now touch me only in my dreams. But if she were living today . . . that little, frail mother of mine . . . would say, 'Son, you be good to the old folks, and God will bless you.'" When the vote came, almost two hundred congressmen, like those California salesmen, had disappeared. Those remaining managed to defeat the bill without recording their votes in a roll call. No matter how mad the proposal, it is not easy to go on record against Mother.

And no matter how mad the Townsend plan was, the size and enthusiasm of its support, particularly in the West, could not be taken lightly.[4]

Security from the Cradle to the Grave

In strength there is weakness, and in weakness there is often potential strength.

In my very young days at Groton School, where I was student manager of the football team, I began to learn that important lesson. When your team is on the offensive most strongly, you are also most vulnerable. The greater the attack, the greater your opponent's opportunity. In football the most dangerous attack of all is the long forward pass. And, of course, the long forward pass is easiest to intercept, which may turn the whole game around.

Our tremendous Congressional victory of 1934 should have—theoretically—made us invulnerable. But there's something about the American political character that makes success breed division. A slim victory forces unity, members of the victorious party hanging together to keep their upper hand. But the more dominant one party becomes, the more likelihood is there of wrangling within it, its strength thus threatening self-destruction.

The dramatic rise of the Long and Coughlin and Townsend movements after the 1934 election placed enormous stress on our victory. So, as coach of the winning team, I had to find a way to preserve our strength by keeping the team united. I had to steal the thunder of these divisive elements, who had the whole country arguing over the pros and cons of pensions and security payments, by attracting their followers to a plan that was practical and feasible.

This I relished doing. Some political "experts" have written that the Social Security Act of 1935 was "forced" upon me as an answer to the demogogues. Absolutely true, yet absolutely untrue. Those demagogues required an answer, but they also created the good timing for a practical plan. I had been waiting for that proper moment for years.

In my first months as governor, even before the economic crash of 1929, my associates and I often talked late into the night about plans that eventually became the Social Security Act. These talks began first with concern for the hazards of unemployment. Security in old age occupied us later. I began to think of unemployment as an industrial hazard, just like factory accidents. The workingman is helpless to control the great economic forces that control him. If our system of competitive enterprise, which has raised the standard of living of most Americans, also brings with it a constant and unavoidable threat of unemployment, even in good times, an individual should not have to suffer its total, crushing cost. I felt sure we could devise a way, as we have done with fire and untimely death, by which large numbers of people could pool their risk in a system of unemployment insurance.

Very few people, other than socialists, had previously thought of this goal as a proper function of government. I began by investigating some private ways that individual New York companies had devised to stabilize the security of their employees. The John A. Manning Paper Company, of Troy, undertook to schedule its production a full year at a time, thus guaranteeing its employees an annual income. Welch's Grape Juice, of Westfield, a seasonal business, added the manufacture of jellies to keep their people more steadily employed, even though on shortened work weeks and workdays. The Hills Brothers Company, led by my friend Ernest Draper, added shredded coconut and canned figs to their basic seasonal business of packing dates, and invested in a cold-storage plant so packing could be stretched over a longer work period. But a few enlightened companies do not an economic system make.

The "right" way for workingmen to provide for unemployment and retirement, some moralists say, is to save, just as country families store wood in the shed against the cold days of winter. Fine! But in the best of times, many families just don't earn enough to do that—and some that can, won't.

During the most prosperous year of our history, 1929, one fifth of our families earned less than one thousand dollars. Another fifth had incomes between a thousand and fifteen hundred. A Brookings Institution study of that year pointed out that "basic necessities" of an average family cost two thousand dollars, so how could those 40 per cent of our families save? The fact is that 80 per cent of American families—those with incomes of $3,100 or less—managed to eke out only 2 per cent of all our national savings. Eighty-six per cent of savings were held by the 10 per cent of families earning more than $4,600.[5]

These statistics have to do with more than personal fears of joblessness, hunger, and cold. They also have to do with the strength of politicians and the foundations of corrupt political machines. We must take a moment to look into the connections between economic security and machine politics.

If 40 per cent of families earned so little that they couldn't buy necessities in good times, how did they stay alive in the terrible days between the crash of 1929 and our first relief measures of 1933? They borrowed from relatives and friends or fell on "charity"—we've gone into that. Many were saved by something else. They were saved by politicians, men who built powerful machines, particularly in the cities, by purchasing the loyalty of unfortunates through handouts of jobs, a few emergency dollars, a food basket here, a few pailfuls of coal there, a stay against eviction.

New York's Tammany Hall, with which I have had my share of unpleasant experiences, grew powerful and bold through such selective charity to the faithful. The entrenched machines of Chicago (Mayor Cermak, followed by Mayor Edward J. Kelly), Jersey City (Mayor Frank Hague), Kansas City (Tom Pendergast), Boston (Mayor Jim Curley), Memphis (Ed Crump), virtually every American city, owed their strength to the wide-open field, neglected by government, of relieving personal insecurity.

In the 1932 campaign—and later in the White House—some of my best friends tried to persuade me not to deal with these powerful and often corrupt machine bosses. I should not, they said, seek the "advice" of these leaders on the location of WPA and PWA projects. I should not, they said, channel patronage through these machines, as if I could pretend these cities had alternative Democratic organizations to insure our election. I should declare independence from them not only for myself but for all Americans, as though some simple proclamation would bring that about.

Harold Ickes, a Chicagoan, pleaded with me not to give Ed Kelly PWA funds to develop the Chicago lake front into a vast park. Did Harold have any ideas as to how the New Deal would carry Illinois if the Chicago Democratic organization rebelled against us and sat on its hands?

It was easy to ignore his pleas, but not so easy to ignore a very difficult situation in New Jersey. Mayor Hague of Jersey City, who controlled the state, gave us trouble in ever so many ways, including virtual warfare on labor organizers, who were vital to the New Deal. We could survive that. Then Hague's henchmen overstepped legality by monitoring the mail of his enemies, spying on letters going through the United States Post Office. We got him to stop that. But I will admit now—for the purposes of instruction in practical politics—that we stopped short of bringing indictments. That episode had forced a most difficult political choice. Yes, perhaps purity would dictate that we indict these politicians for deplorable misbehavior—and make enemies of an organization that alone guaranteed that a major state stood behind our New Deal program. Which was more important? Had New Jersey's more high-minded Democrats worked and troubled themselves to build a Democratic organization in opposition to Hague? If New Jersey Democrats were permitting his machine to endure and flourish, is it the President's job to dismantle it—and throw the state to the opposition?

My course in dealing with the Hagues and Kellys and Tammany Hall, despite the advice of my friends, was not to confront them, but to destroy them more slowly and more surely, by bringing them into camp, enlisting them in the common task of digging their political graves—largely through Social Security.

My plan was to enlist them in the grandest form of political "charity" of all—gathering votes in favor of unemployment insurance and old-age assistance. Let them help me substitute security for insecurity, never quite aware that by undermining insecurity they were undermining the foundations upon which political machines have been built. What would happen, I asked Rex Tugwell one day during the campaign of 1932 when he questioned my attitude toward political machines—what would happen to the organization if handouts were no longer needed, if Mrs. O'Toole didn't have to run to the precinct captain for a food basket while O'Toole was drying out in the clink, or if the Esposito family had their own means, even while Esposito was out of a job, to get a few buckets of coal? If politics were used to help government get security really organized, Tammany's greatest source of power would be ruined. New Deal reform, so appealing to Mrs. O'Toole and Mr. Esposito, and consequently to their political bosses, was the greatest enemy, would be the eventual undoing, of these powerful bosses—and, fortunately, the bosses didn't realize it. No longer could need be traded for votes. If we could build a system of social security that really *belonged* to the people—I don't mean vaguely in principle, I mean specifically in cash, through insurance premiums—politics would never be the same.[6]

Yet in 1931 I was not thinking in terms of a national law. There was no such thing as a federal labor law. Strong government was concentrated in state capitals, not in Washington. But there was a great danger in a state unemployment insurance law. Employers would have to contribute premiums, running up their costs. This would give a competitive advantage to neighboring states in seeking industry, in creating jobs. So, as I was later to do with the NRA, I began to think in terms of co-operation, in this case a compact among neighboring states. I organized a conference of governors of the industrial Northeast—my old friend Gifford Pinchot, the conservationist, who was now governor of Pennsylvania; Joseph B. Ely of Massachusetts; Norman S. Case of Rhode Island; Wilbur L. Cross of Connecticut; Morgan F. Larson of New Jersey; George White of Ohio; William Tudor Gardiner of Maine, and John G. Winant of New Hampshire.

This was not as easy as it sounds. Governors are proud men who do not accede readily to leadership by other persons of equal rank, especially to one being talked about as a possible presidential candidate. I asked Frances Perkins, then my state labor commissioner, to sound out her counterparts in the various states as to whether their governors would be willing to come. We learned that each of them shared my concern about unemployment, and they came. This was a beginning.

Soon afterward I was invited to make a speech at the national conference of governors at Salt Lake City. Mrs. Perkins drafted three or four pages to be included, a forceful argument for unemployment insurance. Too forceful. I made that section shorter, less forceful.

The idea was still radical. I did not want to make enemies before recruiting a few friends. Frances expressed her disappointment—until she saw the newspaper coverage of my speech. The headlines said, in effect, "Governor Roosevelt Comes Out for Unemployment Insurance." It was just right. Had I pressed harder, I would have invited early editorial opposition. So at least the idea was in the air by the time I was elected and inaugurated as President.

Once in the White House, we found ourselves in a family controversy between unemployment insurance and work relief. Harry Hopkins argued that creation of jobs by government was the answer to unemployment. No insurance we could devise, he felt, would be sufficient to take care of families in a long depression. He favored a permanent system of work relief that would be called "unemployment and old-age insurance." Payments should be made from public funds as a matter of right, not requiring the recipient to prove he is destitute. Harry went to great lengths to establish the moral rightness of this position. Eloquent as he was, he failed to see that he was arguing for the very thing we were both against. Such payments, laid out by government, no matter what name they went by, still suggest a dole.

Secretary Perkins argued that if mass unemployment were ever to occur again, some future administration might be too strapped to put out money fast enough for either work relief or unemployment insurance. She felt—as I did—that an insurance fund had to be built up in advance. I let each of them fully develop their arguments, then said:

"I don't see why you can't combine both. Let's go ahead with the plan for unemployment insurance. I think that's right. Let a man have something definite by law for some weeks and then arrange it so he can have relief afterward if unemployment continues and he is in need. When he leaves the unemployment insurance rolls after, say, twelve to sixteen weeks at half to two thirds of his weekly wages, he gets a green ticket and is told he can make another application at another office on this green ticket for work benefits. First the cash benefit, then use up his savings, then a work benefit. The projects to be used as work benefits ought to be thought out in advance, so our enemies can't yell 'boondoggling' to make fun of a useful job."

On this basis we went ahead. I appointed a Committee on Economic Security to bring me all the possible alternatives for a social insurance program.

By this time the nation's first unemployment-compensation law had been passed, by the state of Wisconsin. It required each company to build up its own compensation fund. Companies were "rated" in such a way that those with a history of most layoffs had to make the largest contributions to their funds. The theory was that this would force businessmen to do their best to keep employment stable.

At about the same time, the Ohio Commission on Unemployment Insurance proposed a plan that differed from Wisconsin's in two important ways. First, employees would contribute to the fund as well as employers. Second, size of contributions would be based on size of wages, not on industry "rating," and all contributions would be pooled in a single, state-wide fund. The idea behind that was that unemployment is a social cost that ought to be borne by as many elements of the community as possible, not penalizing unstable industries.

I liked the idea of contributions from both business and labor. Even though both were bound to complain, neither could protest that the entire social burden was on its shoulders. Organized labor, whom one would think would be most enthusiastic for unemployment compensation, was halfhearted about any plan at all. The A. F. of L., still influenced by the ghost of Samuel Gompers, was reticent about legislation to benefit labor. Professional union leaders like to win all their gains through collective bargaining, thus winning credit for themselves rather than government.

The Ohio plan was close to what we agreed upon. Our next problem was whether to centralize insurance in one huge federal fund or to devise a system of separate state funds. On this question the debate went on and on, this way and that, and finally landed on the way I preferred: state funds. I have always shared with Justice Louis Brandeis the notion that a great advantage of having many states in a single nation is that they provide an opportunity for competitive experiment. If Wisconsin wanted industry "ratings," let them have it. If that system proves out, other states will copy it; if it fails, Wisconsin will soon copy other states. This also helped us avoid constitutional troubles. Under a state-by-state plan, the federal government was using only its unquestioned power to tax. Distribution of the funds was local, thus uninvolved with the question of interstate commerce.

Then came the question of retirement pensions. I told my people: "We have to have it. The Congress can't stand the pressure of the

Townsend Plan unless we have a real old-age insurance system, nor can I face the country without having devised . . . a solid plan which will give some assurance to old people of systematic assistance upon retirement."

We all readily agreed that individuals as well as employers should contribute to their own retirement pensions. Should the same size of pension be paid to everyone? While much could be said for that, we knew that would create resentment by skilled workers of higher earnings who had contributed more. We settled on a complex formula of graduated benefits, ranging from ten dollars to eighty-five dollars a month, based on contributions. But then, what about people who were already fifty or fifty-five years old, already within sight of a retirement age of sixty-five? Their relatively small contributions over ten or fifteen years would entitle them to less than half of the full pension their younger coworkers would someday receive. Arithmetic showed us that we could indeed start out paying full pensions to retiring workers by borrowing from the accumulating funds of younger workers. A deficit would show up, however, in about 1980, even accounting for interest the fund could earn. (Regarding this interest, I was attracted to the idea that the Social Security fund could be the biggest, perhaps the sole, purchaser of federal bonds, thus freeing the government at last from the stranglehold of big bankers.)

I refused to go along with such a delayed deficit. If we relied on mere faith that the Congress of 1980 would appropriate money for such a deficit, that Congress, the composition of which we could not know, would also be given the power to destroy Social Security. I was determined to create a system of citizen-owned insurance that politicians could not kill. Pointing out that dependence on Congress was the same old dole under another name, I said, "We can't sell the United States short in 1980 any more than in 1935."

When the state-vs.-federal question came up regarding old-age pensions, this time we came down on the side of a uniform federal system. Under unemployment compensation, a worker laid off in Pennsylvania is entitled to the Pennsylvania system of unemployment benefits. But under old-age assistance, a worker may have worked almost all his life in Pennsylvania, then, at fifty-eight, say, he moves to California; with a state plan, he would have lost his Pennsylvania pension. Americans are starting to move about more than in the past.

This mobility was our main reason for taking the constitutional risks of a federal system, which the Court later upheld.

Unemployment compensation stirred the enthusiasm of some, old-age assistance of others. As I had done with other bills, to strengthen the support of each we put them both in a single Social Security bill. To it, we added other provisions to assist some states with burdens they already had taken on and to encourage other states to take them on. By outright grants-in-aid, the federal government would pay up to one half the costs of state assistance to the needy aged who were ineligible for Social Security; to the blind; to husbandless mothers of dependent children; for the support of indigent Indians; for certain maternal and child-health services; aid to crippled children; and for vocational rehabilitation of the disabled.

How different all this is from a dole! The two main groups of beneficiaries, the involuntarily unemployed and the elderly, pay for their own protection. The other beneficiaries—the blind, the disabled, fatherless children—are victims of the pure chance of misfortune, which could happen to any of us. Nothing in this system encourages idleness of the able-bodied. Everything in it lifts needless fear from the hard-working. And at the end of the line there is an earned, deserved reward of a little leisure for those whose labor has been given.

When I outlined this plan to the Cabinet, I said—although this has not entirely worked out—"The system ought to be operated through the post offices. Just simple and natural—nothing elaborate or alarming about it. The rural free delivery carrier ought to bring papers to the door and pick them up after they are filled out. The rural free delivery carrier ought to give each child his social insurance number and his policy or whatever takes the place of a policy. The rural free delivery carrier ought to be the one who picks up the claim of the man who is unemployed, or of the old lady who wants old-age insurance benefits.

"And there is no reason why just the industrial workers should get the benefit of this. Everybody ought to be in on it—a farmer and his wife and his family. I don't see why not. Cradle to the grave—from the cradle to the grave they ought to be in a social insurance system." (Years later, when Great Britain put in the so-called Beveridge Plan, with enormous fanfare they called it "cradle to the grave" social insurance. Sir William Beveridge's memory is good. He remembered that phrase from the time he came to see me in 1934.)[7]

I chose to make no public use of the "cradle to the grave" phrase. It was a radical-sounding idea that could only stir up unnecessary opposition, of which we already had plenty. The National Industrial Conference Board declared, "Unemployment insurance cannot be placed on a sound financial basis"—thus ignoring our meticulous use of actuarial statistics in planning payroll deductions. Other big-business voices turned to purely emotional propaganda: "The downfall of Rome started with corn laws, and legislation of that type," said George P. Chandler of the Ohio Chamber of Commerce. "The lash of the dictator will be felt," warned Republican Congressman Daniel Reed, "and twenty-five million free American citizens will for the first time submit themselves to a fingerprint test." (Where does the bill say or imply anything about fingerprints?) Even from a more cool-headed Republican, Rep. James W. Wadsworth of New York: "This bill opens the door and invites the entrance into the political field of a power so vast, so powerful as to threaten the integrity of our institutions and to pull the pillars of the temple down upon the heads of our descendants." Social Security, predicted Charles Denby, Jr., of the American Bar Association, "sooner or later will bring about the inevitable abandonment of private capitalism." Mayor Hague's man in the Senate, A. Harry Moore, like many conservatives, objecting emotionally before realizing the immense popularity of Social Security, emoted: "It would take all the romance out of life. We might as well take a child from the nursery, give him a nurse, and protect him from every experience that life affords."

Some Democrats of the South also misgauged the widespread desire for minimum security. The Jackson *Daily News* editorialized, "The average Mississippian can't imagine himself chipping in to pay pensions for able-bodied Negroes to sit around in idleness on front galleries, supporting all their kinfolks on pensions, while cotton and corn crops are crying for workers to get them out of the grass." Another southern voice, that of Senator Thomas P. Gore, amused me. When Frances Perkins testified before a Senate Committee on Social Security, he asked, "Isn't this socialism?" Frances replied, "Oh, no." Gore leaned forward, smiled sarcastically, and—as Frances described it to me—talked to her as though she were a child, saying, "Isn't this a teeny-weeny bit of socialism?"

That kind of opposition didn't worry me greatly. For every such voice there were a million votes on the side of minimum security.

What did bother me was the obstructionism of voices to my left, who insisted on Utopia overnight. They demanded bigger pensions with little or no payroll contributions. Some would have employers pay all, which would kill the bill, or the more mysterious method of having the "government" pay all, as though taxes were not a citizen cost. Their method would permit each succeeding Congress to reconsider the continued life of Social Security, which I found entirely unacceptable.

"If I have anything to say about it," I said once in a private meeting, "it will always be contributed, and I *prefer* it to be contributed, both on the part of the employer and the employee, on a sound actuarial basis. It means no money out of the Treasury." To this some economists argued, perhaps rightly, that such a heavy payroll withdrawal when we were still trying to battle our way out of a depression could itself be a temporary depressant, a form of hoarding money under a great big government mattress. "I guess you're right on the economics," I told one of these objectors, "but those taxes [are not] a problem of economics. They are politics all the way through. We put those payroll contributions there so as to give the contributors a legal, moral, and political right to collect their pensions and their unemployment benefits. With those taxes in there, no damn politician can ever scrap my social security program."

Getting Across to Those
Bridge-Burning Liberals

I could say things like that in private but could not attack my fellow liberals in public. Yet the point had to be made and I asked my wife to make it at one of her press conferences. She waited for a proper time, when a question was asked about the squabbles among friends of Social Security—perhaps she saw to it that the question was asked —and she answered it exactly right: "I have always been amused to note that those who want a great deal more, and those who want a great deal less done, find themselves, unconsciously to be sure, working together and preventing the accomplishment of a moderate middle-of-the-road program."

The strain of these differences involved more than Social Security. For the purpose of clarity, I have described separately the broad array of battles to save agriculture and conserve our resources, to supplant sharecropping with homestead ownership, to enact a public-works bill that would give me freedom to establish WPA, REA, NYA, and all the other emergency relief measures. Also, early in 1935, a National Labor Relations Act was pending in Congress to make permanent the intentions of Section 7a of the NRA. At the same time, I was pressing Congress to pass a major tax bill, called by my enemies a "soak the rich" scheme, which merely shifted proper tax responsibility for our common problem on those best able to pay.

While I have had to describe these battles separately, in 1935 I had to face them all simultaneously. The $4.8 billion public-works bill paralyzed Congress through winter and spring, opposed on the one hand by the economizers, on the other by the prevailing-wage liberals. While millions of needy endured anxiety and suffering during those months, the opponents to the left and right, just as Mrs. Roosevelt said, might just as well have been on the same side.

As a result, some of my friends, needing someone to blame, concluded that I was indecisive or wavering or had somehow lost heart for the fight. Harold Ickes was running all about town whispering—didn't he know that people repeat whispers to me, too?—that I was "distinctly dispirited." Because I would not bludgeon a Congress that would not be bludgeoned, Arthur Krock solemnly concluded in the New York *Times,* "If the President wants control of that body, he must begin to exercise it at once. . . . The legend of invulnerability fades fast."

How easy to be an expert when all you have to do is analyze—but not do anything. A man far closer to the realities of action, Senator Key Pittman, put his finger much closer to the problem: the penalty of our overwhelming victory in 1934. Our party so dominated Congress that, as Pittman pointed out in a letter to me, there was "no Democratic Party in the United States Senate." There were conservative Democrats who "conscientiously believe they are saving you by destroying you." There were Democrats who sympathized more with Progressive Republicans than with my program. Then there was that small, individualistic band of Progressive Republicans, bent on nationalizing almost everything that wasn't agricultural, some equally bent on saving agriculture by free coinage of silver. The remaining few were the "unscrupulous, regular Republican" group—Pittman's words. Pittman concluded in his frank letter:

> Well, of course, the fault is that there is a lack of confidence in the success of the Administration. There is cowardice. There is discontent with regard to patronage. There is complaint . . . that strange and peculiar persons have become advisors; that there is no leadership; that thinking is farmed out; that defeat is inevitable; and every man must take care of himself.

The country was demanding—needed—action, yet I had no choice but to bide my time, regardless of criticism. On March 13, 1935, my National Emergency Council fell into a discussion about the "jittery feeling" that Congress would go through its whole session accomplishing nothing.

"That, I think, is positively childish," I told them. "Give them a chance. After all, they love to talk. Let them talk." To old friends who prodded me about this jittery feeling, I wrote similarly. To Josephus Daniels, my old Navy boss: "I am saying very little, keeping my temper and letting them literally stew in their own juice." To Colonel Edward M. House, President Wilson's close associate, I predicted that the rest of the session would be a madhouse, "every Senator a law unto himself and every one seeking the spotlight."

These things I could say in private, but again, to channel a more public comment I turned to my wife. From our complaining mail we selected one letter, from Molly Dewson, a dependable friend serving Hopkins and me as a traveling observer while on the staff of the Democratic National Committee. Mrs. Roosevelt's letter to her, which I went over carefully, said:

> The fact that people are feeling a lack of leadership in him at present and are worried is perfectly natural. . . . These things go in cycles. We have been through it in Albany and we are going through it here. . . . He says to tell you that Congress is accomplishing a great deal in spite of the fact that there is very little publicity on what they have done. . . . The relief bill and the [social] security bill are bound to go slowly because they are a new type of legislation. If he tried to force them down the committee's throat and did not give them time to argue them out, he would have an even more difficult congress to work with. . . .
>
> Please say to everyone who tells you that the President is not giving leadership that he is seeing the men constantly, and that he is working with them, but this is a democracy after all, and if he once started insisting on having his own way immediately, we should shortly find ourselves with a dictatorship and I hardly think the country would like that any better than they do the delay.
>
> The ups and downs in peoples' feelings, particularly on the liberal side, are an old, old story. The liberals always get discouraged when they do not see the measures they are interested in go through immediately. Considering the time we have had to work in the past for almost every slight improvement, I should think they might get over with it, but they never do.
>
> Franklin says for Heaven's sake, all you Democratic leaders calm

down and feel sure of ultimate success. It will do a lot in satisfying
other people.

Why do liberals have this perpetual problem of disunity while conservatives do not? The reason is simple: Conservatives all want essentially the same thing—inaction. They remain united in saying "no."
Civilization is a tree that, as it grows, produces rot and deadwood.
The conservative says, "Don't touch it." The radical says, "Cut it
down." The liberal compromises. He says, "Let's prune, so that we
lose neither the old trunk nor the lengthy new branches." Sometimes
he says, "Let's graft on a vigorous new limb here." Liberalism is selective action for improvement of society. Naturally, liberals don't
all select the same action; they may not agree on which branches are
dead and which may be saved, which may require pruning shears
and which hacksaws. These are matters of judgment and each tree
"expert" likes to think of himself as right, the other fellow wrong.
That is bound to result among people who are brave enough to undertake what has not been done before. Differences among liberals, quite
understandable, are one thing; mutual destruction of liberals is quite
another, and is never excusable. It remains the task of liberals, if they
are to make their efforts successful, to find common ground, each
making concessions so that all may obtain the substance of what they
commonly desire.

That word "liberal" is one I seldom used, avoided applying to myself, when it entered the political language before the days of the New
Deal. At that time it was mostly used in self-description by muddle-
headed, overly theoretical thinkers who really were intellectual radicals. They liked to spend hours in their armchairs theorizing why free
enterprise would never work and dreaming up elaborate, unworkable
schemes of common ownership that overlooked the realities of human
nature. They were a small band found chiefly in eastern universities
and around copies of *The Nation* and the *New Republic*.

The word "liberalism," however, took on new connotations of
practicality when bold, realistic reform took shape through the New
Deal. So, in about 1935, I adopted the word to describe myself and
those who, in a broad way, stood with me.[8]

Unlike the original "liberals," the Progressives were a large group,
far more influential, mainly from the upper Midwest and Northwest,
with roots in agriculture and silver mining; radical reformers, yes,

militant in their opposition to predatory banks and railroads, but equally militant in their belief in competition and personal enterprise. Their patron saint was Robert M. La Follette, Sr., the once-senator father of now-Senator Bob La Follette and of Governor Philip La Follette of Wisconsin. But the Progressives were a dying breed, weakened by their individual unwillingness to join the mainstream of either major political party. As a result, pessimism and bitterness were becoming their most conspicuous themes.

One night early in 1935 Rex Tugwell held a dinner for several friends, including Senator Burton K. Wheeler of Montana, a Progressive although nominally a Democrat. Throughout the evening— I learned of this not from Tugwell but from one of his guests, William E. Dodd, my Ambassador to Germany—Wheeler railed incessantly against me. For "all his fine talk," Wheeler said, Roosevelt really stood with conservatives, not Progressives. The one man who could smash the conservative leadership in the Senate, especially Joe Robinson and Pat Harrison, according to Wheeler, was Huey Long, whom Wheeler counted among his personal friends. When Dodd protested the methods identified with Long, Wheeler said, as Dodd recalled it to me, "We shall soon be shooting up people here, like Hitler does." The answer, Wheeler went on to argue, was a third party in 1936, to unite Long, Father Coughlin (whose obsession with silver coincided with Wheeler's), Upton Sinclair, the La Follettes, and Governor Floyd Olson of Minnesota. No surprise that some editorial speculations on such a third party mentioned Burt Wheeler as its probable presidential candidate!

At the same time, I knew that Progressive Republicans—La Follette, Cutting, and Nye—were also flirting with the idea of a third ticket. Their hope was that such a third ticket would defeat the New Deal, elect a conservative Republican who would throw us back into Hooverism, and—according to their twisted intellectual theory— would bring about such public disgust that there would be a swing to the far left by 1940. I had a theory of my own: that these Progressive Republican elements were an important source of Huey Long's seemingly unlimited finances.[9]

These strange maneuverings intensely complicated the crisis of inaction in Congress, particularly affecting the Social Security bill and the public-works appropriation. At just the right time, late in April of 1935, Felix Frankfurter forwarded to me a letter from a bright young

man, David K. Niles, a Boston liberal leader (who was later to become an assistant to Harry Hopkins, then to me at the White House).
His letter said:

Dear F.F.:
   . . . I am quite disturbed at the way our cockeyed liberals are
permitting themselves to be used in the campaign to discredit the
Administration. I think it is only fair to assume that most of them are
misled by their inability to grasp fully what it is the President is up
against.
   I am writing you now because before we know it next year will be
upon us with the election and it will be up to us to try to line up the
liberals in order to preserve the gains that we have already made. I
think it is a mistake to wait until next year. . . .
   Some of our liberals are bellyaching because they are mentally
constipated and others because they must have swallowed too big a
chunk of hostile propaganda; but for the most part, I think it is due
to their inability to recognize to the full what it is the President has to
contend with. After all, trying to satisfy a hundred and twenty-five
million people is a somewhat different problem from trying to please a
relatively few thousand readers of the *Nation* and the *New Republic*
and similar journals. By the way have you noticed how many new
so-called liberal magazines and newspapers have been started this past
year? However, these liberals and progressives are an important factor
and will be needed, in my judgment, next year more than in any other
campaign that we've been through. I wish, Felix, we could do something about it before they commit themselves too definitely to these
different so-called progressive and liberal organizations that are cropping
up all over the country. Once they have tied up with these groups it
will be impossible to win them away.
   It occurs to me that a frank talking-things-over between the President
and these liberal and progressive leaders from all over the country
should be of real help. It should be a kind of executive session from
which all reporters are barred and during which these liberal and progressive leaders could tell the President what it is that disturbs them
about his program and have him explain to them why it is so difficult
to progress as rapidly as he and they would like.
   Two years ago was the first time that the liberals and progressives
participated in a victory and it is a new experience for them. They are
naturally impatient and for the most part they are so emotionally constituted that it is easier to be anti-administration than pro; but I think
at the bottom they are honest men and women and at a conference

of this sort a common denominator can be found which will make them want to go out and fight those who would destroy the President's program once they understand better what the President's program is.

. . . Just between you and me, another advantage in getting these liberals together would be to let them see for themselves how divided they are in their criticism.

The idea seemed excellent. I approved a meeting for the evening of May 14. It soon came clear that our problem could not be solved by inviting leaders of liberal organizations; we needed a good talk with liberal senators. One of them, Senator Norris, urged that we keep it as small as possible. Niles then had the happy thought that we could avoid offending sensibilities by limiting invitations to the six senators who had been members of the National Progressive League supporting me in the 1932 campaign. They were Costigan, Cutting, Hiram Johnson, La Follette, Norris, and Wheeler. To make this arbitrary demarcation look right, we added two cabinet members, Wallace and Ickes, who were also members of the Progressive League, So, with Frankfurter, Niles, and myself, we had a good working group of eleven.

What we discussed during our long, frank talk was very much what we have already reviewed in this chapter, the pulls and tugs upon the President of diverse, possibly dangerous political forces to right and left, and the need for liberals each to give up a little in order to win a great deal.

My feeling that the meeting went extremely well was confirmed within the week by a note from Frankfurter: "There is no doubt about the high success of the Tuesday night session. I have heard from all the Senators, except Norris and Hiram Johnson, and they all were truly happy. According to Bob La Follette, 'it was the best, the frankest, the most encouraging talk we have ever had with the President. I know Burt felt that way about it for I went home with him. I told Burt that hereafter if there is anything on his chest he should get it off to the President directly, that he no longer has any excuse for private grousing, now that the President has told him he could get in touch with him through Miss LeHand. The President was fair, and frank, and I felt greatly encouraged that he is going to get into the stride of his old aggressive leadership.' There was real warmth and enthusiasm in Bob as I talked to him, and I know your assertion that 'the time had come' heartened and invigorated them."

The deadlock in the Senate soon broke, committee hearings took a constructive turn, and on June 19 the Social Security Act passed. It had already passed the House in April. Every Republican in the House, save one, had voted to recommit the bill to committee, a standard attempt at killing it. When that maneuver failed, the majority of Republicans, after fighting the elderly and the unemployed every step of the way, hypocritically voted in favor of the "catastrophe" they had so bitterly predicted. The tally was 371 to 33. In the Senate, where most Republicans were equally unwilling to go on record against Social Security after fighting it tooth and claw, the vote was 76 to 6. Our opponents underhandedly battled further to block Senate-House agreement on their two versions of the bill, but finally on August 19 I signed Social Security into law.

Still more trouble: Huey Long took on a one-man filibuster against passage of an appropriation to set up a Social Security office. The only way Congress could end his talking was to adjourn. I decided it was law-stretching time again. The NRA was being liquidated. With the small amount of NRA payroll money left, I assigned NRA workers to set up Social Security machinery. In addition, we set up a WPA "research project" to study "ways and means" of administering the Social Security program—in effect, bringing the Social Security Administration into being. Before doing this I obtained the consent of Republican leaders in Congress, who resented Long as much as I, as well as the support of Comptroller General John R. McCarl, who happened to be a Republican.

Within two years all forty-eight states had passed unemployment compensation laws. None would resist the public demand for protection.

Not long after Social Security became law, I asked my wife to visit the scene of a mine accident that had killed several men. One widow, with three children and a fourth on the way, told her, "I am going to get Social Security widow's benefits of nearly sixty-five dollars a month. I pay fifteen dollars a month on my house and land, and I shall raise vegetables and have chickens and with the money from the government I will get along very well. In the past probably the mine company might have given me a small check and often the other miners took up a collection if they could afford it, but this income from the government I can count on until my children are grown."[10]

A Bill of Rights for Labor

Even before passage of Social Security—about six weeks before—the new unity of liberals had proved the Congressional log jam could be broken. Congress in early July finally passed the National Labor Relations Act, often known as the Wagner Act.

I was thrilled by this victory, not because I was thrilled by the bill itself but because we needed a victory. Actually, earlier in the year I would just as soon have seen the Wagner bill sidetracked. I felt, in the long run, it would create as many problems as it might solve, but certain accidents of history eventually forced me to pretend greater enthusiasm for the Wagner Act method of stabilizing labor-management relations than I actually felt. To trace these accidents and their effects, we must glance back at Section 7a of the NRA.

This section, as I have said, excited labor organizers far beyond our expectations. Instead of encouraging harmony and co-operation, the essence of NRA, it fired up organizers to form unions in factories and mines that had not been organized. Businessmen, wholly inexperienced in dealing with organized labor, were sometimes dumfounded when newly elected union officers marched in to demand written contracts specifying wages and working conditions. Many employers simply refused to meet with workers. They would abide by the NRA industry codes, they said, but they'd be hanged before they'd bargain with "upstarts" who, after all, were paid employees, not stockholders or customers. By midsummer of 1933, only weeks after passage of the NRA, factories were shut down by about one thousand strikes.

To smooth out these disputes we set up a National Labor Board within NRA. I made Senator Wagner, a friend of labor, its chairman. Its members included, among others, Gerard Swope, the public-spirited and fair-minded president of General Electric, and John L. Lewis, the miners' union leader, who had supported Hoover in the 1932 election.

After the initial "accident" of Section 7a, the next was one of those minor incidents that unexpectedly lead to major history. An especially stubborn hosiery manufacturer insisted that his workers belonged to no union, did not want one, and he would not permit them to "horn in" on his business, Blue Eagle or no. The man was a German, and Frances Perkins remarked to me that he "looked like a Nazi." Gerard Swope tried in vain to reason with him and finally said: "I have a suggestion. Let them vote on it. We'll have a free election by secret ballot and every employee of yours can vote whether he wants to be represented by the union or not. That's fair, isn't it? Then you'll know."

"Vy," demanded the mill owner, as Frances mimicked the man to me, "vy should they vote?"

"Because," said Swope, struggling to maintain his customary patience, "this is America and that's the way we do things here."

The employer refused, but a week later the vote was taken anyway and the workers overwhelmingly affirmed that they wanted a union.

That first vote, followed by similar ones elsewhere, became a precedent that Senator Wagner soon formalized as a cornerstone of his bill. I did not feel the Wagner Act was likely to become law, partly because I felt sure, as Secretary Perkins did, that big labor—the A. F. of L.—would not stake its survival and growth on a counting of noses. They were more likely to continue relying on a strike threat by whatever number of workers they could muster, whether a majority or not. Elections, after all, might open the door to employer-influenced company unions, freezing the A. F. of L. out. To our surprise, William Green and Matthew Woll of the A. F. of L. endorsed Wagner's bill, elections and all. (Soon after its passage, when the Congress of Industrial Organizations, under John L. Lewis, began organizing unskilled workers on an industry-wide basis, the

A. F. of L. was among the first to demand that the election provisions of the Wagner Act be amended or repealed.)

The Wagner bill defined and would make illegal certain "unfair
labor practices," among them firing a worker for membership or
activity in a union; formalize the holding of elections to determine
who shall represent workers in bargaining, if anyone; and establish
machinery for hearing and adjudicating cases where labor's rights
were alleged to have been violated or denied. The National Labor
Relations Board, which the bill would create, would not act as a
mediator or conciliator in labor disputes. That function would remain with the Conciliation Service of the Labor Department. Wagner recognized that the judicial function and the mediation function
should not be confused. Compromise, the essence of mediation, has
no place in the interpretation and enforcement of the law.

I did not feel it was the government's job to help unions organize
and thrive, nor to provide the machinery through which unions
ought to establish their majorities, their right to bargain. Workers,
without question, especially unskilled workers, were getting a raw
deal, were unfairly exploited, sometimes intimidated from pursuing
better conditions and, in a large sense, their weak position depressed
the entire national economy. Unions are indeed the best instrument
for balancing their strength against that of employers. I did and do
believe in labor unions—wholeheartedly. But the formation of unions is the job of those workers who see the need for them, not that
of government, once government has established, as we did with
Section 7a, the legal right of workers to form them. If a union recruits only a minority of workers in an industry or plant, the government cannot—should not—do anything to correct the failure of the
union's appeal. If it recruits a majority, a union certainly has its
own ways of making its strength known and felt by an employer.

In addition to these philosophical questions that troubled me
about the Wagner Act, I had no desire to alienate certain influential
liberals who feared the Wagner Act and were already beginning to
fear the New Deal. One of these was Roger Baldwin, the highly
respected leader of the American Civil Liberties Union, who raised
the thought that government involvement in labor relations might
in the long run pose a threat to the independence and freedom of
unions, especially under an anti-labor President. I did not wish to
deepen the misgivings expressed in a 1934 statement of the Civil

Liberties Union: "The enormous increase in the power of the federal government under the New Deal policies carries with it inevitable fears of inroads in the right of agitation. Alarms are widely expressed over alleged dictatorship by the President, the abrogation of states' rights and the vast economic powers of the federal government reaching out to every home and business in the land."

I had enough of that sort of thing to my right. I did not need more of it to my left.

Labor's remedy was not in government intervention but in wiser and more experienced labor leadership. The fact is that labor organizers, especially the new ones, tended to be hotheads and lost many battles they might have won. Only experience would correct this. The best example was the San Francisco general strike of 1934, when I was aboard ship out in the Pacific. As I said off the record to my reporter friends:

"In the San Francisco strike a lot of people completely lost their heads and telegraphed me, 'For God's sake, come back. Turn the ship around.' . . . Everybody demanded that I sail into San Francisco Bay, all flags flying and guns double shotted, and end the strike. They went completely off the handle. Well, I kept in pretty close touch. . . . It appeared very clear to me just as soon as there was talk about a general strike, that there were probably two elements bringing about that general strike. One was the hotheaded young leaders who had had no experience in organized labor whatsoever and said that the only thing to do was to have a general strike. On the other side was a combination of people out there on the Coast who were praying for a general strike. In other words, there was the old conservative crowd just hoping that there would be a general strike, being clever enough to know that a general strike always fails. . . . The general strike started. And immediately the strikers, being young, did silly things like saying to the inhabitants, 'You cannot eat in that restaurant, but you can eat in this restaurant.' Naturally the public resented it.

"Of course they learn by things of that kind. They have got to learn by going through the actual processes, actual examples, and not by interference from the federal government or the President or the United States troops. People will learn from a certain number of examples. We have to conduct the country and essentially to educate labor to their responsibility."

At that same press conference it happened that sitting beside me was a guest, Lord Illiffe, an owner of the London *Daily Telegraph* and other British papers, who joined in the discussion:

"We have a responsible union system now. But, as you know, we have had very considerable troubles. But I think the same thing is going to apply to the United States. You have unions here that have only just begun to feel their power, and when a man gets power at first he does not know how to use it. But he does after a bit. I am perfectly certain it is going to turn out all right in the end. . . . The result of the general strike in England in 1926, I think, is that it gave the unions a greater feeling of responsibility than they felt before. They really thought that it was possible for them to do anything, and they did not consider the interest of the nation as a whole. Before 1926 they played their own hand. After 1926 they realized that they had to consider the general good of the public. In the United States, as soon as they realize that, you will find that the union system will work all right. In these days, when you have organized capital you have to have organized labor, and each side has to realize its responsibility for the public good as a whole."

For all these reasons I had no intention of supporting the Wagner bill when Congress met in January 1935. But as the talkative session dragged on, the lobbyists of labor gathered commitments from the liberal majority far beyond our expectations. Furthermore Senator Wagner's support had become of critical importance to the passage of the $4.8 billion public-works bill and the Social Security Act. Wagner realized the strong trading position in which the Congressional stalemate had placed him. Since I had to go along with his National Labor Relations Act, there was no point in doing it half-heartedly. I got behind it in June with the appearance of great enthusiasm. It passed in July—and in August we had Social Security.[11]

Bridges to Big Business—
Who Really Burned Them?

Union organizers, so often accused of lawlessness, have no monopoly on it. The vice-president of United States Steel in charge of industrial relations, Arthur Young, speaking before the American Management Association, said that he would rather "go to jail or be convicted as a felon" than obey the National Labor Relations Act. The association rewarded Young for his "patriotism" with a medal for "outstanding and creative work in the field of industrial relations."

Stubborn, impetuous, childish opposition not only to the Wagner Act but to all our attempts at reform became the rule among powerful voices of big business. The American Bankers Association, at its convention in the fall of 1935, turned down its own nominating committee's recommendation for—of all things—second vice-president, because the nominee was a business associate of Marriner Eccles, my appointee to the Federal Reserve Board. In his place they named one Orval Adams, like Eccles a Utah banker, who promptly proposed that bankers "declare an embargo" and "decline to make further purchases" of government bonds. "The bankers of America should resume negotiations with the federal government only under a rigid economy, a balanced budget, and a sane tax program." You'd think—in fact, our bankers had long been accustomed to thinking—that they were some independent kingdom unto themselves, treating the upstart United States Government as some foreign rival.

The United States Chamber of Commerce convention of 1935 turned into an unrelieved ritual of denunciation of me and our awful government. As I told my reporter friends, "In all of these speeches made, I don't believe there was a single speech which took the human side, the old-age side, the unemployment side." Well, there was one, from a businessman removed enough from our scene to have a little perspective. I was glad to find this clipping in a newspaper and read it to the reporters:

"Francis E. Powell, head of the United States Chamber of Commerce in London, last night said that the Old World is amazed at the stubborn fight being made by business here against the New Deal. Tall and silver-haired, Powell once was chairman of the Anglo-American Oil Company. He was astonished, he said, at the frosty reception that greeted his attempt yesterday to bring peace between American merchants and the White House. Hundreds of delegates of the United States Chamber of Commerce Convention sat in grim silence as Powell proposed that a group be notified to call on Mr. Roosevelt and pledge co-operation.

"'I was astonished by their attitude,' he told the United Press in an exclusive interview. 'It couldn't have happened anywhere else in the world. I have listened for days to the criticism of the government's policies.'"[12]

Harvard Bridges Falling Down

In one instance, such childish hostility, this time from the academic world, turned comical—although, I admit, it was quite annoying at the time. It was summed up by Felix Frankfurter as "incredible among cultured men and without precedent in this country." The episode began with my receipt of the following letter:

Boston, Mass.
February 20, 1936

Dear Mr. President:

President Conant and the Directors of the Harvard Alumni Association have asked me to take charge of the tercentenary meeting of the alumni on the afternoon of September the eighteenth, and President Conant tells me that you have kindly consented to speak on this occasion. Now, it being a meeting for the mutual congratulation of the graduates at the three hundredth anniversary of their alma mater, we hope you will choose for your theme for a brief address something connected with Harvard and the tercentenary of higher education in this country, and feel that you would welcome this opportunity to divorce yourself from the arduous demands of politics and political speech-making. Do you not think it would be well to limit all the speeches that afternoon to about ten minutes? Does this express your idea?

Yours very sincerely,
A. Lawrence Lowell
[President Emeritus of Harvard]

Mr. Franklin D. Roosevelt
President of the United States

I sent the text to Felix at Harvard with a notation: "The following is a line for line exact copy of the original, against which I compared it by having my wife read the original to me giving every line, punctuation, capitalization, etc., etc." And I added this letter:

Dear Felix:—
Very confidentially, what do you think of this? I felt like replying—
"if I am invited in my capacity as a Harvard graduate I shall, of course, speak as briefly as you suggest—two minutes if you say so—but if I am invited as President to speak for the Nation, I am unable to tell you at this time what my subject will be or whether it will take five minutes or an hour."
I suppose some people with insular minds really believe that I might make a purely political speech lasting one hour and a half. Give this your "ca'm jedgment" and suggest a soft answer "suitable to the occasion."

Good lawyer that he is, Felix wired me asking to see President Conant's original letter and my acceptance, adding: "I should not have been terribly sorry if you had taught the gentleman a lesson in manners and written to him what you felt like replying. However, you shall have my calm judgment after I have had two days to cool off."
Next, I wrote Felix:

On looking over the file there appears an interesting situation. On November 7, 1934, President Conant writes—"Dear Mr. Roosevelt (sic) I am now extending to you on behalf of the University a formal invitation to be present." Am I invited in my official capacity or just as a graduate? I wonder—?
On November 14, 1934, Jerome Greene says—"Dear Mr. President . . . I am . . . writing to you in support of President Conant's official letter . . . the preliminary arrangements for the great day would have to take very largely into account the welcoming of the President of the United States to his own College. . . ."
The plot thickens! It is developing into a detective story. . . .

After some more back-and-forth between the good counselor and me, Felix handed down his judicial opinion:

. . . The controlling letter—that of November 7, 1934—leaves no possible room for doubt that President Conant's invitation was addressed to the President of the United States. I don't want to rely on the minor fact that the Conant letter went to:

Honorable Franklin D. Roosevelt
President of the United States

in contrast to Dr. Lowell's form, "Mr. Franklin D. Roosevelt." What is crucial is that President Conant extended to you "on behalf of the University a formal invitation to be present," so that the "celebration of the 300th Anniversary of the founding of Harvard College may be honored by your presence, as the celebration of the 250th Anniversary was honored by that of President Cleveland."

. . . Grover Cleveland was not an alumnus. He came as President of the United States. The whole tenor of President Conant's letter, with its explicit reference to the Cleveland visit, unequivocally proves that the invitation went to you not as alumnus but as President. Naturally enough, Jerome Greene, as director of the Tercentenary celebration, placed that interpretation upon "President Conant's official letter." No other construction is tenable.

In sum, of course you were invited in "Your official capacity" and not "just as a graduate." I'll bet you a St. Croix rum highball that even the Supreme Court would so rule, the Supreme Court, that is, ex McReynolds. . . .

Felix advised that I write a "brief, courteous, conclusive" letter, which he said "Dr. Lowell will fully understand." I wrote:

The White House
March 6, 1936

My dear Dr. Lowell:—

I have your letter of February twentieth.

In graciously asking me to attend Harvard's Tercentenary Celebration, President Conant of course invited me not as an alumnus but as President of the United States. I am sure you will approve my thought that he did not expect me to do otherwise than to be true to the requirements of the office which I shall represent on that occasion.

The good Dr. Lowell, after taking more than five weeks of deep thought, did not "fully understand":

April 14, 1936

To the President of the United States
Dear Mr. Roosevelt:

You are certainly right that you were invited to come to Harvard on the Alumni Day of the Tricentennial celebration as President of the United States. In that capacity I suppose you will want to say something about what Harvard has meant to the nation. In arranging the occasion there are about half a dozen other speakers—partly alumni, but mainly representatives of other institutions over the world,—who will naturally speak. I am thinking of asking each of them to take about ten, or at most fifteen minutes. Does not this strike you as appropriate?

Memorandum for Felix Frankfurter

The White House
April 16, 1936

Before I get through I shall lose my temper completely and find it necessary to stay in Washington in September to attend the meeting of the International Power Conference instead of going to Cambridge!

Here is the latest. What is your slant on this one? Damn.

F.D.R.

Cambridge, Mass.
April 19, 1936

Dear Mr. President:

If I said what I really thought of Emeritus, Jim Farley wouldn't allow it to go through the mail.

I submit the following as possible ways of returning his ball:

(1) You may assume that I shall speak, within appropriate limits, of the significance of Harvard in the context of our national history.

(2) You will have to assume that I understand the proprieties of an occasion like Harvard's Tercentenary.

(3) You will have to assume that I understand the proprieties.

Not having anything of the careful dullness of a John W. Davis, Marion [Mrs. Frankfurter] says she hopes you will lose your "temper completely."

Very faithfully yours,
F.F.

President Emeritus Lowell paid me and the office I held the extreme and unexpected courtesy of not cancelling his invitation to me to speak after I sent him the following letter, quoted in full:

Thank you for your letter of April fourteenth. You are right in thinking that I will want to say something of the significance of Harvard in relation to our national history.

When the "great day," September 18, 1936, finally rolled around I was careful not to put at ease those who were so uneasy at my presence. For one thing, I returned Dr. Lowell's courtesies by omitting his name from the salutation. For another, I reminded him that my visit was official. And I reassured those Republicans in the assemblage that I was perfectly aware that I troubled them:

"I am here today in a joint and several capacity, first, as President of the United States; second, as Chairman of the United States Harvard Tercentenary Commission, which is composed of five members of the Senate, five members of the House of Representatives, a representative of the United States Army and one of the Navy . . . ; finally, I am here as a Son of Harvard who gladly returns to this spot where men have sought truth for three hundred years. . . . This meeting is being held in pursuance of an adjournment expressly taken one hundred years ago. . . . At that time many of the alumni of Harvard were sorely troubled concerning the state of the nation. Andrew Jackson was President. On the 250th anniversary of the founding of Harvard College, many alumni again were sorely troubled. Grover Cleveland was President. Now, on the three hundredth anniversary, I am President."

My speech, on the general theme of a university's contribution to freedom and truth, had to be endured by Dr. Lowell and his fellow tremblers for less than fifteen minutes.[13]

"They Hate Roosevelt"

I enjoy now telling that episode. One of the delights of being in the public eye is to witness the odd reactions you may induce in intelligent, generally well-meaning men. Far less delightful are the reactions you may induce—or, at least, that I seem to have a special talent for inciting—in less intelligent men. I think it is not self-consciousness but a desire to record the social history of my time as President that obliges me to tell of another kind of fear of Roosevelt, not amusing at all. Marquis Childs wrote of this in *Harper's* of May 1936, in an article called "They Hate Roosevelt." While I often heard these lurid stories, I prefer to let him tell about them:

"A resident of Park Avenue in New York City was sentenced not long ago to a term of imprisonment for threatening violence to the person of President Roosevelt. . . . A phenomenon which social historians in the future will very likely record with perplexity if not with astonishment: the fanatical hatred of the President which today obsesses thousands of men and women among the upper class.

"No other word than hatred will do. It is a passion, a fury, that is wholly unreasoning. . . . The phenomenon to which I refer goes far beyond objection to policies or programs. It is a consuming personal hatred of President Roosevelt and, to an almost equal degree, of Mrs. Roosevelt.

"It permeates, in greater or less degree, the whole upper stratum of American society. . . . The extraordinary fact is that whereas the fanatic who went to prison had lost his fortune and, therefore, had a

direct grievance, the majority of those who rail against the President
have to a large extent had their incomes restored and their bank
balances replenished since the low point of March 1933. . . .

"As the New Dealers themselves have been at pains to point out,
taxes on the rich have not been materially increased. . . . Witness
the long advance in the stock market, which has doubled, tripled,
or quadrupled the prices of stocks—and indeed has multiplied some
of them by ten. . . . A great many liberals, and certainly all radicals,
complain that President Roosevelt's chief mission has been to save
the fortunes of the very rich.

". . . The violence of the hatred varies directly with the affluence of
the social group. The larger the house, the more numerous the servants, the more resplendent the linen and silver, the more scathing is
likely to be the indictment of the President."

Childs submits a "characteristic scene"—at a Florida resort, involving someone he identifies as James Hamilton, a Chicago commodity broker, head of a firm that made a handsome profit from the
New Deal's agricultural and farm-commodities programs. The President, says James Hamilton, is ruining the farmers of the Middle West
by permitting the importation of corn. No matter what he is told in
rebuttal, according to Childs, "It is breath wasted. . . . He will not
hear you if you point out the exact number of bushels of corn that
have been imported, a negligible number. . . .

"With James Hamilton is his son, James Hamilton III, also a
partner in the firm. The younger Hamilton specializes in Roosevelt
horror stories. . . . Many of these are built round the report that
Roosevelt is insane. A number of versions of this story have become
familiar. The commonest one has to do with the strange laughter with
which the President greets his visitors, a laughter that—if one were
to believe the story—continues foolishly and irrelevantly during most
of the interview.

"But James Hamilton III can improve upon these stories. He had
it from a man who had dinner in the White House last week that—
James Hamilton III becomes unprintable. He reveals with a kind of
painstaking delight the horrible details of the intimate life of the first
family of the land. . . . This is not idle talk. It is for James Hamilton
III the gospel, and only slightly less so for his father. . . . For authority for the radical plots in which Mr. Roosevelt has had a hand,
James Hamilton III will quote from a Hearst editorial article, from a

speech by Governor Talmadge, or from any one of a half dozen weekly papers and pamphlet services that are feeding the fiercer anti-Roosevelt fires. . . .

"What one returns to—the incredible, the amazing fact—is that most of these people seem to have no realization whatever of the present plight of the world. The events that occurred between the autumn of 1929 and the spring of 1933 have apparently left no mark upon their memories. The fact that there are in the United States still some twelve million unemployed is seemingly without significance to them. The fact that when Mrs. Skeane dismissed her gardeners and chauffeurs in 1933 the dismissal was more disastrous to them than to her does not lodge in her mind. The fact that in a time when millions are destitute through no fault of their own James Hamilton is very fortunate to have a cabana on the warm sands of Florida has not dawned upon him. Nor does it seem to have occurred to Joshua Thornberry that the plight of hundreds of thousands in his own city, who without governmental relief would speedily starve or freeze to death in the zero weather from which he can so readily flee, may have some logical connection with the taxing of the money which he has cleaned up in a quick and easy stock-market deal. . . . Not that Mr. Thornberry is not, among his peers, a good fellow, kindly and generous. . . . He does not think of the unemployment as *his* problem as an American citizen. He and others of his class who share his views appear to think that they have discharged their full responsibility when they have touched off a string of adjectives, peppered by a few sulphurous epithets. If they cannot have at Washington an administration of their own choosing, they in effect resign from the United States. . . . (One recalls that dinner of New Jersey public utility men at which a toast to the President of the United States was greeted by a roar of laughter.)"[14]

A Strategy for a New Democratic Party

The publication of that article came at a time when we were beginning
to plan the re-election campaign of 1936. During that campaign I
was to be accused of making myself—and the hatred of me by some
of our richest men—the central issue. Well, let's turn now to the true
history of that campaign, which I will try to reconstruct in the frankest way I can.

The passage of the Wagner Act and the Social Security Act signaled a new unity, fragile as it might be, among liberals in the Senate.
But this still left me with the problem of holding together a party
that, unlike the Republican naysayers, had so little to hold it together.

This problem was severe. The Democratic Party, although the
party in power, was not yet the nation's dominant party. It was
truly a majority composed of minorities of every shade of liberal and
conservative, and its differences threatened constantly to shatter it.
Sometimes these differences were over petty things, but symptoms of
larger troubles. An example: In 1935 I had a nasty little problem of
a feud between Senator Millard Tydings of Maryland, investigating
something or other in the Virgin Islands, and Harold Ickes, whose
Interior Department had been placed on the defensive. Tydings, demanding Ickes' scalp, had enlisted Senator Pat Harrison on his side,
and Harrison in turn lined up Majority Leader Robinson.

On July 10, 1935, after a pleasant dinner with Felix Frankfurter
and a New York friend, Ferdinand Pecora, I brought up the matter
(and asked Felix to keep minutes of our conversation). I said, "At

bottom, the leaders like Joe Robinson, though he has been loyal, and Pat Harrison are troubled about the whole New Deal. They just wonder where the man in the White House is taking the old Democratic Party. During their long public life, forty years or so, they knew it was the old Democratic Party. They were safe. When the Republicans got into trouble, the old Democratic Party won nationally. But in any event they—in the South without opposition—were all right and old-fashioned. But now they just wonder where that fellow in the White House is taking the good old Democratic Party. They are afraid there is going to be a new Democratic Party which they will not like. That's the basic fact in all these controversies. And that explains why I will have trouble with my own Democratic Party from this time on in trying to carry out further programs of reform and recovery. I know the problem inside my party, but I intend to appeal from it to the American people."

The overwhelming popular approval of Social Security and the Wagner Act, as well as our record in agriculture and in emergency job creation, gave me the instruments for that appeal. If we could establish these as memorable symbols of Democratic achievement, the Democratic Party would become defined as the party of liberalism —and the majority party. Then the Harrisons and the Robinsons could not so easily threaten to throw us back into the old days. Nor could the Longs and Coughlins threaten to lure us astray with demagogic pipedreams.

On September 8, a startling occurrence disarranged—and rearranged—our whole picture. Huey Long was in the state capitol of Louisiana supervising the passage of bills by the state legislature, which he controlled as completely as he had while governor. About 9:20 P.M., his day's work done, Huey walked across the rotunda of his capitol, surrounded as usual by bodyguards and sycophants, when a young man in a white linen suit stepped out from behind a pillar, drew a pistol from his pocket, pressed it against the senator's abdomen, and fired. The young man was a son-in-law of a district judge whom Long was bent on destroying. Long is said to have declared the judge had Negro blood (an implied offense against the young man's wife and son), and on that very day, one of Long's bills had been aimed directly at the judge. Long was obsessed with fear of assassination, never moving about without an armed platoon. Revolvers and submachine guns were unloosed on the assailant, spraying fifty-nine bullets into his body, two into his head. But this thunderous vengeance could not save Huey Long. On September 10, at the age of forty-one, he was dead.

So was a chapter in our nation's history, which helps answer the question of whether personalities shape history while history shapes men.

Immediately, the southern situation was changed. With Huey gone, suddenly his Louisiana machine was just another political organization. Senators Robinson and Harrison, who had both feared an invasion by Long to defeat them in their states, were now free of that threat. Nationally, Long's No. 2 man, Gerald L. K. Smith, brushed aside by Louisiana politicians in his claim for Long's mantle, took charge of the Share-Our-Wealth movement, injecting it with religious bigotry, particularly against Jews.

In June 1936, Smith, Coughlin, and Townsend created the Union Party, giving the nomination, which might have been Long's, to a far less impressive man, Rep. William Lemke of North Dakota. But, at its birth, the party all but screamed itself to death—over their divided attitudes toward me. Coughlin, ripping off his clerical collar and coat, called me some terrible names. Minutes later, an Oklahoma Democrat, Gomer Smith, got just as much applause denouncing Gerald Smith and upholding me as a "church-going, Bible-reading, God-fearing . . . golden-hearted patriot who had saved the country from communism." A few weeks later Coughlin refused to let Townsend and Gerald Smith speak at his Social Justice Convention. Then Townsend and Lemke denounced Gerald Smith for his fascist sympathies. Coughlin announced he would deliver at least nine million votes for Lemke or quit broadcasting—then proceeded to ignore Lemke's campaign. Like the end of a Shakespearean tragedy, the stage was strewn with bodies.

With a serious third-party threat out of the way, I was able to set my mind on more realistic problems, chiefly that of redesigning the Democratic Party, making it a stable party of the majority.

My closest political adviser for a quarter of a century, Louis McHenry Howe, had been gravely ill all through the tormenting days of 1935. On April 18, 1936, while I attended a Gridiron Club dinner, my old friend slipped away from us. Because of the quiet, self-effacing style of Louis' loyal service and keen intelligence, the nation may never fully know the debt owed him for enabling the New Deal to come into being. Governmental affairs were not Louis' forte perhaps; he was a man of politics, of sensing the public mind and wishes, and turning national sentiment into election victories. Great governmental achievement is impossible without the prior work of such political geniuses as Louis Howe.

Howe's function as personal adviser—distinguished from Jim Farley's role as national organization leader—had to be filled. I called upon another proven friend, Ed Flynn, the Bronx Democratic leader. Those who didn't know Ed well cast him in the caricature of a cigar-smoking political boss. He could be counted on to bring in an 80-per-cent-Democratic vote in the Bronx, proof in the eyes of some that he must be evil. The fact is that not many people know him well. He is not a mixer, as most politicians are. His style is to deal chiefly with district leaders, not being accessible to most others, and seeing few politicians socially. He is a widely read, widely traveled, and cultured man, far more interested in national and international affairs than most local "bosses." His philosophy, like mine, is that clean and efficient government is the surest foundation of political success, and that a corrupt and stupid official, no matter how adept at vote getting (or vote buying) is a liability.

Like Howe, Flynn is also a shrewd analyst of political statistics and trends. In 1935 Flynn began to detect statistically what my eyes and ears and bones were telling me, too. The trend among American voters was toward social and economic reform, toward liberalism. Their political alignments, however, had not yet shifted with changing sentiments. The territory existed for a majority liberal party, which the Democratic Party could claim. Some of the facts making this true saddened me, but they were facts nevertheless and had to be faced. Here is how Flynn put it:

"There are two or three million more dedicated Republicans in the United States than there are Democrats. The population, however, is drifting into the urban areas. The election of 1932 was not normal." (In this observation, Flynn was quite right. We had won because of large defections of Republicans, alarmed by Hoover's inaction, but most of these voters still considered themselves Republicans. The only other Democratic President of this century, Woodrow Wilson, had won twice because of bitter divisions within the dominant Republican Party, including Theodore Roosevelt's third-party venture in 1912.) "To remain in power we must attract some millions, perhaps seven million, who are hostile or indifferent to both parties. They believe the Republican Party to be controlled by big business and the Democratic Party by the conservative South. These millions are mostly in the cities. We must attract them by radical programs of social and economic reform."

All my life I had dedicated myself to reversing this "drifting into urban areas." If it continues, the quality of our national life, of our family and personal lives, will suffer. But it *is* continuing, and no one man at present can reverse it. What kinds of people compose this drift? Of course there are the intellectual liberals, not great in number, who have mainly resided in cities to begin with. Then there are large numbers of Negroes, escaping the lack of opportunity in the rural South, many of whom had been barred from voting by poll taxes, and who embraced the Republican Party as the party of Abraham Lincoln. These colored people were among the most needy beneficiaries of our emergency work programs and Social Security; we could count on their support in 1936 and perhaps win their permanent loyalty. The largest group of all is of factory workers, a growing number unionized, for whom the Wagner Act and Social Security have symbolized a liberation, which could be turned into permanent loyalty to the Democratic Party. In religious terms, Catholics and Jews comprise vast numbers of city dwellers whose votes in turn control major states. Jewish people tend to respond to liberalism; Catholics are prominent in labor organization and urban political leadership. These groups, some of them overlapping, are the minorities that can be welded into a majority, a new kind of Democratic Party.[15]

A Credo of Disunity

The time had come to end the illusion of national co-operation and harmony. That harmony, which I had worked so hard to make real, had remained a sham. I have been accused of ending this harmony by *saying* it was over—by pointing out that it never existed. The dominant elements of big business, while talking co-operation, were "on strike" against government. Democratic conservatives along with Republicans insisted on overlooking people's needs in favor of traditional political theologies. Meanwhile the demagogues of the left proved, if nothing else, how eager, how hungry the people were to wrest power from the privileged few who had always taken for granted that power was solely theirs.

My first statement of the 1936 campaign—my acceptance of renomination at the Democratic Convention at Philadelphia on June 27 —had to be a credo of this new disunity. There is no way to pretend unity in a democracy when a privileged class refuses to reduce its accustomed power by democratizing it. They had to be identified as the enemy.

I named them "economic royalists." That name brought trembles in private clubs, in editorial rooms, and in Capitol cloakrooms— which didn't surprise me one bit. I intended it that way. The first step in remaking the Democratic Party was that speech, aimed at urban industrial workers and shopkeepers while not overlooking their natural allies, family farmers. Franklin Field was full and cheering as I said:

"Philadelphia is a good city in which to write American history. . . . In 1776 we sought freedom from . . . eighteenth-century royalists who held special privileges from the crown. . . .

"Since that struggle . . . economic royalists carved new dynasties. New kingdoms were built. . . . Through new uses of corporations, banks and securities, new machinery of industry and agriculture, of labor and capital, . . . privileged princes of these new economic dynasties, thirsting for power, reached out for control over Government itself. They created a new despotism and wrapped it in the robes of legal sanction. . . . Against economic tyranny such as this, the American citizen could appeal only to the organized power of Government. . . .

"There is a mysterious cycle in human events. To some generations much is given. Of other generations much is expected. This generation of Americans has a rendezvous with destiny.

". . . We are waging a great and successful war. It is not alone a war against want and destitution and economic demoralization. It is more than that; it is a war for the survival of democracy. . . . I am enlisted for the duration of the war."

If the phrases "economic royalists" and "rendezvous with destiny" made this speech memorable to others, something of a very different kind made it memorable for me. I came near to not being able to give it. Moments before I was introduced, as I was walking toward the platform from my car in Franklin Field, one hundred thousand pairs of eyes on me, I happened to recognize the well-known poet Edwin Markham—you couldn't miss him for his full white beard —and reached out to shake his hand. At that instant the brace on my left leg unlocked. Son Jimmy's strong arm had a grip on mine in the almost invisible way I had trained him to do, but my sudden lurch knocked him off balance. The pages of my speech scattered to the ground and I was going down with them. It was the most awful moment I ever had in public. But Gus Gennerich and Mike Reilly of the Secret Service were at me before I went down altogether and they heaved me upright. The first thing I realized after their fullbacks' heave was that those who saw it didn't quite realize what had happened. Believe me, in my position you become extremely sensitive to faces around you—and nobody looked alarmed. I quickly instructed Jimmy and the others to lock my brace and pick up the pages, and resumed my handshake with the bearded poet. It was a close call—

not only for me, but for Markham. Later, Jimmy and I speculated about Markham's fate if some quick-triggered Secret Service agent —who might not be up on his poetry and the faces of poets—had assumed that the old man's extended hand was some kind of attack. When I finally got to the rostrum, the economic royalists were not the only ones trembling.[16]

To oppose me in the election the Republicans nominated the governor of Kansas, Alfred M. Landon. He was the poorest choice possible. Actually I like Alf Landon and, toward the end of my second term, seriously considered inviting him to become a member of the Cabinet. He was a good-enough governor but not a broadly experienced politician equal to the complexities of national leadership. To make matters worse for him, he neither supported the New Deal nor opposed it very enthusiastically (I had that letter of his support for work relief to pull out any time he forced me to). This of course left him the option of a personal smear campaign against me, of the kind Thomas E. Dewey was later to conduct, but Landon is far too decent and upright a man for that.

We put Landon off his guard early. Shortly after the convention I took a train trip West for a firsthand inspection of a widespread and devastating drought. We called it a non-political trip, and, except for my encounters with Governor Landon, it was. I invited all the drought-state governors to meet with me in Des Moines. There was no way he could avoid coming without appearing unconcerned about his state's most urgent problem. That left him no way to avoid being one of many supplicants coming to the President for counsel and help.

Alf, of course, was not unmindful of our imbalanced positions. And we learned that he had his little plan for reversing the balance: He was coming to the meeting with a truckload of charts, tables, and information to show me up before the press by displaying his great familiarity with federal relief programs, whether or not they had anything to do with the drought. I liked and admired the ploy—and went him one better. I stayed up late the night before with Howard Hunter of Harry Hopkins' staff memorizing minute details about one particular WPA project in Kansas—and made sure that before Alf brought out his charts I began questioning him about the progress and status of this project—just making friendly conversation, you know—while the reporters scribbled their notes. Alf, of course, knew nothing about the particular project except its existence. After that, his charts didn't go over very well.[17]

In a way, the advance surrender of the election by the Republicans, represented by Landon's nomination, made things difficult for me, too. If I was to do great battle to rally people into a new majority party, whom would I do battle against? Well, I had fully expected— in fact, had made a couple of small cash bets on it—that the Republicans would renominate Herbert Hoover. I lost those bets—but decided to run against Herbert Hoover anyway:

"In the spring of 1933 we faced a crisis which was the ugly fruit of twelve years of neglect," I said in the opening speech of the campaign at Syracuse on September 29. ". . . A few people—a few only—unwilling to remember, seem to have forgotten those days.

"In the summer of 1933, a nice old gentleman wearing a silk hat fell off the end of a pier. He was unable to swim. A friend ran down the pier, dived overboard and pulled him out; but the silk hat floated off with the tide. After the old gentleman had been revived, he was effusive in his thanks. He praised his friend for saving his life. Today, three years later, the old gentleman is berating his friend because the silk hat was lost."

And then I struck my theme of redefining old labels in such a way that independents and forward-looking Republicans could feel welcome in the Democratic Party, eventually make it their home. I attacked not Republicans but Republican misleaders:

". . . The first essential of doing a job well is to want to see the job done. Make no mistake about this: the Republican leadership today is not against the way we have done the job. The Republican leadership is against the job's being done.

". . . The true conservative is the man who has a real concern for injustices and takes thought against the day of reckoning. The true conservative seeks to protect the system of private property and free enterprise by correcting such injustices. . . . Liberalism becomes the protection for the farsighted conservative. . . .

"I am that kind of conservative because I am that kind of liberal."

A few days later, at Forbes Field in Pittsburgh, I had a more specific problem. Forbes Field was where, in 1932, I had made a campaign speech containing a regrettable promise. I had promised to do what Herbert Hoover had not done—to curtail federal expenditures and balance the budget. This was the place I was sure I would now be

called upon by my critics and the press to talk about the finances of
the nation, to meet the charge that the New Deal was extravagant and
would soon lead to bankruptcy. Of course this charge was utterly
false; what threatened to ruin us was not emergency deficits but
prolonged unemployment, stagnation, and loss of spirit. What could
I say at Pittsburgh that would be true, and at the same time mute
the shrill slogans of our critics?

One night at the White House we went around and around and
around on this, wearily and futilely. When constructive ideas seemed
exhausted, Henry Morgenthau said: "Mr. President, a speech has
been prepared for me to deliver next week at a bankers' convention.
It deals with the finances of the nation. Why don't you deliver that
speech yourself at Forbes Field?" Good old Henry. Only he could
imagine that a technical speech for a bankers' convention could be
transplanted to a ball park for a presidential campaign. I asked him
to read it—of course, he just happened to have a copy with him.
After the second page, when I found myself guessing at the number
of remaining pages we had to endure, my private secretary, Marguerite LeHand, who did not always conceal her feelings, stood up
and said what I could not bring myself to say: "By this time all the
bleachers are empty, and the folks are beginning to walk out of the
grandstand." As Miss LeHand walked out of our meeting, even Henry
joined the laughter.

I decided to rely on a rule I always tried to campaign by: "Never
let your opponent pick the battleground on which to fight. If he picks
one, stay out of it and let him fight all by himself."

So, at Forbes Field in 1936, I just never mentioned that regrettable promise of 1932.

The day of that Pittsburgh speech, October 1, was a typical campaign day. It began with a speech about wildlife conservation at the
Mountain States Forest Festival at Elkins, West Virginia. Then, from
the rear platform of my campaign train I spoke extemporaneously at
Grafton ("The last time I came through, there was no such thing as
the Tygarts Valley Dam. . . . I am not talking politics, but I am calling your attention to the fact that this dam up here is a pretty good
boondoggling idea"); at Fairmont ("I received a telegram a few
moments ago on the train and through you good people I am going
to make an announcement. . . . For the first time in fifty-five years
we have completed one full year without a single national bank failure

in the United States"); at Morgantown, and then across the state line for a rear-platform greeting at Connellsville, Pennsylvania, before going on to Pittsburgh. Quite a day!

I love greeting and being greeted by crowds in these small communities. I will take those meetings any time over big ball-park crowds in cities, where, frankly, I have never felt comfortable. Some candidates, to be sure, prefer the big crowds in big cities, the big roars thundering out of faces they can't see. These city crowds make me feel less personal. Perhaps it's because I am a small-town man myself, but I like to see the faces.

Some candidates complain about the ardors of campaigning. They should find another trade. Campaigning—seeing the faces, the farm houses, the plains, hills, and valleys, the clear rivers and the polluted ones, the smokestacks and the mining shacks—is to experience America. It is an elementary course in the education of a President, and a periodic refresher course is not too much to ask of one who would lead this great land.

I tried to make of the campaign a short course in the people's interdependence, tying the welfare of farmers to that of city workers, and vice versa. A few samples of rear-platform remarks, mostly extemporaneous:

At Oelwein, Iowa, October 9: "I am not making one kind of speech in the East and another kind of speech in the West. I am not making one kind of speech to farm people and another kind of speech to industrial workers. In the last four years we have gained a great knowledge of the interdependence of every part of the Nation with every other part."

Next day, at Red Oak, Iowa: "The city dwellers have to have money to buy food and more food. Last year, somebody in the Department of Agriculture . . . made a survey of what the people of the United States eat. Then they classified as Class A the diet that we all ought to have. Diet B was graded as a pretty good diet but not the best. And they found that as a Nation we are living today in the United States, on the average, on Diet C. That is the actual fact. Why is it? It is because people have not the purchasing power for either a B-diet or an A-diet. Incidentally, if all of us had the proper kind of diet in the United States, we would have to put 40 million acres more land into the production of food stuffs."

Same day, at Pacific Junction, Iowa: "Suppose somebody came to you and said, 'If you will borrow eight hundred dollars, it will increase your income every year by more than twenty-two hundred dollars,' would you do it or not? Well, all you have to do to get a picture of American national finance is just to add a whole lot of zeroes to those figures. In other words, we have gone into debt a little less than eight billion dollars net, but our annual income today is over twenty-two billion dollars more than it was in 1932. I call that a pretty good investment."

And that night at Omaha, Nebraska, I tried to demonstrate to the liberals and progressives back in the Senate that in asking them to bend, I stood ready to bend, too. I would put liberal principle ahead of party label. In that Omaha speech, kept secret until its delivery, I withheld support of the Democratic candidate for the Senate in favor of the leader of Senate progressives, a Republican: "Outside of my own State of New York, I have consistently refrained from taking part in elections in any other State. But Senator Norris' name has been entered as a candidate for Senator from Nebraska. And to my rule of non-participation in State elections I have made—and so long as he lives I will always make—one magnificently justified exception. George Norris' candidacy transcends State and party lines. . . . He is one of the major prophets of America. Help this great American to continue an historic career of service."

At Colorado Springs, Colorado, October 12: "You know, there has been a good deal of difference in tourists. In 1932, when I came through here, there were a lot of tourists—but they were riding in box cars. This year there are more of them—and they are riding in Pullmans."

And in a major address at Chicago on October 14:

"Today for the first time in seven years the banker, the storekeeper, the small factory owner, the industrialist, can all sit back and enjoy the company of their own ledgers. They are in the black. . . .

"Some of these people really forget how sick they were. But I know how sick they were. I have their fever charts. I know how the knees of all of our rugged individualists were trembling four years ago and how their hearts fluttered. They came to Washington in great numbers. Washington did not look like a dangerous bureaucracy to them then. Oh, no! It looked like an emergency hospital. All of the distinguished patients wanted two things—a quick hypodermic to end the pain and a course of treatment to cure the disease. They wanted them in a hurry; we gave them both. And now most of the patients seem to be doing very nicely. Some of them are even well enough to throw their crutches at the doctor."

The crowds along the way are thrilling; yet, in 1936, as I remarked to Harold Ickes, there was something terrible about their response. I would hear people cry out, "He saved my home," "He gave me a job." The people were so excited by the passage of Social Security, the Wagner Act, by what NRA had done for them, by the sudden change from unforgivable government neglect to bold government action, they were beginning to think we could do anything. I recall a most awful jam around my car in New Bedford, Massachusetts, where there must have been twenty thousand people in a little park. A girl about six feet away was trying to reach me with an envelope but a policeman pushed her back. I told him, "Get that note." As I recall, it said: "Dear Mr. President: I wish you could do something to help us girls. We work in a garment factory and a few months ago our minimum pay was $11 a week. Today it is $4 a week. You are the only man that can do anything about it. Please send somebody from Washington to restore our minimum wages because we cannot live on $4 a week." People wrote to the White House all the time asking me to raise wages or stop child labor, as though by executive order I could just do that. Of course, the President has no such power.

These motorcades and rear-platform speeches, this direct contact, by eye and word, by personal greetings and written messages passed by hand, remind a candidate of whom he'll be working for if he gets the job, of the reality of their problems. I like these personal greetings, too, because they bring me back to the exciting days of my first campaign for the New York State Senate, in Dutchess, Columbia, and Putnam counties. I got myself a bright-red Maxwell touring car—cars were new then, and a Democrat in that district had to do anything that would attract attention. For four weeks Richard Connell, the candidate for Congress, and I bumped along two thousand miles of rugged roads. If we had no meeting to attend, no train of commuters to meet, we set up drinks for all comers in the local saloon or inn. We had to learn to turn liability into asset. One day our car struck a farmer's favorite dog. We paid the farmer five dollars, then made sure word got around that he was satisfied. That farmer turned out to be a Republican—and he brought us fifteen Republican votes that fall. Another time, Connell was hit by a baseball from a sandlot game. While he rushed to a doctor I stayed on and cheered—for both sides. When we had a blowout we didn't mind—it collected a crowd.

There is no substitute for meeting the people.

Our 1936 campaign train, hardly a red Maxwell, carried about a hundred people in eleven cars. The excitement of crowd after crowd, town after town, cheers upon cheers, keeps mounting. Between stops, you gulp down your food, you snatch cat naps. Sometimes I'd get a chance to remove my leg braces. The one thing I hated—perhaps this is another reason I was not keen on the big meetings in ball parks— was an arrival in a big station when I had to leave the train. After the meeting, late at night, there would always be a big crowd awaiting our return to the train. I would have to hear that infernal hush as I grasped the handrails of a trainside ramp and slowly worked my way into the train, propelling myself by arm and shoulder muscles. People expect their President to walk. This is something I could never discuss, apologize for, even openly acknowledge. The people's confidence must sometimes be won in odd ways, but it must be won.

Once inside, with shades drawn, we could relax. We'd sip a little refreshment, relive a few humorous sidelights of the night's triumph, then talk about the next day's speeches without altogether letting up on the fun. Stanley High, one of the speech drafters, could never get used to mixing jokes with serious business, but allowed one night that probably no presidential campaign had ever gone forward with so much kidding. I replied, "Can you imagine what it must have been like to campaign with Hoover or Coolidge?"

At another relaxation session I said, "You know, boys, I had a lovely thought last night. I thought what fun it would be if I could now be running against Franklin D. Roosevelt. I don't know whether I could beat him or not, but I certainly would give him a close race —a darned sight closer than Landon is doing.

"First, I would repudiate Hearst. Then I would repudiate the Du Ponts and everything they stand for. Then I would say: 'I am for social security, work relief, etc., etc. But the Democrats cannot be entrusted with the administration of these fine ideals.' I would cite chapter and verse on WPA inefficiency—and there's plenty of it, as there is bound to be in such a vast emergency program.

"You know, the more I think about it, the more I think I could lick myself."[18]

William Randolph Hearst, owner and editorial dictator of America's largest chain of big-city newspapers, had supported me in 1932, and his support was valuable when I was not as well known outside my own state. In 1936, at first we were quite troubled by his vitriolic opposition, along with that of 85 per cent of the nation's newspaper publishers. But the more vitriolic he became in his first-page editorials with key phrases printed all in capital letters ("the RAW DEAL tax program is a nefarious plot to SOAK THE RICH," etc., etc.) and the more our campaign travels showed us the people's true sentiments, the less I was concerned. You can't rant against the interests of the people and keep your influence over them, no matter what your circulation. When Old Willie finally realized that his phrase "SOAK THE RICH" was exactly what many people wanted done, he ordered his editors to substitute "SOAK THE SUCCESSFUL"—but it was too late. His best-known columnist, Arthur Brisbane, I learned, was privately for me, and at least would not add to his boss's smears. Next I learned that Hearst's very special friend, Marion Davies, the movie actress, was strong for me and—according to Steve Early, who had a friend close to Miss Davies—"was working persistently on Hearst."

I had ways of working on him myself. An editorial writer for the Washington *Evening Star* (not a Hearst paper) passed word to Ickes that two stenographic transcripts of a Communist International meeting in Moscow were in this country. An incomplete one was at the State Department—and a complete one was supposed to be in the hands of Hearst. According to the tip, Hearst had assigned a man to prepare a series of articles on one portion of this record: a decision that the American Communist Party should endorse me for re-election if no major radical candidate appeared. Such an endorsement would be "help" I certainly did not need. On the other hand, repudiating it could create difficulties: Labor organizers and liberal pressure groups, almost all supporting me, were so fearfully on the receiving end of unfounded charges of communism, they were oversensitized to the issue. Attacked themselves, they felt defensive about all others under similar attack and distrusted hasty repudiators as allies of their enemies.

I did not wish to contribute to any further division of the left. I chose different ground—international ground—for my countermove. Through Ambassador Bullitt at Moscow, our State Department

sent a sharp note to the Soviet Government charging (but not specifying) that the USSR was encouraging communistic activities in this
country, a violation of our agreement in 1933 to establish diplomatic
relations. The note clearly implied—although it did not directly
threaten—possible severance of those relations. I don't know what
they thought of it in Moscow, but its impact was so unexpected here
that it completely took the air out of Hearst's plan.

Soon Hearst made *his* countermove—this time a private one. A
friend of Hearst came to see me in August 1936, after the convention
but before the campaign. I am sure he came with Hearst's knowledge
and approval, although the man was careful to deny it. He asked
what I thought of Hearst, and I asked whether he meant personally
or politically. Politically, he said. Not yet knowing what this was all
about, I replied that I thought very well of him and believed his
attacks on me might be quite effective in the campaign. Then he
wanted to know whether I intended to criticize Hearst. Interesting!
The publisher was worried about my possible discrediting of him at
least as much as I of his possible campaign damage to me. I said I
didn't know yet, whereupon he said that Hearst was sensitive to public
criticism. Then the man asked whether Victor Watson, former managing editor of Hearst's Chicago *Herald-Examiner*, was a friend of
mine, and I said he had been while I was governor and Watson was
running Hearst's New York *American*. My visitor suggested that I
choose some "prominent Jewish friend" and send him to Watson to
see whether they might work out some sort of truce, pointing out that,
of course, Hearst would have to go through the motions of supporting
Landon. I asked what kind of truce he had in mind, and he said an
apportionment in Hearst papers of equal space for the Democratic
and Republican campaigns. (What a magnanimous concession!)
Twitting the man, I asked whether Hearst was losing circulation. To
my surprise, the man admitted he was. Advertising? The man replied that, of course, advertising follows circulation.

Finally I asked why he suggested I send a Jew as an intermediary.
He replied that Hearst had great respect for the business acumen of
successful Jews. We talked about the possibility of sending one of
the Strauses, who own Macy's in New York. Isidor Straus, Ambassador to France, happened to be on his way home at that time. On
that possibility, we closed the discussion.

This strange proposal didn't appeal to me, but it was worth thinking about. Removing the thorn of Hearst would be a relief. But then what if Hearst, who would stoop to anything, were to break a story that the President of the United States sent an emissary to America's leading publisher to plead for mercy? If he had any truce to propose, let him send the emissary. I did nothing about it.

Other sections of the press, each in their own way, were just as childish or inept, misgauging the American people's awareness of their own best interests. A leading news magazine, the *Literary Digest*, which had never been wrong in forecasting a national election, predicted an easy victory by Landon, who, their poll showed, would carry thirty-two states and 370 electoral votes. Their "poll" consisted of a sampling drawn from telephone subscribers and lists of automobile owners. This, of course, showed how accustomed publishers and their fellow club members were to talking to themselves, how far behind the times they had fallen. The millions of Americans rescued by the WPA, the AAA, the CCC, the TVA, the REA, Social Security, and the Wagner Act could not afford the luxury of a telephone or a motorcar. Under the very noses of these economic royalists the majority of Americans were asserting their political independence—and their former masters had no idea of it. Shortly after the election the oracular *Literary Digest*, discredited, was out of business.

All through the campaign year, papers everywhere, led by the Chicago *Tribune*, ran an editorial-page warning of the coming election: "Only 201 [or 101 or 21] days remain in which to save our country. What are you doing to save it?"[19]

If anything gave our campaign a last-minute uplift and assurance of victory, it was the last-ditch drive of the opposition in the final two weeks—not by newspapers so much as by desperate Republican employers. How unbelievably out of touch they were! Into the pay envelopes of their employees they inserted scares, usually printed on dreaded pink slips. A typical one said: "Effective January 1937, we are compelled by a Roosevelt 'New Deal' law to make a 1 per cent deduction from your wages and turn it over to the government. You might get this money back . . . but only if Congress decides to make the appropriation." One Republican campaign orator predicted that Social Security would require everyone to wear a dog tag—but he made the allowance that the tag would be of stainless steel to avoid skin irritation. Advertising appeared in streetcars and buses warning, "Under Social Security you will be known by a number, not a name." Republican campaign workers warned voters they would have to be fingerprinted. How little these men, who lived on dividends, understood the average American's eagerness for the simple security of unemployment insurance and an old-age pension, a simple hope from which lies would not scare them away.

These desperate falsehoods, while giving me absolute confidence of victory, angered me. If Roosevelt haters and people haters were so bent on making me the personal symbol of all they hated—all that the people yearned for—I would accept their challenge. This time I would strike back on *their* chosen ground. My last major address was to be at Madison Square Garden in New York on October 31. Against the advice of some of my friends I declared in that speech:

"For twelve years this Nation was afflicted with hear-nothing, see-nothing, do-nothing Government. The Nation looked to Government but the Government looked away. Nine mocking years with the golden calf and three long years of the scourge! Nine crazy years at the ticker and three long years in the breadlines! Nine mad years of mirage and three long years of despair! . . . For nearly four years you have had an Administration which instead of twirling its thumbs has rolled up its sleeves. We will keep our sleeves rolled up. . . . We know now that Government by organized money is just as dangerous as Government by organized mob.

"Never before in all our history have these forces been so united against one candidate as they stand today. They are unanimous in their hate for me—and I welcome their hatred.

"I should like to have it said of my first Administration that in it the forces of selfishness and lust for power met their match. I should like to have it said of my second Administration that in it these forces met their master."

Well, didn't the editorialists and columnists tear their hair: Roosevelt wants to make himself the "master" of the American people. Friends urged me to issue an explanatory statement. Even some panicky Democratic leaders wired warnings to clarify. But the American people, who needed no explanation of Social Security, who needed no explanation of the last-minute treachery by their enemies and mine, did not need further explanation of exactly what I meant. Least of all did we have to worry about how the big cities would vote—the big cities of Hearst papers, but also of big labor unions; the big cities of big machine bosses with their old-style political favors, but also of widespread new security based on Social Security. Because the voters were clearly on our side, the machine bosses enthusiastically went along for the ride, a ride that would eventually do them in. Never had they carried a food basket as appreciated as Social Security, and they made the most of it.

In Brooklyn I heard a tale of one Hymie Shorenstein, a minor machine straw boss who enunciated a new big-city political ethic that has become known in his borough as "Shorenstein's rule." Because he could deliver the votes—in 1936 he was to deliver sixty thousand for me against three thousand for Landon—Hymie was given the privilege of personally choosing a candidate for a local judgeship. His candidate made the expected large financial contribution to what he thought was his own campaign, then protested when he saw no billboards emblazoning his name before the people. Shorenstein, as I heard it, informed the candidate of the facts of life in his inimitable Brooklyn manner:

"You're worried? Listen. Did you ever go down to the wharf to see the Staten Island Ferry come in? Did you ever look down in the water at all those chewing-gum wrappers, and the banana peels and the garbage? When the ferryboat comes into the wharf, automatically it pulls all the garbage in too. The name of your ferryboat is Franklin D. Roosevelt. Stop worrying."[20]

On November 3, the boat, by whatever name, was to pull into the dock.

On the afternoon before the election, Jim Farley made a last-minute telephone check with every state Democratic leader outside of the "solid South." His conclusion—although I knew Jim was not given to wishful analysis—appeared preposterous. I would not allow myself the luxury of believing it. He sent me a note by messenger saying, "After looking them all over carefully and discounting everything that has been given in these reports, I am still definitely of the opinion that you will carry every state but two—Maine and Vermont."

On election night, with forty or fifty relatives and Dutchess County neighbors and campaign-staff members munching sandwiches and huddling around the radio in the library of my Hyde Park home, I and Miss LeHand and a couple of other close associates set ourselves up in the dining room two doors down the hall, where we had tickers from the Associated Press and United Press and a direct telephone line to Democratic headquarters in New York City. The figures that came from these sources I assembled on large tally sheets, which I had prepared in advance in accordance with my old election custom. Some of my aides would chide me about taking all this trouble, claiming they kept up with returns just as fast and completely sitting beside a radio. Let them have their efficiency. I like the old way I learned when I ran for state senator—and it gives me a task to do as the tension mounts.

Two early returns told me something extraordinary was happening. First, I learned that I carried a district I had never won in all my political life—the election district of Hyde Park. Next came a report that we carried New Haven, Connecticut, the first complete city count in the nation, by fifteen thousand—where a victory of five thousand would indicate winning the state. I asked someone to go to another phone and check New Haven through a different source. It was true. And that's the way the votes kept pouring in.

Late that night—talk about things extraordinary—a phone call came for John Boettiger, my son-in-law, who was then employed as publisher of the Seattle *Post-Intelligencer*, believe it or not, a Hearst paper! This is what he heard:

"Hello, John, this is Marion Davies. I just wanted to tell you that I love you. We know that a steamroller has flattened us out, but there are no hard feelings at this end. I just wanted you to know that." Then Hearst himself got on the phone to repeat the no-hard-feelings message.

Jim Farley's prediction turned out precisely and astonishingly right. Forty-six states for us, only Maine and Vermont for Landon; 523 electoral votes against eight. The popular vote was 27,476,673 to 16,679,583. Our already one-sided majority in Congress was increased from sixty-nine to seventy-six in the Senate (twelve freshmen would have to be seated with the Republicans to keep the traditional dividing aisle decently near the center of the chamber); and from 322 to 333 in the House.

In the days that followed we analyzed the results more closely. The correctness of the appeal to the growing labor force in large cities was remarkably borne out. Of American cities with populations of one hundred thousand or more, we swept 104; Landon took two. A still closer analysis revealed that we had captured virtually 100 per cent of city districts inhabited by Negroes. This was a dramatic turn-around, without which the national election would have been reasonably close in terms of electoral votes. In 1932, Negro districts of Detroit, Cleveland, Philadelphia, and Cincinnati had gone for Hoover, some overwhelmingly. In Chicago, while winning 59 per cent of the white vote, I had polled only 23 per cent of Negro ballots. Yet even though politics forced me to resist endorsing an anti-poll-tax bill and anti-lynching bill, which would correct old southern injustices, Negroes learned concretely, through our work-relief programs, that we were out to uplift the fortunes of the poor regardless of race.

Negro allegiance to the Republican Party was at last broken. In advance of the 1934 election, Robert Vann, publisher of the Pittsburgh *Courier,* a Negro paper, voiced this break when he told his his readers: "My friends, go turn Lincoln's picture to the wall. That debt has been paid in full." In 1936 the Negro vote for me in Chicago doubled that of 1932. Every Cleveland Negro ward went Democratic. We won Pittsburgh's Negro Third Ward by almost ten to one. Not long after the election, a poll by *Fortune* recorded 85 per cent of Negroes as counting themselves on our side.

The traditionally Republican steelworkers' district of Homestead, Pennsylvania, voted Democratic four to one; the Jones & Laughlin ward in Pittsburgh, 5,870 to 925. The CIO leader John L. Lewis, a lifelong Republican, had contributed $770,000 to our campaign fund, $469,000 of it from his United Mine Workers, a major shift in the financial sources of the Democratic Party. Needless to say, our contributions from bankers and brokers and industrialists, previously our financial mainstay, had dropped to almost nothing in 1936. Labor's funds replaced them. (I am sorry to say that Lewis was soon to demand a kind of stockholder's control in my administration, such as millionaires had previously expected—and got—from some of my predecessors. His "investment" was appreciated and respected, but he soon discovered that he did not hold voting stock.)

Still further analysis revealed that class division, of which I was so often accused, was far less reflected in the votes than the "experts" assumed. We received good percentages, although seldom majorities, in wealthy voting districts. I was endorsed by many farsighted businessmen, such as the Boston merchant Edward Filene (who said, "Why shouldn't the American people take half my money from me? I took it all from them"); Thomas Watson, head of International

Business Machines; Russell Leffingwell of the House of Morgan; and A. P. Giannini, head of the Bank of America.

The Democratic Party was reconstructed as a predominantly progressive and liberal party. If we could hold together, we would remain for a long time to come the nation's majority party.

But there was a sadness and—at least for me—a deep sense of loss in this triumph. We had drifted far, perhaps past the point of possible return, down the river of becoming a nation of cities, of city people, of disconnection from the land and from one another. This drift cannot lead us toward being a happier nation.[21]

BACKGROUND MEMORANDUM TO PART VI

Every campaigner, especially for leadership of a large and complex state or for national office, is a cripple. His legs are bound against running faster than his constituents are able to keep in step. His hands are tied by the limited powers of the office he seeks; he had better not promise what he knows he cannot deliver. His tongue is gagged against pronouncements that may make new friends if those pronouncements will also make new enemies. His balance is threatened by the pulls and tugs of conflicting demands for justice: Shall money go for this urgent need or that one? Shall this group's freedom be expanded at the expense of that one's?

Immobilized by these paralyzing constraints, the candidate has to make himself appear able-bodied, attractive, confident, and powerful—at least, more so than his opponent.

Being crippled—not in metaphor but in reality—is perhaps good schooling for politics.

To this day, more than a quarter century after his death, people keep wondering aloud and speculating, "If Roosevelt had not been a cripple, would he have been the same kind of President?" Of course not. If a different kind, how? Impossible to say. "If he had not been a cripple, would he have become President at all?" Again, imponderable.

Did F.D.R.'s private battle teach him to identify with those who suffer? Unquestionably. Moreover it taught him the uses of patience (never a strong suit with crusaders who relied upon him, upon whom he relied, yet who continually harassed him). It heightened his sense of time and timing. "It made him realize"—an observation of Egbert Curtis, his Warm Springs companion—"that he was not infallible, that everything wasn't always going to go his way." More than anything, it forced him to study the uses of handicap, giving him a leg up in a profession of able-bodied crippled men.

Let's not carry theory and speculation too far. Instead let's try to observe firsthand, in so far as the written word permits, the connections between suffering and Roosevelt's acquired capacity for patience, for tolerance and respect of the wills and ambitions of others, for turning handicap into power.

We begin with his own words. A sufferer identifies with sufferers; and "Doctor" Roosevelt of Warm Springs also identifies with other doctors. In F.D.R.'s early days at Warm Springs, a South Carolina physician, Dr. William Eggleston, writes to Roosevelt for a personal case report that might help him treat a polio patient who came his way. Roosevelt's reply is the only detailed personal account of what he recently endured. The letter, dictated to Missy LeHand during their first stay at Warm Springs, says in part:

. . . I am very glad to tell you what I can in regard to my case and as I have talked it over with a great many doctors can, I think, give you a history of the case which would be equal to theirs.

First symptoms of the illness appeared in August, 1921. . . . By the end of the third day practically all muscles from the chest down were involved. Above the chest the only symptom was a weakening of the two large thumb muscles making it impossible to write. There was no special pain along the spine and no rigidity of the neck.

For the following two weeks I had to be catheterized and there was slight, though not severe, difficulty in controlling the bowels. The fever lasted for only 6 or 7 days, but all the muscles from the hips down were extremely sensitive to the touch and I had to have the knees supported by pillows. This condition of extreme discomfort lasted about 3 weeks. . . . This sensitiveness disappeared gradually over a period of six months, the last remaining point being the calf muscles.

As to treatment—the mistake was made for the first 10 days of giving my feet and lower legs rather heavy massage. This was stopped by Dr. Lovett, of Boston, who was, without doubt, the greatest specialist on infantile paralysis. In January, 1922, 5 months after the attack, he found that the muscles behind the knees had contracted and that there was a tendency to foot-drop in the right foot. These were corrected by the use of plaster casts during two weeks. In February, 1922, braces were fitted on each leg from the hips to the shoes, and I was able to stand up and learned gradually to walk with crutches. At the same time gentle exercises were begun, first every other day, then daily, exercising each muscle 10 times and seeking to avoid any undue strain by giving each muscle the correct movement with gravity. These exercises I did on a board placed on the bed.

The recovery of muscle paralysis began at this time, though for many months it seemed to make little progress. In the summer of 1922 I began swimming and found that this exercise seemed better adapted than any other because all weight was removed from the legs and I was able to move the legs in the water far better than I had expected. . . .

I still wear braces, of course, because the quadriceps are not yet strong enough to bear my weight. One year ago I was able to stand in fresh water without braces when the water was up to my chin. Six months ago I could stand in water up to the top of my shoulders and to-day can stand in water level with my arm pits. This is a very simple method for me of determining how fast the quadriceps are coming back. Aside from these muscles the waist muscles on the right side are still weak and the outside muscles on the right leg have strengthened so much more than the inside muscles that they pull my right foot forward. I continue corrective exercises for all the muscles.

To sum up I would give you the following "Don'ts":

Don't use heavy massage but use light massage rubbing always towards the heart.

Don't let the patient over-exercise any muscle or get tired.

Don't let the patient feel cold, especially the legs, feet or any other part affected. Progress stops entirely when the legs or feet are cold.

Don't let the patient get too fat.

The following treatment is so far the best, judging from my own experience and that of hundreds of other cases which I have studied:

1. Gentle exercise especially for the muscles which seem to be worst affected.

2. Gentle skin rubbing—not muscle kneading—bearing in mind that good circulation is a prime requisite.

3. Swimming in warm water—lots of it.

4. Sunlight—all the patient can get, especially direct sunlight on the affected parts. It would be ideal to lie in the sun all day with nothing on. This is difficult to accomplish but the nearest approach to it is a bathing suit.

5. Belief on the patient's part that the muscles are coming back and will eventually regain recovery of the affected parts. There are cases known in Norway where adults have taken the disease and not been able to walk until after a lapse of 10 or even 12 years.

I hope that your patient has not got a very severe case. They all differ, of course, in the degree in which the parts are affected. If braces are necessary there is a man in New York . . . who makes remarkable light

braces of duraluminum. My first braces of steel weighed 7 lbs. apiece—
my new ones weigh only 4 lbs. apiece. Remember that braces are only
for the convenience of the patient in getting around—a leg in a brace
does not have a chance for muscle development. This muscle development must come through exercise when the brace is not on—such as
swimming, etc.[1]

At Hyde Park, before discovering Warm Springs, this powerful man, to
the shock of his children and friends, practices dragging himself crablike
across the floor, explaining that the one fear he ever knew was that of being caught in a fire. Then, showing off his inordinately strong shoulders
and arms, he fills the house with laughter, wrestling his boys on the floor,
two at a time. Mama orders an electric tricycle from Europe, but F.D.R.
uses it only once. He doesn't want his muscles *worked;* he wants to work
them himself.

John Gunther describes Roosevelt's determination to get from floor to
floor unaided: "Day after day he would haul his dead weight up the stairs
by the power of his hands and arms, step by step, slowly, doggedly; the
sweat would pour off his face, and he would tremble with exhaustion.
Moreover he insisted on doing this with members of the family or friends
watching him, and he would talk all the time as he inched himself up
little by little, talk, talk, and make people talk back. It was a kind of
enormous spiritual catharsis—as if he had to do it, to prove his independence, and had to have the feat witnessed, to prove that it was nothing."

At Warm Springs in 1924, coached by Dr. LeRoy Hubbard, "surgeon-
in-chief," and Helena Mahoney, head physiotherapist, he concentrates on
the day he will be able to walk unaided with braces. Braces, which he once
said he "hated and mistrusted," which he cannot put on or take off by
himself, make him like a man on stilts. Unable to flex his toes, he has no
balance. In 1928, after seven years of immobility and more than four years
of daring and persevering, one day, finally, triumphantly, he hobbles most
of the way across the living-room floor of his cottage—with braces, but
without human help. The achievement is exhausting—and is never to be
accomplished again. Years later, according to Grace Tully, "Missy's eyes
filled up when on occasions she reminisced about those days." Roosevelt
likes to maintain the belief that if he had had another year before the demand that he run for Governor, he'd have mastered walking with a single
brace.

In the summer of 1928 at Warm Springs, shortly after Roosevelt agrees
to address the Democratic National Convention at Houston, son Elliott,
eighteen, is visiting. One evening, Roosevelt is lost in concentrated thought
when suddenly he bursts out:

"With my hand on a man's arm, *and one cane*—I'm sure. Let's try it!"

A fellow polio, Turnley Walker, Roosevelt's dinner guest, describes what then happens over and over:

"First Roosevelt would get over to the wall and balance there with his cane. It was an ordinary cane but he held it in a special way, with his index finger extended down along the rod from the handle. This finger acted as a rigid cleat . . . so that the strength of the massive arm and shoulder rammed straight along the cane to its tip against the floor.

" 'Now, Elliott, you get on the left, my weak side.' Elliott watchfully took his place and Mahoney came forward to show him how to hold his right arm against his middle at the proper angle and lock it there with a clenching of his biceps.

" 'Remember that a polio needs more than a fingertip of guidance—he needs an *iron bar*,' said Mahoney. 'Make a habit of *holding that arm there*. Never forget the job it's got to do.'

" 'Let's go,' said Roosevelt, and he reached out to find the proper grip. Elliott had never felt his father's hand touching him that way. He had been grabbed and hugged, and even tossed and caught with wild energy when he was younger. But now the fingers sought their grip with a kind of ruthless desperation. . . . The pressure became stronger than he had expected as his father pressed down to hitch one braced leg forward for the first step. 'You must *go right with him*,' said Mahoney sternly. 'Watch his feet. Match your strides with his.' Elliott stared down as the rigid feet swung out slowly, and through the pressing hand he could feel the slow, clenching effort of his father's powerful body.

" 'Don't look at me, Son. Keep your head up, smiling, watching the eyes of people. Keep them from noticing what we're doing.'

"The cane went out, the good leg swung, the pressure came, the weak leg hitched up into its arc and then fell stiffly into the proper place against the floor. Elliott carefully co-ordinated his own legs, and they moved across the room.

"Roosevelt set his hips against the far wall and told Elliott to rest his arm. 'We'll do beautifully,' he said.

"They went across the room and back again. It was becoming somewhat easier.

" 'As soon as you feel confident, Son, look up and around at people, the way you would do if I weren't crippled.'

" 'But don't forget,' Mahoney warned, 'if he loses his balance, he'll crash down like a tree.'

" 'Don't scare us,' said Roosevelt.

" . . . The cane, the swing, the pressure, the swing. Elliott found that he could look up now and then as they advanced. He caught his father's eyes, the broad smile which was held with a very slight rigidity. . . . Only then did he notice that his father was perspiring heavily."

Yet, except when a public show requires such extraordinary exertion, Roosevelt is as helpless as a baby. When no strangers are around to see, he lets himself be carried by practiced attendants. When F.D.R. becomes governor, his cousin Nicholas Roosevelt spends a weekend at Hyde Park, and is to recall: "His mother and I stood on the veranda watching his son Elliott and Gus Gennerich, the state trooper who acted as his personal bodyguard, carry him down the steps and place him in the car. As they turned and left him, he lost his balance (his powerful torso was much heavier than his crippled legs), and he fell over on the car seat. I doubt if one man in a thousand as disabled and dependent on others would have refrained from some sort of reproach, however mild, to those whose carelessness had thus left him in the lurch. But Franklin merely lay on his back, waved his strong arms in the air and laughed. At once they came back and helped him to his seat behind the wheel, and he called me to join him."

Early on, Louis Howe sets an iron rule—one that F.D.R. is scarcely inclined to resist—that he must never be carried in public.[2]

Frances Perkins recalling the gubernatorial campaign: "I saw him speak in a small hall in New York City's Yorkville district. The auditorium was crowded. . . . The only possible way for any candidate to enter the stage without being crushed by the throng was by the fire escape. I realized with sudden horror that the only way he could get over that fire escape was in the arms of strong men. That was how he arrived.

"Those of us who saw this incident, with our hands on our throats to hold down our emotion, realized that this man had accepted the ultimate humility which comes from being helped physically. . . . He got up on his braces, adjusted them, straightened himself, smoothed his hair, linked his arm in his son Jim's, and walked out on the platform as if this were nothing unusual. . . . I began to see what the great teachers of religion meant when they said that humility is the greatest of virtues, and that if you can't learn it, God will teach it to you by humiliation."

Is humility—or humiliation—Roosevelt's great teacher? Many have speculated. Ickes, after a day in a campaign car with Steve Early:

"[Early] recalled the campaign trips that he had made with Roosevelt when the latter was a candidate for Vice President in 1920. He said that if it hadn't been for the President's affliction, he never would have been President of the United States. In those earlier years, as Steve put it, the President was just a playboy. . . . He couldn't be made to prepare his speeches in advance, preferring to play cards instead. During his long illness, according to Steve, the President began to read deeply and study public questions."

Perkins: "I saw Roosevelt only once between 1921 and 1924, and I was instantly struck by his growth. He was young, he was crippled, he was physically weak, but he had a firmer grip on life and on himself than ever before. He was serious, not playing now. . . . He had become conscious of other people, of weak people, of human frailty. I remember thinking that he would never be so hard and harsh in judgment on stupid people—even on wrongdoers. . . . I remember watching him [as governor] in Utica. . . . Certainly some of the Democratic rank-and-file were pretty tiresome, with a lot of things to say that were of no consequence. However, he sat and nodded and smiled and said, 'That's fine,' when they reported some slight progress. I remembered, in contrast, how he had walked away from bores a few years earlier when he was in the State Senate.

"Now he could not walk away when he was bored. He listened, and out of it learned . . . that 'everybody wants to have the sense of belonging, of being on the inside,' that 'no one wants to be left out,' as he put it years later in a Columbus, Ohio, speech. . . . He became thoroughly familiar with the concept that good and evil, hope and fear, wisdom and ignorance, selfishness and sacrifice, are inseparably mixed in most human beings."

A considerably more speculative observation, by Noel F. Busch, childhood neighbor of the Oyster Bay Roosevelts who grew up to be a *Time* correspondent and avid F.D.R.-watcher: "Loss of the use of one's legs has several effects on the human psyche. One is that, when deprived of the power to move around, the mind demands a substitute or compensation for this power, such as the ability to command other people to move around. That is why almost all invalids tend to be peckish and demanding. However, . . . Roosevelt sublimated and refined the pardonable peevishness of the normal invalid into an administrative urge which would have had profound consequences for him even if he had never become President."

Biographer Emil Ludwig: "The privilege of remaining seated, which everyone concedes him because of his affliction, starts him off with an advantage in his intercourse with others, in the same way as the smallness of Napoleon's stature compelled everyone standing before him to bend his back a little. Certainly giants like Bismarck or Lincoln had an advantage when they appeared before men, but the same effect can be produced by the opposite, by a weakness, and as Roosevelt looks up at everyone standing in front of him, he has accustomed himself to an upward and therefore very energetic gesture of the chin which counteracts the danger of his conciliatory smile."

Gunther (who, it should be pointed out, was not many times in Roosevelt's presence but who was fascinated by the psychological implications of his affliction, and probed those closest to F.D.R. about it): "He loved gossip so much because he himself could not get around; talk was an outlet for all his suppressed energy. He loved holding the tiller of a boat because this gave him a sense of controlling motion."[3]

While never mentioning his paralysis in public (until his last speech to Congress in 1945) and seldom privately, F.D.R. can come down fiercely on those he feels mention it unfairly. Huey Long's tapping a straw hat on the useless presidential knee he can take as bad manners—the other fellow's problem, not his. But when Fulton Oursler brings him a manuscript of a profile of F.D.R. by Jay Franklin to be published in *Liberty*—the editor courteously seeking F.D.R.'s reaction—Oursler sees "a red flush rise on his neck like the temperature in a thermometer." Assuming that Roosevelt is angered over some political needling, he learns otherwise:

"Mr. Oursler, there is only one statement in this article that I want corrected. The author says in this line here that I have 'never entirely recovered from infantile paralysis.' *Never recovered what?* I have never recovered the complete use of my knees. Will you *fix* that?"

His reluctance to mention it—and the released heat that accompanies exceptions—are shared by Mrs. Roosevelt. At an Akron, Ohio, lecture she is asked: "Do you think your husband's illness has affected his mentality?" Betraying no emotion as she reads the written question aloud, she pauses for an extra, cooling moment and replies: "I am glad that question was asked. The answer is Yes. Anyone who has gone through great suffering is bound to have a greater sympathy and understanding of the problems of mankind." The audience rises in an ovation.

He is frequently torn between keeping his silence and protesting his case. On April 6, 1938, he writes to an "old friend"—Elliott's description—mentioning his affliction. The important thing is not what he writes but his decision not to mail it. Instead, he marks it "Written for the Record" and files it away. It says in part:

. . . I do not mind telling you, in complete 100% confidence, that in 1923, when I first went to Florida . . . my old running mate, Jim Cox, came to see me on my house-boat in Miami. At that time I was, of course, walking with great difficulty—braces and crutches. Jim's eyes filled with tears when he saw me, and I gathered from his conversation that he was dead certain that I had had a stroke and that another one would soon completely remove me. At that time, of course, my general health was extremely good. . . .

Jim Cox from that day on always shook his head when my name was mentioned and said in sorrow that in effect I was a hopeless invalid and could never resume any active participation in business or political affairs. As late as 1931—I think it was—when I was coming back from the Governors' Conference in Indiana, I stopped off at Dayton to see

Jim Cox. He had had a very serious operation, followed by a thrombosis in his leg, and was very definitely invalided. His whole attitude during the two hours I spent with him alone was the same—that it was marvelous that I could stand the strain of the Governorship, but that in all probability I would be dead in a few months. He spent the greater part of the time asking me solicitously how I was, though he was a much sicker man than I was.

He made a fine come-back and is furious today if anybody ever refers to the thrombosis he had in his leg—but I still think he expects me to pop off at any moment.

While deciding not to mail that letter, at other times he can be as open as a billboard. Son Jimmy recalls that on one of Madame Chiang Kaishek's visits to the White House, the grande dame thoughtlessly tells the President not to stand up as she rises to leave the room. He gently replies, "My dear child, I couldn't stand up if I had to."

In a wheelchair or an automobile, getting F.D.R. into or out of an overcoat is an awkward exercise. With a stage sense of costume, F.D.R. takes to a velvet-collared, braid-looped regulation Navy cape, which, along with his cigarette holder, becomes a personal mark. Again, disadvantage is the fabric from which, with flair and style, he fashions advantage.

Out of deference to his office as well as personal affection, newsmen virtually never mention the President's disability. So effective is their conspiracy, even upon themselves, that, as Gunther recalls, "hard-boiled newspaper men who knew that he could not walk as well as they knew their own names could never quite get over being startled when F.D.R. was suddenly brought into a room. The shock was greater when he wheeled himself and, of course, was greatest when he was carried; he seemed, for one thing, very small. . . . During the 1930's when I lived in Europe I repeatedly met men in important positions of state who had no idea that the President was disabled."

The people of the United States—his constituents, those from whom he draws strength and, more importantly, those who draw strength from him —know, yet don't know. They, too, waiting at tiny railroad depots, straining to see through the autumn sunshine the commanding figure of their President, freeze with shock at seeing the painfully slow-motion, brace-supported step-pause-step, what seems a tortuous mile from the train's rear door across the tiny observation platform to the microphone.

It is an unexpected, unforgettable drama of frailty and strength.[4]

Part VII

Saving Liberalism and Liberty: The Battles Join

How it did rain on the morning of January 20, 1937, as again I stood before our majestic Capitol to be sworn into office. Without my knowledge, the Secret Service—or someone—had ordered the construction of a glass protection around the speaking stand. When I learned of it I ordered the glass taken down. If all those people could stand in the downpour to hear me, I could stand in the rain to address them.

Although dampened by the skies, how much cheerier a day this was than four years before.

"The greatest change we have witnessed has been the change in the moral climate of America," I said in my address. ". . . Shall we pause now and turn our back upon the road that lies ahead? Shall we call this the promised land? Or, shall we continue on our way? . . . Many voices are heard as we face a great decision. Comfort says, 'Tarry a while.' Opportunism says, 'This is a good spot.' Timidity asks, 'How difficult is the road ahead?' . . . Let us ask again: Have we reached the goal of our vision of that fourth day of March, 1933? Have we found our happy valley?"*

Looking over that vast throng of supporters ready to march with

* The delivery of an address, when you know that the eyes of the world are upon you, can sometimes be burdened by peculiar risks. This speech contained a sentence to twit my conservative adversaries: "Hard-headedness will not so easily excuse hard-heartedness." In rehearsing the speech aloud for Cabinet, friends, and family, I found myself stumbling over that tricky sentence, transposing the head and the heart. So, on my reading copy, I drew a head over the syllable "head"; over "heart" I drew a heart with a little arrow through it. In delivery the sentence turned out fine.

me along the tougher but imperative road of progress, I spoke of
work yet undone:

"I see a great nation, upon a great continent, blessed with a great
wealth of natural resources. . . .

"I see millions of families trying to live on incomes so meager that
the pall of family disaster hangs over them day by day. . . .

"I see millions denied education, recreation, and the opportunity to
better their lot and the lot of their children.

"I see millions lacking the means to buy the products of farm and
factory and by their poverty denying work and productiveness to
many other millions.

"I see one-third of a nation ill-housed, ill-clad, ill-nourished.

"It is not in despair that I paint you that picture. I paint it for
you in hope—because the Nation, seeing and understanding the injustice in it, proposes to paint it out. We are determined to make
every American citizen the subject of his country's interest and concern; and we will never regard any faithful, law-abiding group within
our borders as superfluous. The test of our progress is not whether we
add more to the abundance of those who have much; it is whether
we provide enough for those who have too little.

"If I know aught of the spirit and purpose of our Nation, we will
not listen to Comfort, Opportunism, and Timidity. We will carry on."

After the speech, I remarked to Sam Rosenman, "When the Chief
Justice read me the oath and came to the words 'support the Constitution of the United States' I felt like saying, 'Yes, but it's the Constitution as *I* understand it . . . not the kind of Constitution your
Court has raised up as a barrier to progress and democracy.'"[1]

We were about to undertake in full force the battle to save the
country—indeed the Constitution—from an arrogant Supreme Court
which had stubbornly dug its heels into an earlier century.

Nine Old Men

After four years of struggle to establish the New Deal—mandated by the people in 1932 and 1934, overwhelmingly reaffirmed by them in 1936—we had at this point almost no New Deal at all. Virtually everything we fought for and won, the Court, usually by a majority of one old man, systematically destroyed. The TVA, and that alone, was left to stand, of all the major reforms enacted by Congress, signed by the President, and willed by the people. In consecutive order the Court killed our effort to end chaos in the petroleum industry, striking down our right to prescribe state quotas for oil production. While upholding the government's power to abrogate gold clauses in public contracts, the Court struck down our right in private ones. Then the Court killed the Railroad Retirement Act, with the astonishing declaration that *any* attempt by Congress to pass a compulsory pension act for railroad workers was invalid because it would not be related to the business of interstate *transportation*. If railroads and the welfare of their workers are not related to interstate transportation, what in the world is?

In a single day, May 27, 1935, the Court ruled the President could not remove a member of the Federal Trade Commission; invalidated the Frazier-Lemke Act, designed to help farm mortgagors; and, most fatefully of all, killed the National Industrial Recovery Act. Then, striking again at the very heart of our program, the Court killed the Agricultural Adjustment Act, with full knowledge that states by themselves were helpless to lift farm income and reduce surpluses. Blow after blow after blow, each one an arrogant assertion that despite national need, despite human suffering, despite the evolution of an interdependent national economy, despite the threat of desperate revolution that would end the Republic, the federal government—the Congress, the Executive, the majority will itself—was powerless to enact any reasonable economic law to save ourselves and improve our lot.

That was not all. The climax of this course of destruction was a 5-to-4 decision in June 1936 denying even a *state's* right—in this case, New York—to establish a minimum fair-wage system for women in industry. If the federal government could establish no such minimum, and now neither could a state, there seemed to be a complete "no-man's land." They left no way for law to protect laboring women from oppressive sweatshop wage scales, which were so prevalent and traditional.

The language and temper of these decisions left little hope for the future. The Court condemned the United States Government to paralysis and impotence. Government by and for the people, in modern times for modern needs, lay virtually dead.

Was there some fatal fault in our Constitution? Or were we victims of the fault of human beings who, in our generation, were torturing its meaning, twisting its purposes, to make it conform to their own outmoded economic prejudices? There is nothing wrong with the Constitution as I read it. I stand with—and the Court repudiated— John Marshall's conception of our Constitution as an instrument adequate to all times, flexible, able to adjust itself as new needs of new generations arise.

The fault lay with frozen-minded Justices, most of them born during the life of Abraham Lincoln: Butler was age seventy, Sutherland seventy-four, McReynolds seventy-five, Van Devanter seventy-seven. This horse-and-buggy quartet, augmented by Roberts, at sixty-one the Court's "youngster," composed the irreducible majority of five which stood against the needs of our century. The remaining four, while occasionally more modern of mind, were hardly symbols of youth: Stone was sixty-five, Cardozo sixty-six, Chief Justice Hughes seventy-four, Brandeis eighty. What needed to be changed was not the Constitution but the composition of the Court.

As I took my oath to uphold the Constitution on January 20, 1937, amid the corpses of those duly enacted New Deal laws, all we had for certain to help us restore the health of the nation, besides the single permanent reform of the TVA, was an emergency program of work projects and public works. At that moment, our later New Deal measures were working their way up to the Supreme Court: the Social Security Act, the National Labor Relations Act, the Public Utility Holding Company Act. Were these to die, too, at the hands of a superannuated "super-legislature," which is exactly what the Supreme Court had made of itself? Were eight years of a New Deal administration—popularly elected twice—to melt into history with nothing done, erased by nine old men?[2]

In my State of the Union Address to Congress of January 6, 1937, I referred in the broadest, most unspecific way to this crisis, merely pointing out that the Preamble and Article I of the Constitution confer "the legislative powers upon the Congress of the United States." Equally broadly, I said that "means must be found to adapt our legal forms and our judicial interpretation to the actual present national needs." That was all—only the broadest hint of a great battle to come. The Justices of the Supreme Court apparently expected I was going to take my gloves off right then and there. Not a single member showed up for the joint session of Congress to hear my address, although it is custom for them to do so.

What were the "means" to be that had to be found?

The one certain way with which the Court could not interfere would be a Constitutional amendment. That way, however, was out of the question. Any group of thirteen states could block an amendment—and, in this case, probably would. Even if such a course could succeed, the time involved would make it out of the question. By the time Congress approved such an amendment—if they would—every state legislature would have adjourned for the year. The following year, 1938, only about one third of the legislatures were scheduled to meet. That would bring us to 1939. I anticipated that our extraordinary Democratic majority in Congress would be somewhat reduced in the 1938 mid-term election, and that reduction would most surely be used as an argument in 1939 legislatures that the public no longer supported us—therefore, ratification would be contrary to the popular will. So, in all probability, we would go into the 1940 election with the amendment unratified, the government still paralyzed —and eight years of the New Deal would lie dead.

Furthermore, I did not like any of the amendments out of the dozen or so proposed. For example, one senator's proposal, supported more than most, provided that any decision of the Court declaring a law unconstitutional could be overridden by a two-thirds vote of the Congress next elected after the decision was handed down. The theory, of course, was that a Congressional election would have given the people an opportunity to express their will. The trouble with that proposal was that it *did* undermine the intent of the Constitution by attacking the legitimate function of the Court. Just as I rebelled against seeing the Court usurp the functions of Congress, I did not want to see Congress usurp the rightful powers of the Court. Our trouble was not with the design of the Court, but with the individuals who sat on it.

We had to rely on simple legislation—but of what kind? Some senators and congressmen suggested a law to require that any Court decision declaring a statute unconstitutional had to be by unanimous vote, or by an 8–1 opinion, or 7–2. Suppose the Court invalidated *that* law? Surely there is some legal doubt as to whether Congress may control the operation of the Court in such manner.

Another set of proposals called for expanding the size of the Supreme Court. That would be legal, all right. The Constitution does not specify the size of the Supreme Court, and, in fact, its size has been altered by law several times since the founding of the Republic —sometimes for the very purpose of changing decisions. But that course would be a mere expedient, which could lead to the same trouble. An expanded Court and its successors could likewise fall into the same obstructionist mold, which so often happens when men grow old, protected by life tenure, and get out of touch with swiftly moving social and economic changes. What we needed was a way in which the Court could constantly refresh and reinvigorate itself with new minds, new ideas, new youth.

To work out such a plan, I took into my confidence nobody except my Attorney General, Homer Cummings, and the Solicitor General, Stanley Reed. I emphasize that, because there has been so much speculation—almost all of it erroneous—as to who "influenced" me in the plan I was soon to propose.

Under this plan the size of the Court would be flexible. As soon as a Justice reached the age of seventy, a new Justice would be appointed—not to replace him, but as an additional Justice. The old men would remain, but the voices of younger men would be heard, too. What could be more fair and sensible than that? Applied to the Court as it stood, my plan would enable me to appoint six additional Justices, for a total membership of fifteen.

I prepared a message to Congress proposing this plan, but for a few days showed it to no one. Just three days after its completion, the annual White House Judiciary Dinner was scheduled, on February 2. That would be an embarrassing time to send up the message, not only for the Court but perhaps for me—I might wind up dining alone! On the other hand, six days after the dinner, on February 8, Solicitor General Reed was scheduled to argue several major cases before the Court, among them the National Labor Relations Act. I wanted the message to go to Congress before that argument. Frankly, I fully expected that the message would give the Court pause to consider. I decided to submit it on Friday, February 5.

Usually, after making a decision of that kind, I can put it out of mind as something done. This one left me uneasy. I called in Sam Rosenman to touch up some of the language of the message. We arranged for the office girls to mimeograph the text at 6:30 A.M. on February 5—not before—thus reducing the danger of a leak.

The message, I was soon to realize, contained a major strategic mistake—and, I suppose, sensing that was what made me uneasy. Homer Cummings had provided me with bureaucratic statistics, the kind that cabinet members can conjure to prove any case, which purported to show that the whole federal court system was loaded down with too many cases. Homer convinced me to use that "simple fact" as camouflage to justify a "reorganization" of the entire federal judiciary. Imbedded in that grand setting, the reorganization of the Supreme Court was supposed to look like a mere added detail.

As a Senate hearing soon bore out, that "simple fact" was simply not a fact at all. And it gave us great trouble. I should have assaulted the real problem directly, putting the emphasis on the obstructionist decisions of the Supreme Court. I soon corrected that mistake in speeches and statements, but we never fully overcame its damage.[3]

The very first opposition witness before the Senate Judiciary Committee—my old, reliable Democrat-Progressive-liberal friend Senator Burton K. Wheeler, upon whom I could count every time to be as unpredictable as possible—started off by reading into the record a letter signed by Chief Justice Hughes and concurred in by Justices Brandeis and Van Devanter. I had already abandoned the argument that the lower courts were overworked, but the Chief Justice took full advantage of that error in my message with laboriously detailed counterargument that this was not so—that the dockets were indeed reasonably up to date—and, of course, totally ignoring my main concern, the age and attitude of the Supreme Court. Tangential as it was, Hughes's intervention was quite harmful to our cause.

Before long, Wheeler was to order from the Public Printer twenty-one thousand dollars' worth of reprints of his speeches against our Court plan, mailing them out under his senatorial frank to millions of voters. I would like to know where he got that money, and the thought crossed my mind to investigate whether his tax return reported it as income.

On Monday, March 29, less than a week after that treacherous Wheeler testimony, a great turnabout took place—what eventually amounted to full victory for what we sought. By a 5–4 decision, the Court upheld a minimum wage law for the state of Washington almost identical with the New York statute the same Court had recently struck down. A turnabout vote by Justice Roberts reversed the result. Two weeks later, the Court upheld the National Labor Relations (Wagner) Act. Again the vote was 5–4, again the swing vote was Roberts'. The reasoning of the new majority was almost exactly contrary to the opinion that had killed the NRA in the "sick chicken" case. Hugh Johnson, immensely enjoying the vindication, sent me one of his inimitably biting notes: "I was taken for a ride on a chicken truck in Brooklyn two years ago and dumped out on a deserted highway and left for dead. It seems this was all a mistake." Even Felix Frankfurter, seldom given to cynicism, wired me, "After today I feel like finding some honest profession to enter."

In my heart I feel certain that the turnabout of Roberts (and the favorable vote of Hughes, who was always a question mark) can be directly attributed to my having challenged the composition of the Court.* They were going to "weaken" my case by showing that the Court didn't really have to be changed at all. Which, of course, was just fine with me.

---

* Author's note: Here I am faced with a special problem which is bound to occur for a ghost writer of a posthumous memoir—a conflict between truth as seen by the President and facts as later revealed. When the Court surprisingly changed its stance on March 29, 1937, Roosevelt believed—and had substantial reason to believe—that the pressure of his Court plan was primary in forcing the change, particularly in chang-

And before many days the suddenly enlightened Supreme Court upheld the Social Security Act.

What utter cynicism! What politics, from that august body supposedly above politics! I drew up a memo—just a private record for my files—listing Court actions *before* my Court message and *after* my message. The AAA had been struck down on almost precisely the same ground on which Social Security was now upheld—the right of the federal government to tax and spend. The Guffey Act had been killed on the same ground on which the Wagner Act was now upheld —federal power to regulate commerce. And the New York Minimum Wage Law had been voided for the same reasons that the Washington Minimum Wage Law was now validated.

Now many of my friends began to urge me to drop the Court bill. This I would not do. What assurance had we that the change of heart was really a change of philosophy and not just an expedient ploy by political-minded members of the Court? Furthermore, even if the Court had suddenly gone liberal and modern, the basic principle of insuring some semblance of young blood on the Court was still perfectly sound. I was determined to press on.

The battle was long and bitter—and overblown and tiresome. I have no intention of recounting here all the emotion and chicanery and tomfoolery of that battle. For 168 days, from dead of winter to heat of summer, the first pages of newspapers blared the ups and downs of "Roosevelt's Court-packing plan," as though the depression itself and the rising threat of war in Europe were mere details in human affairs. Yet they all missed the point: The *major* news was not the daily details of how one liberal after another deserted ship during those noisy months, but how the *threat* of Court reform indeed reformed the Court. Under cover of so-called defeat we accomplished complete victory.

---

ing the position of Justice Roberts. We now know what F.D.R. had no way of knowing: In December—well before the President's message of February 5, 1937—Roberts had privately informed Chief Justice Hughes that he would vote to sustain the Washington minimum wage law, bringing about a reversal of the New York decision a few months earlier. Aware that Roosevelt was preparing an assault on the Court, Hughes apparently did not want the surprising new majority vote to appear a direct response to the President. So he took the unusual step of delaying the announcement of the decision (ostensibly because of an illness of Justice Stone) until the end of March. Roosevelt's belief, as set down here, that his action directly changed the stance of the Court was what he truly believed—at least, repeatedly said he believed.

The pressure of my plan impinged upon the comfort of different men in different ways. While already forcing change in the votes of the Court itself, in the Senate my continued pressure forced other actions. Senators Borah and Wheeler, opposed to my plan but fearful that it might pass, put tremendous personal pressure on Justice Van Devanter to retire, which supposedly would take the air out of "Roosevelt's Court-packing" plan. On May 18, Van Devanter resigned. Thus, after four years of my first term with no opportunity to appoint a Justice, I finally had a vacancy to fill.

Immediately an enormous drive arose in the Senate to get me to name Majority Leader Joe Robinson for that vacancy. A lot of progress that would have been! Joe was certainly a friend and a loyal fellow. He worked admirably to maintain support behind the Court bill, even though I know that he privately had misgivings about it. But he was also one of the most conservative members of my party. Dear a man as he was, Joe was scarcely my idea of how to liberalize the Supreme Court. Yet to ignore him—and his many supporters—would destroy support for the bill.

I had Joe to the White House one evening for a private talk and told him I wanted to appoint him to the Court. I added, however, that "if there is to be a bride there must also be bridesmaids"—at least four. Joe tried to urge upon me a too-risky compromise, claiming he could get the Senate to agree to "a couple of extra Justices tomorrow." So I would be left with one new conservative and two perhaps liberals. So uncomfortably thin a margin scarcely justified the battle. The senators avidly advancing Robinson's candidacy apparently didn't realize it, but they were making it impossible for me to compromise. There was no way I could convey this either to Joe or to other senators, but his desire to sit on the Court forced me to stand stubbornly behind the bill. And by now, I suppose I must admit, I had my Dutch up.

Then a terrible thing happened. Early in the morning of Tuesday, July 13, Joe Robinson was found dead on the floor of the bathroom of his apartment, the victim of a coronary thrombosis.

This was saddening to us all, but I cannot forgive the emotionalism of two senators, which, if nothing else, made it quite impossible for me to back off, even in light of the changed situation. Senator Royal S. Copeland, a New York Republican, rose to "warn" the Senate that others of their number would die if I did not withdraw the bill and let them adjourn and go home. And my dear friend and liberal ally, Senator Wheeler, rushed into print with a statement that if I stood by the Court bill I would be "fighting God." (And to think that, later in my term, some people suggested I support Wheeler, of all people, for the Democratic nomination to succeed me!) In July the Court bill suffered another blow, which I recount here just to demonstrate how great issues often turn on the most petty and irrelevant matters of personal pique. My successor as governor of New York, Herbert H. Lehman, addressed a public letter to Senator Wagner bitterly opposing the bill. In light of Lehman's close identification with me in the past, this letter was most damaging. Some months earlier, many governors had publicly gone on record for or against the bill, but coming at this late date, when feelings had grown bitter, Lehman's attack was conspicuous and disastrously timed. Oh, how the papers and the experts speculated on Lehman's reasons! But none of them got near the real story, which was simply this:

In 1936 word had reached me that Lehman did not want to run for a third term as governor. The state ticket needed him—and in New York he might bring added strength to the national ticket. I asked Henry Morgenthau, his nephew by marriage, to have a talk with Lehman. This did not work out well; Lehman told Henry that when the President had something to say to him he should say it in person. In a few days Lehman sent a letter to the newspapers saying he would not run. Such decisions, of course, are often subject to change, and one way to change the mind of a prima donna is to treat him like a prima donna.

Jim Farley arranged to make Lehman a speaker at the close of the Democratic National Convention at Philadelphia—and arranged more than that. At the conclusion of his lengthy and not-very-rousing speech, from every corner of the hall delegates "spontaneously" arose and marched up and down the aisles, bobbing and dancing and cheering, waving their state standards, in a personal tribute usually reserved for ex-Presidents. The tribute visibly moved Lehman. Then, after my Franklin Field acceptance address, I asked Governor and Mrs. Lehman to ride to Hyde Park with me in the presidential train. Next morning we talked for an hour and a quarter about his running. I pointed out that Al Smith had served three terms and wouldn't it be nice for Lehman to equal his record. I also stressed that the honor of three terms given to a man of the Jewish faith would do much to allay prejudice. Finally, Lehman gave me the standard change-of-mind response: repeating that he did not want to run but would have to do so if the President asked him to. I put the request directly, and Lehman withdrew his letter declining to run, and made the race.

Of course I wanted Lehman's help, but it appears he thought I was asking him to *save* me. He carried the state by a handsome five-hundred-thousand-vote margin. But apparently my state margin of 1,100,000 put his nose out of joint. Then Lehman telephoned me to ask that I attend his inauguration on January 2. I told him I would go anywhere for him, but at that moment, with both an annual message and a budget to complete, it was just impossible to leave Washington. Jim Farley represented me there. Unfortunately, the Morgenthaus, who had spent Christmas on the Lehman farm, left for Washington the day before the governor's inauguration, for which Lehman seemed to hold me responsible. As a climax, someone—I don't know who—told Lehman that the Philadelphia demonstration had all been staged as a prelude to my persuading him to run. What was meant as a tribute to him he now decided was all an attempt to play him for a patsy.

So that queer little chain of events strained the feelings of this sensitive man, and those feelings now erupted, sad to say, in a vengeful manner, in the form of his letter on the Supreme Court issue. That's the simple story as I see it—the kind of story that so often occurs in politics, picayune personal feelings turning the course of major events.[4]

Of all my supposed shipmates who jumped ship, none irked and distressed me more than Vice-President Garner. A senator turning coat on a President of his own party can try to excuse himself on the ground that he is independently elected by a local constituency, as though he has no obligation to a national party and program. But a Vice-President, elected by no independent votes of his own? Placed on the ticket—and in office—by the consent of the presidential candidate as his running *mate?* That is mutiny. A President may at least expect unquestioned loyalty of the man who at any moment fate may make his successor.

Garner's disloyalty did not take the form of his speaking in public against my Court bill. It was more underhanded. More than most Vice-Presidents, he enjoyed close associations in Congress, buttressed by his years as Speaker of the House. He knew I would like to rely on him to work out an acceptable compromise on the Court bill. Instead, however, he used his influence to undermine the bill, to talk it down, to wreck it. At the end of each legislative day Garner and his leadership cronies—among them, Joe Robinson—would gather for drink and story swapping in an out-of-the-way room of the Capitol basement that Jack liked to call the "board of education." Much of the nation's lawmaking business was negotiated in that sanctum, and that was where I needed Jack's support. Instead, what emitted from him —did Garner think that tales did not get back to me?—was down-in-the-mouthing, defeatism. What kind of compromise can there be when a most influential "spokesman" for my side talks surrender? Compromises are negotiated from strength, not defeatism. By weakening my position, my Vice-President helped make compromise impossible.

After a trip that brought me through Garner's state, Texas, I reported at a cabinet meeting—for Jack's benefit more than anyone's— that a lot of precinct committeemen told me that the people were overwhelmingly behind my Court plan. I warned that Democratic congressmen opposing it could expect harsh treatment from their constituents in the 1938 mid-term election.

I was soon to make a tour of several national parks, one of them Yellowstone, in Wyoming. This was a good opportunity to put my warning into visible form. I made a point of not inviting Wyoming's Senator Joe O'Mahoney to board my train as we crossed into his state.

O'Mahoney's sniping at the Court bill was unforgivable. That man would still be an inconsequential local politician if Jim Farley and I had not plucked him from obscurity to appoint him Assistant Postmaster General, then recommended him for appointment to the Senate to fill out an unexpired term. When O'Mahoney was elected in 1936 "in his own right"—thanks to my national landslide—suddenly Joe fancied himself a statesman. His "independence" wouldn't let him support the Court bill, but he never hesitated to come running to me asking favors for his state's sugar-beet interests. Letting Joe feel my cold shoulder before the people of his own state would give Joe— and by example, some of his Congressional colleagues—a little demonstration of who needed whose loyalty most.

That plan didn't quite work. When we crossed into Wyoming, Joe, without invitation, simply boarded my train. It was the only thing I admired about him in the whole Court episode. I have a soft spot for gate crashers.[5]

Eventually the Congress passed a Judiciary bill adopting every major suggestion I had made in my February message—except the change in the personnel of the Supreme Court. But a series of Court vacancies occurring before the end of my second term insured an overwhelming victory in the larger war.

One vacancy was already before me, the seat left open by Van Devanter. I now faced for the first time this most important of presidential opportunities.

In narrowing the choice down to a single man, many considerations must be balanced—and they don't always balance in the way the President might have expected at the outset. My first thought was geographical—a preference for appointing someone from the Wisconsin-Illinois-Indiana judicial district, which had not had a man on the Supreme Court for many years. The candidate who looked best was Senator Sherman Minton of Indiana, an effective young fighter for the New Deal who was outstanding in the Court-bill debate. Any senator is almost certain of confirmation by his colleagues. Yet I knew that reactionaries would be jarred by the nomination of one of the Senate's most conspicuous liberals. Naming Minton would not help heal the wounds that lay open in the Senate.

Another candidate on my mind was Senator Hugo Black of Alabama. His nomination would throw the geographical consideration out the window. Also, he was every bit the stanch liberal that Minton was. Yet, nominating Black would outwit my conservative friends in a way that was most appealing. Conservative Democrats, in the main, are Southerners. If senators are reluctant to disfavor one of their own, southern senators are especially reluctant to turn on one of *their* own. Nominating Black, the only true liberal among them, would make my southern friends furious—but they wouldn't dare raise a voice against him.

Another consideration: putting Black on the Court might be the only way to keep this great liberal in the service of the nation. He had recently mentioned to me that his re-election campaign coming up in 1938 was bound to be a hard fight, that he was too liberal for his state; that perhaps he ought to retire from public service and seek financial security, which his family sorely needed. His only child, a seven-year-old boy, suffered from deafness. A Court seat would make Black more secure—and make liberalism more secure as well.

In the end perhaps these personal considerations helped sway me. In any case I enjoyed the surprise that burst upon the Senate when I sent up the nomination of Hugo La Fayette Black.

The effect on Southerners was a delight to see: "Cotton Ed" Smith of South Carolina was chairing an Agriculture Committee hearing when someone passed him a note to inform him of the nomination. He levitated from his chair, emitting an unprintable oath heard in the back row—but Cotton Ed, like his southern colleagues, was compelled to support the nomination.

My dear southern friend and shipmate, Vice-President Garner, "supported" it, too—in his reliable, underhanded way. The Senate's custom is to confirm a nomination immediately, without sending it to committee, when the nominee is a senator. As the story was told to me, when Black's nomination was read on the floor, the Vice-President asked, "Are there any objections?" None was heard. Again he asked, "Are there any objections?" Again silence. As though someone was failing to respond to a prearranged cue, Garner asked it still again. This time, Hiram Johnson, the California Republican, who had once numbered himself among the progressives, murmured, "I object." So the nomination was forced into a Judiciary Committee hearing. Of course the committee reported favorably with dispatch, and the Senate confirmed.

What seemed ended was not yet over. A month later, a news reporter dug up the skeleton of Hugo Black's short-lived membership, many years earlier, in the Ku Klux Klan. There had been a time, of course, when Klan membership was virtually a requisite for running for office in Alabama—but the revelation now created a major sensation.

The important thing to me was Black's long record in the Senate. That's what really told where he stood. Yet many liberals got quite upset over the disclosure. Conservatives, too, tried to make hay, charging I should have asked Black if he had ever been in the Klan. Frankly, it had never crossed my mind. Arthur Krock, the columnist, asked Joe Kennedy why Black had not volunteered the information to me. Joe, who seldom overlooks an opportunity to be risqué, told me he replied, "If Marlene Dietrich asked you to make love to her, would you tell her you weren't much good at making love?"

The affair blew over when Black went on the radio with a frank statement of his past, which seemed to satisfy most people. Within a few weeks Justice Sutherland retired, and in his place I appointed Solicitor General Stanley F. Reed. Before my second term was over, I appointed Felix Frankfurter; William O. Douglas, chairman of the Securities and Exchange Commission, a former law professor at Columbia and Yale; and Frank Murphy, former Governor of Michigan, who, at the time of his appointment in 1940, was my Attorney General. What a changed situation—what a changed Court!—since the message of 1937. Five of the nine seats were now occupied by new men, of forward-looking viewpoint, and—by Supreme Court standards—relative youth.[6]

Shearing the Wolves in Sheep's Clothing

If I am to believe what was printed in the newspapers and magazines all during 1938 and later—and if I am to believe what I know some of my best friends have been saying—I was hopping mad over the "defeat" of my Supreme Court plan. If I am to believe these experts, the Supreme Court "defeat" was what led me into the so-called "purge" of reactionary Democrats in the 1938 primaries.

That is not true. The Supreme Court fight—I kept saying this, but might as well have been talking to the wind—had nothing to do with it. I was hopping mad, all right, but over something far deeper than a single vote on a single bill. I was angered over politically dishonest men who invoked the use of my name to help them get elected, who embraced the name of the New Deal, playing upon the people's trust of me and the progressive measures I stood for—then, once in office, fought me, fought the New Deal, fought liberal principles on every inch of ground. If these reactionaries—Democratic reactionaries—wanted to try to win their elections on *their* principles, that was all right with me. But they would not, if I could help it, defraud their way into office under the banner of *my* principles.

What was at stake in 1938—indeed, for the future of the Democratic Party—was the validity of the great coalition achieved in 1936 and the tremendous victory that resulted from it. Did such a coalition really exist? Could a liberal party, composed of a majority of minorities, endure?

The biggest question mark was in the South. The political history of the South is unlike that of any other region. That is where poverty is most appalling, where the need for progress is most sore. That is where the one third of the nation that is ill-housed, ill-clothed and ill-nourished is most concentrated. That is where, more than any other place, the principles of the New Deal can change all of American life forever. And that is where, among the plain and needy and hopeful people of this land, I and the New Deal found our greatest trust and loyalty.

But the history of the South has cursed it with a flaw, the curse of racial bitterness born of the time of slavery. The irrational feelings of mutual fear, of economic competition, sometimes of hatred, between white people and Negroes of the Southland are indeed what have kept so many so poor. Yet the feelings have persisted. Politicians ride to power playing on these feelings, then fan the flames of the bitterness as a means of holding power. It is a terrible thing to observe, but true: Given a choice between economic progress (based on co-operation and harmony) and maintenance of outdated racial customs (based on fear), Southerners too often permit themselves to be swayed emotionally by old racial fears.

I know this remains true. Yet I know that this need not be.

In the earliest days of 1938 I saw clear evidence that it need not be. In a Democratic primary in Alabama in January a demagogue named Tom Heflin, playing on racial traditions, challenged Representative Lister Hill, as loyal a New Dealer as any in the South. The issue of progress-vs.-fear was clear as day. The people chose Lister Hill—and progress.

A few days later in Florida, through an announcement by my son Jimmy, the administration endorsed Senator Claude Pepper, whose two years filling an unexpired term proved him a fighting liberal, one who, I believed, could become a model for a new kind of southern political leader. Again the issue was clear—and Pepper swept through with a clean majority over all his primary opponents combined.

My eye was on more than the South. The Democratic Convention of 1940 was where the future of liberalism would be determined. Was our party to be forever hobbled by the Cotton Ed Smiths, whose resemblance to, say, Robert F. Wagner, is only the coincidence of party name? The Democratic Party of the South—at least its leaders —had nothing in common with the party against privilege we were building elsewhere. Indeed, the *people* of the South had much in common with people elsewhere. But southern misleaders had to be shed—driven out—if our party was to make sense. Driven where? Let them go into the Republican Party. Let conservatives join conservatives. Let those people who would follow them go. To lead those who remain Democrats, true national Democrats—and I am confident the vast number will remain—new liberal leaders will emerge, leading the South into the forward march of the nation at large.

Some Democrats take comfort in the one-party Democratic South —the "safe" South. I find it neither comfortable nor safe. In the South of all places I would happily and confidently pit a New Deal program of a true Democratic Party against a let-things-be program of the Republican Party. But the present one-party system, forcing a President to accommodate Republicans in Democrats' clothing, is unfair to the people of the South, a drag on the national Democratic Party, on liberalism, on the nation itself.

Conversely, liberal Republicans who valiantly—but futilely—battle to make their party liberal should give up that hopeless fight and become Democrats. As long as each party remains weighed down by a minority of its own opposites, which each party tries to accommodate, both parties shall remain Tweedledum and Tweedledee to each other. We shall be a healthier nation if the philosophies of liberalism versus conservatism are fought *between* our two major parties rather than *within* them. The British have long enjoyed an honest choice between a party of liberals and a party of conservatives. Americans had fairly clear choices of party direction in Jefferson's day, in Jackson's day, in Lincoln's, in Theodore Roosevelt's, and in Wilson's day. More than ever, we need it now.

Solidifying the Democratic Party as the party of militant liberalism, begun with our great coalition in 1936, would not be accomplished in a single election. But continued steps had to be taken. Those continued steps took the form of a few interventions I made in the Democratic primary elections in 1938, which the newspapers facilely —but incorrectly—labeled a "purge." Actually I took a personal stand in only four elections, although some writers tried to make my "interference" appear more widespread.

While I had always been careful as President not to interfere in local primaries, I made an exception in the spring of 1938, when Senator Alben Barkley of Kentucky was challenged in a primary by Governor A. B. "Happy" Chandler. My reasoning was that Barkley's re-election was of national concern, since he had replaced Senator Robinson as Majority Leader. I was especially concerned because I consider Chandler a dangerous man of the Huey Long type, except that he is far less able. So, passing through Kentucky, I stopped at Covington and made known my respect and fondness for Barkley. The action was as aboveboard as could be—Chandler, as governor, was sitting right there on the platform. (In fact, when I began reciting my surprise endorsement of Alben, Happy, who is resourceful if nothing else, tried to divert attention from my speech by waving and calling greetings to old friends in the crowd.)

Later, in Georgia, with Senator Walter George sitting right behind me, I stated my personal friendship and respect for George but made clear that "on most public questions he and I do not speak the same language." I pointed out that many of my friends were conservatives —but that they were Republicans. A man does not have a right to run, the way George did, as a friend of the New Deal when, deep down in his heart, he opposes the New Deal.

In Maryland I similarly made it known that Senator Millard Tydings, trying to clothe himself with the banner of the New Deal and Roosevelt, was no political ally of mine.

Up North—in my own New York City—we singled out one congressman, John J. O'Connor, a member of the all-powerful House Rules Committee, who unceasingly sabotaged the New Deal and made vitriolic attacks upon me. Democrats had a right to know that this man was actively undermining his own party. I had discussed O'Connor with Jim Farley, who agreed to make sure that a New Dealer would challenge O'Connor in a primary for his seat, giving Democrats of that district a real choice. In May and June I asked Farley about this again; both times he agreed to take care of it. In July, when I knew that Farley was about to leave for Alaska, I reminded him again; he promised to attend to it before leaving. On July 21, with only two weeks left for a potential opponent to file a primary petition, Farley departed, not having done the job. There has been much speculation as to why my long and happy relationship with Jim Farley cooled before the end of my second term. The cooling began right then and there. Farley could not bring himself to perform surgery, no matter how necessary, within his own party. While a peerless campaign technician, he was far more interested in political victories than in political issues. In the nick of time, Tom Corcoran arranged the candidacy of James H. Fay, and Ed Flynn quietly supervised a superb campaign that defeated O'Connor.

As far as I am concerned, the re-election of Majority Leader Barkley and the removal of O'Connor from the Rules Committee as well as the House itself were far more important than my failure to defeat Senators George and Tydings. On balance, my intervention in these few primaries was, despite what the "experts" said, a success.

The mistake the "experts" made was to measure the results only at the polls. Their narrow vision, typical of experts, prevented them from seeing the direct effects in the Congress itself, where party loyalty took a sharp upturn, lasting through the 1940 convention. An immediate and historic result was the passage in June 1938 of the Fair Labor Standards Act, often called the Wages and Hours Act. Congress had refused to act on this bill when Senator Hugo Black first introduced it, in May 1937. The bitterest opposition had come from southern Democrats in both houses who insisted that the South be permitted to pay lower minimum wages than other sections of the country. During a special session in the fall of 1937, these Southerners had joined with a majority of Republicans in narrowly defeating the bill.

But in June 1938—after I held the disloyalty of selected Democrats up to public view—the House, suddenly converted to "the light and the way," passed it overwhelmingly, 313–97.[7]

Going Broke Again
on a Balanced Budget

Passage of the Wages and Hours Act was the final major reform accomplished by the prewar New Deal. But our work was far from complete. We had still not yet learned how to free ourselves from the paralysis of economic depression. We were still in the "dark ages" of 1929 to 1933 as far as economic theory was concerned. The economists were producing few new ideas that were politically feasible; the politicians were still too cautious to give us a free hand in trying large-scale economic experiments. Before my second term was done, we were indeed to learn some important lessons, but in a most tragic way—the way of war. Will we ever be ready to apply the economic lessons of war to a world of peace?

In 1937, when the nerves of Congress were raw over the Court fight, when confused liberals had surrendered the initiative to conservatives, the demand by big business and big publishers to reduce government spending hampered recovery as never before. Over the anguished protests of my New Deal friends, I decided to let conservatives in Congress try things their way. I submitted a balanced budget.

A balanced budget, as Herbert Hoover had so sadly learned, exists only on paper. You cut expenses, regardless of social cost, down to the level of *anticipated* government income. This is what Hoover did year after year—but government income never came up to what he anticipated. As the economy shriveled, so did tax collections, and he went deeper and deeper into debt. Of course, there is another way to balance a budget, the way businesses do, temporarily going into debt in anticipation of later profits. We could spend to stimulate the economy, then balance the budget through rising tax collections. After four years of battling for this latter course, I gave in to Congress, letting them try the former.

By April we began to see—those of us who were willing to see—the coming disaster. I kept peppering the men and women of the press with the danger signs.

On April 2, 1937: "Everybody who has been reviewing the existing economic situation is pretty well agreed that the present increase in the production of durable goods is more rapid than the production of consumer goods and that that, judging by the past—going back over thirty or forty years—does constitute a danger sign . . . a falling off in the production of both consumer and durable goods within the next twelve to eighteen months. . . . We need more expenditures at the bottom and less at the top . . . funds at the bottom go primarily to people, millions of people, who are the consumers of consumer goods. . . ."

June 15, 1937: "When one-third of the nation hasn't got any buying power, it ought to be to the interest of every business man to try to help that one-third of the country to get buying power. . . . The more we attack the basic problem of getting a better standard of living for the one-third at the bottom, the quicker we shall get rid of relief. . . . Otherwise we shall always have them with us and always have relief with us. If we can increase the share of the national income of this one-third, while at the same time increasing the total of the national income, we can automatically balance the federal budget."

The spurious "budget balancing" demands of big business and big publisher-editorialists had stampeded not only Congress but the people as well. An opinion poll showed that even two out of three of the unemployed believed in balancing the budget by cutting expenses. So my 1937 budget cut back relief and ordered PWA to stop building and RFC to stop lending. For a short time the treasury actually showed a small cash surplus. Of course it did.

It was an especially risky time to "balance" the budget, because 1937 was the first full year that 2 per cent of the aggregate national payroll would be withheld from the market place because of Social Security deductions. Benefits payable during that first year were negligible compared to the withholding. Yet, knowing this, big business insisted on the "balance," to give them *confidence*—that old word again—to invest. What did they do with their great victory? Exactly what they had done before the budget reduction—nothing. They did not extend themselves to provide new jobs. The banks did not make it easier for a wage earner to borrow money to build a house. They did not begin vast ventures to provide low-cost homes and apartments, one of the fastest and surest ways of spurring employment. They did not risk cutting the price of cars so that more people could buy them, more cars would have to be produced, manufacturing cost would come down, etc., etc. For four long years since Hoover they had echoed the Hoover slogan of "restoring business confidence." Confidence to do *what?* Judging by what they did in 1937, the answer is perfectly clear: Do nothing.

Then, on October 19, 1937—known as "Black Tuesday"—the stock market broke. During the next few months production and jobs collapsed faster than after the 1929 crash. Was the infinite economic wisdom of big business ready to come to our rescue? When a Senate committee in January 1938 sought the wise counsel of the president of General Motors, William Knudsen, that great Dane (who apparently had not kept up with my press conferences the previous year) had only this to offer: "I don't think anyone in God's world could have told me that the outlook was going to drop fifty percent in two or three weeks."

By midsummer 1938 the unemployed were swelled by five million. Fourteen per cent of all Americans—one out of seven—were receiving public relief. Starvation was upon us again. In Chicago, children again were discovered picking food from garbage cans. In Cleveland, relief money ran out and sixty-five thousand men, women, and children went for a week without food or clothing allotments; one reliefer committed suicide. In the automobile towns of the Midwest, WPA rolls expanded alarmingly—Toledo's by 194 per cent, Detroit's 434 per cent. Steel business was slashed by two thirds. On March 25, 1938, after a feeble rise the stock market cracked again.

By June, Congress had had enough. They suddenly couldn't wait to give me a $3.75 billion "spend-lend" fund—a billion for PWA, $1.4 billion for WPA, smaller amounts for low-cost public housing, NYA, farm-security payments, and a substantial sum to lend to private business to encourage employment and recovery. (How readily businessmen are willing themselves to accept "relief," whether by loan or subsidy, when they feel the pinch.)

Sure enough, within weeks unemployment and relief rolls again began to show a steady decline.

But was that the best answer we could provide? Were we to have suffered this greatest of depressions and learned nothing other than creating emergency jobs to buy our way out when human conditions became unbearable? There has to be a better way to keep the elements of economics—manpower, materials, machines, and money —in harness so that major depressions do not happen at all.

And except for the ancient way of war, we had not found that way.

I still do not know the way, but I think I know the general direction. The direction must lie in a method that is as yet so politically unpopular that I had to drop its name from my vocabulary some years earlier. Its name is *planning*. The direction must lie in a method we tried crudely and hurriedly in the NRA, which did not survive to be refined by experience. If nobody yet has an exact prescription, at least I tried in 1938 to do some rough thinking out loud with my reporter friends about the disease and the cure:

"I will tell you a story. Last August, the last week of August, I was at a little village, and I happened to know the fellow who runs the garage, and who is also the agent for one of the larger automobile companies. We used to play on the same ball team together.

"I said, 'Bill, how are you getting on?' He said, 'I am getting on too well.'

"I said, 'What do you mean?'

"He said, 'It is this way: You know, people in this vicinity to whom we cater, own a total of about one hundred automobiles— pleasure cars—which they use. Well, these people are not rich and they do not get a new car every year. They get their cars every three years or four years or five years or six years. I figure the average turnover is about one car—one new car—every three years, perhaps a little bit more. I figure they ought to buy about thirty new cars every year.' Then he said, 'This year, in this community, they have bought sixty-two new cars. . . . I have sold over half of them myself. I had no right to and they had no business buying sixty-two new cars. That means that next year I am going to have an awful year. . . . I don't think next year I will sell more than ten or fifteen cars. That is why I say I am doing much too well.'

". . . That is one illustration. Another one is this: I said to a very large steel manufacturer the other day, "How is it that you suddenly dropped from 90 per cent [of production capacity] to around 28 per cent?' 'Oh,' he said, 'a lot of factors entered into it. One was automobile steel. Then there was another curious thing that happened. The railroads in the country last spring suddenly came to us and gave us orders for all the steel rails that they needed for a full year and they said, "We want them now." So all through the summer we were working seven days a week, turning out steel rails, to fill these orders. . . . Now they do not need, or want, any more for another nine months.'

"I said, 'What do you think of it?' He said, 'I call it highly unintelligent.' "

Then a reporter intelligently asked me, "How can the government do anything to prevent this type of unintelligent business operation?"

I replied, ". . . Under NRA it was perfectly legal for the heads of all the companies in a given industry to sit down around the table with the government and . . . figure out much more clearly than they ever had before, as an industry, what the probable demand of the country would be for a period of six months or a year ahead. . . . Now done that way, it is a perfectly legitimate thing for them to do . . . just so long as it is done without any attempts at price-fixing or driving competitors out of business or things like that as a result of the conference.

"There is a question today whether a meeting of that kind, around a table, is legal under the anti-trust laws. A lot of people are afraid of it. I would very much favor making it a completely legal thing to do: to meet around a table to find out, with the help of government, what the demands are, what the purchasing power of the country is, what the inventories are."

I recognize, of course, that such a system of industry planning in co-operation with government would present problems in preserving the advantages of competition—of how each of these companies could compete for its slice of a pie, the total size of which is planned. No one knows the answers to those problems. They must be learned by experiment, by patient trial and toleration of error. But I do know that those problems will be far less difficult to solve—far lower in human as well as economic cost—than the intolerable problems of depression and starvation and loss of faith in democracy and the threat of desperate revolution.[8]

There is another way as well. And as those very words were spoken by me to reporters on January 4, 1938, that other way was being tried elsewhere in the world—threatening the continued existence of humankind.

The End of Isolation

While we were battling to solve our internal economic problems, other nations, led by a new breed of tyrants, turned to the ancient way of inventing external enemies and external solutions. Chief among these was Germany, led by Adolf Hitler, a fanatic nationalist whose madness was so hard to believe that many indeed refused to believe it. Otherwise good Americans found it within themselves to make excuses for Hitler's invention of an "international conspiracy" of Jewish bankers as the source of Germany's economic problems. These same people remained unalarmed as Hitler mobilized every atom of his country's human and industrial resources into a terrifying war machine that surely had to find a place to spend itself.

Yes, regimentation for war is one way to halt a depression—temporarily. Get the factories going, get people to work by *ordering* them to work. Make the regimentation palatable by the motivation of fear—not fear of want, not fear of the loss of liberty, but fear of lost nationality, fear of becoming choked by hostile outsiders. Hitler cried *"lebensraum,"* space for living, as though being crowded by her neighbors was the cause of Germany's share of the world-wide economic depression.

Germans give themselves easily to such a call for regimentation. They love rules, regulations, strict codes of behavior—and those who enforce them. I know this from personal experience. When I was fourteen years old and on a bicycle tour of Germany with my tutor, Arthur Dumper, we had our little taste of the German mania for regulation. In one day we were arrested four times: for picking cherries from trees alongside a road, for wheeling our bicycles into a railroad station, for riding into Strasbourg after sundown (the specific violation was "entering a fortified city of the Empire on, with, or in a wheeled vehicle after nightfall"), and for running over a goose. As for that last crime, actually I did not run over the goose. The bird committed suicide by sticking its neck into the spokes of my wheel.

Germans, led by Hitler, appointed themselves the bullies of the Western world, arming to the teeth. As I wrote to Ambassador Straus at Paris as early as February 1936, "The armaments race means bankruptcy or war—there is no possible out from that statement. . . . I am initiating nothing new unless and until increases by other nations make increases by us absolutely essential to national defense." Barely a month later, however, I wrote to Ambassador William E. Dodd in Berlin, "All the experts here, there and the other place say 'There will be no war.' They said the same thing all through July, 1914, when I was in the Navy Department. In those days I believed the experts. Today I have my tongue in my cheek. This does not mean that I am become cynical; but as President I have to be ready just like a Fire Department!"

This is not the place, in an account of the domestic affairs of the New Deal, to reconstruct the earth-trembling international events of the 1930s: of the rise of the Nazi war machine; of Hitler's Fascist junior partner to the south, Benito Mussolini; or of Hitler's aggressive affiliate in the Far East, Japan; of the overthrow in Spain of a democratic government by a rebel army armed by Germany and Italy; or of the quavering appeasement of Hitler at Munich, where British Prime Minister Neville Chamberlain, declaring "peace in our time," joined with France in permitting Hitler to dismember Czechoslovakia; or of how Soviet Russia, alarmed over the designs of Hitler, committed the unjustifiable brutality of overrunning the defenses of independent Finland.

Through all these events I adhered, as I was required to do, to strict observance of the embargo provisions of the Neutrality Law, which by this time I regretted that I had ever signed. By requiring me to declare an arms embargo against both sides of a foreign conflict, the law actually encouraged the aggressor nations. It assured them that the peaceful, democratic nations, upon whose continued existence our security ultimately depended, could get no help from us.

The arms embargo, I became convinced, led to the downfall of republican Spain and had encouraged Italy in her ruthless invasion of Ethiopia. Now it threatened to encourage war throughout Europe by guaranteeing Hitler and Mussolini that America would be helpless to stand with her natural allies.

In July 1939 I met with Republican and Democratic leaders of Congress to urge the repeal of the arms embargo. Repeal was urgently needed to stave off an immediate threat of European war. The leaders told me that practically all the Republican members of Congress would vote against repeal, and so would about 25 per cent of the Democrats. Republican Senator Borah informed me that his own "private information" was more reliable than that collected by the State Department and that his own "private information" was that there would not be any war in 1939. The Congress adjourned without action. Less than two months later, in September 1939, the inevitable happened: Europe was at war. Before the month was out, Congress met in extraordinary session to repeal the arms embargo, which action, had they done it when I asked for it, would have delayed Hitler's march, perhaps stopped it in its tracks.

Having already accomplished lightninglike occupations of the remainder of Czechoslovakia and Austria, Hitler, under the cover of indiscriminate bombing, now blitzed his armed hordes across the lowlands of Luxemburg, Belgium, and Holland, northward through Denmark, Sweden, and Norway, finally into France and to the surrender of Paris. All this with scarcely the firing of a shot on the ground.

Meanwhile Japan was invading China, rattling swords in the direction of all of Southeast Asia, and "inadvertently" sank an American gunboat, the USS *Panay*.

Freed from the unneutral Neutrality Law embargo, the United States moved rapidly to become an "arsenal of democracy." The vast detail of this conversion also is out of place here. Let me pause, however, to tell the background of one major step, passage of the Lend-Lease Act, since it had enormous consequences for domestic industry and the beginning of full re-employment of idle Americans. The island of Great Britain now stood alone against the power of a Nazified Europe. Requiring her to pay cash for the war matériel she needed (as many Americans demanded) would be almost as bad as keeping an embargo upon her; she had no such cash. Yet her successful defense was our best immediate defense. How could we legally help her—and help ourselves? I hit upon the lend-lease idea and first made it known at a press conference on December 7, 1940:

". . . There is absolutely no doubt in the mind of a very overwhelming number of Americans that . . . from a selfish point of view of American defense, . . . we should do everything to help the British Empire to defend itself.

"I have read a great deal of nonsense in the last few days by people who can only think in what we may call traditional terms about finances. . . . Now, what I am trying to do is to eliminate the dollar sign. . . . Let me give you an illustration: Suppose my neighbor's home catches fire, and I have a length of garden hose four or five hundred feet away. If he can take my garden hose and connect it up with his hydrant, I may help him to put out his fire. Now, what do I do? I don't say to him before that operation, 'Neighbor, my garden hose cost me $15; you have to pay me $15 for it.' What is the transaction that goes on? I don't want $15—I want my garden hose back after the fire is over. All right. If it goes through the fire all right, intact, without any damage to it, he gives it back to me and thanks me very much for the use of it. But suppose it gets smashed up—holes in it—during the fire; we don't have to have too much formality about it, but I say to him, 'I was glad to lend you that hose; I see I can't use it any more, it's all smashed up.' . . . He says, 'All right, I will replace it.' Now, if I get a nice garden hose back, I'm in pretty good shape.

"In other words, if you lend certain munitions and get the munitions back at the end of the war, if they are intact—haven't been hurt—you are all right. If they have been damaged or have deteriorated or have been lost completely, it seems to me you come out pretty well if you have them replaced by the fellow to whom you have lent them.

". . . There is no use asking legal questions about how you would do it . . . but the thought is that we would take over not all, but a very large number of future British orders. And when they came off the line, whether they were planes or guns or something else, we would enter into some kind of arrangement for their use by the British on the ground that it was the best thing for American defense, with the understanding that when the show was over, we would get repaid sometime in kind, thereby leaving out the dollar mark in the form of a dollar debt and substituting for it a gentleman's obligation to repay in kind. I think you all get it."

What a battle that started! Conservative naysayers, who can be counted upon to stand in the way of domestic reform, always say that the chief function of federal government—almost the only function—should be national defense. How was their philosophy now matching up against their actions? Bombs were raining on two sides of the world, and these naysayers now insisted that we need do nothing, that it was none of our business. In 1940, before the lend-lease proposal, I asked for defense preparation of the most basic kind, a National Selective Service and Training Act to prepare some of our young men for possible defense of our own shores. A majority of Republicans in the House, joined by ostrich-head Democrats, tried to block it; it passed by an uneasy majority of 185 to 155, almost a hundred members absenting themselves from the vote—there's a display of courage for you in a moment of national peril. Once taken off the hook by the House, the Senate approved it overwhelmingly.

The following year, only four months before the United States was viciously attacked by the Japanese, the naysayers really ganged up, *coming within a single vote* of defeating an extension of the draft.

Those who turned their backs on the world battle for freedom were by no means all Republicans. Senator David I. Walsh, chairman of the Naval Affairs Committee, a Massachusetts Democrat, whose eye was more on the coming election than the survival of the free world, fought me at every turn. Joe Kennedy, my Ambassador to London until I was forced to relieve him, sputtered defeatism in every direction. A broad band of isolationists, gathered in the America First Committee, made a political celebrity of Charles A. Lindbergh, who, after accepting a medal from Nazi Germany, spread the message throughout America of Nazi "invincibility." And my great liberal ally, Senator Wheeler, declared that passing the lend-lease bill would mean "ploughing under every fourth American boy."

These isolationists and defeatists had a devastating effect. Opinion polls showed that only 30 per cent of Americans believed, during Britain's darkest hour, that an Allied victory was possible. Yet at every critical turning the American people stood behind my determination to do what we could, short of war.[9]

The Failure to Find a Successor

The timing of these perilous events forced upon me a most excruciating personal decision: The events were culminating as my second—and presumably final—term was drawing to a close. Judging by the Republican record in Congress, a victory by almost any Republican candidate would turn us toward isolationism. Within my own party, too, however, the threat of an isolationist candidate loomed large—Wheeler, for example. I also had another urgent concern: The battle to solidify my party as a liberal party had scarcely begun. Would the new Democratic nominee be one who, after steering us through the world crisis, could be counted upon to carry on the fight for liberalism? These two requirements—international leadership and liberal leadership—in my mind were essential. Who was that man to be?

When talk of a third term first emerged I brushed it aside as foolishness. It is a flattery that has been paid to almost every two-term President. The earliest I recall hearing of third-term talk was in the fall of 1937, when such a thought was as remote from my mind as could be—in fact, unthinkable. My private secretary, Missy LeHand, was visiting New York and called on her friend Fulton Oursler, the editor of *Liberty* magazine. *Liberty* had just polled newspaper editors and leaders of industry and labor as to whom they thought the 1940 Democratic candidate would be. The "overwhelming" belief, so I was told, was that I would be the nominee and would be elected as the nation's first third-term President.

Since no other candidates were clearly on the horizon at that early date and since I had so recently won re-election, that poll result was predictable, if unimaginative. By 1939, however, as the world crisis developed, and especially in early 1940, third-term talk became more common. Many times I felt forced to put an end to it, but could not. As any second-term President knows, the surest way of relinquishing national leadership is to make it clear that he expects to leave office. It is useful to keep that tiny question alive, just barely breathing.

In my mind the only question mark was who the nominee was to be. Soon after my re-election I discussed his possible candidacy with Harry Hopkins. I suppose he took it seriously—but, frankly, I did not. By the summer of 1937, Harry was ill with cancer, which had killed his father and from which his wife was then dying. He soon underwent surgery that left him physically impaired. I later appointed him Secretary of Commerce, as much to build up his morale as anything else. Secretary of State Cordell Hull was looked upon with considerable favor. Of course, I knew better than others that Hull, fine man that he is, was not the strong leader in international affairs that his office suggested. Furthermore I had serious doubts about Hull as a New Dealer, although (perhaps *because*) he seldom commented on domestic matters.

Another man widely talked about as a candidate—mostly by himself—was Postmaster General Farley. While he was a first-rate party leader, his grasp of public affairs matched his lack of interest in them. He had told me so himself. I once suggested to him that the Democratic National Committee ought to conduct an educational campaign on the administration's economic positions. His instant response was, "Why, Boss, you know I don't know anything about economics." Another time, when I brought up international affairs with Jim, he replied, "Why, Boss, you know I don't know anything about international affairs."

Perhaps the most widely discussed possibility was a Hull-Farley ticket. I could hardly support such a compounding of errors. I did, however, try to urge Farley to run in New York State either for governor or senator, where his national ambitions, if they had merit, could be properly tested. Jim refused.

Some people, with apparent sincerity, expected me to give serious consideration to supporting Vice-President Garner, who, besides being totally ignorant of international affairs, would turn the domestic calendar back a decade. I would certainly make my feelings known about

that absurdity if I had to, but I didn't have to. I think his chances
ended the day John L. Lewis, the CIO leader, testifying before the
House Labor Committee, called Garner a "poker-playing, whiskey-
drinking, evil old man" who was trying to drive his knife into the
heart of labor. It was an astonishing attack, from a man whose genius
for verbal assault was seldom used without forethought. A friend of
mine, Walter A. Jones, a Pittsburgh oilman and Democratic contributor, asked Lewis why he did it. Lewis coolly told him, "I had
made up my mind to destroy Garner as a candidate, and in spite of
what anyone may say, I have done that." He certainly had. No matter
how low the blow, recovery from it was virtually impossible. House
Majority Leader Sam Rayburn tried to salvage his fellow Texan with
a resolution by the entire Texas Congressional caucus in defense of
Garner. This plan was upset by one young representative, Lyndon
Johnson. Under terrific pressure, Johnson refused to endorse the "ridiculous" statement that Garner was a friend of labor and that he
was not a whiskey drinker. Without the signatures of all, none had
validity, and the resolution was dropped.

Wearing two hats, as party leader and as hopeful candidate, Farley
kept peppering me with unacceptable suggestions for our ticket, and
I could do nothing to convince Farley that I would withhold my support from any but a strong New Deal ticket. He'd say, "But, Boss,
you can't do that. Think what the Democratic Party has done for you."
To which I'd reply, "Yes, but think what the American people have
done for me. If the occasion arises, I'll speak as an American first and
a Democrat second." On one occasion I added that if the candidates
were not acceptable, during the election campaign I might suddenly
discover urgent national business to take care of in the Philippines.
On another occasion I had to tell him:

"Only liberal candidates on a liberal platform can win next year.
I will not support anyone but a liberal. I will not support either a conservative or a straddlebug. I will not support a tweedledummer. I am
too old for that sort of thing and I have done my share. I supported
John W. Davis when I knew there wasn't a chance. I ran on the ticket
with Jim Cox when I knew beforehand that we were doomed to defeat."

Farley then asked me point-blank if I would be a candidate, or, if
not, would I dare support a third-party ticket. I told him:

"I am not a candidate for anything. In certain circumstances I would support a third-party ticket. For instance, if both the old parties should nominate reactionaries, the American Labor Party in New York will run a third ticket. In such circumstances, I would vote for their candidate. I not only won't support a reactionary on the Democratic ticket, I will not support anyone who apologizes for the New Deal."

Then I added, because in this frank talk with an old associate I had to, that in the event of war "all bets will be off. I don't know what I would do and you don't know what you would do."

Farley couldn't get my point through his head. One day he asked how I'd feel about Senator Wheeler. If Wheeler should be nominated for President, I told him, I'd sooner vote for a Republican.

"Boss, you couldn't do that as head of your party."

I told him simply, "Oh, yes I could."

Closer to home, pressure for a decision also was great. Mrs. Roosevelt urged me to give assurance—at least privately to her—that I would not run again. My son Elliott, involved in business in Texas, assumed my decision was made when he made a public endorsement of Garner, which as a free American he had his right to do. Meanwhile, Missy LeHand was trying to convince me that I had to run again. I assured her that a good man would yet rise to the surface, that out of the ferment of an election year God had a way of always providing a candidate. Her response was that God had better get busy pretty soon.

Of course, that's what I was counting on. There were a number of good men who would make fine liberal leaders, but none had yet become the center of a national movement. Time would make one of them ready. One possibility was Henry Wallace, who could start from a good base among farmers. Another was William O. Douglas, who, although not well known, would surely leave his new seat on the Supreme Court to run if sufficient support gathered for him. Some people mentioned Fiorello La Guardia, the colorful mayor of New York. His background as a crusading Republican would be a great asset to our ticket, although I had doubts about the acceptability of his combined Italian and Jewish ancestry. Time would tell.

Having neither desire nor intention of being available, I went ahead with my personal plans of what to do after January 20, 1941. At one point I had Felix Frankfurter quietly look into a possible purchase of the Boston *Transcript,* which he ascertained could be bought for a hundred thousand dollars. Nothing would have pleased me more than to demonstrate the right way to run a newspaper. I once advised my son-in-law John Boettiger how he ought to run the Seattle *Post-Intelligencer:*

"John, cut out your editorial page entirely. . . . You are a *news-*paper. You are in a labor-dispute town. The next time you have a strike down on the waterfront, take two of your best men and say to Mr. A, 'You go down and you cover . . . the story of the strikers from their point of view, and write your lead that the strikers claimed yesterday that so and so and so and so, and that the leader of the strikers, Harry Bridges' man, said so and so and so and so.' And then say to Mr. B, 'You go down there and you write your story from the point of view of the shippers. . . .' You run those two stories in parallel columns on the front page, and do not make them too long, so that the reading public will get both sides at the same time."

John didn't take my advice, but he did get honest reporting and put a losing paper in the black.

On January 27, 1940, I concluded a contract with *Collier's* magazine to write twenty-six articles a year for three years as a contributing editor. They were to furnish me several editorial assistants and a salary of seventy-five thousand dollars a year. Actually, their salary offer was higher than that, but I did not think it proper to exploit my position as an ex-President by accepting more than the presidential salary.[10]

If France had not fallen before the Hitler onslaught in May 1940, I would not have considered accepting renomination in July 1940. Moreover, if any liberal, international-minded Democrat had emerged who had a fair chance of election, there would have been no reason at all for me to consent to nomination.

We entered the summer, the convention suddenly close upon us in July, and the boiling pot of politics had brought no strong liberal candidate to the surface. A few delegates had been gathered by Farley and Garner. Considerably more got behind Speaker William Bankhead of Alabama. Whether or not his New Deal record was acceptable, I happened to have learned through my personal physician, Admiral McIntire, that the Speaker was afflicted with an ailment that would soon take him from us. A last-minute boomlet developed for Senator James F. Byrnes of South Carolina. Jimmy is a devoted New Dealer, far more so than most Southerners. I could have happily supported him except for a fact of his background that I felt certain would make him unelectable. The fact that he had been born a Catholic might possibly be overcome, a risk worth taking; but the fact that he later became an ex-Catholic would affect him fatally at the polls. I sustained my hope that support would gather around Henry Wallace, but it did not materialize.

A few nights before the convention I met in my oval study with Mayor Kelly of Chicago, Ed Flynn, Frank Walker, and Jimmy Byrnes, to discuss convention strategy. These men, who intimately knew our party from several vantage points, insisted I had to run and, by now, I could see no alternative. Our discussion turned to the means of making my availability known. I favored doing so through a letter to Bankhead, who, as keynote speaker, would address the convention on opening night. I had already penciled out such a letter and showed it to them:

Dear Will:

When you speak to the Convention on Monday evening will you say something for me which I believe ought to be made utterly clear?

You and my other close friends have known and understood that I have not today and have never had any wish or purpose to remain in the office of President, or indeed anywhere in public office after next January.

You know and all my friends know that this is a simple and sincere fact. I want you to repeat this simple and sincere fact to the Convention.

Kelly and the others urged me not to send it—in fact, to say nothing, and permit a nomination which they thought would be made by acclamation. I insisted on some form of statement, however, and gave that letter to Harry Hopkins, who was to be my personal observer at the convention, with instructions that he give it to Bankhead.

In the next couple of days it became apparent that Farley and Garner were going to go through with their efforts to get the nomination. I felt it would be improper for me to use my influence to hold delegates. If they were to name me, it had to be by free and open choice, not because of any previous pledge or commitment. Then a call from Chicago informed me that Bankhead would not go on the air until 10 P.M. and probably would not finish until almost midnight Eastern time. Alben Barkley, however, would be speaking early in the evening of the second day's proceedings and would have a far larger radio audience. Because I wanted the people to understand my views firsthand, I decided to send my message to Barkley—and a somewhat fuller one. I asked Alben to include the following text at the end of his address, which he did:

> I and other close friends of the President have long known that he has no wish to be a candidate again. We know, too, that in no way whatsoever has he exerted any influence in the selection of delegates or upon the opinions of delegates.
>
> Tonight, at the specific request and authorization of the President, I am making this simple fact clear to the Convention.
>
> The President has never had, and has not today, any desire or purpose to continue in the office of President, to be a candidate for that office, or to be nominated by the Convention for that office.
>
> He wishes in all earnestness and sincerity to make it clear that all the delegates to this Convention are free to vote for any candidate.
>
> That is the message I bear to you from the President of the United States.

The nomination came not by acclamation, which I think stands as evidence that the Convention was indeed open and free. The first and only ballot was: Roosevelt 946½, Farley 72½, Garner 61, and Millard Tydings, 9½.[11]

The convention's most anxious moments were yet to come, as things turned out. A vice-presidential candidate had to be nominated. It was impossible for me to make my decision on a running mate before witnessing the currents and crosscurrents that the convention would develop during the presidential nomination. With the overwhelming vote for me that did develop, I was now more determined than ever that an unwavering liberal had to—and could—complete the ticket. For days I had questioned many Democrats, listened carefully to them all, collected a list of candidates, and considered them all.

The names most often mentioned were Cordell Hull, Jimmy Byrnes, Will Bankhead, Jesse Jones, and Henry Wallace. Bankhead and Jones were out. If I had ever been able to consider Bankhead, that became impossible after his keynote speech, in which he not

once mentioned the New Deal or the name of the President. Clearly
he was aching to return the party to the control of his fellow Southerners. Jones (whose name was later seconded at the convention by
Elliott) represented "making peace" with—meaning surrender to—
big business, and an end to the coalition of 1936.

Hull would have been a very good choice. Despite his shortcomings on domestic matters, he symbolized our new focus on foreign
affairs and had fine standing with the people, the party, and in
Congress. On one occasion, when he had asked me if I would run
for a third term, without directly replying I asked if he would run
with me. He left no question that he would not. Remaining at the
State Department appealed to him far more. "If you don't take it,
I'll have to get Henry Wallace to run," I said, knowing that that
prospect would rankle him. Not rising to the bait, he said, "That's
all right with me." Then I knew he didn't want to run.

The White House was a quiet place during the national convention. Mrs. Roosevelt had gone to Chicago, where, before the roll
call, she gave a perfectly worded unifying speech. Hopkins was there,
too. At a quiet dinner with Sam Rosenman and Missy LeHand I felt
free to state for the first time my strong preference for Wallace.

Almost the moment the presidential roll call was over, the vice-
presidential pressure exploded. Mayor Kelly called me late at night
and I told him I wanted Wallace. It didn't go down too well. Like
Farley and other party professionals, Kelly could not stand the idea
of running a man who had been a Republican most of his life.
Early next morning, Hopkins called asking me to confirm that Wallace was my choice and reporting that he would be hard to put
across. I told Sam at breakfast, "I suppose all the conservatives in
America are going to bring pressure on the convention to beat Henry.
The fellow they want is either Jesse or Bankhead. I'm going to tell
them that I won't run with either of those men or with any other
reactionary. I've told them that before and I'll tell them that again."
Then I added, "I won't deliver that acceptance speech until we see
whom they nominate."

Next to call was Farley, who dragged out the tired myth that Wallace is a "mystic." I replied, "Jim, Henry's not a mystic, he's a philosopher, a liberal philosopher, and I'm sure that he'll be all right."
When Farley began pushing for Jones or Bankhead, I had to cut
him off abruptly.

Within minutes a grand solution arrived in the form of a telegram from Harold Ickes, who was at the convention. Blowing up the opposition to Wallace, his suggestion was that he, Ickes, would make a very good candidate. "Dear old Harold," I remarked to Sam. "He'd get fewer votes even than Wallace in that convention."

And then Bankhead called, frankly angry that he had been passed over and angrier that a non-organization man and a liberal to boot was my choice. And Byrnes phoned to argue against Wallace. Of course I knew what he had in mind, and I expressed great regret that I could not have chosen him, Byrnes, for reasons with which he was already quite familiar. I have to hand it to Byrnes. Although greatly disappointed, he went right out among the delegates, so I was told, and put on a fine display of loyalty, rounding up support for his rival.

That night at the White House we had a little crowd—General and Mrs. Edwin Watson, Steve Early, Ross McIntire, Sam, Missy and her assistant Grace Tully, and others, all listening to the convention proceedings on the radio. I was playing solitaire at a card table, growing angrier as the speeches at Chicago grew more acrimonious. Finally I asked Missy for a pad and pencil and wrote a message to the convention that filled five pages. Aware that I was writing in pique, I instructed Sam to take it into the next room and smooth it out. I told him, "I may have to deliver it very quickly, so please hurry it up." As he departed, followed by Missy and Pa Watson, I returned to my solitaire to help me simmer down.

In fifteen minutes or so, Sam returned with his text, little changed from my own. By this time everyone knew what was in it. And everyone urged me not to convey it to the convention—except Missy, who was beaming with joy, the only one there who understood the necessity of my taking a stand. The essence of the message, to be read to the convention if Wallace were not chosen as the nominee, said:

July 18, 1940

Members of the Convention:

In the century in which we live the Democratic Party has received the support of the electorate only when the party, with absolute clarity, has been the champion of progressive and liberal policies. . . . The Democratic Convention, as appears clear from the events of today, is divided on this fundamental issue. . . . It is without question that certain political influences pledged to reaction in domestic affairs and to appeasement in foreign affairs have been busily engaged behind the scenes in the promotion of discord since this Convention convened.

Under those circumstances, I cannot, in all honor, and will not, merely for political expediency, go along with the cheap bargaining and political maneuvering which have brought about party dissension in this Convention.

It is best not to straddle ideals. . . . It is best for America to have the fight out here and now.

I wish to give the Democratic Party the opportunity to make its historic decision clearly and without equivocation. The party must go wholly one way or wholly the other. It cannot face in both directions at the same time.

By declining the honor of the nomination for the Presidency, I can restore that opportunity to the Convention. I so do.

And then over the radio came the vote. I put aside my cards and kept a tally myself. The division in the convention was deep and, until the final moments, it could have gone either way: to Wallace or to the sole remaining opposition candidate, Speaker Bankhead.

By a bare majority of 627 out of 1,100, Henry Wallace was nominated. Division, yes; but a liberal had emerged as victor, and the ticket could speak with one voice. I was satisfied.

The room broke out in hurrahs—all but Missy, who was in tears. This most loyal person had not been able to accept that my nomination was not unanimous, and that now my choice for the vice-presidency had not been received unanimously. But, of course, the battle to establish a liberal party is a long and hard one, in which bitterness must be swallowed, and victories, no matter how thin, must be seized and welcomed.[12]

The Republican Convention had taken place almost a month earlier. Just five days before they convened I am afraid I gave them quite a shock. I appointed prominent Republicans to the two most important defense posts in the Cabinet—Henry L. Stimson (Hoover's Secretary of State) as Secretary of War, and Frank Knox, a Chicago newspaper publisher, as Secretary of the Navy. My purpose, of course, was to encourage a maximum of national unity in our defense effort. Republican Chairman John Hamilton, throwing a childish tantrum, announced that he was "reading them out of the party," which, of course, is beyond his or anyone's power.

As it turned out, partisan sniping at the defense effort was mini-
mized by the Republican choice of a presidential nominee. The nomination of Wendell L. Willkie, my old adversary over electric-power
rates, was a stunning surprise. Until two years earlier this man had
been a lifelong Democrat and, except for the power question, even
something of a liberal. As recently as six weeks before the Republican Convention, virtually no one took his chances seriously. Republicans, however, saw sure defeat in their two leading candidates,
Senator Robert Taft of Ohio, a bedrock conservative and isolationist,
and Thomas E. Dewey, a much-publicized but utterly inexperienced
youngster who was then, of all things, a county prosecutor in New
York City. What a qualification for the presidency!

The Republicans turned to Willkie in the last minute because they
did not know him—and the Republican old guard turned away from
him after the campaign because by then they *did*. He refused to put
the election before the national interest. Soon after his nomination
I sent an emissary to Willkie to tell him I wanted to arrange giving
England fifty over-age American destroyers in exchange for Western
Hemisphere bases, but that I could not do it at that time if it were
to become a campaign issue. Willkie agreed with the step, agreed
not to attack it, and kept his word. Old-guard Republicans urged
him to play on the pacifist instincts of Americans by attacking Selective Service, trying to persuade him—perhaps correctly—that such
an attack would win him the election. Willkie, sharing my belief
that the draft was essential to our national interest, refused. Rather
than undercutting my call for an all-out defense effort, he tried to
distinguish his stand from my own by saying we weren't helping
Britain enough, thus actually strengthening the cause we both believed in.

He was an effective campaigner, but an inexperienced one, and he
made blunders. For example, he tried to invade the base of my
greatest support by promising to appoint a Secretary of Labor from
the ranks of organized labor—an effective promise—but then made
the mistake of adding the words, "And it won't be a woman either."
That lost him more housewives than it gained him laborers.

Our victory was not as one-sided as in 1936 but was greater than
I expected. The popular vote was 27,243,000 to 22,304,000. I had
estimated winning 340 electoral votes. Actually, I won 449 from
thirty-eight states, against Willkie's eighty-two from ten states.

Shortly after the election, Willkie met with me to discuss ways of making a common effort in the terribly dangerous days ahead. I developed a real affection and respect for this man, leading to an important meeting of minds I will soon describe.

As a last word on that election, I will not forget a conversation at dinner a few nights before my third inauguration, when I took Chief Justice Hughes aside to go over arrangements for taking the oath. The Chief Justice, whom I had admired ever since he was governor of New York and I was a state senator, in a tone of conspiracy asked me, "Mr. President, after I have read the oath and you have repeated it, how would it do for me to lean forward and whisper, 'Don't you think this is getting just a little monotonous for both of us?' "[13]

December 7, 1941:
The New Deal Goes to War

All through 1941 we became in a sense a nation at war while at peace. The American genius for organization, which had never been fully released to free us from economic depression, now came into full flood. Industry accepted the leadership of government (but not until we devised contracts guaranteeing industry a fixed rate of war profits). Labor leaders pledged—and delivered—co-operation. The United States indeed became an arsenal of democracy, for our own defense as well as to save beleaguered England. Unemployment as a national problem began to disappear, replaced by a dangerous shortage of skilled workers and even of the unskilled.

In June of 1941, after Germany and the Soviet Union had signed a pact of mutual non-aggression, Hitler unloosed an attack on Poland and drove his armies toward the heart of Russia. The war was now in full and furious scale. Our entry appeared more inevitable with each passing hour.

We knew that Hitler wanted Japan to provoke the United States into a Pacific war, calculating that such a diversion would cut down our ever-rising flow of supplies to Britain and the Soviet Union. Japan's threatening naval maneuvers throughout the Pacific, added to her aggression against China, sustained a constant tension, although I had already resolved that, no matter what, Hitler would remain targeted as the number-one enemy of world peace and freedom.

In late November the situation appeared temporarily quiet enough to permit me to make my annual Thanksgiving visit to Warm Springs.

Arriving Saturday morning, November 29, I drove directly to the cottage of Missy LeHand, who had suffered a stroke the previous June. I had hardly settled down in my own new cottage, the Little White House, when a call from Secretary Hull informed me that a large Japanese fleet was at sea, destination undeterminable by our intelligence forces. Our best guesses were that they might be headed for Singapore or other Malay ports, conceivably—yet unbelievably—for the Philippines. There was also the possibility they might turn north to cut Russian supply lines around the Bering Straits. As Cordell remarked, "You can count on them to do something unexpected." I had to return to Washington. Next morning, our visit abruptly ended, Grace Tully and I paid a farewell call on Missy. I knew it would be a long time before I would return to Warm Springs in the carefree holiday mood I always associated with that restful place.

Knowing how ominous was our situation with Japan, I began to prepare a message to Congress, to be sent on December 8, giving the full history of our tensions and negotiations with Japan. It was necessary to make clear that, yes, we had been furnishing Japan with some quantities of steel and oil, but by no means as a form of appeasement. On the contrary, these actions were a deliberate maneuver to delay Japan's known aggressive designs, to give us time to build our defense capacities—industrial, coastal, and naval—which we had done.

During the week of my return to Washington I received a peculiar message from Bernard Baruch. Through Ray Moley, Baruch had been approached by Saburo Kurusu, a Japanese special envoy, then engaged with Ambassador Nomura in discussions with our State Department. Kurusu wanted to see me personally, without the presence of Secretary Hull. I authorized Baruch to accept a message that would be delivered personally to me. The essence of the message was that Kurusu himself wanted peace and that the Emperor wanted peace but that the warlords of Japan were "sitting with a loaded gun in each hand determined to shoot." He urged me to set aside protocol and appeal directly and personally to the Emperor, which he felt would immobilize the military. On Saturday evening, December 6, through Ambassador Joseph Grew in Tokyo, I sent such an unprecedented message directly to Emperor Hirohito, urging that the Japanese movements toward Indo-China be withdrawn.

Early next afternoon, a Sunday, I was sitting at my desk chatting with Harry Hopkins, planning a restful hour catching up on my stamp collection—and, not incidentally, awaiting a call from Hull about his discussions with Nomura and Kurusu, which at that very moment were taking place. At 1:47 P.M. a call came, not from Hull but from Secretary of the Navy Frank Knox. The message was astounding: "Mr. President, it looks as if the Japanese have attacked Pearl Harbor!"

The incredible report was followed by others: They attacked Guam; Wake, Midway, and Howland islands; Hong Kong; and there were unconfirmed reports that they also had attacked Manila and Singapore.

At Pearl Harbor, where sailors were on weekend shore leave, the waves of Japanese planes, launched from aircraft carriers, sank the battleship *Arizona* and several lighter craft, and severely damaged several warships in dry dock. A great section of our fleet was snugly tied up, side by side, at docks, with no steam up. They presented an easy and helpless target. Incomplete as those first reports were, I knew we had suffered the worst naval disaster in American history. Lives of Americans lost were as yet uncounted, but we knew the loss was terrible.

That day of infamy hurled us into full-scale war against Germany, Italy, and Japan. And thus our story of the prewar New Deal ends as this mightiest of American undertakings begins.[14]

I cannot close this narrative without acknowledging the Divine Providence which guided our nation into the national mobilization of the New Deal as preparation for a mobilization of survival.

In work aimed solely at helping our people live more fruitful lives in peace, we prepared ourselves to survive in war.

By organizing our streams to prevent floods, to irrigate, to electrify, we developed water power ready when needed to turn the wheels of war factories. TVA alone furnished more power than that of many whole nations.

By stringing wires to illuminate our farmhouses we made it possible to locate war factories in remote rural communities and engage the labor of farm hands in the national war effort.

The miles of roads paved by men on WPA were highways to transport soldiers and jeeps and foodstuffs and munitions.

A United States Employment Service, revived by the Social Security Act, with a network of three thousand offices, was ready-made for mobilizing willing men and women for war jobs, wherever each might be.

The CCC camps had provided experience for reserve officers and given the first taste of group labor and order to hundreds of thousands of young men now called into the military.

The National Youth Administration helped hundreds of thousands complete their education despite poverty, enabling them now to lead as military officers and industrial engineers and technicians and planners.

The NRA, short-lived as it was, introduced American businessmen to co-operation with government in joint accomplishment of large-scale national policy. It also introduced government to businessmen, who could now be called upon to come to Washington to organize the total mobilization of industry.

The AAA preserved the condition of the land as well as the state of the farm family, so that both could now provide sustenance for fighting men of all the world's free nations.

If the New Deal in peace had helped us prepare for war, war now taught us what the New Deal might truly have accomplished in peace. There was never enough money, so the naysayers said, to care for impoverished Americans. For example, as recently as January 1940, I had asked the Congress for a paltry $7.5 million to $10 million to finance WPA construction of fifty 100-bed hospitals in remote communities that had none. Congress never acted upon it, as if the sum would break us. Now we discovered that 49 per cent of the nation's young men had to be rejected for military service for physical reasons. In one rural state alone, Mississippi, the figure ran to 70 per cent. As the need to conscript young men rose, we learned that we could accept many of those young men, that we had the resources to correct their disabilities. Could we not have undertaken this most direct of humanitarian services in time of peace?

War proved to us that virtually no one is "unemployable," that no one willing to work need be poor. There was work for the aged, the blind, the lame, the disoriented, who, once provided with work, eagerly took it and performed it well. Millions of the "one-third of a nation" found themselves with more spending money than they had ever known. Those remote souls who remained poor in wartime were those whom the national hunger for labor had failed to find. By the millions, reliefers became taxpayers.

War taught us that even the husbandless mother, the special concern of the Aid to Dependent Children provision of the Social Security Act, could contribute—and be better off for doing so. Because every hand was needed, we passed the Lanham Act, providing nursery care for children not yet of school age, as well as play for their older brothers and sisters before and after school hours, so that their mothers could take jobs. Among the millions of women who took home-front jobs, tens of thousands were ADC mothers who found work more attractive than dependence. ADC rolls diminished from 390,000 families in 1941 to 254,000 in 1944. The children, of course, benefited by their mothers' full pay envelopes, enabling far better nutrition, clothing, and housing. We found no evidence that the children's well-being was impaired while their mothers were making their contribution to victory.

War taught us that our capacity for "spending"—meaning our willingness to cultivate an economy to fully serve our needs—is not limited, except by our needs. We *are* a land of plenty, limited in realizing our plenty only by timidity and fear. War taught us, to the amazement of the very senators and congressmen who now voted to spend, that the expense of huge war preparations—for all of our allies as well as the United States—could indeed be scheduled and met, and provide a good and continuing income for every American family while doing so. What would happen if each million dollars spent on a battleship were to be spent instead—in peacetime—on schools and hospitals and national parks, helping make human beings better educated and healthier, thus better able to contribute to their neighbors' lives? What a practical and economically sound investment!

War proved that in the long and terrible depression we had "spent" not too much but too little.

War taught us, above all, that *planning*—by industry and labor, co-operating with government—*can* work, and can indeed work miracles.

War proved our capability of cultivating abundance in peace. War was proof of the economic principles of the New Deal. When those activist principles are one day adopted by every nation, every government, there will be no more war. The roots of war—hunger, fear, national envy, aggressiveness—will no longer infest the earth.[15]

Regarding the future of liberalism, I have one final episode to tell. The incident came to an unfulfilled end because of the untimely death of a fine American.

The thought occasionally crossed my mind after the election of 1940 that the Democratic candidate for President in 1944 might very well be Wendell Willkie. He would represent both postwar internationalism and liberalism. Moreover, a man such as he could lead Republican liberals into our party, strengthening us to drive out the conservatives who shackled us. This thought, of course, became buried under the tremendous preoccupations of war. By the time the 1944 election came near, our forces had invaded the Normandy beaches, the tide of Axis victories had been reversed, and it was clear that this was no time to change captains. I consented to run for a fourth term.

The Republicans nominated Dewey, who by this time was governor of New York. Willkie maintained silence on that candidacy, which I know was unacceptable to him. On the other hand, he was reluctant to sever his influence among Republicans by endorsing me. In June 1944 Gifford Pinchot, my old conservationist friend and former governor of Pennsylvania, came to see me after having had an extraordinary discussion with Willkie. Willkie, who sought the nomination again, had been rejected by the dominant conservatives of his party, and he correctly observed that reactionary Democrats, particularly in the South, were out for my scalp, too—more specifically, they were determined that liberals were not to control our party after the war. Willkie expressed a thought to Pinchot that I had been thinking since 1936: the need for a single, united liberal party.

I called in Sam Rosenman, the most dependable man I knew for an extremely delicate political mission. I asked Sam to go to New York to see Willkie, tell him how interested I was in his thought, and ascertain if and when Willkie would be willing to talk personally with me about it. I instructed Sam to make clear in advance that his conversation would have nothing to do with the coming election. It was most important that Willkie be assured that his silence regarding

Roosevelt-vs.-Dewey was in no way connected with what we wanted to bring up. On that assurance, Willkie agreed to meet with Rosenman. Sam arranged for lunch in a private suite of the St. Regis Hotel on July 5. As Sam tells it to me, they were so concerned about secrecy that when a waiter knocked on the door to deliver lunch, Willkie slipped into an adjoining bedroom.

The two men reviewed the situation in both parties: how the 1944 Republican convention was completely in the control of the reactionaries, who would give no quarter to Willkie-type liberals; how the majority of Democrats, time after time, adopts a sound liberal platform only to have southern conservatives subvert it.

"Both parties," said Willkie, in full agreement, "are hybrids."

Sam told him that I would like to team up with Willkie in constructing a truly liberal party immediately after the November election, whether I was to win or lose it.

Willkie talked at great length about his particular concern that the United States take leadership in the formation of "One World," a phrase that had become his personal identification, and that a new political grouping was needed to guarantee it. He concluded: "You tell the President that I am ready to devote almost full time to this. A sound, liberal government in the United States is absolutely essential to continued co-operation with the other nations of the world. I know some of these reactionaries—especially those in my own party. They'll run out on the other nations when the going gets tough—just as soon as they can."

Then they got down to more specific talk, of what groups would naturally adhere to a truly liberal party: labor, racial and religious groups, small farmers, students, small merchants and businessmen, and the liberal university and intellectual crowd. They went over the names of outstanding Republicans who felt isolated in their party and those of Democrats who would feel more at home in a new conservative alliance. Willkie said he did indeed want to discuss it with me personally and more fully, but not before election day. There was no way, he felt, that such a meeting could be kept secret, and the press would surely conjecture that Willkie was conspiring with Roosevelt against Dewey in the current campaign.

The prospect was so exciting to me that in mid-July I sent Willkie a letter, about which no one knew but Grace Tully, who took the dictation:

July 13, 1944

Personal

Dear Wendell:

I will not be able to sign this because I am dictating it just as I leave on a trip to the westward.

What I want to tell you is that I want to see you when I come back, but not on anything in relationship to the present campaign. I want to talk with you about the future, even the somewhat distant future, and in regard to the foreign relations problems of the immediate future.

When you see in the papers that I am back, will you get in touch with General Watson? We can arrange a meeting either here in Washington or, if you prefer, at Hyde Park—wholly off the record or otherwise, just as you think best.

Unfortunately the existence of a letter from me to Willkie—not its contents, just its existence—became known to someone and leaked to the press. That made a meeting before Election Day impossible.

The meeting was never to take place.

In the fall Willkie entered a hospital in New York. There was no hint given out that his illness was serious. On Sunday, October 8, 1944, to the shock of the nation and the world, Wendell Willkie died.[16]

So ended, at least for the time being, that hope of his and mine to reconstruct our two-party system along natural lines of liberalism versus conservatism. No one of his party was left who matched Willkie's stature to lead the Republican side of so great an enterprise.

The unification of liberalism in a single political force, unhampered within by its opposite philosophy, remains an imperative task.

By liberalism I do not mean the specific ideas and methods and experiments of the New Deal. Liberalism is not a program that is fixed for all time. As the needs of the nation changed from the horse-and-buggy days to the depression days of the 1930s, so they will keep changing. Some of the specific measures of the New Deal will no longer serve the needs of a new America that they will have helped create.

The central principle of liberalism, however, is constant and simple: It is a never-ending search to discover the human uses of government appropriate to each generation. Always we will have among us those who say, "The tree we have now is perfect; don't touch it."

Always we must have those who say, "Let's see how, by grafting a limb here, pruning a branch there, we can make of it a finer tree."

The New Deal stands as our first large-scale venture to find the best ways that government in its time might serve the human beings governed by it. The continuation and continual refreshing of that search is the constant of liberalism.

BACKGROUND MEMORANDUM TO PART VII

On the seventh of September, 1941, a day that will live in memory at Hyde Park, without advance warning—there was no storm, no wind, no lightning—the mightiest oak on the Roosevelt estate groaned and toppled to the ground. Geologists were later called in to investigate. They explained that, because of a thin layer of earth over a rocky base, such occurrences in Dutchess County were quite normal.

The people around the Roosevelts—the secretaries, the Secret Service men, the household workers and gardeners—never quite accepted that. They preferred to rely on a more symbolic explanation. Barely five minutes before the great tree fell, Sara Delano Roosevelt, lying in her bed on the second floor of the mansion, gave up her last breath.

Later in the afternoon of that somber day her only son, Franklin, was taken by a strong urge. He wished to go out among the trees and quiet roads of the place, driving in his little car—alone.

He was not permitted to do so. Even at so private a moment, Mike Reilly, chief of the Secret Service detail, insisted that he must ride by the President's side. And a car full of Secret Service men had to follow behind.

A man can get very lonely never being able to be alone.

The presidency, they say, is the loneliest job in the world. As it was for the thirty men who preceded him, so it was for Franklin Roosevelt. But never had he been left so lonely—personally lonely—as during the year that ended with his nation at full war. And so it was to remain for all his remaining days.

There was, first, a new political loneliness: desertion by friends during his personal challenge to the Supreme Court; then abandonment and defeat (which he tried to call a victory) when he placed his name—his person—on the line to rid his party of a couple of southern senators; and the barely forestalled mutiny of his own party in the vice-presidential balloting at the convention. These were humiliations to which no experience, political or otherwise, had accustomed him.

At such a time one turns for strength to those he has known intimately and long. But who—where—were they? Louis Howe, the spine of continuity through all F.D.R.'s political years, was dead. Eleanor Roosevelt by now headed what was virtually a separate household and social circle, and, in fact, except for keeping up appearances, lived in a separate house; most of her time at Hyde Park was spent at her Val-Kill cottage. This left only Missy.

And by the time of Mama's death even Missy was gone. Alive, yes, but he knew she would never be back, never be Missy again.

In June 1941 there was a party at the White House for the staff. Toward the end of dinner Missy, looking strangely drawn, told Grace Tully she felt ill. She refused, however, to go upstairs to bed before the Boss left, which he did at about 9:30. A few minutes later Missy slumped to the floor, unconscious. Dr. McIntire rushed her to her room. The signs of a stroke were unmistakable. Her left arm and leg were paralyzed. Her speech was gone. The constant vigilance and care she required was difficult at the White House; after some days Missy was taken to Doctors Hospital and, after a few weeks there, at her request, to Warm Springs, where she could get both medical attention and rest.

The visit by F.D.R. to Warm Springs in late November was awkward and painful for him. It would have been for anyone, but especially for a man who could scarcely bring himself to talk of illness, let alone be in its presence. Worn now by the immense tensions of national mobilization and impending war, he could barely endure the ordeal of trying to cheer Missy—the old cheery, talkative, loyal Missy—who could now say without great effort only a single word, "Yes."

He took Grace Tully along. "You had to have at least two people," explains Egbert Curtis, "so you could talk across Missy to the other person. Suppose I could only say 'yes—yes,' it would be very difficult for you or anybody else to talk with me. She could only participate by listening, maybe by small signs of her face. And, you know, people who have had strokes are very prone to cry easily."

It was minutes after that ordeal that Roosevelt heard from Hull of the threatening Japanese maneuvers and decided to return to Washington immediately. Roosevelt began now to do what he had to do, what he had learned so well by example from his mother to do, to blot the unpleasant out of his consciousness: blotting out Missy's illness, even Missy herself.

This requirement of his personality was reinforced by the all-consuming demand of war.

Back in Washington, on the night of the terrible Sunday of Pearl Harbor, Roosevelt sat with his Cabinet, who had gathered hurriedly from all over the East, as tense and grave a meeting as any Cabinet had ever held. During the meeting a call came from Warm Springs. Grace could not put it through. Instead she typed out on a note what she knew the caller was struggling to convey:

> December 7, 1941
> 10:05 P.M.
>
> MEMORANDUM FOR THE PRESIDENT
>   Missy telephoned and wanted to talk with you. She is thinking about you and much disturbed about the news. She would like you to call her tonight. I told her you would if the conference broke up at a reasonable hour—otherwise you would call her in the morning.
>
> G.G.T.

The next night Roosevelt, after going to Congress for a declaration of war, spoke to the nation on the radio. This time no after-speech poker game, no letting his hair down quietly in the Oval Room. Roosevelt sat upstairs at his big desk, drawing on a cigarette, poring over his stamps. Sam Rosenman appeared at the door. He observed, and later wrote:

"He was all alone. If Missy had been well, she would have been sitting up with him in the study that night. She always did in times of great stress, to see whether there was anyone he wanted to call or talk to."

The President looked up with a "sad and tired" smile, saying merely, "Come in and sit down. Help yourself to a drink."

Weeks later, Eleanor, whose conflicts over Missy never supplanted a motherly protectiveness, asked Franklin if he had called to greet her on Christmas Eve. Perhaps he resented the intrusion, perhaps the discomforting obligation. (Trying to sustain a conversation on the phone was agony.) He irritably replied that he had not and was not planning to do so. Eleanor, who could always override her feelings to attend to an obligation, could not fathom Franklin's incapacity to do so. Years later, still resenting him for it, she told friends that she "could not understand that."

Franklin had his own ways of doing what he had to do. He altered his will to provide for Missy's medical expenses up to 50 per cent of his estate, the remainder being left to Eleanor.

Franklin Roosevelt, at the nucleus of a world at war, could bury his loneliness. But how could Missy? That cursed cottage in Warm Springs was like a berth in a speeding, hurtling train suddenly stopped. She had lived at the power center of the nation, the world; the great names of her time, waiting edgily for an audience with the greatest name of the time, would stop at her deskside chair to chat. What the great did not know, what that man inside would not tell them, he would often confide to her. To the fortunes of this man, to his responsibilities and to his person, she had committed her life. While never to have him, she had as much of him as anyone, and for that she had long decided to have no one else. Now that whirling, exciting life was suddenly stilled. And the man was not with her. It could never again be as it was. She knew that. At forty-one, now *she* was crippled. Without speech. It was all over.

One night—in the middle of the night—the telephone rang in the home of Dr. C. E. "Ed" Irwin, medical director of the Warm Springs foundation. He dressed and left quickly for the Alva Wilson cottage. Before dawn he returned weary and puzzled, saying to his wife, Mabel, "I don't know what I'm going to do about Missy. I think she tried to kill herself tonight." Then, shaking his head in disbelief, in distress over this old friend, he added, "Tried to do it by swallowing chicken bones."

Over a cup of coffee, the doctor and his wife speculated on the bizarre occurrence, and agreed that perhaps Missy was going berserk.

Missy was soon brought back to the White House, to her third-floor apartment. Three nurses were assigned to her care around the clock. A favorite White House maid was called from retirement to look after her dinner, then sit in her room all night. During those long nights, Missy, unable to sleep, needed someone to talk to her, and someone to listen to the words she would struggle to form.

A speech therapist was brought in to teach Missy, as one would a baby to speak again, but progress was slight. The worst of the suffering is that a stroke-damaged brain, while having lost the memory of how to form words, while sometimes in a mist of disorientation, has its periods of clarity and understanding, of awareness of events and people, of despair and desire—and a surging need to express. Yet she was dumb, looked dumb, *knew* she looked dumb. Those who came to see her—Grace and F.D. himself—although knowing otherwise, were hard put to treat her except as dumb. Bracing himself for the evening visits, F.D. would assemble in his mind a string of the day's tales, then, setting his face in a wide smile, wheel into her room. Spurred by her eager eyes, he'd unreel his monologue complete with self-propelled laughter. Suddenly there were no more stories to his string, no response to egg him on. They'd look at each other. Before silence could shatter the masquerade, another cheery smile—"See you tomorrow!"—and he'd wheel around. Gone.

What she could not speak she could yet in ways communicate. The all-night maid once told her daughter, a White House seamstress, that Missy knew she was dying.

"Because she could read," says Grace Tully, "I used to bring her the State Department decoded messages that used to go across her desk and now went across mine. I thought she'd enjoy knowing what was going on around the world. I wanted her to feel that she was keeping up with things. I don't know how much she took in of it, but she seemed to appreciate my bringing them before I sent them back to the State Department."

And she could write, too. She began to write letters to people who had been close. Passages in the letters were manic, tormented outbursts of fantasy of a life she had not permitted herself to live. "The letters," says an informant not wishing in this connection to be named, "told of this one being in love with her, and that one wanting to marry her. Everyone realized that she could no longer be trusted with important information. These friends and the family drew together to get the letters out of sight, to hush up Missy's lapse."

The White House was clearly not a good place for her to be. Missy was sent to Somerville, to the house on Orchard Street from which two decades earlier she had set out for New York in search of excitement and a career. According to Grace Tully, she wanted to go: "She felt there was nothing for her to do, she was getting depressed and thought, well, she'd go up to her family, her two nieces and a sister. She was very fond of those two nieces, although she couldn't care less about the sister who would go out and charge everything to Missy that she could lay her hands on."

In July of 1942 the Curtises visited Missy, and Curtis wrote cheerily to the President, "She is certainly improving. She has gained twelve pounds, they tell me, since she has been home and is now able to walk with a cane." A few months later, on the morning of the Congressional mid-term election, Missy sent a wire to F.D. at the White House, which was forwarded to him at Hyde Park:

I AM FIGHTING FOR YOU LOVE MISSY.

In February 1944, as Eleanor was preparing for a tour among American troops in the Caribbean and South America, she discovered that Missy had been invited to visit the White House during her absence. This was the period when Eleanor was most annoyed that other women—Mrs. Hopkins and Jimmy's wife, Betsey—were assuming prerogatives she felt were solely hers. She wrote Missy to postpone the visit: "I was away last week when Grace and Franklin arranged for you to come down on the 7th of March. I am terribly sorry that they did not realize that I want to be here when you come. . . . I am very sorry that they did not consult me before making plans but it is hard to get everyone together and I have been away for a few days at a time."

On the tenth anniversary of Roosevelt's first inauguration, Felix Frank-furter, always a close student of how to touch F.D.R. most personally, took a moment from Court business to send a note: "What a day. If only Missy were also here to rejoice!"

On the evening of July 30, 1944, Missy went to the movies. "As I recall being told," says Barbara Curtis, "she saw a newsreel of Franklin Roose-velt and was shocked at the way he looked and the way his voice sounded. At home, she went to bed and was looking at some old pictures. Her arm that had been useless was moving and jumping just like this, and they thought that life was coming back. They thought she was getting better. She called her sister in, and then Missy slumped over."

The President was aboard ship, just having departed from Honolulu, where he had conferred on the Pacific campaign with General MacArthur and Admiral Chester Nimitz. A radio message arrived from the White House:

July 31, 1944

MEMORANDUM FOR THE PRESIDENT:

REGRET TO INFORM YOU THAT MISS LEHAND DIED IN THE NAVAL HOSPITAL AT CHELSEA, MASSACHUSETTS, AT 9:05 A.M. TODAY. ADMIRAL SHELDON, OF THE BUREAU OF MEDICINE AND SURGERY, STATES THAT THE CAUSE OF DEATH WAS CEREBRAL EMBOLISM. MISS LEHAND WAS TAKEN TO THE HOSPITAL AT 2:00 O'CLOCK THIS MORNING. ADMIRAL SHELDON SAID SHE HAD ATTENDED THE THEATRE LAST EVENING AND THAT THE CHANGE FOR THE WORSE WAS UNEXPECTED. HAVE NOTIFIED MRS. ROO-SEVELT AND MISS TULLY. AWAIT INSTRUCTIONS. WILL ISSUE STATEMENT IN THE PRESIDENT'S NAME AND WILL SEND TEXT TO YOU FOR YOUR IN-FORMATION.

EARLY—HASSETT

Grace Tully, recalling his return to Washington: "I naturally said to him, 'You and I lost a very dear friend.' And he was about to cry and so was I, and he said, 'Yes, poor Missy.' But he never liked to talk about those things because he was—well, being a man, he didn't want to show any emotion. At least I never saw him show any."

Actually, she had—only once. Concealing emotion after his mother's death, Miss Tully has written, his reserve broke and he fell into tears when "he discovered one day in my presence shortly after the funeral that she had carefully saved and tagged his christening dress, his first pair of shoes, his baby hair, and some of his childhood toys and many of the little gifts he had sent or brought to her through the years."

Franklin Roosevelt, lover of the sea and ships, found his own way of arranging his personal salute. On March 27, 1945, on the eve of his departure for what was to be his last visit to Warm Springs, the White House dispatched a night letter to the Ingalls Shipbuilding Corporation at Pascagoula, Mississippi, builder of C-3 cargo vessels:

MRS. ROOSEVELT AND I SEND WARM GREETINGS TO ALL WHO ATTEND THE LAUNCHING OF THE S.S. MARGUERITE A. LEHAND IN THE HOPE THAT A CRAFT WHICH BEARS SO HONORED A NAME WILL MAKE MANY A SAFE JOURNEY AND ALWAYS FIND A PEACEFUL HARBOR.

FRANKLIN D. ROOSEVELT[1]

From the time Missy was taken ill, before Pearl Harbor, Roosevelt, for the first time since his own illness twenty years earlier, had no shield of woman to protect him from woman. In Missy, almost twenty years his junior, he had found the consuming devotion that Mama had early taught him was his due, but without the price of demand; he had found the self-sacrifice to his ambition that Eleanor had early signaled and pledged, but without the price of solemnity and heavy virtue.

Perhaps this was to be found only in a younger, worshipful woman. The wariness of women taught him by Mother, he had transformed to an extreme wariness of motherly wives. He had a habit, when talking about influential men, of turning the talk to their influential wives. William Hassett recalls a conversation in which "the President fell to musing about the wives of Presidents from Lincoln onward. . . . Of Mrs. Theodore Roosevelt he spoke with great appreciation, said a life of 'Aunt Edith' should be written. . . . She managed T.R. very cleverly without his being conscious of it." Jim Farley quotes F.D.R. in a denunciation of Senator Wheeler: "Of course, he is tremendously ambitious and wants to be President. His wife is even more ambitious for the White House and it's a well-known fact that she runs him. He can't control her." Wheeler himself quotes Roosevelt on Justice Brandeis' opposition to the Court bill: "Justice Brandeis was all in favor of it at first, but the old lady—the nice old lady —kept dropping little drops of water on his head until he changed his mind." Wheeler adds, "The President was very suspicious about the influence of wives. He was reported to have called Mrs. Wheeler the 'Lady Macbeth of the Court fight' . . . The President was represented as believing that Mrs. Wheeler hated him and influenced me against him."

If this distrust was a legacy from a meddlesome mother, transferred to wife and other men's wives, the transfer was complete. F.D.R. had long before learned to take Mama's interferences, which never let up, with humor. When Mama went abroad, the President and son Jimmy would read aloud to each other what they called her "Assistant Secretary of State bulletins." Received by Mussolini on her visit to Italy in July 1937, she reported with delight that "the Duce sent me a grand bunch of flowers" and that "all seems very flourishing & peaceful & the devotion to the 'Head of the Government' is general in all classes. . . ." In the same letter she relayed intelligence acquired from a Spanish-born countess that "there is great hope that the 'rebels' under Franco will win, as they are the only hope for poor Spain. . . ." F.D.R., after gleefully reading the bulletins, would say, "Well, Mama is having a grand time!"

But the influence of Mama remained; even after her death the distortion she had wrought in her son's marriage by her subjection of his young wife —and the wife's surrender to and resentment of it—persisted. The month following Mama's death Eleanor, after talking with the President, confided to Joseph Lash, who wrote in his diary: "She had suggested changes should be made in the Big House so that it would be more livable. But he did not want that. He wanted the Big House kept as it was and as it had been left by his mother—as a museum. She could not live in it. She would live in the cottage at Val-Kill and come over to the Big House when the President was there."

"The fact that Granny was dead," says daughter Anna, "didn't suddenly solve a lot of personal problems, because long before Granny died Mother had become a fully evolved person. Their patterns were quite permanent."[2]

And in at least one way their patterns had become quite similar. Eleanor writes this complaint about Mama's behavior at Hyde Park: "If, as sometimes happens, he did not want to see some old friends or various other people she wanted him to see, she would calmly invite them for luncheon or dinner anyway, and simply not bring them into the dining room until after Franklin was seated and it was too late for him to do anything about it." Such "old friends" were generally people from his earlier social milieu, often boring, with whom Mama did not want him to lose contact.

When she could, Eleanor protected him from such ordeals. But at the White House she used the same device to force upon him people whose causes she felt deserved a presidential hearing. Grace Tully recalls that on some mornings in the office he'd confide, "Eleanor had a lot of 'do-gooders' for dinner and you know what that means." From these ordeals Missy tried to protect him, going over in advance the list of guests and warning him when he'd better stay away. Now Missy was no longer there. The dinner table was again a place of family crisis, as it had been in the early days of Albany and the Brains Trust. Tugwell recalls of those days:

"Really serious talk at table was avoided if Roosevelt could manage it. Eleanor, so humorless and so weighed down with responsibility, made this difficult. . . . Sam [Rosenman] and Doc [Basil O'Connor] were so disillusioned with the cuisine and so prone to be annoyed with Eleanor's well-meant probing that they often turned up after dinner rather than before. . . . [Sam] could stand it as long as Missy LeHand was there. Her presence was like a quiet blessing on any company she graced. She never said much, but when she did speak, it was softly, and always sensibly, about something immediate. . . ."

As Mrs. Roosevelt's stature and involvements grew, so did Rosenman's regard for her; yet, years later, writing of her during the war, he is still critical: "She was invariably frank in her criticism of him—and of his speeches. Sometimes I thought she picked inappropriate times to discuss matters with him—as when he was engrossed in some other problem or perhaps during a social and entertaining dinner. . . . Her objectives were the same as his. She had none of his give, however, that is one of the great essentials of a successful political leader. It was hard for her to compromise. . . . She advocated the direct, unrelenting approach. If she had had her way, there would have been fewer compromises by Roosevelt, but also, I am afraid, fewer concrete accomplishments."

Grace Tully: "On one occasion of a dinner party cross-examination by Mrs. Roosevelt, I recall Anna speaking up jokingly: 'Mother, can't you see you are giving Father indigestion?' "

Anna: "She pushed him terrifically. This I know. But you can't ask somebody to be your eyes and ears and then not—."

What was most irksome was not that she pushed—but *what* she pushed: her pushing was always for some cause of justice and right, lost or obscured in the larger web of politics and war. Justice, being indivisible, was to her as urgent on the smallest scale as on the large. Her eye was forever on the sparrow as well as the flock. To her table she brought pleaders for refugees, righteous spokesmen of youth, impassioned guests who urged that if the decency of desegregation were ever to begin, the time was now —in the armed forces.

How do you say, "Yes, but—" to justice? What plea of the practicality of national-unity politics will satisfy? The confrontation itself is an assault on that most tender of places, conscience. It is an affront. And yet this marriage of conscience and practicality at the same tense dinner table was indeed a marriage, holding both parties in line, each strengthening the other by permitting neither to run loose.

The pressures of conscience were hers, the necessity of cold decision his. It was he who had to weigh conscience against necessity when Mrs. Roosevelt in 1942 became caught up in a case of a Negro tenant farmer named Waller who had been sentenced to death for the murder of his landlord. She tried to intervene with the governor of the state where the trial had taken place, then asked the President to do so. He wrote a "very strong letter" to the governor, urging a commutation to life imprisonment. At that moment of history, in other places, young men, unaccused of crimes, were dying by the thousands. The Germans were at the gates of Cairo, the Japanese menacing India. The man-power crisis at home was at its most severe. Harry Hopkins, observing the pressure and resistance between President and First Lady, jotted down a private memo:

> The Governor had given six different reprieves and the President felt that he could not interfere again. He thought the Governor was acting entirely within his constitutional rights and, in addition to that, doubted very much if the merits of the case warranted the Governor's reaching any other decision.
>
> Mrs. Roosevelt, however, would not take "No" for an answer and the President finally got on the phone himself and told Mrs. Roosevelt that under no circumstances would he interfere with the Governor and urged very strongly that she say nothing about it.
>
> This incident is typical of things that have gone on in Washington between the President and Mrs. Roosevelt ever since 1932. She is forever finding someone underprivileged and unbefriended in whose behalf she takes up the cudgels. While she may often be wrong, as I think she was in this case, I never cease to admire her burning determination to see that justice is done, not only to individuals but to underprivileged groups.
>
> I think, too, in this instance Mrs. Roosevelt felt that I was not pressing her case with the President adequately, because in the course of the evening he was not available on the phone and I had to act as a go-between. At any rate I felt that she would not be satisfied until the President told her himself, which he reluctantly but finally did.[3]

"When he became President," John Gunther, in a surprisingly unnoticed passage, quotes an unidentified informant, "F.D.R. cut every really personal relationship out of his life except his love for Missy." If his need for unchallenging, undemanding feminine attention had once made him largely replace Eleanor with Missy, now he needed somehow to fill a void left by Missy. He did so during the war by bringing closer to him a circle of "lovely ladies who worshipped at his shrine," to use the phrase once written teasingly by Eleanor. First among these was Anna. Her husband being in uniform and overseas, she moved into the White House to look after her father, look after his relaxation, his meals—what she describes as "this business of *guarding* that he did not get during the previous year. He did not get his swim, his massages, he didn't get the things he needed to keep circulation going, his rest."

There was also Betsey Cushing Roosevelt, Jimmy's wife; and Louise

Hopkins, Harry's wife. There were two cousins from Dutchess County whom Roosevelt now took on his trips to Warm Springs: Laura Delano, whose penchant for dyeing her hair unpredictable shades of purple was in itself a constant entertainment, and Margaret Suckley, who had given Franklin his famous dog, Fala. Both were maiden ladies. Of Miss Suckley, Anna says, "Here's a gal who never married, who was simply devoted to him. She'd do anything, anything for Father. Her life was entwined with his." Was he aware of this? "I think he was perfectly aware of it."

With the influx of royalty fleeing the occupied countries of Europe, there was Crown Princess Martha of Norway, with whom F.D.R. would go motoring through the hills of Berkshire County, Massachusetts, not far from Hyde Park, helping the Princess house-hunt. (From the Hassett diary: "The President and Princess Martha to tea with the Morgenthaus this afternoon. How they must have been bored, and I don't mean the Morgenthaus.") And there was Princess Juliana of the Netherlands, who never quite attained the closeness to him of Princess Martha, possibly because of her formidable mother, old Queen Wilhelmina, whose hauteur oddly affected Roosevelt. (Hassett: "He hasn't said so, but I have a feeling the President dreads her. . . . Nevertheless the Boss will call her 'Minnie' and make her like it.")

While this bevy saw to his entertainment, Anna became increasingly concerned about his health. She began to wonder whether Admiral McIntire was quite the man her father needed, beyond the Navy talk F.D.R. enjoyed, beyond his skills as an ear, nose, and throat specialist. Did McIntire look far beyond Roosevelt's ever-troublesome sinuses? "I wasn't married to a physician then as I am now, but I didn't think McIntire was an internist who really knew what he was talking about. I felt Father needed more care, more general care. Since then, of course, we've learned that he had arteriosclerosis even before the Casablanca Conference, but nobody recognized this. This was not Father's fault or Mother's fault, but you've got to realize that these two were brought up in a generation when you just *didn't talk* about what's wrong with you physically. I can remember going to Mother at that time, after Casablanca, and saying, 'I think Father has to have such-and-such and I've already talked to Dr. McIntire.' She said, 'Well, dear, I agree with you, I think this is very important.' Of course, by then Bruenn [Dr. Howard Bruenn, a heart specialist] was in the picture. But there were no anti-coagulants or whatever then, and I don't think there is the slightest doubt that Father must have had times when the blood was not pumping the way it should through one hundred percent of the body. I saw this with my own eyes, but I don't think Mother saw it. She wasn't looking for him to be any different. Father wasn't interested in physiology—that was all there was to it. But neither was Mother interested in physiology. She seemed to be cerebrating one hundred percent, *all* the time.

"She couldn't see why, at a moment when he was relaxing—I remember one day when we were having cocktails. This is upstairs in the oval room. A fair number of people were in the room, an informal group, nobody important. I was mixing the cocktails. Mother always came in at the end so she would only have to have one cocktail—that was her concession. She would wolf it—she never took it slowly. She came in and sat down across the desk from Father. And she had a sheaf of papers this high and she said, 'Now, Franklin, I want to talk to you about this.' I have permanently blocked out of my mind what it was she wanted to bring up. I just remember, like lightning, that I thought, 'Oh God, he's going to *blow*.' And sure enough, he blew his top. He took every single speck of that whole pile of papers, threw them across the desk at me and said, 'Sis, you handle these tomorrow morning.' I almost went through the floor. She got up. She was the most controlled person in the world. And she just stood there a half second and said, 'I'm sorry.' Then she took her glass and walked toward somebody else and started talking. And he picked up his glass and started a story. And that was the end of it.

"Intuitively I understood that here was a man plagued with God knows how many problems and right now he had twenty minutes to have two cocktails—in very small glasses—because dinner was served at a certain hour. They called you and out you went. He wanted to tell stories and relax and enjoy himself—*period*. I don't think Mother had the slightest realization."[4]

It appears no longer possible to pinpoint exactly when Franklin Roosevelt, presumably following Missy's stroke and the shock of Pearl Harbor, reopened a place in his life for Lucy Rutherfurd. Jonathan Daniels, son of F.D.R.'s old Navy boss, Josephus Daniels, and White House Press Secretary during the final weeks of Roosevelt's life, became absorbed in recent years with the "lifelong romance" viewpoint of the Roosevelt-Rutherfurd relationship—in fact was its creator and publicist. Shortly after publication, in 1961, of my book *When F.D.R. Died,* describing for the first time details of Mrs. Rutherfurd's presence during the President's final visit to Warm Springs, Daniels undertook correspondence with me as well as with numerous others who might furnish pieces of the story he sought to put together. Although the conclusions he drew were not shared by me, I furnished him with passages from my manuscript that I had deleted from the book because Mrs. Roosevelt was still alive. In October 1963 Daniels wrote me: "The big blank in the story, as far as I am concerned, are the years between 1920 and 1942. I'm filling them."

Daniels' research was assiduous and broad, but the "filling" for those years turned out far from convincing. If his findings fail to portray the continuation of a "lifelong romance," they do, however, suggest the preliminaries to a resumption of a relationship long dormant. "White House files show," Daniels was to write in his book *Washington Quadrille,* that on June 26, 1941, Roosevelt received Winthrop Rutherfurd at the White House. Presumably, this was Lucy's thirty-seven-year-old stepson; the elder Winthrop, then seventy-nine, was confined to his Aiken mansion, having suffered a stroke. Then, for almost two years, no trace of a Rutherfurd contact, until May 1943, when a pair of tickets were sent by Roosevelt to John Rutherfurd, young Winthrop's brother, for Winston Churchill's address to a joint session of Congress. This was followed by three more chats at the White House, on May 18, July 8, and September 8, with young Winthrop, by then an Army officer. Also, in May 1943 Roosevelt sat for a water-color portrait by Elizabeth Shoumatoff, the picture to be given as the President's gift to Lucy's only daughter, Barbara.

(The truth is, of course, that the President could afford little time to sit. After the face and head were done, he called in William D. Simmons, asking the puzzled Secret Service man to try on his famous Navy cape, booming "Fine! Fine!" and F.D.R. returned to his office. Simmons was not entirely new to the role. On the 1936 campaign train rolling through Arkansas, Roosevelt had summoned Simmons to the presidential car and asked with mock sternness, "Bill, how would you like to be President for a while?" Weary of waving through a window at crowds in every passing town, he had instructed Simmons to pull up a chair, fastened his pince-nez glasses to Simmons' nose, showed him how to hold his cigarette holder in a wide-arc wave while smiling a big smile, then pronounced, "Fine! Fine! Now every time we pass a town, just sit there and wave. I'm going to take a nap.")

It was Simmons, in fact, who told me of the meetings that now resumed, somewhere around 1943, and that Daniels reports similarly, with variations in detail. The President's car would stop at a house on Q Street near Georgetown to pick up a lady for whom the Secret Service had a code name, "Mrs. Johnson." (In Daniels' version, "the President rode out to a meeting place on a road beyond Georgetown. Lucy would be waiting there in what Secret Service men remembered as an old car.") As he and Missy used to do afternoons, they would go riding through the Virginia countryside for an hour or so, the President and "Mrs. Johnson" in quiet conversation behind a glass that sealed them from the chauffeur, and then the President would return to face the burdens awaiting him at the White House.

Later in 1943, hounded by a lingering cold and persistent sinus pain, Roosevelt accepted an invitation for an extended rest at Bernard Baruch's South Carolina estate, Hobcaw Barony. He thought at least twice before accepting, harboring a distrust of Baruch, a lavish Democratic contributor who, Roosevelt once ruefully remarked, "owns sixty Congressmen." Bill Hassett was later to note: "The Boss paid a heavy penalty in accepting Bernie Baruch's hospitality. Bernie added himself to the household and so was there most of the month." The month had its moments. Lucy visited him from Aiken, Baruch providing her with some of his own precious gasoline ration tickets to get there. Mrs. Roosevelt, to whom the Rutherfurd visit was not known (although to Anna it was), flew down one day for lunch, later commenting that his stay at Hobcaw "was the very best move Franklin could have made."

According to Daniels, White House employees recall that "during this period Lucy came to the White House for dinner more than once."[5]

In mid-1944, Lucy's aged and ailing husband died.

Roosevelt's wartime travels, of course, were shrouded with heavy security protection. Three reporters, one from each wire service, went with him almost everywhere under a rule of "voluntary censorship." The travel itself went unreported, except for public appearances. One of Roosevelt's secret trips was to Hyde Park to spend the Labor Day weekend in advance of the limited campaigning he was to do in 1944. Perhaps the reporters were surprised when the train stopped unexpectedly in northwestern New Jersey and they saw Roosevelt being transferred from his wheelchair to an automobile. They resumed their card playing upon being informed that he was dropping by to see an old friend whose husband had died a few months before. The visit was to Tranquility Farms, the Rutherfurd summer estate near Allamuchy. The only man to write of it was Bill Hassett, who later expunged two pages from his diary before its publication. The visit was short, enabling a late-afternoon arrival at Hyde Park, where Eleanor met the train.

Almost three months later, the fourth campaign over and victorious, the President, accompanied by Laura Delano and Margaret Suckley, entrained for his annual Thanksgiving visit to Warm Springs. Lucy motored down from Aiken to share the first few days of his visit, presumably staying at Roosevelt's tiny guesthouse, across a driveway from his cottage, which she was to occupy during a later, final visit.

The secrecy of these rendezvous, necessitated by a wife as well as a war, invites speculation, evokes a leer of curiosity. To Anna, most of the visits were not secret. After these many years, she now speaks of them readily—almost eagerly—with the anxiety of a daughter brought up in an atmosphere of history, with a respect for history and truth, yet with a feeling that a little bit of truth, blown out of shape, has wronged her father. She was aware—perhaps the only one then aware—that her father's energy was declining, that he was lonely, that in his last days he reached back for gentle friends, gentle memories.

Having known of—and seen—the resumed relationship between her father and Lucy from 1943 to 1945, she describes it today as "an important friendship to both of them." It presented special difficulties to her, she adds, because she was also concerned that her mother not be injured again. Anna recalls:

"Soon after that Thanksgiving 1944 visit to Warm Springs—you see, this is all *late* in his life—Lucy Rutherfurd told me something that, although she probably didn't know it, was very revealing to me about the kind of relationship it was. She told me, 'You know, your father drove me in his little Ford up to'—what's the name of that mountain where he loved to go on picnics?—'Dowdell's Knob.' And she said, 'You know, I had the most fascinating hour I've ever had. He just sat there and told me of some of what he regarded as the real problems facing the world now. I just couldn't get over thinking of what I was listening to, and then he would stop and say, "You see that knoll over there? That's where I did this-or-that," or "You see that bunch of trees?" Or whatever it was. He would interrupt himself, you know. And we just sat there and looked.'

"As Lucy said all this to me—Father was right there in the room—I realized, Mother was not capable of giving him this—just listening. And of course, this is why I was able to fill in for a year and a half, because I could just listen. I remember, when we were starting out for Yalta, it was almost dusk. We sat out on deck watching. He started telling the history of various parts of Virginia that were going by. It was quiet, and at one point he said, 'That's where Lucy's family used to live. That's where they had their plantation.' This was so open, above board, not hanky-panky or whatever you want to call it. That is why I think this whole thing has become such a—."

What reserves of strength he gathered during that Thanksgiving visit he knew were soon to be invested in the long, arduous journey to Yalta, where, with victory soon at hand, life around the globe was to be reshaped. From the stresses of that conference, and the travel by plane and ship, he was never fully to recover.

In late March of 1945—again a quest to renew lost vigor at Warm Springs.

The secret bond between Franklin Roosevelt and Lucy Rutherfurd seemed ironically fated to disclosure—not once, but twice. Each time, the disclosure burst in the face of a wife at a moment when her emotions were already under the severest stress. In the first instance, in 1918, the discovery of Lucy's letters came when her husband was gravely ill. In the second, the discovery of Lucy's presence at the time and place of his last days on earth.

Lucy drove to Warm Springs accompanied by her friend Elizabeth Shoumatoff, who was to do a second water color. Also accompanying them was a color photographer, Nicholas Robbins, to take pictures of the President from which Mrs. Shoumatoff could complete the portrait. Before his death several years ago, Robbins told me his recollections of his assignment. Some of these went unpublished in my earlier book. While these recollections are of little importance, they are vivid. Mrs. Roosevelt now being beyond injury, there is no reason not to refer to the original draft of that manuscript:

Dusk was approaching on Monday, April 9, when a dark Cadillac convertible pulled into a gasoline station in a tiny settlement a few miles from Warm Springs. The owner of the car, Elizabeth Shoumatoff, was at the wheel. Beside her was an acquaintance of some years' standing, Lucy (Mrs. Winthrop) Rutherfurd, a woman in her early fifties with striking blond hair and distinguished beauty of face. . . . In the back seat of the car sat a thin man in his late fifties, with sleepy gray eyes under great tufts of eyebrow and a bald dome. . . . This was Nicholas Robbins. . . .

A young attendant at the gas station, wiping the windows of the Cadillac, had just experienced a unique excitement and he couldn't keep from telling it:

"You should have been here five minutes ago. President Roosevelt just went down the road."

He shouldn't have said it. The President, as far as the plain folk of America knew, was supposed to be in Washington. . . . It was easy to get powerful newspaper editors to clam up in the interest of a wartime leader's safety. But gas station attendants are a less manageable breed.

"Which way did he go?" Madame Shoumatoff asked eagerly. Who wouldn't have asked?

"Down that way," the attendant said.

A few hundred yards down the highway, Madame Shoumatoff slowed her car as she recognized certain landmarks where she had been told her party was to be met. Sure enough, parked there at a crossroad were two closed black Lincolns. She stopped. The two women got out of the car. In the back seat of one of the Lincolns sat Franklin D. Roosevelt. They talked gaily for a minute and then the two women entered his car. The President was sitting to the left, Madame Shoumatoff settled herself on the right, Mrs. Rutherfurd sat between them.

Robbins took the wheel of the Cadillac. A Secret Service man told Robbins to pull away immediately behind the President's car; the Secret Service car would follow in the rear. The three-car procession made a U-turn and headed for the Little White House. . . .

The morning after they arrived at the Little White House, Robbins made three photographs of the President, Mrs. Rutherfurd sitting nearby. To relax his subject, Robbins, a Russian by birth, engaged the President with questions about Yalta, explaining that he had gone to high school there. F.D.R. said that Yalta looked bad, very bad, that the Germans had ruined it. Robbins, bitter over being driven from his homeland by the Revolution of 1917, remarked, "Are you sure it was the Germans? Maybe the ruins were still there from the Bolsheviks." F.D.R. looked at him queerly and said nothing.

When they were done, Roosevelt asked if Robbins would take a picture of Mrs. Rutherfurd. The photographer engaged her in conversation until her blue-gray eyes were lit by a certain quality of reserved warmth he had come to admire.

A romantic as well as an artist, Robbins says, "I have seen two smiles like that in my life. One was on Leonardo da Vinci's 'Mona Lisa'; the other was Mrs. Rutherfurd's."

Later that day, Tuesday, April 10, Roosevelt accepted an invitation by the tiny town's leading local dignitary, Mayor Frank Allcorn, a transplanted New Yorker, and Ruth Stevens, manager of the Warm Springs hotel, to attend an old-fashioned Georgia barbecue on Thursday afternoon, Miss Stevens having announced that she had "just bought a goddamned pig that weighs three hundred pounds."

On Wednesday, the President rode with his bevy of lady guests—Mrs. Rutherfurd and the Misses Delano and Suckley—through the mountains and to a picnic at Dowdell's Knob.

Thursday morning was for sleeping late; because of bad weather in Washington, a courier plane with the presidential mail was delayed. A few minutes before noon, Bill Hassett arrived with a mail pouch stuffed with papers. With him was Dewey Long, White House Transportation Officer. As Hassett sorted mail, Long sat with the President in the sunny living room to review travel plans for the President's forthcoming trip to San Francisco for the official founding of the United Nations. This was the first time in Long's memory that Roosevelt seemed indifferent about a railroad routing, setting speed above a scenic adventure.

Hassett handed Roosevelt a letter for his signature prepared by the State Department. Perusing it, F.D.R. remarked, "A typical State Department letter. It says nothing at all." Next, a bill just passed by Congress increasing the borrowing power of the Commodity Credit Corporation. Boyishly Roosevelt remarked to the ladies, who had joined him in the room, "Here's where I make a law."

Mrs. Shoumatoff arrived with clatter, carrying an easel, setting it up near the windows in the dining area of the room. She placed his Navy cape on the President's shoulders, meticulously arranging its folds, then stepped behind her easel.

As the President continued to read papers before him, the room grew quiet. His right profile was lit by the sun from the long windows. Mrs. Rutherfurd sat by the windows, Miss Suckley across the room on a couch, crocheting. Miss Delano stepped quietly about, filling vases with flowers she and Miss Suckley had picked that morning.

At one o'clock the President, glancing at his watch, said to the artist, "We've got just fifteen minutes more."

These have been quoted, erroneously, as the President's last words, perhaps because they bore an irony of truth.

"I noticed," the artist was later to say, "as his face would turn partly away from me, that he looked younger than he had on the previous day. As I studied him he looked like a portrait done of him several years ago by Salisbury. . . . He looked strangely well."

The President slid a cigarette into his holder and lit it. Mrs. Shoumatoff noticed that he raised his left hand to his temple and pressed. He slid the hand around his forehead, squeezing. Then his hand flopped gracelessly down, as though fumbling for the arm of his chair.

Miss Suckley's attention was caught by the gesture. She thought he was groping for a dropped cigarette, and asked, "Did you drop something?"

The President pressed the palm of his left hand behind his neck. His head was leaning forward. His eyes were closed. He said very quietly: "I have a terrific headache."

Then his body sagged deeply into the chair.

The time was one-fifteen. At that moment, the consciousness of Franklin Delano Roosevelt came to an end.[6]

Mrs. Shoumatoff was at the wheel of her Cadillac, Mrs. Rutherfurd beside her. Both were silent, yet clearly upset. The passenger in the back, Nicholas Robbins, puzzled by their hasty departure, sensed that he should ask no questions. Mrs. Rutherfurd asked to take the wheel. Slowing the car near a crossroad, she said, "Isn't this the place where he came to meet us the other night?" Mrs. Shoumatoff nodded. Then they exchanged places at the wheel again and drove on.

For three hours the women sat almost wordless. At last Mrs. Rutherfurd asked if it would be all right if she turned on the radio. Mrs. Shoumatoff said, "Go right ahead."

Music floated softly from the loudspeaker, but it seemed to ease no taut nerves. Abruptly the music stopped. An excited announcer said, "We interrupt this program to bring you a special bulletin. . . ."

When the message was given, Mrs. Rutherfurd gasped and covered her eyes.[7]

Appendixes

Appendix I
Letter from Herbert Hoover to F.D.R.

THE WHITE HOUSE
WASHINGTON

Feb. 18, 1933

My dear Mr President-Elect:

A most critical situation has arisen in the country of which I feel it is my duty to advise you confidentially. I am therefore taking this course of writing you myself and sending it to you through the Secret Service for your hand direct as obviously its misplacement would only feed the fire and increase the dangers.

The major difficulty is the state of public mind—for there is a steadily degenerating confidence in the future which has reached the height of general alarm. I am convinced that a very early statement by you upon two or three policies of your admistration [sic] would serve greatly to restore confidence and cause a resumption of the march of recovery.

The large part which fear and apprehension play in the situation can be well demonstrated by repeated experience in the past few years and the tremendous lift which has come at times by the removal of fear can be easily demonstrated.

One of the major underlying elements in the broad problem of recovery is the re-expansion of credit so critically and abruptly deflated by the shocks from Europe during the last half of 1931. The visible results were public fear hoarding, bank failures, withdrawl [sic] of gold flight of capital falling prices increased unemployment etc. Early in 1932 we created the agencies which have steadily expanded available credit ever since that time and continue to expand it today. But confidence must run

THE WHITE HOUSE
WASHINGTON

Feb. 18. 1933

My dear Mr President-Elect:

A most critical situation has arisen in the country of which I feel it is my duty to advise you confidentially. I am therefore taking this course of writing you myself and sending it to you through the Secret Service for your hand direct as obviously its misplacement would only feed the fire and increase the danger.

The major difficulty is the state of public mind — for there is a steadily degenerating confidence in the future which has reached the height of general alarm. I am convinced that a very early statement by you upon two or three policies of your administration would serve greatly to restore confidence and cause a resumption of the march of recovery

Opening page of President Hoover's ten-page letter to me, delivered by hand as I attended the Inner Circle dinner in New York.

parallel with expanding credit and the the instances where confidence
has been injured run precisely with the lagging or halting of recovery.
There are of course other factors but I am only illustrating certain high
lights.

Within the last twelve months we have had two profound examples of
the effect of restoration of confidence. Immedeatly [sic] after the passage
of the measures for credit expansion ect [act?] early in 1932 there was a
prompt response in public confidence with expression in rising prices employment decrease in bank failures hoarding etc even before the actual
agencies were in action. This continued until it was interrupted by the
aggregate of actions starting in the House of Representatives last spring
again spread fear and practical panic across the country. This interruption brought back all the disasterous [sic] phenomena that I have
mentioned but near the end of the session when it became clear to the
country that the revenue bill would be passed that inflation of the
currency and bonus were defeated that the government credit would be
maintained that the gold standard would be held etc. Promptly for a
second time confidence returned and ran parallel with the expansion and
reconstruction measures. The country resumed the march of recovery.
At once there was a rise in farm, commodity, and security prices production, industry employment. There was a practical cessation of bank
failures hoarding and gold returned from abroad. This continued during
the summer and fall when again there began another era of interruptions
to public confidence which have finally culminated in the present state of
alarm and has transformed an upward movement into a distinct downward movement.

The facts about this last interruption are simple and they are pertinent
to the action needed. With the election there came the national and inevitable hesitation all along the economic line pending the demonstration
of the policies of the new adminstration. But a number of very discouraging things have happened on the top of this natural hesitation.
The break down in balancing the budget by the House of Representatives
[sic]; the proposals for inflation of the currency and the wide spread
discussion of it; the publication of R.F.C. loans and the bank runs
hoarding and bank failures from this cause; increase in unemployment
due to imports from depreciated currency countries; failure of the Congress to enact banking, bankrupcy [sic] and other vital legislation; unwillingness of the Congress to face reduction in expenditure; proposals to
abrogate constitutional responsibility by the Congress with all the chatter
about dictatorship and other discouraging effects upon the public mind.
They have now cumulated to a state of alarm which is rapidly reaching
the dimensions of a crisis. Hoarding has risen to a new high level the

bank structure is weakend [sic] as witness Detroit and increased failures in other localities, there are evidences of flight of capital and foreign withdrawls [sic] of gold. In other words we are confronted with precisely the same phenomena we experienced late in 1931 and again in the spring of 1932. The whole has its final expression in the increase of unemployment suffering and general alarm.

During all this time the means of credit expansion has been in [sic] available but neither borrowers or [sic] lenders are willing to act in the initiation of business. While the financial agencies of the government can do much to stem the tide and to localize fires and while there are institutions and situations that must be liquidated these things can only be successfully attained in an atmosphere of general confidence. Otherwise the fire will spread.

I therefore return to my suggestion at the beginning as to the desirability of clarifying the public mind on certain essentials which will give renewed confidence. It is obvious that as you will shortly be in position to make whatever policies you wish effective you are the only one who can give these assurances. Both the nature of the cause of public alarm and experience give such an action the prospect of success in turning the tide. I do not refer to action on all the causes of alarm but it would steady the country greatly if there could be prompt assurance that there will be no tampering or inflation of the currency; that the budget will be unquestionably balanced even if further taxation is necessary; that the government credit will be maintained by refusal to exaust [sic] it in issue of securities. The course you have adopted in inquiring into the problems of world stabilization are already known and helpful. It would be of further help if the leaders were advised to cease publication of R.F.C. business.

I am taking the liberty of addressing you because both of my anxiety over the situation and my confidence from four years of experience that such tides as are now running can be moderated and the processes of regeneration which are always running can be released.

Incidentally I will welcome the announcement of the new Secretary of the Treasury as that would enable us to direct activities to one point of action and communication with your good self.

I wish again to express my satisfaction at your escape and to wish you good health.

Yours sincerely
Herbert Hoover

President-Elect
   Franklin Roosvelt

Appendix II

PHYSICAL ACCOMPLISHMENT ON WPA PROJECTS

Through October 1, 1937

UNITED STATES SUMMARY

CONSTRUCTION ACTIVITIES

		Number or Amount		
Type	Unit of Measurement	New Construction	Repairs and Improvements	Additions
Public Buildings—Total	Number	11,106	30,542	1,172
Schools and other educational buildings	Number	1,634	16,421	574
Gymnasiums, stadiums, park, and other recreational buildings	Number	3,722	2,033	203
Hospitals and other institutional buildings	Number	262	2,270	58
Courthouses, offices, and other administrative buildings	Number	537	2,263	106
Other public buildings (fire houses, hangars, storage structures, etc.)	Number	4,951	7,555	231
Demolition of Buildings	Number	xxxx	6,141	xxxx

| | | Number or Amount | |
Type	Unit of Measurement	New Construction	Repairs and Improvements
Highways, Roads, Streets, and Related Facilities			
Highways, roads, and streets—			
Total	Miles	43,870	146,901
Rural primary roads	Miles	6,961	15,337
Rural secondary roads	Miles	29,742	115,703
Urban	Miles	6,319	14,848
Other (parks, cemeteries, etc.)	Miles	848	1,013
Bridges	Number	19,272	13,166
	Length in feet	612,521	520,665
Culverts	Number	183,084	30,061
	Length in feet	4,902,451	774,031
Sidewalks and paths	Miles	4,581	3,003
Curbs	Length in miles	3,938	917
Roadside landscaping	Miles	xxxx	38,685
Street signs	Linear ft. line painted	12,495,773	xxxx
	No. signs made	769,924	xxxx
	No. signs erected	320,352	xxxx
Airports and Airway Equipment (Excl. Buildings)			
Landing fields	Number	105	109
	Acres	14,348	15,070
Runways	Length in feet	852,834	244,676
Air markers	Number	8,357	xxxx
Recreational Facilities (Excl. Buildings)			
Athletic fields	Number	1,335	1,234
	Acres	7,213	9,702
Parks	Number	770	2,866
	Acres	22,072	158,193
Playgrounds	Number	1,107	3,583
Swimming and wading pools ..	Number	1,883	173
Golf courses	Number	103	167
Tennis courts	Number	3,076	1,094
Water Supply, Sanitation and Drainage Systems			
Water mains, aqueducts, or distribution lines	Miles	3,865	1,382
	No. of consumer connections	107,634	154,152
Storage tanks, reservoirs, and cisterns	Number	1,150	298
	Gals. capacity	1,788,052,000	2,402,878,100
Storage dams	Number	3,330	283
Wells	Number	1,526	1,271
Treatment plants (excl. cesspools and septic tanks)			
Sewage	Number	228	131
Water	Number	51	55
Garbage incinerators	Number	24	22

Type	Unit of Measurement	New Construction	Repairs and Improvements
		Number or Amount	
Pumping stations	Number	229	86
Storm and sanitary sewers	Miles	5,692	1,624
	No. of service connections	114,725	19,904
Mine sealing	No. of mines	7,523	xxxx
	No. of openings	66,750	xxxx
Sanitary toilets	Number	779,587	10,943
Mosquito control	Linear ft. of ditch	26,820,125	17,504,776
	Acres drained	835,950	455,038
	Gals. of spray used	1,184,819	xxxx
Drainage (other than roadside and mosquito eradication) ..	Acres drained	807,452	5,335,587
Flood and Erosion Control— Navigation Aids—Irrigation			
Dredging (other than channels)	Cu. yds. of material dredged	9,656,574	xxxx
Dams (other than storage or power)	Number	15,855	145
Riprap (other than river bank)	Sq. yds. surfaced	3,376,950	361,505
Retaining walls and revetments	Number	9,347	1,029
	Linear feet	1,985,873	166,614
Levees and embankments	Linear feet	815,610	1,532,956
	Cu. Yds. placed	9,164,621	6,903,296
Irrigation	Acres	193,918	1,283,314
	Miles of flume or canal	230	2,453
Miscellaneous			
Police and fire alarm signals ..	No. of boxes and signals	23,570	xxxx
	Linear ft. of line strung	3,063,702	xxxx
Lighting airports, parking lots, athletic fields, etc.	No. of places lighted	245	20
	Acres lighted	4,690	2,065
Fish hatcheries	Number	134	74
	Annual fingerling capacity	308,154,800	168,663,000

OTHER THAN CONSTRUCTION ACTIVITIES

Type	Unit of Measurement	Number or Amount
Conservation Activities (Not Elsewhere Classified)		
Reforestation	Acres	21,131
	No. of trees planted	9,789,184
Firebreaks	Miles	1,196
Fire and forest trails	Miles	2,481
Plant and tree nurseries	No. of nurseries	115
	No. of plants or trees planted ...	9,485,158

Type	Unit of Measurement	Number or Amount
Bird and game sanctuaries	No. of sanctuaries established ...	825
Noxious plant eradication	Acres	3,601,177
Spray treatments, disease, and insect pest eradication (except mosquito control).	Acres sprayed	639,159
	Gallons of spray used	11,256,776
	Tons of poisoned food used	6,097

Work in Libraries

New branch libraries	No. established	2,305
New traveling libraries	No. established	5,824
Cataloging for existing libraries ..	No. of volumes cataloged	18,272,529
Renovation of books	Number	29,855,417
Sewing Rooms	No. of articles made	108,427,938
Canning and Preserving	Net pounds	24,026,581
School Lunches Served	Number	128,057,654

Medical, Dental and Nursing Assistance

Medical and dental clinics conducted	No. of clinics	1,654
	No. of persons examined	1,355,373
	No. of persons treated	601,543
Nursing visits	No. of home visits made	2,093,182
Nursing aid at immunizations	No. of immunizations	550,749

Art

Art classes	Average monthly attendance	55,231
Drawings, easel paintings, murals and sculptured works	Number	54,244
Etchings, lithographs, woodblocks, etc.	No. of originals	3,519
	No. of prints	21,341

Music

Music classes	Average monthly attendance	140,321
Musical performances	Average number per month	4,549
	Average monthly attendance	3,107,345

Theater

Theatrical productions	Number	1,501
Theatrical performances	Average number per month	2,833
	Average monthly attendance	1,043,478
Writing	No. of books and pamphlets written	116
	No. of copies distributed	401,928
Local, State and National Planning and Research Surveys	Number	1,620
Engineering Surveys	Square miles of mapping survey .	75,597
	Miles of line survey	60,191
	No. of permanent markers set ...	57,883
Braille	No. of Braille pages transcribed .	1,146,913
	No. of Braille maps made	40,635
Housekeeping Aides	No. of visits made	3,473,472
	No. of families aided	517,945
Museum Activities	No. of articles constructed or renovated	3,269,496

		Number or Amount
Type	*Unit of Measurement*	
Education (Month of October 1937)		
—*Total*	No. of classes	100,145
	No. of enrollees	1,144,689
Literacy	No. of classes	17,195
	No. of enrollees	192,481
Vocational	No. of classes	10,596
	No. of enrollees	159,430
Nursery schools	No. of classes	1,481
	No. of enrollees	40,243
Other	No. of classes	70,873
	No. of enrollees	852,680
Recreation		
Community centers operated	Number	9,068
Community centers assisted	Number	6,220

Appendix III

"A History of the United States"
Begun by F.D.R. Aboard Larooco, February 1924

. . . for lack of general record.* It is therefore more correct to say that the Columbus discovery was the first which became a part of the world's knowledge.

Many other factors contribute to the thought that the period itself was the discoverer of America and Columbus the agent of his time. Medieval history, the "feudal age" was coming to a close; modern history—the revival of learning—was arriving. To understand the next century of further discoveries it is needful to examine the background.

Europe in the year 1000 was highly primitive. Peoples were not far past the tribal state. Horrible barbarities were still the rule. Learning was looked down on by the war lords, unknown to the populace, indulged in only by a minority of the priesthood. From this chaos came the feudal system, a beginning of the modern permanent organization of society. With it arose a defining of land ownership, a clear division of humanity into classes, a lessening of barbarous and inhuman practices, an institution of a code of conduct, and a distinct surge of religious faith.

This last found voice in the epoch of the Crusades. It is little realized that the spiritual enthusiasm which launched seven major expeditions and a dozen minor efforts against the Mohammedan from 1096 to 1270 accomplished in the end more for civilization and democracy than any previous event. Knighthood and overlordship took on responsibilities to others. Feudal barons were taught to look beyond their own castle

* Page one of handwritten manuscript is lost.

domains, and to work with other individuals to a common end. With travel came the desire for the products of other lands and organized trade commenced by land and sea throughout Europe. From this quickening of intercourse and growth of travel came however the most important result, for the Crusades required money, and equipment, and the interchange of goods and supplies. It was natural that at once the growth of villages into towns and cities became marked. Merchants became a class, skilled artisans developed the dignity of trades, money lenders who financed the needs of the feudal lords grew into bankers. Thus a middle class grew up, different from the serfs upon the land, different from the fighting men-at-arms, and with their acquisition of money and property came the demand for certain rights of government. By the end of the fourteenth century the burghers of the cities of Europe were to be reckoned with as a factor in wealth, in learning and even in battle.

One other element had entered into the political life of the times. The great Ecclesiastics wielded powers more secular than priestly. Bishops made and unmade kings, led armies, owned vast tracts of land and exercised wholly feudal relations to their countless tenants. The Church became a political factor.

Down at the bottom of the heap of humanity, but comprising by far the greater part of the whole, lay the serfs—slaves to their barons or bishops—servants to their burghers. Actually there was far less freedom as we know it for the great mass of the European population than their ancestors had enjoyed under the tribal conditions which prevailed in the days of Roman supremacy. In all Europe, even in England, the land was wholly owned by the greater and the lesser nobles and the dignitaries of the Church. A mere handful of humanity, certainly less than one in a hundred, owned and controlled the very lives and fortunes of the other ninety-nine.

All through the eleventh, twelfth, thirteenth and fourteenth centuries Europe was an armed camp. When the overlords were not making a mad dash for the Holy Land they were waging hot war against their neighbors. Ruling houses rose and fell. Kingdoms and duchies were created and fell apart. Brothers fought brothers, sons overthrew their fathers, rival Popes excommunicated one another, whole fair provinces were bartered away, and to us moderns these years seem a mad kaleidoscopic scramble for power and plunder. The rule was that the man went under who did not attack and crush his neighbor first.

Yet through these centuries up to the year 1400 certain events of truly great significance to the future of civilization took place. Commerce produced better roads on land and better ships at sea. The Crusades gave some knowledge of the East and an interest in geography. Independent communities in which at least some fair share of the inhabitants had a voice in the government came with the growth of towns. In England the bill of rights called Magna Charta was granted. The beginnings of the Swiss Confederacy were formed, and it is safe to say that by the early part of the 15th Century a larger number of people than ever before were talking of what we would call the rudiments of science and art and letters and government. At best this number was but a handful, yet it gave promise of the great strides to come.

In 1450 came the discovery of printing; in 1453 occurred the fall of Constantinople resulting in the search for a new way to the East, and a dispersal of the Eastern scholars through Europe carrying with them the classics, and a new enthusiasm for the sciences. Beginning in 1461 Louis XI of France put down the power of the great feudal lords and established his absolute monarchy. In all countries a growing protest over the abuses of the churchly power; in Spain the conquest of Granada and in Portugal the important discoveries of the Madeira, Cape Verde and Azore Islands, and the West Coast of Africa under the patronage of Henry the Navigator. Universities had increased in number and patronage.

In short, by the year 1492 the imagination of thousands in Europe was on fire. Not the populace by any means, but at least more than a handful of people were thinking in larger terms than ever before. Scholars were interchanging theories and facts by means of printed books, and these very books were being read by mere laymen. So too the commercial needs of times demanded new worlds to conquer. The short route to the East was shut off by the Turk, yet the story of what Marco Polo had found in the Far East was still remembered. New profits were dreamed of by the merchants, new adventures by the knights and sailors, new kingdoms by the rulers and princes.

This was the atmosphere in which Columbus grew to manhood, and that is why it has been said that America was discovered by the era. It is perhaps not stretching the point to assert that definite knowledge of America to the European world was bound to come at the end of the 15th Century.

EXPLORATION

For nearly a century and a quarter colonization of America held back. The time was not yet ripe. By colonization we mean an emigration from the older world by men and women and children who, leaving their homes, intend to establish new homes and with their descendants live and die in the new land. Thousands of Europeans came to the New World from 1492 to 1607, but they came for exploration, for conquest, for gold, for fur, for fish—all, except a handful, intending to return richer in pocket or in knowledge or in power to their Old World homes.

We are often inclined to think that aside from the Spaniards in Panama and Peru and Mexico only a very few explorers visited the other parts of North and South America. We have read for instance of the voyages of the Cabots, of Vespucius, of Balboa, of Cortez and Pizarro, of Jacques Cartier, of deSoto and Ponce de Leon, of Coronado and Frobisher, Landonnière and Grenville. Our school histories tell of these and a dozen more, and historical research has revealed the names of several score others who led expeditions to the new land. Are we then to assume that in all that century a few hundred ships only crossed the Atlantic to North America? Such is the impression given, yet it is wholly false. What a ridiculous assumption to teach that Henry Hudson in 1609 was the first to enter the river that bears his name; or that Chesapeake Bay was first seen by the Virginia colonists in 1607; or that the Pilgrims were the first to see Cape Cod in 1620.

First of all Spain obtained the honor of capitalizing the discoveries. During the whole of the 16th Century, indeed, no other nation seriously undertook to develop the new world. English mariners grew rich indeed in the occupation of robbing the Spanish galleons, but these galleons were heavy laden with treasure because of the enterprise and imagination of the subjects of His Most Catholic Majesty. The conquest of Mexico, and of Peru, the founding of great cities in Central and South America, the building of cathedrals, the establishment of universities, the whole creation of a new civilization in the Spanish parts of America—all had been undertaken, had reached their zenith and had commenced to decline before ever Jamestown or Plymouth were conceived. It was a false glory, that of Spain. For mostly men came, leaving behind them their mothers and sisters and wives. So it was that a hybrid race grew up, part cavalier, part Indian, later on in part negro. All was staked on the great adventure. Glorious riches to be gained for little labor, all in a land whose fabled wealth was magnified a thousand times beyond reality. Nothing in the method of these Spanish cavaliers made for a sound and permanent colonization. Their whole object from King to soldier was exploitation—to get as much out of it in as short a time as possible.

Everything from Mexico and Florida southward to Magellan's Straits, was under the influence of the Spanish and the Portuguese, and their ships in vast numbers plied the waters on both the Atlantic and Pacific coasts. It would be unwarranted to assume that their mariners, well versed by now in the arts of navigation, were never visitors to the more northern coasts of what are today the United States and Canada. When we consider that the records of only a very small percentage of the Spanish voyages to the southward have survived to this day, it is not to be wondered at that we know practically nothing of their navigators who saw and visited the shores of the Carolinas, the Virginias and New England.

From the other approach came many vessels also. As early as 1504 French fishermen were on the Grand Banks, and soon hundreds of vessels from France and Northern Europe were drying their nets on Newfoundland and Nova Scotia. Surely some of them, seeking new grounds, became familiar with our whole Atlantic coast line. Other shipmasters seeking furs or the ever hoped for Northwest Passage to the Indies skirted our shores.

Thus it was that before even the English colonies were settled scores, probably hundreds of vessels, had visited the region. It is easy to understand why we have such scanty records of these voyages: Everything militated against their recording. First of all there was the need of secrecy. To publish the news of a new harbor, or of a place to fish, or of a friendly tribe of Indians ready to sell furs meant competition the following year; furthermore it might mean armed attack by other nations. If some French fishermen established a base in some safe harbor from which to conduct their operations, a printed recital of their doings might bring down on them English or Spanish marauders. So it was that there came to be a premium on secrecy, much to the loss of history.

The other cause of the paucity of records is the lack of learning of the time. Shipmasters could navigate by rule of thumb but it did not follow that they could read or write or draw maps, and it was an exceptional case when any record of a voyage was set down on paper at all. Books, even a hundred years after Gutenberg, were an event; publication only of facts of apparent grave importance to the world was undertaken. Newspapers were non-existent; their predecessor handbills were read and used to light the fire. The only wonder is that we have any surviving records of the voyages of those early days. All we can surely say is that thousands saw and knew our shores, but none remained.

Bibliography and Sources

Once again I am indebted, as for an earlier book, to the devoted and knowledgeable staff of the Franklin D. Roosevelt Library at Hyde Park, New York. Research for this volume spanned the tenure of three directors: Elizabeth Drewry, James E. O'Neill, and J. C. James, all of whom extended co-operation and utmost courtesy. A previous director, Herman Kahn, also was most generous in sharing his knowledge and wisdom concerning the subject material of this book. In particular, I again thank two staff members of the F.D.R. Library to whom no request for assistance in tracking down an elusive fact is ever too bothersome to engage their interest. They are Jerome V. Deyo, archivist, and Joseph W. Marshall, librarian.

References to the Franklin D. Roosevelt Library in the chapter notes are indicated by the abbreviation FDRL.

A long list of generous people contributed their firsthand recollections of F.D.R. in direct interview. They are identified in the text and the chapter notes. One of these good people, Mrs. Mabel Irwin, a neighbor of the President at Warm Springs, died before the manuscript was completed. My gratitude goes to them all.

Certain primary sources are indicated by codes as follows:

PPF   President's Personal File, FDRL, followed by file number.

PSF   President's Secretary's File, FDRL, followed by file number.

OF   Official File, FDRL, followed by file number.

Personal Letters   These indicate the volume number of *F.D.R., His Per-*
I, II, III, and IV   *sonal Letters,* edited by Elliott Roosevelt, New York:
                     Duell, Sloan & Pearce. In order, they are subtitled
                     Early Years (1947); *1905–1928* (1948); *1928–
                     1945,* 2 vols. (1950).
PPA   *Public Papers and Addresses of Franklin D. Roose-
                     velt,* Samuel I. Rosenman, ed., 1928–36, 5 vols., New
                     York: Random House (1938); 1937–40, 4 vols.,
                     New York: Macmillan Co. (1941); 1941–45, 4 vols.,
                     New York: Harper & Bros. (1950). The code PPA
                     is accompanied in each reference by the year e.g. PPA
                     1933, PPA 1939, etc.

Certain multivolume memoirs, diaries, and histories are listed with
Roman numerals to identify volumes. They are:

The Secret Diary of Harold L. Ickes, New York: Simon & Schuster.
Cited as Ickes I: *The First Thousand Days: 1933–36* (1953); Ickes II:
The Inside Struggle: 1936–39 (1954); Ickes III: *The Lowering Clouds:
1939–41* (1954).

Raymond Moley, *After Seven Years,* New York: Harper & Bros.
(1939), cited as Moley I. *The First New Deal,* New York: Harcourt,
Brace & World, Inc. (1966), cited as Moley II.

Eleanor Roosevelt, *This Is My Story,* Dolphin Books edition, Garden
City, N.Y.: Doubleday & Co., Inc. (1961), cited as ER I. *This I
Remember,* Dolphin Books edition (1961), cited as ER II.

Arthur M. Schlesinger, Jr., *The Age of Roosevelt* (3 vols.), Boston:
Houghton Mifflin Co. *The Crisis of the Old Order: 1919–1933* (1957),
cited as Schlesinger I. *The Coming of the New Deal* (1958), cited as
Schlesinger II. *The Politics of Upheaval* (1960), cited as Schlesinger III.

Other books are identified in full only in the first instance each is cited
in a chapter. Subsequent reference in that chapter to the same book cite
only the surname of the author.

FOOTNOTES

Part I: President-Elect

1. Rexford G. Tugwell, "Roosevelt and Hoover," *Antioch Review,* Winter 1953–54.

2. F.D.R. letter to Donald R. Richberg, Dec. 28, 1934, Personal Letters III, 442.

3. The ideas of the "personalized presidency" and of "legislating directly for people" drawn from a series of invaluable conversations with Herman Kahn, former
director of FDRL.

4. Moley I, 139–40.

5. PPF 820.

6. William Starr Myers and Walter H. Newton, *The Hoover Administration,* Charles Scribner's Sons (1936), 341.

7. PPF 820.

8. PPF 820.

9. PPF 53.

10. Moley II, 128–29.

11. Frank A. Vanderlip, formerly president of the National City Bank of New York, in an article, "What About Banks?" in *The Saturday Evening Post,* Nov. 5, 1932, pp. 3–4.

12. Schlesinger I, 474.

13. Moley II, 130–31.

14. Caroline Bird, *The Invisible Scar,* Pocket Books edition (1967), 86.

15. William Manchester, "The Great Bank Holiday," *Holiday,* Feb. 1960. Caroline Bird, "The Day the Money Stopped," *Look,* March 12, 1963.

16. Myers and Newton, 343.

17. From a daily syndicated article by Coolidge as quoted in *Home Book of Quotations,* 10th edition, Burton Stevenson, ed., Dodd, Mead & Co. (1967).

18. Arthur M. Schlesinger, Jr., "The First Hundred Days of the New Deal." In *The Aspirin Age: 1919–1941,* Isabel Leighton, ed., Simon & Schuster (1949), 283–84.

19. PPF 70.

20. Schlesinger II, 5.

21. PPF 745.

22. Moley I, 144–45, 148, 152. Proclamation No. 2039, March 6, 1933, PPA 1933, p. 25.

23. Moley I, 146, 148.

24. *The Memoirs of Herbert Hoover: 1929–41,* Macmillan Co. (1952), 212. Schlesinger I, 5.

25. Anne O'Hare McCormick, "Roosevelt's View of the Big Job," New York *Times* Magazine, Sept. 11, 1932.

26. Moley I, 144–46; James Roosevelt with Sidney Shalett, *Affectionately, F.D.R.,* Harcourt, Brace & Co. (1959), 251–52; Grace Tully, *F.D.R. My Boss,* Charles Scribner's Sons (1949), 57, 60–65.

Background Memorandum to Part 1

1. Interview with Anna Roosevelt Halsted.

2. Frank Freidel, *Franklin D. Roosevelt;* Vol. I, *The Apprenticeship,* Little, Brown (1952), 16–24.

3. Mrs. James Roosevelt with Isabel Leighton and Gabrielle Forbush, *My Boy Franklin,* Ray Long & Richard R. Smith, Inc. (1933), 12–13. F.D.R. letter to James Roosevelt, June 7, 1890, Personal Letters I, 16.

4. James Roosevelt, *Affectionately, F.D.R.,* 17. John Gunther, *Roosevelt in Retrospect,* Harper & Bros. (1950), 161.

5. Rita Halle Kleeman, *Gracious Lady,* D. Appleton-Century Co. (1935), 144, 154, 188. Mrs. James Roosevelt, 19, 33.

6. Personal Letters I, 6. Kleeman, 172–73. ER I, 83.

7. Freidel, 30–31, 33. Personal Letters I, 13. Kleeman, 160–61, 183, 193.

8. Freidel, 48. Mrs. James Roosevelt, 44–46. Personal Letters I, 205.

9. Personal Letters I, 172–73, 249, 362, 378.

10. Moley I, 138–41. Rudolph Marx, M.D., *The Health of the Presidents,* G. P. Putnam's Sons (1960), 364–65. Michael F. Reilly with William J. Slocum, *Reilly of the White House,* Simon & Schuster (1947), 48–52.

11. Moley II, 115.

12. Ernst is quoted by Robert E. Sherwood in *Roosevelt and Hopkins,* Harper & Bros. (1948), 8. Funeral instructions, Bernard Asbell, *When F.D.R. Died,* Holt, Rinehart & Winston (1961), 197–99.

Part II: My Friends . . .

1. New York *Sun,* March 4, 1933.

2. William Manchester, "The Great Bank Holiday," *Holiday,* Feb. 1960. Caroline Bird, "The Day the Money Stopped," *Look,* March 12, 1963. ER II, 86–87.

3. Moley I, 148–49. PPA 1933, 24–28. The Bankers' Special anecdote was related by F.D.R. to the European author Emil Ludwig, as quoted in his biography, *Roosevelt: A Study in Fortune and Power,* Viking Press (1938), 161. Glass, Wheeler, and Johnson quotes, William E. Leuchtenburg, *Franklin D. Roosevelt and the New Deal: 1932–40,* Harper & Row (1963), 22.

4. Manchester, op. cit. Schlesinger II, 6. Bird, op. cit. Moley I, 152. Moley II, 164, 188.

5. Moley I, 155. Moley II, 171, 178. Schlesinger II, 7.

6. Grace Tully, *F.D.R. My Boss,* Charles Scribner's Sons (1949), 88–89. New York *Times,* March 19, 1933. *Memoirs of Herbert Hoover: 1920–1933,* Macmillan Co. (1952), 199. Presidential use of telephones, Charles Hurd, *When the New Deal Was Young and Gay,* Hawthorn Books (1965), 117; *Telephone News,* Southern New England Telephone Co., Oct. 1967; John Gunther, *Roosevelt in Retrospect,* Harper & Bros. (1950), 125.

7. Samuel I. Rosenman, *Working with Roosevelt,* Harper & Bros. (1952), 93. Hurd, 119. Tully, 92–93. Michael F. Reilly, *Reilly of the White House,* Simon & Schuster (1947), 76.

8. Alfred B. Rollins, Jr., *Roosevelt and Howe,* Alfred A. Knopf (1962), 21. Text of Fireside Chat, PPA 1933, 61–65. Tully, 66. James Roosevelt, *Affectionately, F.D.R.,* Harcourt, Brace & Co. (1959), 292. *Roosevelt and Frankfurter: Their Correspondence, 1928–1945,* Max Freedman, ed., Little, Brown (1967), 130.

9. PPA 1936, 391–92, a detailed comment by F.D.R. on preparation of his speeches. Moley II, 96–124. (This is Moley's version of the preparation of the first inaugural address, in which he was an intimate participant. It contradicts in many respects an account in Rosenman, 89–91. Rosenman was not a participant in the preparation and bases his account on an examination of the manuscript at the Hyde Park Library. I accept the Moley version because it answers many questions not explained by the manuscript, including the probable derivation of the phrase, "the only thing we have to fear is fear itself"). ER II, 80–81. Moley II, 173–74, 194–95. Rosenman, 3, 94.

10. Moley II, 196–98. PPF 3795. Personal Letters III, 339.

Background Memorandum to Part II

1. Frances Perkins, *The Roosevelt I Knew,* Harper Colophon edition (1964), 43. Moley I, 388–89. Rosenman, 16. *Roosevelt and Frankfurter,* 752. Ickes I, 240. James Roosevelt, 3, 236, 315, 319. Joseph P. Lash, *Eleanor Roosevelt: A Friend's Memoir,*

Doubleday & Co. (1964), 209, 211. Interview with Anna Roosevelt Halsted. Reilly, 57.

2. Personal Letters I, 12.

3. Personal Letters I, 19.

4. Personal Letters I, 42, 43, 46, 48, 185.

5. Personal Letters I, 78, 97. Frank Freidel, *Franklin D. Roosevelt;* Vol. I, *The Apprenticeship,* Little, Brown (1952), 43–45.

6. Gunther, 22–24, 55. Moley I, 10–11. Rosenman, 54. Margaret Suckley quoted to me by a mutual friend.

7. Orrin E. Dunlap, Jr., New York *Times,* March 19, 1933.

Part III: The First Hundred Days

1. The phrase "economic and social collapse" may seem intemperate for the President's description of the national condition. In his introduction to the 1933 volume of his *Public Papers and Addresses,* pp. 5–6, F.D.R. writes: "A frank examination of the profit system in the spring of 1933 showed it to be in collapse. . . . A frank examination of the social system showed that it, too, was in collapse. . . . A vocal minority had already begun to cry out that reform should be placed on a shelf. . . . They would have been more content if Government had restricted itself at that time to saving the banks which were closing. . . . For in spite of the lessons of 1931 and 1932, they were still willing to believe that this kind of help by Government to those at the top of the financial and business structure of the country would trickle down and ultimately save all."

2. Caroline Bird, *The Invisible Scar,* Pocket Books edition (1967), 18–19, 22–25, 28. William E. Leuchtenburg, *Franklin D. Roosevelt and the New Deal: 1932–40,* Harper & Row (1963), 28.

3. New York *Times,* May 22, 1932; July 27, 1932. Bird, 42.

4. George Soule, "Are We Going to Have a Revolution?" *Harper's,* Aug. 1932. Leuchtenburg, 25, 27. New York *Times,* Jan. 21, 1931; Feb. 26, 1931.

5. Leuchtenburg, 23–23. Mary Heaton Vorse, "Rebellion in the Corn Belt: American Farmers Beat Their Plowshares into Swords," *Harper's,* Dec. 1932.

6. Avis D. Carlson, "Deflating the Schools," *Harper's,* Nov. 1933.

7. Wilson quotation recalled in F.D.R. letter to Robert W. Bingham, Sept. 29, 1931, Personal Letters III, 219. The views on Wilson's use of his "honeymoon" are reported by Rexford G. Tugwell in *The Brains Trust,* Viking Press (1968), 442–43, based on entries in Tugwell's diary. F.D.R.'s contrasting decision on management of patronage, Moley I, 127–28.

8. Ernest K. Lindley, *Half Way with Roosevelt,* Viking Press (1936), 47–48, provides one of countless firsthand testimonies of F.D.R. saying "repeatedly that his method is to try something and, if it fails, to try something else." 13th Press Conference, PPA 1933, 139. *Roosevelt and Frankfurter: Their Correspondence, 1928–1945,* Max Freedman, ed., Little, Brown (1967), 254. Rexford G. Tugwell, "The Experimental Roosevelt," *Political Quarterly* (1950), 266–67.

9. Moley II, 228. Lindley, 37–41.

10. Leuchtenburg, 61, for a description of the June 17 signing ceremony, also quotes of Essary and White. The Lippmann quote, New York *Herald Tribune,* Jan. 8, 1932.

11. The essay on election campaigns, the presidency, and the Progressives that completes this chapter is consistent with innumerable fragments of diaries and memoirs

by F.D.R.'s associates in which these topics are touched on—but they are seldom more than touched on. Among these are Moley I, 23, 60–63; Moley II, 232, 234, 246–47, 338–39; and Samuel I. Rosenman, *Working with Roosevelt,* Harper & Bros. (1952), 85–87. A fascinating report of Roosevelt's extensive and developed thinking on these topics, however, appears in Tugwell, 122–23, 160–61, 286–87, 307–9, 317, 320–21, 410–11, 419–20, 422–24, 441, 444–46, 488, 493, 500–4.

Background Memorandum to Part III

1. Emil Ludwig, *Roosevelt, A Study in Fortune and Power,* Viking Press (1938), 295. Grace Tully, *F.D.R. My Boss,* Charles Scribner's Sons (1949), 66. ER II, 75–76.
2. Frances Perkins, *The Roosevelt I Knew,* Harper Colophon edition (1964), 34. Moley II, 4–6.
3. John Gunther, *Roosevelt in Retrospect,* Harper & Bros. (1950), 119. Frank Freidel, *Franklin D. Roosevelt;* Vol. I, *The Apprenticeship,* Little, Brown (1952), 31. ER II, 125. Ludwig, 338.
4. Perkins, 97, 99, 20, 32–33. Moley I, 11. Bernard Baruch, *The Public Years,* Holt, Rinehart & Winston (1960), 258.
5. Moley II, 225. Moley I, 20–21.
6. James P. Warburg, *Hell Bent for Election,* as quoted in Ernest K. Lindley, *Half Way with Roosevelt,* Viking Press (1936), 76–77. Gunther, 64–67. Moley I, 192. Rosenman, 55.
7. Perkins, 163, 153.

Part IV: Trees, Crops, Water and Power

1. Ernest K. Lindley, *Half Way with Roosevelt,* Viking Press (1936), 138–40. William E. Leuchtenburg, *Franklin D. Roosevelt and the New Deal: 1932–40,* Harper & Row (1963), 172. F.D.R. speech, Lake Placid, N.Y., Sept. 14, 1935 (Speech File, FDRL). F.D.R. speech, Troy, N.Y., March 3, 1912 (Speech File, FDRL). Alfred B. Rollins, Jr., *Roosevelt and Howe,* Alfred A. Knopf (1962), 38–40. F.D.R. column in the Macon *Daily Telegraph,* April 18, 1925, as reproduced in *F.D.R., Columnist* (Donald Scott Carmichael, ed.), Pellegrini & Cudahy (1947), 33–35.
2. F.D.R. speech, Lenox, Mass., June 20, 1921 (Speech File, FDRL).
3. Ickes I, 5, 21. F.D.R. acceptance speech, Democratic National Convention, Chicago, July 2, 1932 (Speech File, FDRL). First Inaugural Address, PPA 1933, 13. Moley I, 172–75. Moley II, 269. 3rd Press Conference, PPA 1933, 69–71, 80–81. 7th Press Conference, PPA 1933, 95. Rollins, 403–4. Frances Perkins, *The Roosevelt I Knew,* Harper Colophon edition (1964), 177–81. James Roosevelt with Sidney Shalett, *Affectionately, F.D.R.,* Harcourt Brace & Co. (1959), 47–48.
4. PPA 1933, 109–10. Ickes I, 78–80. Letter to Owen Johnson, Sept. 29, 1937, PPF 611; memo to Daniel W. Bell, Feb. 24, 1938, OF 6-P. PPA 1934, 424–25. PPA 1936, 172–73.
5. PPA 1933, 74–79. F.D.R. statement on AAA, Oct. 25, 1935 (Speech File, FDRL).
6. Moley II, 248–53. Rexford G. Tugwell, *The Brains Trust,* Viking Press (1968),

448–53; Rexford G. Tugwell, *FDR: Architect of an Era,* Macmillan Co. (1967), 103–4. Leuchtenburg, 53, 74. 120th Press Conference, May 11, 1934, PPA 1934, 229–30. F.D.R. speech, Amarillo, Texas, July 11, 1938 (Speech File, FDRL). Transcript of conversation, Dec. 1934, between F.D.R. and Secretary of Commerce Roper, apparently on telephone, Personal Letters III, 437–40.

7. Moley II, 255. Leuchtenburg, 72–73. Schlesinger II, 62–63. PPA 1935, 178.

8. F.D.R.-Roper conversation transcript, *supra.* 66th Press Conference, Nov. 3, 1933, PPA 1933, 441–44. Leuchtenburg, 77. Lindley, 120, 132–33.

9. Moley II, 260–63. 267th Press Conference, Jan. 17, 1936, PPA 1936, 55–56. F.D.R. statement on signing the Soil Conservation and Domestic Allotment Act and accompanying Note, PPA 1936, 95–102.

10. PPA 1936, 592–93. Leuchtenburg, 137–41. Moley II, 258. PPA 1937, 81–85.

11. It would be extravagant to footnote sources showing F.D.R.'s interest in social planning. One is singled out, however, a chat F.D.R. had with newsmen upon sending a committee of three men abroad to inspect European co-operatives, particularly in the field of power. F.D.R. said he had just read "a very interesting book," *Sweden: The Middle Way,* by Marquis W. Childs, about European co-operatives. He said, "I was tremendously interested. . . . In Sweden, for example, you have a royal family and a socialist government and a capitalistic system, all working happily side by side. . . . They have these co-operative movements existing happily and successfully alongside of private industry and distribution of various kinds, both of them making money." 303rd Press Conference, June 23, 1936, PPA 1936, 226–17.

12. Moley II, 322–29. *The Memoirs of Herbert Hoover: 1920–33,* Macmillan Co. (1952), 232, 303–4. PPA 1928–32, 887–89. Leuchtenburg, 54. 339th Press Conference, Jan. 26, 1937, PPA 1937, 23–24. Harold L. Ickes, *Back to Work: The Story of PWA,* Macmillan Co. (1935), 128–31. ER II, 144. PPA 1933, 122–29. 160th Press Conference, Nov. 23, 1934, PPA 1934, 465–68.

13. Figures regarding absence of electricity on farms and, later, the spread of electricity through REA are largely taken from F.D.R.'s "Note" following Executive Order No. 7037, "The Establishment of the Rural Electrification Administration," PPA 1935, 172–75. Steinmetz reference from F.D.R. speech to the Third World Power Conference, PPA 1936, 354. Story of Corinth, Miss., PPA 1934, 459–60, and 160th Press Conference, PPA 1934, 468–72. See also Ruth Stevens, *"Hi-Ya Neighbor,"* Tupper & Love (1947), 66–67. PPA 1933, 122–29 (F.D.R. "Note" following "A Suggestion for Legislation to Create the Tennessee Valley Authority"). Leuchtenburg, 55. Ernest K. Lindley, *Half Way with Roosevelt,* Viking Press (1936), 180–81 (for comparisons of electric rates, 1933 and 1935, as well as appliance-sale data). Ickes, 127. Leuchtenburg, 157–58. Caroline Bird, *The Invisible Scar,* Pocket Books edition (1967), 174.

14. Address to the Third World Power Conference, Washington, Sept. 11, 1936, PPA 1936, 352–55. Interview by Anne O'Hare McCormick, New York *Times,* July 8, 1934.

Background Memorandum to Part IV

1. Lindley, 71. Interview with Anna Roosevelt Halsted. The incident about the Hyde Park title search is from a confidential government source. Rexford G. Tugwell, *The Brains Trust,* Viking Press (1968), 67–68, 88–89. Letter to Van Loon, PPF 2259.

2. James Roosevelt, *Affectionately, F.D.R.,* Harcourt, Brace & Co. (1959), 186–88.

Alfred B. Rollins, Jr., *Roosevelt and Howe,* Alfred A. Knopf (1962), 203. Charles Hurd, *When the New Deal Was Young and Gay,* Hawthorn Books (1965), 196, 199. Stevens, 16–17, 33, 35, 53, 56–58. Tugwell, *The Brains Trust,* 91–92, 103.

3. Rexford G. Tugwell, *FDR: Architect of an Era,* Macmillan Co. (1967), 142–43. PPA 1937, 136–37. PPA 1939, 182–83. Stevens, 20, 36.

4. PPA 1928–32, 457–58. Lindley, 72.

Part V: The Ethics and Politics of Work

1. ER I, 86. ER II, 107. Alfred B. Rollins, Jr., *Roosevelt and Howe,* Alfred A. Knopf (1962), 414. Fayetteville letter, OF 444.

2. F.D.R.'s reasons for opposing the Soldiers' Bonus are best detailed in a letter of Dec. 27, 1934, to Commander Garland R. Farmer, American Legion Post, Henderson, Texas, PPA 1934, 503–6. Caroline Bird, *The Invisible Scar,* Pocket Books edition (1967), 56–57. *The Memoirs of Herbert Hoover: 1929–41,* Macmillan Co. (1952), 225–26. Edmund W. Starling (and Thomas Sugrue), *Starling of the White House,* Simon & Schuster (1946), 296, 300. Roosevelt's reaction to the newspaper display of the Bonus March rout is reported in detail by Rexford G. Tugwell in *The Brains Trust,* Viking Press (1968), 352–59. His feelings about MacArthur are in Tugwell, 432–34, to which the following footnote is appended: "I report this conversation verbatim. I made notes about it that afternoon, but afterward tore them up. It remains so vivid a recollection that I am willing to stand on its accuracy." The outmaneuvering of MacArthur in the appointment of his successor is reported by James A. Farley in *Jim Farley's Story: The Roosevelt Years,* Whittlesey House, McGraw-Hill Book Co., Inc. (1948), 55.

3. The observation that Hoover seemed an "expensive President" is found in Moley I, 153–54. Rollins, 386–88. Frances Perkins, *The Roosevelt I Knew,* Harper Colophon edition (1964), 111–12. ER II, 120–21.

4. Samuel I. Rosenman, *Working with Roosevelt,* Harper & Bros. (1952), 51. *The Memoirs of Herbert Hoover: 1929–41,* 174–75. Bird, 26–27. Hoover, 144. Perkins, 183–86. Robert E. Sherwood, *Roosevelt and Hopkins,* Harper & Bros. (1948), 44–45.

5. William E. Leuchtenburg, *Franklin D. Roosevelt and the New Deal: 1932–40,* Harper & Row (1963), 47, 56. Perkins, 192–96.

6. Moley II, 284–90. Perkins, 197–200. Harold L. Ickes, *Back to Work: The Story of PWA,* Macmillan Co. (1935), 12–13. Bird, 151.

7. Ickes I, 48. Perkins, 200–5.

8. Third Fireside Chat, PPA 1933, 300–1. Moley II, 292–93. Postage-stamp letter, Personal Letters III, 358. Perkins, 216–23.

9. Ickes I, 71–72, 195–98.

10. Ernest K. Lindley, *Half Way with Roosevelt,* Viking Press (1936), 155–57. Hopkins memo to F.D.R., Aug. 29, 1933, OF 444. Personal Letters III, editor's note, 382. Moley I, 292–93.

11. Interview with F.D.R. by Anne O'Hare McCormick, New York *Times,* July 8, 1934. Message to Congress on gains under NRA, Feb. 20, 1935, PPA 1935, 80–83. Perkins, 208. Article, "NRA: A Trial Balance," by M. D. Vincent, head of NRA Textile Division, *Survey Graphic,* July 1935, 333–37, 363–64.

12. Leuchtenburg, 143–45. *Roosevelt and Frankfurter: Their Correspondence, 1928–1945,* Max Freedman, ed., Little, Brown (1967), 259–60. Moley II, 296, 208th Press Conference, May 29, 1935, PPA 1935, 198–222.

13. M. D. Vincent, *Survey Graphic*, July 1935, 333–37, 363–64. Moley II, 291. Schlesinger III, 286–90.

14. Moley II, 273–75. Ickes I, 28–29, 34, 84–85. Interview with F.D.R. by Anne O'Hare McCormick, New York *Times*, Nov. 25, 1934. PPA 1933, 242.

15. Sherwood, 48–51, 54–56. 66th Press Conference, Nov. 3, PPA 1933, 445–46. Ickes I, 116, 256. Executive order creating CWA, PPA 1933, 454–55, 458. Lindley, 193. Extemporaneous speech by F.D.R. to CWA conference, PPA 1933, 469. Leuchtenburg, 121. Schlesinger II, 270, 274–77. Bird, 109. McCormick, New York *Times*, Nov. 25, 1934.

16. PPA 1934, 3. Fireside Chat, PPA 1934, 314–15. Rosenman, 96–97.

17. Annual Message, PPA 1935, 19–22. Paul L. Benjamin, "Unemployment and Relief," *The Family* (Family Service Association of America), May 1935, 67–71.

18. Perkins, 225–26, 273. Tugwell, 517. *Roosevelt and Frankfurter*, 170–71, 183.

19. PPA 1935, 167–68. Lippmann quoted by Sherwood, 67. Schlesinger III, 343. Leuchtenburg, 124–25. Schlesinger II, 295–96. PPA 1935, 118.

20. Executive order creating WPA, PPA 1935, 163–68. Ickes II, 35. Sherwood, 70–71, 78–79. John Morton Blum, *From the Morgenthau Diaries*, Vol. I, Houghton Mifflin Co. (1959), 240–42. Ickes I, 360–61, 386–88, 409–10, 426–27, 436, 438, 628. Schlesinger III, 352.

21. The joke told to Hopkins was told in the presence of—and retold to me by—Mrs. Mabel Irwin of Warm Springs, Ga. Jacob Baker (WPA official), New York *Times* Magazine, Nov. 11, 1934. Memo, Hopkins to Louis Howe, letter to F.D.R., and Hopkins memo to all state relief administrators, OF 444. PPA 1935, 284–87. On "stretching of the law," F.D.R. extemporaneous speech to state superintendents of education, Dec. 11, 1935, PPA 1935, 496–99.

22. On F.D.R.'s taste in paintings, Perkins, 76. Leuchtenburg, 126–27. Perkins, 188. Sherwood, 60. Jerre Mangione (National Co-ordinating Editor of Federal Writers Project), New York *Times* Book Review, May 18, 1969. Robert Bendiner, *Saturday Review*, April 1, 1967.

23. "Unemployment in 1937," *Fortune*, Oct. 1937. Hopkins letter to F.D.R., June 9, 1936 OF 444. F.D.R. to Hopkins and reply, Aug. 26 and Sept. 13, 1935, OF 444. Perkins, 190. Lindley, 202–3. Atlanta speech, PPA 1935, 474.

24. PPA 1933, 331–32. Schlesinger II, 287–88. Ickes I, 498. Personal Letters III, 573. Ickes, *Back to Work: The Story of PWA*, Macmillan Co. (1935), 19, 65–66, 150–53. Burton K. Wheeler with Paul F. Healy, *Yankee from the West*, Doubleday & Co. (1962), 304–6, F.D.R. memo to Hopkins, OF 444. Press Conference, Hyde Park, Oct. 7, 1938, transcript in FDRL.

Background Memorandum to Part V

The inscription preceding this background memo is quoted by James Roosevelt in *Affectionately, F.D.R.,* 315.

1. John Morton Blum, *From the Morgenthau Diaries*, Vol. I, Houghton Mifflin Co. (1959), 253–54. Personal Letters I, 238–40, 242–45, 340–41, 368, 376–77, 437, 459–60, 463, 469. Frank Freidel, *Franklin D. Roosevelt;* Vol. I, *The Apprenticeship*, Little, Brown (1952), 27.

2. Mrs. James Roosevelt, *My Boy Franklin*, Ray Long & Richard R. Smith, Inc. (1933), 18. ER I, 83–88. James Roosevelt, *Affectionately, F.D.R.*, Harcourt Brace & Co. (1959), 30. Joseph P. Lash, *Eleanor and Franklin*, W. W. Norton & Co. (1971),

101–2, 106–7. Personal Letters I, 474, 486, 489–90, 499–500, 516. Coded diary entry and deciphering, New York *Times*, Jan. 22, 1972.

3. Lash, 107, 109, 111–12. ER I, 88. Mrs. James Roosevelt, 62–63. James Roosevelt, 29–31. Personal Letters I, 518–20.

4. ER I, 97–100. Lash, 29–30, 146. Interview with Anna Roosevelt Halsted. Robert M. Goldenson, *The Encyclopedia of Human Behavior*, Doubleday & Co., Inc. (1970), 485, 1240–41. ER I, 102, 106, 109–11, 116, 122–23, 126, 139. ER II, 154, 158.

5. Lash, 157, 163, 197–98. Freidel, 86. Personal Letters II (Elliott's notes on state senatorial election), 151–52.

6. ER I, 151–52. Personal Letters II, 219, 349–50. Jonathan Daniels, *The End of Innocence*, J. B. Lippincott Co. (1954), 80–81, 159–60. Daniels, *Washington Quadrille*, Doubleday & Co. (1968), 67, 70. Lash, 221.

7. Personal Letters II, 347, 352, 358, 361. Daniels, *The End of Innocence*, 228. Lash, 223–27

8. Rudolph Marx, M.D., *The Health of Presidents*, G. P. Putnam's Sons (1960), 358–60. Emil Ludwig, *Roosevelt: A Study in Fortune and Power*, 87–88. ER I, 244–48, 252. The Draper letter in John Gunther, *Roosevelt in Retrospect*, Harper & Bros. (1950), 225–26. Other items on Louis Howe in James Roosevelt, 144, and Rollins, 181, 185.

9. Doris Fleeson, "Missy—To Do This," *Saturday Evening Post*, Jan. 8, 1938. Fulton Oursler, *Behold This Dreamer!* Little, Brown (1964), 368, 402. Grace Tully, *F.D.R. My Boss*, Charles Scribner's Sons (1949), 338–39. Also, interview with Grace Tully. ER I, 255. Log of *Weona II* and log of *Larooco* in FDRL. Description of *Larooco* (by F.D.R.) and quotation from John S. Lawrence in an unpublished paper by Donald S. Carmichael, "An Introduction to the *Log of the Larooco*—Being Chiefly the Correspondence of Franklin D. Roosevelt and John S. Lawrence," in FDRL. James Roosevelt, 164. Lash, 510, 723.

10. Log of the *Larooco*, FDRL. Draft of F.D.R.'s "A History of the United States," Personal Letters II, 545–52. Letter to Sara Roosevelt, Personal Letters II, 543–44. James Roosevelt, 169. ER II, 34–35. Freidel, 191.

11. Personal Letters II (notes), 560–64, 577–78. Ruth Stevens, *"Hi-Ya Neighbor,"* Tupper & Love (1947), 4.

12. Personal Letters II, 564–68, 599, 610–11, 616–17. The Loyless anecdote is retold by Donald S. Carmichael in *F.D.R., Columnist*, 5–6. Interview with Mr. and Mrs. Egbert T. Curtis, Aug. 1968. Other sources, interviews with Anna Roosevelt Halsted and Grace Tully. The will of Marguerite A. LeHand, FDRL, PPF 3737.

13. Medical report, Gunther, 267. Gunther does not cite his source for the technical portion of the medical report, which he quotes in full. FDRL has only the publicly released summary.

14. Interview with Raymond Moley.

15. Oursler, 428–31.

16. Personal Letters II, 622. Interviews with Grace Tully and Mr. and Mrs. Curtis.

17. Interview with Mr. and Mrs. Curtis. Lash, 321, 326, 336, 339, 508. ER II, 354–55. James Roosevelt, 313. Interview with Anna Roosevelt Halsted. Missy's Christmas letter at FDRL, PPF 3737.

18. ER II, 63–64, 80, 84, 132–33. Perkins, 69–70. Interview with Anna Roosevelt Halsted. Interview with Raymond Moley. Lash, 355, 432, 482.

19. Doris Fleeson, *Saturday Evening Post*, Jan. 8, 1938. *Newsweek*, Aug. 12, 1933, 15–16. Interview with Grace Tully. Lillian Rogers Parks, *My Thirty Years*

BIBLIOGRAPHY AND SOURCES443

Backstairs at the White House, Fleet (1961), 244–46. Description of lawn party is in Ickes I, 537, 633–35. Oursler, 423–25, 433–35. James Farley, 43, 180–81. Ickes II, 184, 312; Ickes III, 193. The McIntire anecdote is from an interview with Raymond Moley. Marguerite A. LeHand folder at FDRL, PPF 3737. Interview with Barbara Curtis. *Roosevelt and Frankfurter,* 258. ER II, 176–77. Rosenman, 459–60. The palmist anecdote appears in the Fleeson article. Raymond Moley, "What Every Woman Should Know," *Newsweek,* Aug. 14, 1944. Tugwell, 65. Moley I, 390.

Part VI: Demagogues, Democrats, and Demography

1. The Hyde Park lunch, including F.D.R.'s "cross a bridge with the devil" remark, is described by Grace Tully in *F.D.R. My Boss,* Charles Scribner's Sons (1949), 323–24.

2. Edward J. Flynn, *You're the Boss,* Viking Press (1947), 95–96, 101. Schlesinger III, 53–56, 59–65. Personal Letters III, 460–61. James A. Farley, *Jim Farley's Story: The Roosevelt Years,* Whittlesey House, McGraw-Hill Book Co., Inc. (1948), 51.

3. Schlesinger III, 20–25. For description of F.D.R.'s mimicry of Coughlin, Fulton Oursler, *Behold This Dreamer!* Little, Brown (1964), 425–26. William E. Leuchtenburg, *Franklin D. Roosevelt and the New Deal: 1932–40,* Harper & Row (1963), 101–3.

4. Schlesinger III, 35–40. Leuchtenburg, 103–4.

5. Raymond Moley recalls F.D.R. using the phrase "steal Long's thunder" in Moley I, 305. F.D.R. spoke of the ripe timing of Social Security to Anne O'Hare McCormick, reported by her in the New York *Times* Magazine, Nov. 25, 1934. Frances Perkins, *The Roosevelt I Knew,* Harper Colophon edition (1964), 92–94. Brookings Institution survey discussed by Mary Ross, *Why Social Security?* published by Social Security Board, 1936, 11–32.

6. For the Hague episode, Thomas J. Fleming, " 'I Am the Law,' " *American Heritage,* June 1969, 40–43. Rexford G. Tugwell, *The Brains Trust,* Viking Press (1968), 368–71.

7. Frances Perkins, *The Roosevelt I Knew,* Harper Colophon edition (1964), 103–7, 188–89, 282–97. Schlesinger II, 301–3. PPA 1935, 324–26.

8. For conservative opposition to Social Security, Schlesinger II, 311–14. Leuchtenburg, 131. Perkins, 299. Anne O'Hare McCormick, New York *Times* Magazine, Oct. 16, 1938. On the political importance of employee contributions, Schlesinger II, 308; Rexford G. Tugwell, "Roosevelt and Hoover," *Antioch Review,* Winter 1953–54. Joseph P. Lash, *Eleanor and Franklin,* W. W. Norton & Co. (1971), 438–39. On Roosevelt's temporizing with Congress, Schlesinger III, 5, 7–9; Lash, 437. Discussion of liberals: "civilization is a tree," etc. quoted by Anne O'Hare McCormick, New York *Times* Magazine, Sept. 11, 1932; F.D.R. address at Los Angeles, Oct. 1, 1935, PPA 1935, 404.

9. The Wheeler incident at the Tugwell dinner, including Dodd's report that he repeated the diatribe to F.D.R., is drawn from William E. Dodd, Jr., and Martha Dodd, *Ambassador Dodd's Diary,* Harcourt, Brace & Co. (1941), 212–13. Wheeler's name (which Dodd omits) is confirmed by the diary of Tugwell, as reported in Schlesinger II, 141–42. Progressive "flirtations" with a third party and Huey Long speculated on by F.D.R. in letter to Colonel Edward M. House, Feb. 16, 1935, Personal Letters III, 452–53.

10. The Niles letter, meeting with liberal senators, and trouble with conservative

Democrats, *Roosevelt and Frankfurter: Their Correspondence, 1928–1945,* Max Freedman, ed., Little, Brown (1967), 261–62, 269–71, 282–83. Aftermath of Social Security passage, Perkins, 298–300. ER II, 140.

11. Perkins, 236–44. Presidential statement upon signing National Labor Relations Act, PPA 1935, 294–95. ACLU statement quoted by Carl N. Degler, *The New Deal,* Quadrangle Books (1970), 25. 141st Press Conference, Sept. 5, 1934, PPA 1934, 396–99. Moley I, 304.

12. Leuchtenburg, 177. Ickes I, 471. 201st Press Conference, May 3, 1935, PPA 1935, 162.

13. *Roosevelt and Frankfurter,* 322–27, 355. F.D.R. Harvard Address, PPA 1936, 362–65.

14. Marquis W. Childs, "They Hate Roosevelt," *Harper's,* May 1936.

15. *Roosevelt and Frankfurter,* 282–83. Schlesinger III, 338–40, for a vivid retelling of the Long assassination. Ickes I, 462. Leuchtenburg, 180–82. The Flynn conversations, while not detailed in Flynn's own cautious memoirs, are recorded in Moley II, 377–79, 525–27.

16. Acceptance Speech, PPA 1936, 230–36. Perkins, 122–23. Samuel I. Rosenman, *Working with Roosevelt,* Harper & Bros. (1952), 106–7. The Markham incident, James Roosevelt, *Affectionately, F.D.R.,* Harcourt, Brace & Co. (1959), 157–58.

17. F.D.R.'s assessment of Landon, Tully, 213, and Perkins, 115. The Des Moines meeting, Rexford G. Tugwell, *FDR: Architect of an Era,* Macmillan Co. (1967), 136–37, and Tully, 203.

18. Syracuse Speech, PPA 1936, 383–90. Pittsburgh speech and others on that trip, PPA 1936, 396–408. The agonizing over the Pittsburgh speech told to me by James H. Rowe, Jr., F.D.R. administrative assistant; also Rosenman, 45, 112–13. Not comfortable speaking in big cities, Moley II, 9. Campaigning as an education, Anne O'Hare McCormick, New York *Times* Magazine, Jan. 15, 1933. Speech fragments, PPA 1936, 415, 425, 427, 431–32, 450, 487–88. Ickes I, 695. 332nd Press Conference, Dec. 29, 1936, PPA 1936, 624–25. Campaigning for the state senate, Personal Letters IV, 756; Alfred B. Rollins, Jr., *Roosevelt and Howe,* Alfred A. Knopf (1962), 20. Campaign train, Rosenman, 118, 122–25, 131–32.

19. Hearst: Ickes I, 428–29, 519, 660–61. Literary Digest: Robert E. Sherwood, *Roosevelt and Hopkins,* Harper & Bros. (1948), 86. Chicago Daily *Tribune,* April 17, 1936.

20. F.D.R. letter to Josephus Daniels, Nov. 9, 1936, Personal Letters III, 626–27. Caroline Bird, *The Invisible Scar,* Pocket Books edition (1967), 170–71. Madison Square Garden speech, PPA 1936, 566–73. The Shorenstein anecdote is recalled by Theodore H. White, *The Making of the President 1960,* Atheneum (1961), 54.

21. Personal Letters III, 624. Rosenman, 137. The Marion Davies call, Ickes I, 704. PPA 1936, 582. Leuchtenburg, 185–90, 196. Arthur Krock, New York *Times,* Aug. 24, 1938.

Background Memorandum to Part VI

1. F.D.R. letter to Dr. William Eggleston, *Journal of the South Carolina Medical Association,* Spring 1946.

2. John Gunther, *Roosevelt in Retrospect,* Harper & Bros. (1950), 229–31. Tully, 36. Turnley Walker, *Roosevelt and the Warm Springs Story,* A. A. Wyn, Inc. (1953), 148–50. Nicholas Roosevelt, *A Front Row Seat,* University of Oklahoma Press (1953), 224.

3. Perkins, 30, 44. Ickes I, 699. Noel F. Busch, *What Manner of Man?* Harper &

Bros. (1944), 96–97. Emil Ludwig, *Roosevelt: A Study in Fortune and Power,* Viking Press (1938), 321. Gunther, 237.

4. Fulton Oursler, *Behold This Dreamer!* Little, Brown (1964), 369–70. Joseph P. Lash, *Eleanor and Franklin,* 424. Personal Letters IV, 771–72. James Roosevelt, 154–55. Tully, 16. Gunther, 238–39.

Part VII: Saving Liberalism and Liberty

1. Ickes II, 52–53. Second Inaugural Address, PPA 1937, 1–5. Samuel I. Rosenman, *Working with Roosevelt,* Harper & Bros. (1952), 144.

2. F.D.R.'s account of Supreme Court decisions (prepared with the aid of Frankfurter and Rosenman), PPA 1935, Introduction, 3 to 14; PPA 1937, pages LIV–LXI.

3. Message to Congress, Jan. 6, 1937, PPA 1936, 634–42. Ickes II, 31–33. F.D.R. letter to Felix Frankfurter, *Roosevelt and Frankfurter: Their Correspondence, 1928–1945,* Max Freedman, ed., Little, Brown (1967), 381–82. PPA 1937, Introduction, LXII–LXV. Rosenman, 147–49, 154–56.

4. The Hughes-Wheeler episode, Ickes II, 103–4, 251; *Roosevelt and Frankfurter,* 396–98. The Court's turnabout, PPA 1937, LXVI—LXXI; Personal Letters III, 685–86 (F.D.R.'s private memo "for the record"); Ickes II, 106–7; William E. Leuchtenburg, *Franklin D. Roosevelt and the New Deal: 1932–40,* Harper & Row (1963), 236–37. The Robinson episode, Grace Tully, *F.D.R. My Boss,* Charles Scribner's Sons (1949), 224; Ickes II, 144–45, 153, 161–62. F.D.R.'s version of the Lehman episode reported in Ickes II, 166–68. The basis of the author's footnote regarding the Roberts change of position is cited by Samuel I. Rosenman in *Working with Roosevelt,* Harper & Bros. (1952), 161, and in more detailed form by James MacGregor Burns in *Roosevelt: The Lion and the Fox,* Harvest Books edition, Harcourt, Brace & World (1956), 303–4.

5. Ickes II, 108–9, 140–41, 176–77, 179, 222–23.

6. President's Statement on Attaining the Objectives of the Court Fight, Aug. 7, 1939, PPA 1939, 422–24. Ickes II, 182–83, 190–92, 215. Richard Whalen, *The Founding Father,* New American Library (1964), 200.

7. F.D.R. letter to Josephus Daniels, Nov. 14, 1938, Personal Letters IV, 827. Rosenman, 176–80. Ickes II, 143, 342, 387, 471, 475–76. Leuchtenburg, 266–67. PPA 1938, XXVIII–XXXIII. Alben W. Barkley, *That Reminds Me—,* Doubleday & Co. (1954), 165. Joseph P. Lash, *Eleanor Roosevelt: A Friend's Memoir,* Doubleday & Co. (1964), 166 (for Mrs. Roosevelt's account of "the beginning of the bad feeling between the President and Farley"). Edward J. Flynn, *You're the Boss,* Viking Press (1947), 150.

8. 357th Press Conference, April 2, 1937, PPA 1937, 140–41. 374th Press Conference, June 15, 1937, PPA 1937, 266–67. Personal Letters IV (Notes), 740. Leuchtenburg, 249, 256–57. Caroline Bird, *The Invisible Scar,* Pocket Books edition (1967), 183, 187. 422nd Press Conference, Jan. 4, 1938, PPA 1938, 31–34.

9. Young F.D.R.'s encounters with German law and order, mentioned in several sources, are told most closely firsthand in the diary of his wartime staff secretary, William D. Hassett, *Off the Record with F.D.R.,* Rutgers University Press (1958), 200. PPA 1939, Introduction, XXIV–XL. Letters to Straus and Dodd, Personal Letters III, 555–56, 571. 702nd Press Conference, Dec. 17, 1940, PPA 1940, 604–8. Reaction to Wheeler quote, Rosenman, 273. Opinion polls, Leuchtenburg, 302.

10. For the *Liberty* poll, memo from Stephen Early to F.D.R., Sept. 3, 1937, Personal Letters IV, 410–11. Robert E. Sherwood, *Roosevelt and Hopkins,* Harper &

Bros. (1948), 92–93. Rosenman, 201. Ickes II, 576–77, 590, 600, 688, 690–94, 699. Ickes III, 117. James A. Farley, *Jim Farley's Story*, Whittlesey House, McGraw-Hill Book Co., Inc. (1948), 110–11, 224. *Roosevelt and Frankfurter*, 459–60. Advice to Boettiger, PPA 1938, 293–95. The *Collier's* contract, corroborated by Ickes, Mrs. Roosevelt, Dr. Ross McIntire, and others, is detailed by Gunther, 308.

11. Rosenman, 203, 206–12. Ross T. McIntire, *White House Physician*, G. P. Putnam's Sons (1946), 123–24. Farley, 288.

12. *The Memoirs of Cordell Hull*, Macmillan Co. (1948), 860–61. James Roosevelt, 324. Rosenman, 204–19.

13. Ickes III, 215. Farley, 157. Rosenman, 253–55. Frances Perkins, *The Roosevelt I Knew*, Harper Colophon edition (1964), 117–19. The Hughes anecdote, William D. Hassett, *Off the Record with F.D.R.*, Rutgers University Press (1958), 66–67.

14. Rosenman, 303, 307–9. Tully, 248–53. Bernard Baruch, *The Public Years*, Holt, Rinehart & Winston (1960), 288–91. John Gunther, *Roosevelt in Retrospect*, Harper & Bros. (1950), 319. Ickes III, 662–65. Perkins, 378–80. F.D.R. memo to Frank Knox, Personal Letters IV, 1253–54.

15. Perkins, 349–51. Health items, message to Congress, Jan. 30, 1940, PPA 1940, 65–68; Ickes III, 626–27. ADC statistics, U. S. Census Bureau. Rexford G. Tugwell, *FDR: Architect of an Era*, Macmillan Co. (1967), 171–73. PPA 1938, 7. 470th Press Conference, June 28, 1938, PPA 1938, 406–8.

16. Ickes III, 427–28. Rosenman, 463–70.

Background Memorandum to Part VII

1. Michael F. Reilly, *Reilly of the White House*, Simon & Schuster (1947), 84–85. Tully, 246, 249–51, 257. Interview with Mr. and Mrs. Egbert Curtis. Tully's memo on Missy LeHand's call, PPF 3737. Rosenman, 312. Joseph P. Lash, *Eleanor and Franklin*, W. W. Norton & Co. (1971), 510, 715. Interview with Mabel (Mrs. C. E.) Irwin. Interview with Grace Tully. Lillian Rogers Parks, *My Thirty Years Backstairs at the White House*, Fleet (1961), 245–46. Interview with Anna Roosevelt Halsted. Egbert Curtis letter to F.D.R. and Missy's election wire, PPF 3737. Postponement of Missy's visit, Lash, 699–700. *Roosevelt and Frankfurter*, 695. On death of Missy, Curtis interview; Tully, 105; PPF 3737.

2. Hassett, 40. Farley, 125. Burton K. Wheeler, *Yankee from the West*, Doubleday & Co. (1962), 335, 368. James Roosevelt, 302. Lash, *Eleanor Roosevelt: A Friend's Memoir*, 260. Interview with Anna Roosevelt Halsted.

3. ER II, 25. Tully, 78, 110. Rexford G. Tugwell, *The Brains Trust*, Viking Press (1968), 53–55. Rosenman, 347. Hopkins memo in Gunther, 196–97.

4. Gunther, 73. Eleanor Roosevelt quote on "lovely ladies," James Roosevelt, 22. Listing of the "lovely ladies," various sources, including James Roosevelt, 318; Hassett, 48–49, 74, 76, 139. Interview with Anna Roosevelt Halsted.

5. Jonathan Daniels, *Washington Quadrille*, Doubleday & Co. (1968), 293–98. Interview with William D. Simmons, May 1960, partially used earlier in Bernard Asbell, *When F.D.R. Died*, Holt, Rinehart & Winston (1961), 102–4. F.D.R. opinions on Baruch in Tugwell, xxviii; Ickes II, 328; Hassett, 241.

6. Daniels, 289–90, 302. Interview with Anna Roosevelt Halsted. Hassett, 332. Tully, 360. Asbell, 30–38, based on interviews with William D. Hassett, Dewey Long, and Margaret Suckley.

7. Asbell, 99–100, based on interview with Nicholas Robbins.

Index